D0365196

BIRMINGHAM-SOUTHERN COLLEGE
5 0553 01119537 4

WITHDRAWN
FROM B'ham-Sou.
College Lib.

KEEPING ABREAST OF SCIENCE AND TECHNOLOGY

Technical Intelligence for Business

EDITORS

W. Bradford Ashton
Pacific Northwest National Laboratory

Richard A. Klavans
Center for Research Planning

BATTELLE PRESS
Columbus • Richland

Library of Congress Cataloging-in-Publication Data

Keeping abreast of science and technology : technical intelligence for business / edited by W. Bradford Ashton, Richard A. Klavans.
p. cm.
Includes bibliographical references and index.
ISBN 1-57477-018-7 (alk. paper)
1. Business intelligence. I. Ashton, W. Bradford. II. Klavans, Richard A., 1948– .
HO38.7.K44 1997 96-31063
658.4´7—dc20 CIP

Printed in the United States of America

Copyright © 1997 Battelle Memorial Institute

All rights reserved. No part of this book may be reproduced or transmitted in any form or by any means, electronic or mechanical, including photocopying, recording or by any information storage and retrieval system, without permission of the publisher.

Battelle Press
505 King Avenue
Columbus, Ohio 43201-2693
614-424-6393; 1-800-451-3543
FAX: 614-424-3819
http://www.Battelle.org

HD 38.7 .K44 1997

Contents

L10879 6-10-98

PART III
Producing Competitive Technical Intelligence: Approaches and Tools

PART IV
Using Competitive Technical Intelligence: Applying Results to Obtain Value

PART V
Contemporary Business Intelligence Issues

Preface

The practice of applying intelligence principles to science and technology (S&T) in business is a new field, and this is the first book that brings together information on this topic from professionals who are skilled in intelligence production and use. The motivations for this volume are straightforward. We have been intimately involved in technology management for over twenty years. Until recently, we have observed only a gradual acceptance of competitive intelligence as a management tool by U.S. businesses. The S&T aspects of competitive intelligence have been slower to evolve, but the pace of interest in this field is accelerating. An increasing number of business, research, technology, and investment professionals are now focusing on use of intelligence to exploit technology in the commercial world. For some time, we have recognized the need to integrate these experiences in a practitioner-oriented volume at a time when the field is still young.

Historically, most commercial technology development has been focused inside the firm. In research and development (R&D) laboratories and company test sites, new technology was expected to emerge from internal sources. Company attention was therefore directed at day-to-day management of in-house ideas, projects, and technical operations. Now these behaviors are changing and R&D laboratories are seeking more information about developments outside their walls. Market competitors (such as General Electric and Westinghouse or IBM and Apple) are now becoming R&D competitors, often pursuing similar technical objectives for improved products and processes. Company laboratories and development centers recognize that technology is available from many parts of the world and that gaining an R&D edge requires more attention to exploiting the know-how developed by others. No matter where new technology comes from, the first firm to commercialize an advance is likely to capture the significant returns.

In the past, formal methods for monitoring R&D in competitor organizations were not considered necessary because scientists and engineers could learn about advances informally from colleagues and other professionals. But in today's global business world, informal watching of the players, developments, and trends is usually not sufficient. What is needed is often called competitive technical intelligence (CTI)—systematic methods carried out by professionals to collect, analyze, and communicate (to relevant users) action-oriented information on external S&T threats and opportunities.

This distinction between external and internal attention is critical. CTI addresses the future needs of decision-makers and analysts from a uniquely external viewpoint to complement each company's tendency to focus inside the organization. One way to understand the shift from internal technology development to external technical intelligence is to examine the United States' response to the R&D strategies of firms from other nations. Thirty years ago, the United States' internal orientation was reflected in its R&D expenses—more than 90% of private R&D expenses in the United States were for internal operations, and the tools and techniques for technology management were applied inside the R&D lab.

However, over the past thirty years, R&D managers in other nations (such as Japan, Germany, France, the Netherlands, and Finland) have improved the position of their firms, at least in part, by focusing more on technical intelligence. The success of these efforts is evident in industries such as automobiles, specialty chemicals, textiles, electronics, and pulp and paper. Responses by United States businesses have already been reflected in shifting R&D expenditures: recent Industrial Research Institute estimates are that now only about 60% of private U.S. R&D dollars are for strictly internal operations. U.S. firms are increasing their commitment to alliances, joint ventures, and a variety of external networking mechanisms and scanning activities. This trend is a significant adjustment in the attitudes and outlook of technology development managers.

Unfortunately, at this time, information on the practice of CTI in business is diffuse and fragmented. This book is designed to address that gap by drawing on the insights of a group of experienced authors who are professionals in this and related fields. We expect that over the next decade or so, CTI will become an active part of many more firms and that academics and managers will work together to develop specialized tools and techniques for this emerging field. We hope this book provides a useful baseline for that future work.

W. BRADFORD ASHTON
RICHARD A. KLAVANS

Acknowledgments

We are grateful to a number of individuals whose assistance was essential in completing this book. First and foremost, the Pacific Northwest National Laboratory, operated for the U.S. Department of Energy by Battelle, provided the financial and organizational support necessary to complete the coordination and writing tasks. Individuals who were particularly important to us in this regard are Charlette Geffen, Bobi Garrett, Marylynn Placet, and Ronald Nesse. Ms. Geffen had the vision to initiate the work for this book, and the other individuals continued support in her absence. The book would not have been possible without their encouragement and patience.

The editors also gratefully acknowledge the authors who contributed chapters to the book. Many of them endured a long period of waiting until the work was completed. In addition, extensive conversations with these authors, as well as with friends and colleagues around the world, have added depth and additional perspectives to our thinking.

Finally, we owe a special debt of gratitude to our editor, Ms. Judy Danko of the Pacific Northwest National Laboratory, for her vital help in all aspects of getting the book completed. She edited the text, coordinated the graphics and communications with authors, produced the index, and provided the editors with cheerful encouragement throughout the entire project.

W. BRADFORD ASHTON
Pacific Northwest National Laboratory

RICHARD A. KLAVANS
Center for Research Planning

KEEPING ABREAST OF SCIENCE AND TECHNOLOGY

Technical Intelligence for Business

PART I

Introduction and Basic Concepts: Technical Intelligence Foundations

PART I
Editorial Introduction

The general need for technical intelligence in business is not controversial. Virtually all firms that depend on technology for their competitive position and outlook recognize that keeping track of technology trends for business applications is essential in today's economies. But there are a vast range of attitudes about the importance of systematic intelligence efforts and an even wider range of practices for actually gathering, analyzing, and using intelligence information. On one hand, most firms do not have formal technical intelligence programs; they expect intelligence information to emerge as a routine part of all or some staff members' jobs. On the other hand, a small, but growing number of firms have implemented some form of deliberate technical intelligence effort in their organization.

The three chapters in this first section of the book deal with technical intelligence fundamentals. These fundamentals provide the background for the remaining sections of the book, as well as for readers who are interested in formal intelligence organizations.

In the first chapter, Brad Ashton and Dick Klavans introduce a number of fundamental topics that are important for an understanding of technical intelligence in business. This introductory chapter outlines basic concepts and definitions for competitive technical intelligence (CTI) programs and activities. The chapter also provides introductory material on current practices in technical intelligence for business, drawing attention to basic concerns such as technical intelligence objectives, types of user information needs, and applications of CTI in companies.

The other two chapters also address basic ideas in technical intelligence. In his chapter on the research areas that underlie the practice of technical intelligence, Dick Klavans uses co-citation analysis of 10,000 management-related articles from eight management disciplines to identify the main research communities whose work supports technical intelligence. The results suggest that the CTI research base is organized around two bodies of scientific literature—R&D management and information management systems/science. But Klavans also identifies a fundamental schism in the knowledge areas that are emphasized (or discouraged) in different nations. Two profiles emerge from an analysis of these data. These profiles suggest that there are identifiable biases in management knowledge that explain this difference.

In the last chapter in this section, Justin Bloom takes a careful look at the practice of business intelligence in Japan. The Japanese economy has one of the most successful track records of using technical intelligence in business. Bloom explores this success through topics such as acquisition of S&T from overseas, mechanisms for transfer and absorption of technical information, and Japanese intelligence organizations and systems (including public agencies, private firms, trading companies, universities, trade associations). According to Bloom, a combination of historical, social, and institutional factors account for Japan's technological success, including a cultural preference for a collaborative approach to problem-solving. In addition, Japan, unlike certain other countries, has always been very receptive to the introduction of foreign ideas and technologies. This interest in foreign intellectual capital is manifest in the government's heavy investments in education (particularly foreign languages), in support for students and professionals studying and working abroad, in the establishment of subsidiaries overseas, and in the creation of a vast network of public and private sector organizations devoted to technology intelligence-gathering. Bloom illustrates how the Japanese business intelligence mindset is reflected in institutional arrangements throughout the nation's economy and institutional infrastructure and suggests that this is a model other nations could adapt.

An Introduction to Technical Intelligence in Business

W. BRADFORD ASHTON and RICHARD A. KLAVANS

To attain or preserve business success, companies must often adapt rapidly to unforeseen moves from competitors, customers, or suppliers. Thus, firms must continually be alert for indications of shifting conditions in their business environment. Improved product, process, and support technologies are especially important in this picture because technology surprises from outside a company can be highly disruptive, and even minimal responses can require long lead times. More than ever, firms must stay abreast of external technology changes that might affect them and be alert for chances to exploit science and technology (S&T) progress.

In the past, most companies concentrated on internal innovation for future growth. New products and processes were developed within company laboratories to protect competitive advantage and were usually not based on research and development (R&D) from players outside the firm. However, in many industries, this situation has been changing. Now, the number of companies, both foreign and domestic, that are capable of successful technological innovation is rising. Exploiting new developments is the key to future growth for these companies. Their progress in applying new technology can be an unrecognized threat or a lost opportunity for unaware firms. Competitive technologies being rapidly introduced can unseat current products or outperform current processes with little warning, while other technologies can open entirely new lines of business for firms that recognize and capitalize on the right intelligence. These prospects, along with the rapid pace and global scope of technological change and the escalating costs of internal R&D, make it imperative that firms keep track of technology activities outside their R&D walls.

Technological surprises and lost opportunities are an inevitable part of business, but a great deal can be done to minimize their occurrence and adverse effects. An effective intelligence effort focusing on science and technology can prevent or mitigate severe losses or provide unique insight into potential new business advantages. Competitive intelligence efforts of various types are on the rise in business and many of them—such as those at Motorola, 3M, Kodak, and Monsanto—have demonstrated their value several times over.

This book describes the foundations, characteristics, and methods of competitive technical intelligence (CTI) for business as currently practiced by many firms. Broadly, CTI refers to the practice of collecting, analyzing, and communicating the best available information on S&T developments and trends occurring outside one's own company. But CTI is more than just information. CTI produces actionable findings (on threats and opportunities) that are essential inputs to company managers. This book discusses how successful business technical intelligence programs help provide and apply this key information in their companies, thereby helping to ensure long-term business success.

This first chapter provides introductory information on technical intelligence as background for the other chapters. Comments on the importance of technology as an intelligence target are provided, along with a discussion of basic definitions, objectives, applications, and a process description for CTI in companies. Several references to other relevant literature are included to help identify where more information on key topics is available. This chapter is not a framework for the other chapters. This book has been designed to contain conceptual diversity—preserving a variety of viewpoints is important in the early evolution of this emerging field.

WHY INTELLIGENCE ON TECHNOLOGY IS IMPORTANT

Future opportunities for competitive business advantage can come from a variety of sources. Among the most common are advantages from location (owning land that contains valuable minerals), government regulation (favored supplier status), marketing (gaining a unique position in the customer's mind), manufacturing (developing a flexible, low-cost and high-quality manufacturing facility), technology (developing a stream of new products from a technology-based platform) and science (developing new technology platforms based on developments in worldwide sciences). When these future opportunities arise from technology—or the underlying science—outside the firm, CTI can be an important business management tool for exploiting them.

Technology-driven business environments where CTI is valuable are relatively easy to identify. CTI is (and has been) most evident in industries such as pharmaceuticals, chemicals, electronic devices, photography, telecommunications, and computers. This set will be expanded as other industries become more dependent on current developments in science and technology (for example, food products, energy, specialty chemicals, soaps, and detergents). Managers in these industries are "placing bets" that the specialized training of their scientists and engineers will provide a source of competitive advantage in the future. When technologies of interest are external, technical intelligence is crucial to investments because it helps ensure that companies can make their investments pay off. CTI helps establish the odds and, more important, keeps the odds current (Cohen and Levinthal 1994).

Technical intelligence can also be important in environments that are susceptible to or are in the midst of competitive disruption—companies in these industries will face new dimensions of competition (Bower and Christensen 1995). Such industries cannot follow their established business patterns if even one disruptive player changes the rules of competition. Competitive disruptions cause highly antagonistic behavior between firms until a new competitive equilibrium is reached. The result can be hypercompetition and conditions that are analogous to warfare (see D'Aveni 1994). Examples of such technological disruptions are evident in some of the industries that championed use of CTI ten years ago:

- Pharmaceuticals—The disruptive prospect of managed health care made competition more cost-based, forcing many firms to track new chemicals for potential drug applications and to monitor competitors' R&D activities.
- Computers—A disruptive shift from hardware to software as the key driver of performance for many products made keeping up with changes vital for many companies in the industry.
- Consumer electronics—A disruption from the stream of rapid product introductions from Japan prompted many other manufacturers to reverse engineer Japanese devices.
- Telecommunications—Competitive disruptions from industry-wide deregulation and advances in computer and chip technology led to efforts by companies to monitor competitors.
- Photography—A disruptive shift from chemistry to digital electronics in the technology approach to image processing made tracking technology important.

These circumstances suggest several reasons why technology is a natural focus of intelligence activities in business. First, technology is a basic determinant of a company's competitive position. The influences of technology are apparent in the features and performance of company products and in the capacity, yield, quality, and efficiency of its production processes. Technology helps determine the unit costs of making and delivering products and the nature of capital investments the company makes to reduce those costs. Even more important from an intelligence viewpoint, technology advances are the source of new products and processes for future growth, so collecting intelligence on technology can be essential for planning future investments (Porter 1980).

Second, intelligence on technology is important because new technology can be acquired from many global sources. Technology still comes from internal sources such as company laboratories and development centers, but technology from external sources is now essential in many industries. Acquiring technology through mechanisms such as licenses, purchases, or joint development with other organizations is especially important in industries such as pharmaceuticals, chemicals, and electronics (Cutler 1991).

Third, company technology is a valuable intelligence focus because it can be a direct source of business revenue. Firms like IBM and Texas Instruments have generated substantial income from licensing, selling, or trading unwanted elements of their intellectual property holdings. Many other firms have also successfully cross-licensed portions of their technology to acquire property that was more useful to their future business directions.

Fourth, technology should be a major component of competitive intelligence because technology eventually becomes obsolete, sometimes quite rapidly, and emerging technology from external sources is not always "visible" to outsiders. As a result, a company that is not aware of what is going on in a particular technical field may be vulnerable to technology surprises, finding out about the new option only after valuable time has been lost. Keeping abreast of technology is especially important because, as evidenced in industries like computers, telecommunications and consumer electronics, technology has the potential to create or destroy entire markets or industries in a short time.

Finally, in the same vein, technology information can have substantial intelligence value in assessing a competitor's future business position because it is one of the earliest opportunities to gain insight into next-generation products and processes. Because of long development times and extensive development activities, an early look at a company's R&D pipeline provides a unique opportunity to assess a competitor's future directions (Foster 1986, Porter 1983).

INTELLIGENCE DEFINED

The terms competitive intelligence (CI) and business intelligence (BI) are often used interchangeably. Both CI and BI refer to "actionable information about the external business environment that could affect a company's competitive position" (actionable information goes beyond just findings to include explicit recommendations for responding to observations, analyses, or conclusions [see Fuld 1995; Gilad and Herring 1996]). Business intelligence focuses on relevant external events, usually emphasizing information on competitors, suppliers, customers, and the general business or market environment.

Intelligence on science and technology, or S&T intelligence, is a particular type of competitive or business intelligence, obviously directed at technology (and its underlying science) as a component of business. In business settings, S&T intelligence is often referred to using terms such as competitive technology intelligence (Vatcha 1993) or scientific competitive intelligence (Bryant et al. 1993), which are appropriate for particular needs. In our thinking, however, the more comprehensive term "competitive technical intelligence" (CTI) incorporates broader information needs covering BOTH science and technology matters (hence our use of the term "technical"). Unless specifically defined otherwise, our use of the term "technology" intelligence will always imply information on the underlying science aspects of a technological matter. No matter what the precise definition, CTI is a management tool for meeting threats and seizing opportunities from science and technology.

Technical intelligence emphasizes the R&D functions of an organization, but it can also encompass other technology-driven activities such as strategic planning, technology acquisition, and process equipment investments. The relevant S&T topics span the technology development spectrum—basic and applied research, engineering development, system testing, product and process development, and commercialization support. Basic research is scientific investigation designed to produce new basic knowledge of interest to the firm, whereas development is the use of basic knowledge and know-how to produce new or improved products and processes. Testing means systematically checking the operation of prototypes or demonstrations to make sure that specifications and customer needs are being met. Commercialization activities include process and product development, as well as support functions such as product service, maintenance, repair, and replacement. The particular intelligence needs vary for these areas, but together they represent important CTI customers for many companies in high-tech and other industries.

Although it is usually not called "intelligence," many firms employ some technical intelligence methods directed at collecting, analyzing, and using information to assess external threats, opportunities, or other developments (see, for instance, Serapio and Dalton 1993; Moffat 1991). Informal intelligence practices were sufficient when firms faced a few well-known competitors. However, formal technical intelligence collection and analysis are important when companies must also react quickly to the discoveries (or failures) of hidden competitors. Technical intelligence emphasizes both the informal nature of knowledge transfer (developing "trading rules" for the luncheon discussion among researchers in competitive labs) and the more formal mechanisms (for example, using groupware to help scan the environment more effectively and improve internal communication).

With this background, CTI can be thought of in the broad terms below:

> *CTI is business-sensitive information on external scientific or technological threats, opportunities, or developments that have the potential to affect a company's competitive situation.*

This conception indicates that CTI is concerned with external S&T developments that can potentially help or harm business success in a competitive environment. Three key features distinguish CTI from a company's other general S&T information, such as strategic plans or R&D portfolio justifications.

First, the focus of CTI-produced information is on *external competitive matters*—on outside organizations or technology developments representing threats or opportunities that could harm or enhance a company's future business performance.

Second, CTI information is business-sensitive and therefore should be (and usually is) *protected*. Even when identical in content to typical business planning information, intelligence is distinct from information because producers and users secure it against unauthorized disclosure (either purposeful or inadvertent). Intelligence is information whose value is heightened because unauthorized discovery by others could harm a company's competitive position or prospects.

Third, CTI is *action-oriented*, that it, it includes recommended actions that managers can or should take to deal with the intelligence findings. An essential part of the intelligence analysis process is to identify practical options for responding—through management decisions or actions—to the conclusions the intelligence analyst develops.

Competitive technical intelligence has the potential to affect the competitive situation; therefore, it **must be acted upon** if it is to have an impact. One of the most serious problems in any intelligence setting is the failure of decision-makers to take action based on intelligence findings and recommendations (see, for instance, Herring 1993).

Technical intelligence is not spying (Carlton 1992). As advocated in this book, CTI refers to collection and use of information on external S&T matters *using legal and ethical means*. (For a discussion of intelligence ethics, see Fuld 1995.)

OBJECTIVES FOR COMPETITIVE TECHNICAL INTELLIGENCE

Typically some form of the following three objectives is the basic justification for CTI activities in business:

- To *provide early warning* of external technical developments or company moves that represent potential business threats or opportunities
- To *evaluate new product, process, or collaboration prospects* created by external S&T activities in time to permit appropriate responses
- To *anticipate and understand S&T-related shifts or trends in the competitive environment* as preparation for organizational planning and strategy development.

Achieving these objectives can provide important benefits to companies. Good intelligence can eliminate technical surprises or lessen their impact by allowing a better opportunity to respond. The reaction time a company has to respond to moves by others can be lengthened, permitting more careful consideration of follow-up actions. Finally, good intelligence can alert company staff to new technical opportunities or approaches to addressing business problems.

THE COMPETITIVE TECHNICAL INTELLIGENCE PROCESS

Most businesses usually require far more information than can be obtained with available intelligence resources. Thus, CTI efforts must be carefully designed, organized, and conducted with specific objectives, resources, and products in mind. Intelligence activities are usually organized around a six-stage process shown in Figure 1 (Ashton and Stacey 1995).

Planning, collection, and analysis compose intelligence *production*; delivery and use, the intelligence *application or use*; and evaluation, a *process review* or feedback function to identify problems and make improvements.

The first stage of the process—for either an on-going intelligence organization or a single exercise to address a one-time information need—is a planning effort to identify information needs, establish intelligence objectives, define actions, and identify and deploy resources to address user needs.

The collection stage involves activities to obtain, screen, and organize raw data and processed information relevant to the needs being addressed or to overall organizational interests. Collection is either on-going, as in company technology monitoring programs, or is targeted to obtain specific data known to be needed. Collection mechanisms can involve human or technical methods. Human sources and methods, such as networking with colleagues, attending technical meetings, or hiring experts, are usually less expensive. Technical collection methods employ some form of technology-based data collection system such as computer search and storage

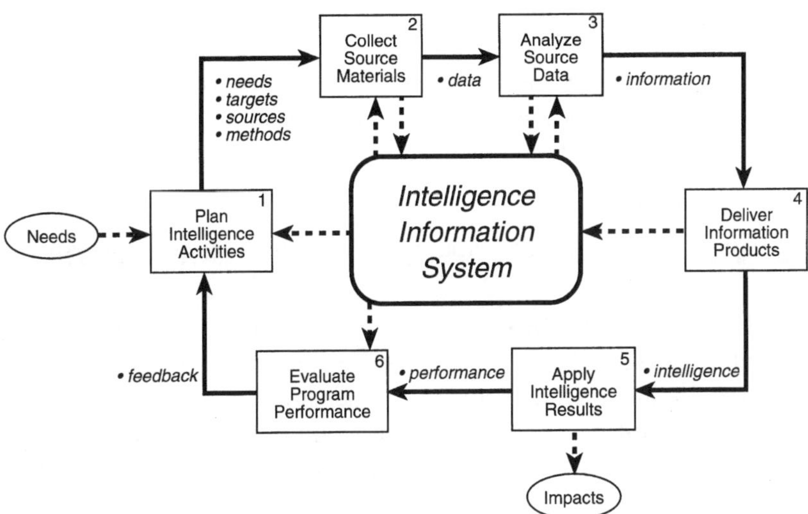

FIGURE 1. The scientific and technical intelligence process (Ashton and Stacey 1995)

mechanisms, photo or electronic imaging systems, or chemical detection of emissions from a facility. Collection also involves screening raw sources to keep only what is relevant and useful, as well as organizing and storing potentially useful raw materials (Fuld 1995).

The analysis stage adds meaning to the collected materials. Such materials may have relevance to the organization's known information needs, to emerging topics, or simply to organizational interests. Analysis is done with the help of tools and methods, some of which are sophisticated and costly. However, excellent analysis does not preclude use of basic, inexpensive data organization and display methods to make sense out of facts or ideas collected (Ashton 1996; Porter et al. 1991).

Delivery is the stage in which analysis products are disseminated to users and discussed and revised. At this point, through interactions with users and other relevant parties, information becomes intelligence. This transformation is based on the fact that the intelligence is designed to guide company moves or actions that must be protected against disclosure.

The use stage is where the intelligence efforts pay off. Intelligence is applied to management decisions, such as which R&D investments to make, or to company actions, such as implementing an external technology acquisition in stages (Walton et al. 1989).

The final stage is an effort to evaluate the intelligence program (or effort) and findings to ensure that organizational needs are being met in a cost-effective way. If necessary, corrective actions are designed and provided as inputs to the planning stage as the intelligence cycle repeats itself (Herring 1996).

TECHNICAL INTELLIGENCE APPLICATIONS TO COMPANY FUNCTIONS

Although general business intelligence can affect virtually any aspect of business life, CTI results are focused on use of technology in company products and processes and on efforts to acquire, develop, exploit, and retire effective technologies. Based on recent company practices, current intelligence on external S&T activities has a significant affect on five main business areas:

- Business and technology strategy

- Technology acquisition
- Management of the R&D portfolio
- Technology deployment
- Production operations.

These five areas represent important types of decisions or actions which are influenced by external S&T developments and which, therefore, must be addressed with more complete information.

At strategic levels of the company, two major CTI applications involve company strategy and external acquisitions. First, business and technology strategy concerns—such as the role of technology in business strategy, the decision to enter new technology-driven markets, and the need to protect key technology property from exploitation by others—all depend on what competitors are doing in S&T and on the direction and pace of technological change in areas relevant to a firm (Metz 1996; Roussel et al. 1991; Porter 1983). Second, selecting technology acquisition approaches and assessing the value of technology partnerships in product or process development are aided by information on S&T trends and on technology-oriented organizations (Cutler 1991; Chatterji and Manuel 1993).

Three other main CTI applications focus on technology development and use. The third major S&T function in a firm—managing the R&D portfolio—includes setting R&D priorities and designing technical approaches in specific R&D projects. Promising R&D portfolios depend on S&T experiences in organizations outside the firm, especially those engaged in similar or competing R&D work (Kokubo 1992; Steele 1989). Fourth, with regard to technology deployment, knowledge of competing technology developments in the market is essential for making capital investment and divestiture choices that will generate an attractive economic return (Souder and Sherman 1994). Finally, conducting production activities so as to preserve and maintain capital investments also depends on progress in supplier and resource technology outside the firm (Betz 1993).

Beyond these five main areas, a range of other business functions outside the R&D organization can benefit from technical intelligence. In particular, strategic business planning, marketing, and customer service can benefit from CTI products (see Krol et al. 1996).

BASIC COMPETITIVE TECHNICAL INTELLIGENCE ACTIVITIES

Technical intelligence in business is directed at two basic aspects of the competitive marketplace: technologies and organizations. Intelligence topics often involve the potential for scientific breakthroughs, projections of future market niches or emerging industries, and S&T issues such as the impact of environmental regulations. Both technology and the organizations are at the heart of these efforts. This dual focus suggests two basic types of technical intelligence activities in firms: technology surveillance and organization or company surveillance.

TECHNOLOGY SURVEILLANCE AND ANALYSIS

Technology surveillance and analysis refers to systematic, continuous watching or searching of an organization's external environment for relevant technology developments or trends. The purpose of technology surveillance is to provide focused S&T information to users in time for them to formulate and execute moves with the best current knowledge of what has been going on. (The external organizations involved in an emerging technology can be identified through technology surveillance, but they are not the primary information target—the primary target is the characteristics of and prospects for the technology).

Technology surveillance can include various collection and screening efforts, such as scanning, monitoring, and scouting, as well as analysis or assessment activities. Technology scanning means continual, broad surveying and screening of the external technical environment to identify S&T developments from many arenas that may be of further interest (Lenz and Engledow 1986; Aaker 1983). Technology monitoring refers to routine, focused tracking of designated S&T topics of interest to stay abreast of current developments and to detect trends (Ashton et al. 1994; Kydd 1996). Finally, technology scouting is collecting and screening targeted information items on particular technologies, experts, or organizations in response to user requests (Serapio and Dalton 1993).

Once surveillance data are collected and screened, various kinds of more detailed analyses can be performed to create technology status reports, trend analyses, or other intelligence for organizational decisions or actions. For instance, S&T assessments or evaluations are often done to describe and value a technology's current or potential features, status, or impacts (for example, development needs, operating characteristics, resource requirements, performance or cost-effectiveness, competitive and market effects, profitability, and economic value). Technology-focused intelligence can be used to

- Provide technical descriptions of existing or emerging technology systems, developments, events, trends, or capabilities; for example, developing an intelligence brief on technical progress and applications of fuzzy logic to process or equipment control
- Identify or predict significant shifts in the rate of progress in an area or the occurrence of technical breakthroughs that will make a new capability technically or economically feasible; for example, describing the impacts of high-temperature superconductivity on advances in scientific instrumentation
- Identify when substitute or competing technologies are becoming available; for example, recognizing the potential for composite materials to substitute for the metallic components now widely used in a firm's products
- Assess the impact on the directions and rate of technology development from new market-influencing technology forces such as government regulations or shifts in consumer preferences; for example, assessing the implications of high consumer interest in "green products" (that is, products produced with low- or zero-emission processes that minimize or eliminate harmful wastes).

To implement these and other technology-focused intelligence efforts, many firms have developed proprietary computer-based systems and databases, with unique features that allow them to search, acquire, compare, and display data. The payoff from these efforts is often smooth acquisition and adoption of a new technology developed through some other organization's R&D efforts.

ORGANIZATION SURVEILLANCE AND ANALYSIS

The second major type of technical intelligence activity—organization surveillance and analysis—focuses on relevant organizations in the competitive environment such as competitors; customers; suppliers; partners; universities; laboratories; and, sometimes, government agencies. The intelligence concern here is to stay abreast of what other organizations are doing, planning to do, or are capable of doing that might affect a firm's own current or future competitive position. Existing or emerging competitor firms, suppliers, or customers could either pose a threat or hold an opportunity for a company's current business or future plans. In a technical intelligence context, the technology characteristics of particular competitors or other organizations are the focus; the broader features of the technology outside of the target organization either are not included or are of secondary importance.

Organization surveillance focuses on evaluating another firms's technology strategy or R&D programs; profiling key technical managers, engineers or scientists; or assessing the role of technology in a competitor's cost structure. Just as with technology surveillance, once organizational surveillance data are collected and screened, various kinds of detailed analyses can be performed; examples include assessing competitive threats, evaluating partnering opportunities, or monitoring changes periodically to detect how other firms make technology-oriented decisions. To illustrate, organization-focused technical intelligence would seek to

- Recognize patterns of activity (by competitors, suppliers or customers) that can have consequences for a firm's market relationships; for example, formation of joint ventures between competitors, customers or suppliers; developments in university research programs; issuance of patents or licenses; announcements of new R&D contracts; or release of a new high-technology product
- Identify emerging capabilities (new distinctive technical competencies) or strengths and weaknesses in a competitor, supplier, or customer that could affect a firm's position; for example, recognizing that a competitor has the ability to recycle and sell materials formerly disposed of as waste products
- Compare the technical state of the art of company product lines

or production methods with those of other companies; for example, finding a means of chemically treating the surface of a product that could be used in place of widely used mechanical polishing equipment

- Compare a competitor's product or process technology performance or cost data with past records to discern potential future impacts or trends; for example, comparing the technical performance and cost of new modular manufacturing techniques against older batch processing methods.

To address these concerns, intelligence analysts tend to use either organizational tracking or organizational assessment approaches. Organizational tracking involves continuously monitoring and evaluating the assets, performance, plans, and personnel of a target organization. Competitor tracking—that is, following all activities and news about a particular competitor—is a good example. In one recently published company example, the objectives of a competitor tracking program are, first, to keep R&D staff regularly informed on all important technical news, publications and patents from key competitors and, second, to develop an annual strategic profile for each major competitor using a computerized profile of all technical information collected during the year (Kydd 1996).

Organizational assessment can take a variety of forms, but generally means an effort to describe or characterize the technological features of an organization and evaluate the consequences or impacts of these features for a firm's business. Examples include intelligence efforts to develop a competitor profile or to analyze the competitor's R&D pipeline. In both cases, the objective is to gain a detailed understanding of a competitor's capabilities, intentions, and chances for success (Vella and McGonagle 1987).

THE PLAN FOR THIS BOOK

This book is organized in five parts. Part I covers introductory material and foundations for understanding technical intelligence. Drawing on the experience of several practitioners, Part II focuses on establishing and managing a CTI unit in business. Parts III and IV move into the production and use of technical intelligence. Part III contains chapters that discuss several approaches, tools, and methods for developing intelligence findings; Part IV contains chapters that describe potential uses or applications of technical intelligence. Finally, Part V (one chapter) offers some thoughts about the future of technical intelligence in business.

REFERENCES

Aaker, D. A. 1983. Organizing a Strategic Information Scanning System. *California Management Review* 25:76-83.

Ashton, W. B. 1996. An Overview of Business Intelligence Analysis for Science and Technology. *Advances in Applied Business Strategy: Business Intelligence Theory, Principles, Practices and Uses.* B. Gilad and J. P. Herring (eds). JAI Press, Inc., Greenwich, Connecticut.

Ashton, W. B., and G. S. Stacey. 1995. Technical Intelligence in Business: Understanding Technology Threats and Opportunities. *International Journal of Technology Management* 10(1):79-104. (Special issue on the management of technological flows across industrial boundaries). Inderscience Enterprises Ltd., Geneva, Switzerland.

Ashton, W. B., G. S. Stacey, and A. Johnson. Spring 1994. Monitoring Science and Technology for Competitive Advantage. *Competitive Intelligence Review* 5(1):5-16.

Betz, F. 1993. *Strategic Technology Management*. McGraw Hill, Inc. New York.

Bower, J. L., and C. M. Christensen. Jan-Feb 1995. Disruptive Technologies: Catching the Wave. *Harvard Business Review*, pp. 43-53.

Bryant, P. J., T. F. Krol, and J. C. Coleman. 1993. Scientific Competitive Intelligence: A Tool for R&D Decision Making. *Competitive Intelligence Review* 5(2):48-50.

Carlton, S. A. November-December 1992. Industrial Espionage: Reality of the Information Age. *Research Technology Management* 35(6):18-24.

Chatterji, D., and T. A. Manuel. November-December 1993. Benefiting from External Sources of Technology. *Research Technology Management* 36(6):21-26.

Cohen, W. M., and D. A. Levinthal. February 1994. Fortune Favors the Prepared Firm. *Management Science* 40(2):121-132.

Cutler, W. G. May-June 1991. Acquiring Technology from Outside. *Research Technology Management* 34(3):11-18.

D'Aveni, R. 1994. *Hypercompetition: Managing the Dynamics of Strategic Maneuvering*. Free Press, New York.

Foster, R. N. 1986. *Innovation: The Attacker's Advantage*. Summit Books, New York.

Fuld, L. 1995. *The New Competitor Intelligence*. Wiley & Sons, New York.

Gilad, B., and J. P. Herring (ed). 1996. *Advances in Applied Business Strategy: Business Intelligence Theory, Principles, Practices and Uses.* JAI Press, Inc., Greenwich, Connecticut.

Herring, J. P. May/June 1993. Scientific and Technical Intelligence: The Key to R&D. *Journal of Business Strategy* 15(3):10-12.

Herring, J. P. 1996. Measuring and Communicating Intelligence Effectiveness to Management. *Proceedings SCIP 1996 Annual Conference*. Society of Competitive Intelligence Professionals, Alexandria, Virginia.

Kokubo, A. January-February 1992. Japanese Competitive Intelligence for R&D. *Research Technology Management* 35(1):33-34.

Krol, T. F., P. J. Bryant, and J. C. Coleman. 1996. Range of Services Provided by Competitive Technical Intelligence. *Keeping Abreast of Science and Technology: Technical Intelligence for Business*. W. B. Ashton and R. A. Klavans (ed). Battelle Press, Columbus, Ohio.

Kydd, P. H. January-February 1996. Tracking Your Competitors. *Research Technology Management* 39(1:)12-14.

Lenz, R. T., and J. L. Engledow. 1986. Environmental Analysis Units and Strategic Decision-Making: A Field Study of Selected Leading Edge Corporations. *Strategic Management Journal* 7:69-89.

Metz, P. D. May-June 1996. Integrating Technology Planning with Business Planning. *Research Technology Management* 39(3):19-22.

Moffat, S. March 25, 1991. Picking Japan's Research Brains. *Fortune*, pp. 84-96.

Porter, A. L., A. T. Roper, T. Mason, F. Rossini, and J. Banks. 1991. *Forecasting and Management of Technology*. John Wiley & Sons, Inc., New York.

Porter, M. E. 1980. *Competitive Strategy.* Free Press, New York.

Porter, M. E. 1983. The Technological Dimension of Competitive Strategy. *Developments in Research and Development Management*, Vol. 4. JAI Press, Inc., Greenwich, Connecticut.

Roussel, P. A., K. N. Saad, and T. J. Erickson. 1991. *Third Generation R&D*. Harvard Business School Press, Boston, Massachusetts.

Serapio, M.G., and D. H. Dalton. November-December 1993. Foreign R&D Facilities in the United States. *Research Technology Management* 36(6):33-39.

Souder, W. E. and J. D. Sherman. 1994. *Managing New Technology Development*. McGraw Hill, New York.

Steele, L. W. 1989. *Managing Technology: The Strategic View*. McGraw Hill, New York.

Vatcha, S. R. May 1993. Competitive Technology Intelligence. *CHEMTECH* 23(5):40-45.

Vella, C. M., and J. J. McGonagle, Jr. 1987. *Competitive Intelligence in the Computer Age*. Quorum Books, New York.

Walton, K. R., J. P. Dismukes, and J. E. Browning. September-October 1989. An Information Specialist Joins the R&D Team. *Research Technology Management* 31(5):32-37.

Identifying the Research Underlying Technical Intelligence

RICHARD A. KLAVANS

Tools and techniques for management have their roots in the open scientific literature. For example, such tools/techniques as portfolio analysis, core competency analysis, process reengineering, groupware, or competitive intelligence can be traced to earlier work that appears in the open scientific literature, usually literature for the social sciences, applied social sciences, applied mathematics, and applied engineering. The work on the experience curve built on prior literature on cost curves. The concept of a portfolio matrix for business was based on earlier literature on portfolio matrices for stocks. The work on personality profiling (a tool associated with competitive intelligence) has its roots in personality theory. The total quality management movement was preceded by an extensive literature on statistical control theory specifically applied to the measurement of quality. The tools used in R&D management (scenario planning, technology forecasting, technology planning, and even third generation R&D) have roots in the open literature.

This chapter examines today's science to anticipate tomorrow's tools and techniques in technical intelligence (TI). New terms—disciplines, research community, research region, and research universe—are introduced in the first part of this chapter. Indicators of "good science" (science-driven, technology-driven, and dollar-driven research) and dynamic indicators (science that disrupts the status quo) are defined. A process for developing a research universe—the research that is directly or indirectly related to a client's interest—is described.

The second part of this chapter identifies and describes the research universe for technical intelligence. Technical intelligence is defined as the intersection between two universes. One universe deals with R&D management, the other with information management/systems/science. These two universes comprise 75 regions of science. These regions are prioritized according to the likelihood that the research would form the basis for new tools/techniques for technical intelligence.

The third part of this chapter (analysis and synthesis) highlights the major findings and identifies gaps in research. Those familiar with the concept of disciplines, research communities, research regions, and the geography of a research universe (core, boundary, and cross-border research) may want to proceed directly to the third part of this chapter. Those unfamiliar with this terminology should read all three.

This chapter uses data provided by the Center for Research Planning (CRP). The data are embedded in a model of scientific activity in 1994 (the 1994 Science Model). This model uses co-citation analysis of the scientific literature to identify research communities. All subsequent references to research communities assume that the CRP algorithms were used to identify these research communities.[1]

DEFINITION OF TERMS

This chapter forecasts the development of new tools/techniques by rigorously analyzing the science on which tools/techniques are based. Terms are defined in order to develop a common language about the structure and performance of science. A step-by-step approach for creating a research universe (the research directly or indirectly related to a client's interests) is described.

DISCIPLINES

A discipline is an area of academic instruction, such as condensed matter physics, biochemistry, surface chemistry, or electrical engineering. Academics self-organize into disciplines for the purpose of instruction. The composition and boundaries of these disciplines are constantly in flux as academics debate what should or should not be included in a program of instruction.

One method for identifying the composition and boundaries of disciplines is to cluster journals based on journal-to-journal citation patterns. This technique is based on the tendency for professors to maintain the boundaries of their discipline by defining journals that are "appropriate" for tenure/promotion decisions. Physicists must publish in physics journals or chemists in chemistry journals in order to establish their reputation within the discipline. An analysis of these groups of journals provides insights into the way disciplines evolve.

In the 1994 Science Model, 5103 journals were clustered into 819 disciplines. The distribution (number of journals per discipline) is log-normal. At one extreme, the largest discipline (biochemistry) is composed of 529 journals. At the other extreme, 468 disciplines have only one journal. The average discipline has 5.6 journals.

Five disciplines will be used as a starting point in this study. Two of the disciplines are associated with R&D (see Figure 1). One discipline was found by starting with *Research Technology Management*, the journal associated with the Industrial Research Institute. This discipline included another journal, *R&D Management*, which deals explicitly with R&D. The remaining journals in this set deal much more with development, espccially new product development. The paradigm journal (the journal in the center of the network that is used to describe the discipline) reflects this development orientation: the *Journal of Product Innovation Management*.

The second discipline associated with R&D was found by searching for research on technology forecasting and research policy. This discipline is much more oriented toward research than toward development. The paradigm journal, *Scientometrics*, reflects this orientation. This discipline deals more with the role of

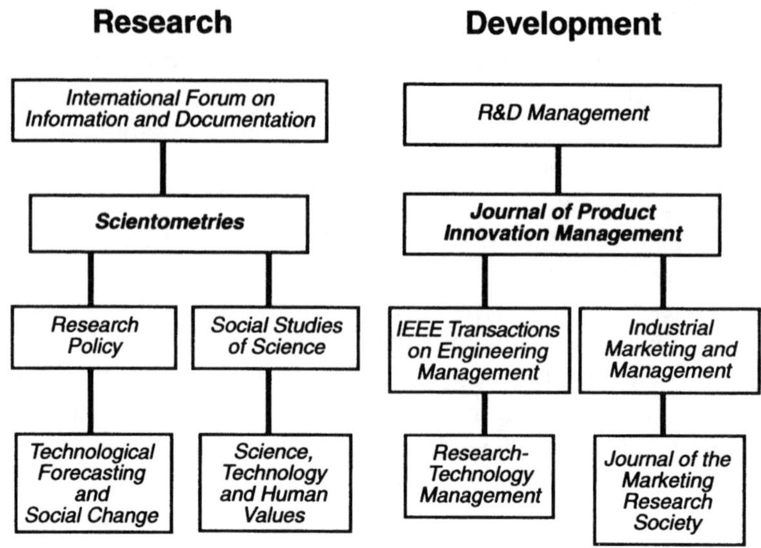

FIGURE 1. R&D disciplines (two clusters of journals).

science in the broader context and has a strong orientation toward objective measurement.

The three disciplines most associated with information dealt with information management, information systems, and information retrieval. The information management discipline is relatively small (see Figure 2). The paradigm journal is *Information & Management*; the other two journals are *MIS Quarterly* and *Database*.

Figure 2 also illustrates the network of journals for information systems. The paradigm journal is *Communications of the ACM*. The remaining five journals deal with different aspects of information systems, especially as they relate to computers and computer systems.

The relatively large network that deals with information retrieval is also presented in Figure 2. The central journal is the *Journal of the American Society for Information Science* (JASIS). This network of journals deals with a broad set of issues that appears to be particularly important to the information professional.

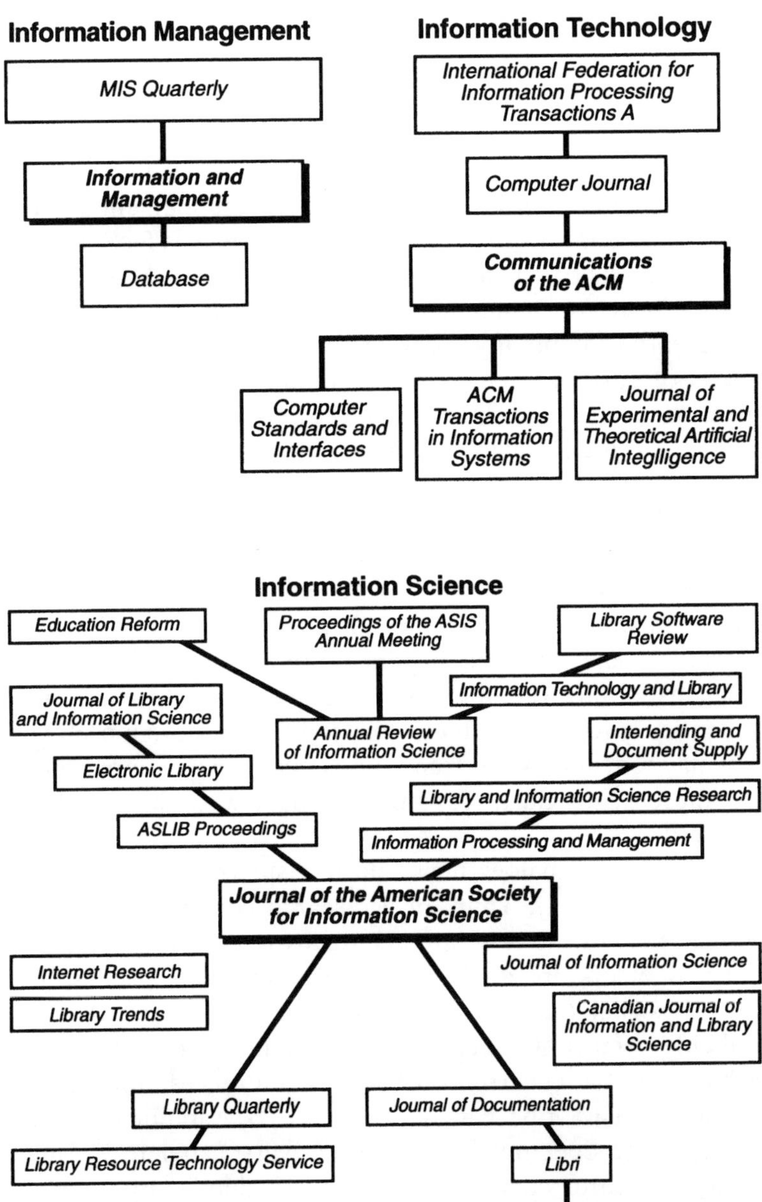

FIGURE 2. Information disciplines (three clusters of journals).

RESEARCH COMMUNITY

A research community is a group of researchers following a similar route to the solution to a scientific/technical problem. A research community is bound by intellectual interests, not by geography.

The concept of a research community is well established. Research communities are considered the fundamental unit of analysis in science. Both science historians (such as DeSolla Price) and sociologists of science (such as Kuhn) refer to research communities as the key component of scientific activity.

A research community is defined by two sets of papers. One set consists of current papers (reports of the work being done and appearing in the open literature), the other of reference papers (the base of intellectual work the research community is building upon).

The number of research communities varies by year. The 1984 Science Model had only 28,128 research communities; by 1994, there were 42,415. The number of research communities is related to the number of current papers appearing in the yearly model of science. In some years, the papers are more tightly clustered, and fewer clusters are required to describe the structure of science. The tendency for papers to be more tightly (or more loosely) clustered may reflect a macro trend in science between harvesting science (more tightly clustered) and planting new ideas (more loosely clustered).

The following analogy may help in visualizing the nature of a research community. Think of a research community as a tribe. The members of the tribe are analogous to current papers, while the tribal elders are analogous to the reference papers. Tribal members signal their membership by acknowledging the **set** of tribal elders (current papers are clustered into research communities based on the occurrence of **sets** of references, not individual references.) The tribe can be identified by sampling the tribal members; one does not have to have every paper to be able to identify a research community—just a sufficiently large sample of papers. (Over 90 percent of all literature that will be cited in the scientific literature is used to generate the CRP Science Model.)

Research communities are assigned to disciplines because most of the current papers and reference papers in a research community appear in a single discipline (a single cluster of journals).

Approximately 90 percent of all research communities are assigned to a single discipline; 9 percent are assigned to two disciplines. The remaining communities are highly interdisciplinary areas of research.

Table 1 lists the number of research communities, the number of reference papers, the number of current papers, and the average age of these papers for the five disciplines mentioned previously. These data illustrate the amount of data that is being summarized: over 3000 papers published in one year and 668 citations to earlier work that researchers in 1994 considered to the basis for their research.

The size (number of current papers, number of reference papers) and age (of the reference papers) are used to develop indicators of the degree to which a research community is science-driven, technology-driven, and/or dollar-driven. Following is a more formal definition of each indicator.

TABLE 1

Seed disciplines for the technical intelligence universe

Name of Paradigm Journal	Research Communities	Reference Papers	Current Papers	Average Age of Reference Papers (years)
Seed Disciplines for the R&D Universe				
J. Product Innovation Management	12	95	238	9.11
Scientometrics	25	93	505	12.77
Seed Disciplines for the Information Universe				
Information & Management	21	89	289	11.74
Communications of the ACM	81	228	1539	8.46
J. of the American Society for Information Science	44	163	570	9.06
Total		668	3141	

PERFORMANCE INDICATORS

Performance indicators have been developed for each research community in the 1994 Science Model. These performance indicators deal with status and dynamic characteristics. The status indicates whether the research is science-driven, technology-driven, or dollar-driven; the dynamics indicate whether the research is disruptive or part of a trend that is growing, in stasis, or declining.

Science-driven research communities are ones in which researchers quickly incorporate new findings into their efforts to solve problems. The incorporation of new findings is reflected in the age of the reference papers. Science-driven research communities have reference papers that, on average, are only a few years old. Conversely, research communities that are not science-driven have reference papers that could be 10 to 20 years old, on average.

The criterion for identifying science-driven research communities is from an algorithm that analyzes the *age distribution of reference papers* and sets an appropriate criterion based on the characteristics of this distribution.

The research communities associated with technical intelligence are less science-driven (4.8 percent versus 12 percent for the entire 1994 Science Model). This is not uncommon for research communities that draw more from the social sciences than from the hard sciences. In general, social sciences are less science-driven.

Technology-driven research communities are ones in which the researchers use new technology, usually a new measurement technique or measurement protocol, to solve problems. The indicator of a technology-driven research community is a very large number of reference papers.

A very large set of reference papers occurs when a technology is calibrated by remeasuring older phenomena. It is the tendency to remeasure (and to reference the studies representing the older technology) that increases the number of reference papers. Approximately 2 percent of the research communities in the 1994 Science Model are technology-driven. On average, they have 25 reference papers (the average is only 4 reference papers per research community). The criterion for identifying technology-driven research communities is derived from an algorithm that analyzes the *size distribution of reference papers* and sets an appropriate criterion based on the characteristics of this distribution.

The research communities associated with technical intelligence are less technology-driven. Only 2 of the 186 research communities are technology-driven (1 percent compared with the baseline level of 2 percent). Technical intelligence is not a technology-driven area.

Dollar-driven research communities are ones in which there is a great deal of research activity. The indicator for dollar-driven research communities is the number of current papers. This indicator assumes that there is an input-output relationship between the money invested in an area of research and the number of research papers published in that area.

A very large set of current papers occurs when researchers are pursuing a "hot" area of research. Only about 2.5 percent of research communities in the 1994 Science Model are dollar-driven. On average, they have 85 current papers, about 25 to 30 current papers per research community. The criterion for identifying dollar-driven research communities is derived from an algorithm that analyzes the *size distribution of current papers* and sets an appropriate criterion based on the characteristics of this distribution.

None of the research communities in the five disciplines listed in Table 1 is dollar-driven. Technical intelligence is not an area in which there is a great deal of investment.

Disruptive science research communities are ones that are not linked to research communities from previous years. The base bibliography (the set of papers co-cited by the research community) is used to link research communities from one model year to another. Approximately 53 percent of the research communities in the 1994 model were disruptive over a 2-year period (the previous model year was 1992). This means that approximately one fourth of all research in any given year is new, and three fourths is an extension of prior research.

The level of disruption in the five disciplines associated with technical intelligence is higher than expected (73 percent versus a baseline of 53 percent). This level is not uncommon for the social sciences. In general, the hard sciences (biology, chemistry, physics, etc.) are less disruptive. One interpretation of this observation is that hard sciences tend to build on previous research. A research community in the hard sciences is more likely to be linked to the research communities from previous years. The social sciences (economics, sociology, psychology) and the applied social sciences (management, R&D management, marketing, finance, manufacturing) tend not to build on previous research as much as do the hard sciences. These research communities are less likely to be linked to the research communities from previous years.

REGIONS

A region is a group of related research communities that appear during the same time period. "Relatedness" is based on the tendency for current papers from one research community to cite the reference papers of another research community at a level that is not sufficient to combine these communities into one larger community, but is sufficient to indicate that these research communities are related.

Regions represent complex problems that require the participation of a diverse set of research communities. Stated in another way, the solution to complex problems emerges from the linkage of distinct research communities. These complex problems are usually multidisciplinary, that is, the research communities are associated with a diverse set of disciplines.

Figure 3 represents Region 714, which is composed of seven research communities. All but one of these research communities are associated with the scientometric discipline (367). This is also the region of science that underlies the methodology used in this chapter.

The upper half of Figure 3 represents the structure of this region of science. The structure is relatively simple: three substructures (one triplet and two pairs) based on cross-community citation patterns. These substructures were combined and linked based on cross-substructure citation patterns.

Behind three of the research communities in Figure 3 is a "shadow," indicating a link to prior research. Four of the research communities are new (not linked to research communities that were identified in previous models). As previously mentioned, the number of new research communities appearing in a region is an indicator of disruption. The level of disruption in this region is less than average for the set of 186 communities (average of 73 percent), but more than average for the entire Science Model (53 percent).

The lower half of Figure 3 represents the content of this region of science. The content of each research community is described by listing frequently occurring idiosyncratic phrases from the titles

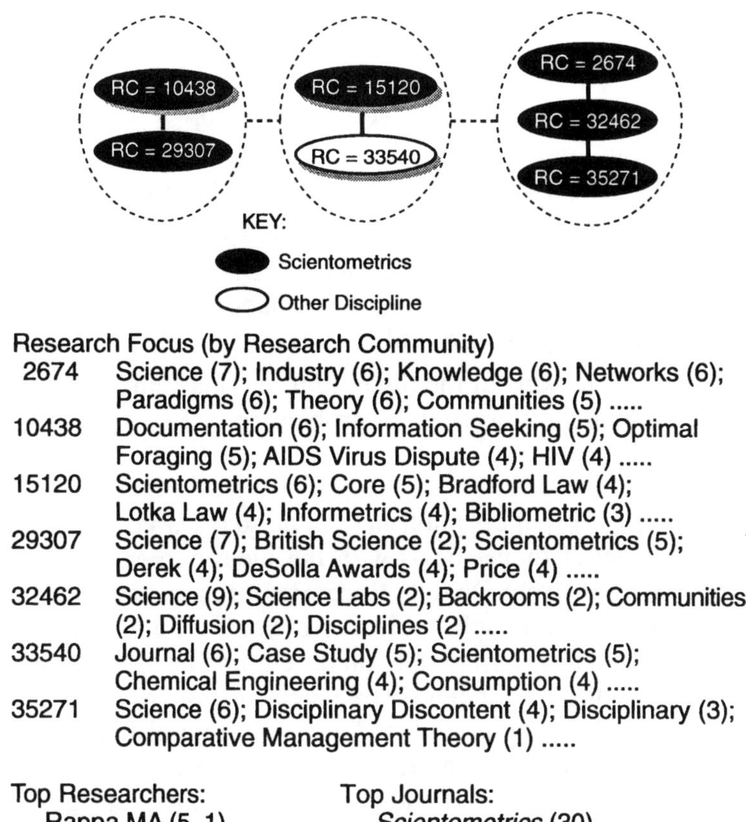

FIGURE 3. Analysis of Region #714.

of the papers. Titles are "parsed" (broken up into single- and multi-word phrases). (Commonly occurring words, such as "a," "the," "and," that do not describe content are deleted.) Researchers recognize the nature of the research problem from these phrases if they are familiar with the research problem.

For example, four research communities have the word "science" as the primary word. Each community is, however, interested in a slightly different problem.

- RC 2674 is focusing more on the role of science in industry by looking at the theory of networks and research communities.

This draws from Kuhn (who emphasized the sociology of knowledge and defined a paradigm as the language of a research community).

- RC 29307 is based on the work of DeSolla Price (a historian of science who emphasized scientific progress and introduced the concept of a research community much earlier than Kuhn).
- RC 32462 builds more on Kuhnian concepts and looks at communication patterns among science laboratories. These communication patterns are improved if both laboratories are from the same disciplinary background.
- RC 35271 is looking at the discontent that may emerge because of disciplinary differences, a problem related to 32462, but slightly different.

There were 166 papers published on these research problems in 1994. The overall theme deals with the measurement of science and draws mostly from DeSolla Price. Researchers have self-organized around different subproblems (research communities). One of the best ways to get up to date on developments in this region is to contact the top researchers. The names of researchers who are most active in the region are listed at the bottom of Figure 3. For example, a few follow-up phone calls would reveal that Rappa MA (5,1) is a professor at MIT. In addition to the five papers published in 1994 and one reference paper, he has a dissertation that builds on DeSolla Price and a number of important working papers. Most of the other top researchers are outside the United States. A few phone calls would verify the hypothesis that the center of excellence for this research is split between the Netherlands and Belgium. An association dealing specifically with these issues (ISSI) is located in Paris.

Another example of a region is presented in Figure 4. This region is predominately associated with discipline 367 (8 out of 15 research communities). But there are more research communities in other disciplines. The disciplinary profile provides some insights into the focus of this region, which seems to deal with R&D, government policy (suggested by the economics and world development disciplines), and strategic management. The content of the region seems to deal more with technology (instead of science). Some of the same researchers appear in this region (Rappa and

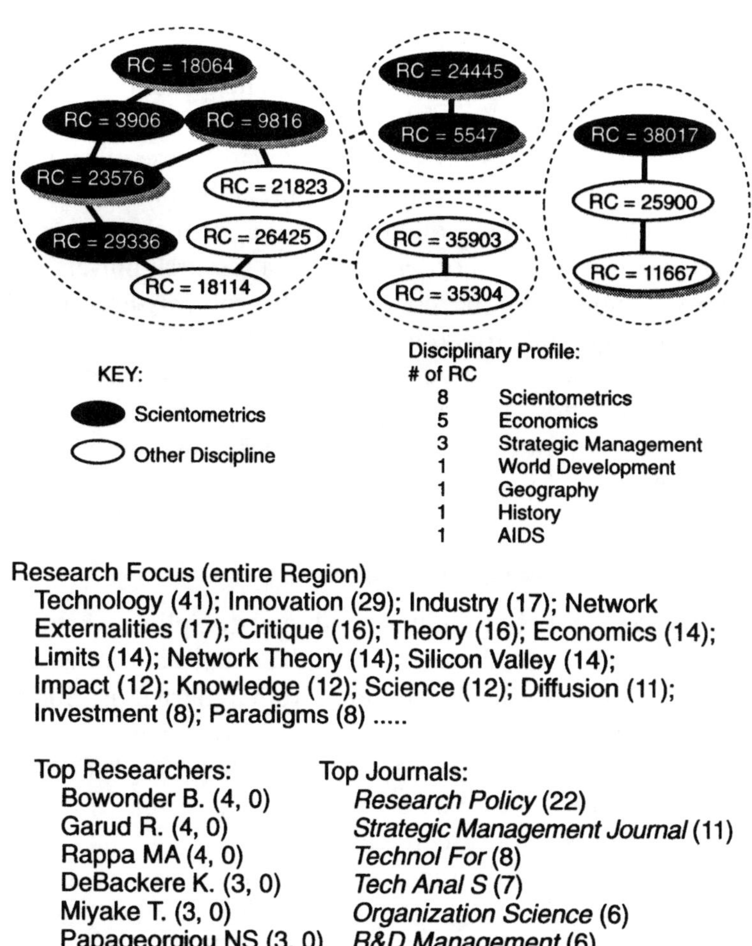

FIGURE 4. Analysis of Region #367.

DeBackere), while new names also appear. The top journals are different—instead of *Scientometrics*, most of the publications are in *Research Policy* and the *Strategic Management Journal*. One could conclude that this is a multidisciplinary region, an interesting region where there is "spillover" to (or from) those interested in R&D management, strategic management, and government policy.

RESEARCH UNIVERSE

The purpose of a research universe is to help clients find "out of the box" solutions to their problems. "In the box" solutions emerge from the activities of researchers in the core of a research universe. "Half in/half out" solutions emerge from the border of a research universe. Out-of-the-box solutions emerge from the activities of researchers in the cross-border sector of a research universe.

Steps 1 and 2 describe how research problems are placed in core, boundary, and cross-border sectors. Step 3 allows clients to "prune out" areas of a research universe that clearly are not relevant to their needs. Step 4 suggests that performance indicators should be used to prioritize the remaining research problems. The goal is Step 5: the formulation of a strategy that can be acted upon.

Step 1—Identify the Seed Disciplines

A research universe is built around seed disciplines, that is, disciplines that are most associated with the client's concerns. These seed disciplines are usually identified from a journal list. Identifying the seed disciplines for a research universe is an iterative process. The objective is to develop a highly focused set of seed disciplines that will generate a highly relevant research universe, but not miss important research problems.

For purposes of illustration, we will identify two research universes. One research universe will be based on the two R&D disciplines as the seed disciplines (356 and 367), the other will be based on three information disciplines (167, 244, and 633) as the seed disciplines.

Research communities associated with a seed discipline are called seed communities.

Step 2—Assign Research Communities to Core, Boundary and Cross-Border Sectors of the Universe

Research communities in the *core sector* are in regions that are dominated by the seed discipline. These regions are in-the-box solutions to research problems. This is a matter of definition. The seed discipline was the discipline identified as the major source of in-the-box solutions. One can expect, then, that regions dominated by the seed discipline would be sources of in-the-box solutions.

Out-of-the-box solutions occur when the regions are not dominated by the seed discipline. One part of the region (research communities associated with the seed discipline and the neighboring research communities) is placed in the *boundary sector*, while the remaining part of the region (research communities that are at least two steps away from a seed community) are placed in the *cross-border sector*.

Region 714 (refer back to Figure 3) is an excellent example of a set of research communities that would be in the core (if the seed discipline were #367/Scientometrics) or split between boundary and cross-border (if the seed discipline were not #367/Scientometrics). The scientometrics discipline dominates this region (all but one of the research communities are assigned to this discipline). If the discipline associated with scientometrics is the source of in-the-box solutions, this region is in the box.

Region 714 has one research community that is not linked to scientometrics. If the seed discipline were associated with this research community only (RC 33540—the only white oval in Figure 3), then RC 33540 and its neighbor, RC 15120, would be in boundary and the remaining research communities would be cross-border. If the discipline associated with the white oval is in the box, then the region consists mostly of out-of-the-box research.

Step 3—Identify the Research Most Relevant to Client Needs

A number of approaches are used to determine which part of the research universe is of particular importance to the client. One approach is to develop a disciplinary profile of relevant research (a disciplinary profile is the number of research communities by discipline). A desired disciplinary profile can be developed deductively from an examination of the disciplinary profiles for the core, boundary, and cross-border areas of the universe. A desired disciplinary profile also can be developed inductively, from a review of individual regions and research communities and an analysis of the disciplinary profile emerging from these choices.

Identifying the relevant reearch is an iterative process. Occasionally clients will reject a discipline as being unimportant and later find these disciplines to be the sources of new scientific discoveries that can seriously affect the client's likelihood of success.

Step 4—Analyze

The analysis focuses on indicators of performance for each section of the universe (core, boundary, and cross-border) and the choices in step 3 (those regions/research communities that are most relevant to client needs). For example, does the universe have more (or less) research that is high momentum (science-, technology-, or dollar-driven)? Is the core "better" or "worse" than the boundary and cross-border research? Are the research communities of interest more or less disruptive than the research communities in the universe?

Step 5—Synthesize and Form a Science Strategy

Two of the major advantages of the CRP model are in the formulation and implementation of a science strategy. A precise and detailed view of the scientific options (e.g., research communities, regions, and disciplines) can help managers test their assumptions about the way the science is organized; resolve conflicts between the way different people believe the science is organized; and identify blind spots, that is, research options that are below the level of conscious awareness but, once mentioned, are usually recognized as important.

The formulation of a science strategy results in a statement of domain (which research communities or regions are of interest) and type of involvement

- Central strategic value
- Listening posts to monitor the region
- Areas of increased/decreased efforts.

Statements about the firm's strengths (capabilities in high-value research communities); weaknesses (no capabilities in high-value research communities); direct threats (competitors in research communities that are of high strategic value); indirect threats (high-momentum/disruptive research in competing regions); and opportunities (research communities where the firm has a historical strength) are grounded in objective data.

The implementation of a strategy involves actions such as reallocating budgets, redirecting monitoring efforts, and seeking alliance partners or acquisitions. Data on research communities, regions, and/or disciplines can greatly facilitate this process. For example, the data are used to rank alliance partners or potential acquisition targets to assess the degree to which the target organization contributes to the strategic goals of R&D. Sudden competitive moves (such as alliance formations) can be quickly assessed in terms of the implications to the firm.

IDENTIFYING THE TECHNICAL INTELLIGENCE UNIVERSE

The identification of a research universe is an iterative process that depends in great part on the identification of the seed discipline. Identifying the seed discipline for technical intelligence is difficult because no journals deal explicitly with this topic. The following discussion on identifying the seed discipline illustrates one way of overcoming this problem. Two universes (one based on R&D management and one based on information) were created to illustrate the biases and omissions that result in the selection of seed disciplines.

IDENTIFYING THE SEED DISCIPLINES

Seed disciplines are disciplines (journal clusters) that are the logical starting point for defining a research universe. Unfortunately, there are no journals that explicitly focus on technical intelligence.

The most active journal in technical intelligence is the *Competitive Intelligence Review*. Because it is a trade journal, it does not have a cross-journal citation influence and, therefore, is not considered a member of worldwide science. Journals that are mentioned in the syllabi of competitive intelligence courses provided additional leads. Here again, the most frequently mentioned journals are also trade journals (the *Competitive Intelligence Review* and the *Journal of Business Strategy*). The non-trade journals mentioned in these syllabi were part of information (*Electronic Library*), corporate decision-making (*Harvard Business Review*), or political decision-making (*World Politics, International Security).*

The disciplines that deal with information and R&D management were selected as the seed disciplines for this study. This choice was based on an understanding of the history of competitive intelligence in the United States (Prescott 1996). Competitive intelligence (CI) emerged from management (especially the planning function) and information (especially the information retrieval function that provided information for the planning function). Competitive intelligence in the United States also emerges from political decision-making (for example, involvement of people from the Central Intelligence Agency and the Defense Intelligence Agency). No discipline associated with political decision-making led to related research on competitive intelligence. Intelligence (in the political context) was reported in a journal that also did not have a strong cross-journal citation pattern, the *Journal of Intelligence and Counter Intelligence*.

The specific choice of the R&D disciplines listed in Figure 1 was based on key journals (*R&D Management* and *Research Technology Management*). The choice of the information disciplines listed in Figure 2 was based on an examination of the research agendas of different information disciplines. These are the disciplines that describe the development of information systems for management (such as groupware), advanced information retrieval techniques (such as search engines for the Internet), and the design of advanced information management systems.

IDENTIFYING CORE, BOUNDARY, AND CROSS-BORDER SECTORS OF ACTIVITY

Table 2 summarizes the size and intersection of the R&D universe and the information universe. The R&D universe is smaller (316 research communities) than the information universe (1183 research communities). While the two universes have 167 research communities in common, the overlap is mostly in cross-border areas. Only 11 research communities are common to the core and boundary sectors of both universes.

TABLE 2
Size and overlap in the R&D and information universe

Sectors	R&D	Information
Core	8	34
Boundary	52	208
Cross-border	256	941
Common to both	167	167
Unique to one	149	1016

IDENTIFYING RESEARCH MOST RELEVANT TO TECHNICAL INTELLIGENCE

A bottom-up approach was used to determine the most relevant research areas. Using data on the regions and the research communities and a literature search of recent publications by key authors, the author assessed the relevance/irrelevance of each region to technical intelligence and consulted experts, as needed. A disciplinary profile was then generated to determine criteria for inclusion/exclusion, and the regions were re-assessed. In total, 20 of the 75 regions were considered relevant to technical intelligence.

Table 3 reorganizes the 20 regions according to the first three parts in this book. Part I is the overview with a chapter on Japan. These topics correspond with regions 3251, 396, 1845 and 2044.

Region 3251 is a multidisciplinary network of research communities dealing with technology strategy, innovation processes, learning processes, embedded knowledge, and computer-assisted cooperative work. This network represents a major research agenda for R&D management and is probably the single best region to describe the context of technical intelligence. From this perspective, technical intelligence is a computer-assisted process for developing technology and innovation strategies around learning/knowledge concepts. This region is also associated with the chapters in Part IV.

TABLE 3
Identifying relevant regions of research

Part I (Overview and Chapter on Japan) and Part IV (Managerial Use of TI)	
3251	Tech Strategy/Innovation/Learning/Embedded Knowledge/ Computer-Assisted Cooperative Work
396	Technology/Innovation/Industry/Network Externalities
1845	Patent Analysis/Knowledge Flow/US-Japan
2044	Innovation/Development Teams/Japan
Part II (Technical Intelligence Management Processes)	
762	Process Reengineering/Information Systems for Decision-Making
Part III (Patent Analysis/Bibliometrics/Scientometrics/Co-citation Analysis/Scouting)	
714	Scientometrics/Measurement of Scientific Activity
Part III (Computer Support Systems, Exploiting Computerized Databases)	
1338	Computer Mediated Communication
5569	IS System Design (Rockhart/MIT)
3856	Manager's Use of IS
667	Satisfaction of IS/ITS systems
24	Info Retrieval/Tabu Searches/etc.
843	Document Relevance Criteria/Searching
4096	Database Design
Analytical Techniques	
2828	Pattern Recognition
1391	Analogy/What makes things similar
2713	Visual Display of Quantitative Data
Expert Systems	
550	Calibration/Experts/Overconfidence in Decision-Making
3352	Modeling Knowledge Systems
3127	Experts/Belief Systems/Evolution

One reason for a separate chapter on Japan in Part I is that Japan's success is tightly linked with research on technology. For example, regions 3251, 396, 1845 and 2044 use Japan as a model of success. Region 396 takes a political/economic perspective and examines knowledge flows across nations—especially the flow to Japan. Region 3251 is more focused on the formation of the U.S. government in regards to these knowledge flows, especially those between the United States and Japan, and uses different analytical techniques, such as patent analysis, to document the flow. Region 3251 looks at innovation strategies and knowledge-based technology strategies. Region 2044 looks at innovation processes and the use of development teams. All four regions are linked to the observation that Japan's technology-based innovation strategies were successful in the 1970s and 1980s.

Part II of this book deals primarily with the design of a technical intelligence system. The corresponding research dealing with this issue is embedded in Region 762. This region of 11 research communities deals, in part, with process reengineering of the information system that supports executive decision-making. The authors in Part II of this book are addressing this problem by providing practical "best practice" accounts.

Part III deals with a diverse set of problems linked primarily to the information disciplines and to scientometrics. The first three chapters correspond to the research in nine regions that draw from the information disciplines. All nine regions are dealing with more advanced issues of information retrieval and systems design.

The remaining three chapters draw from one region (714), which is at the interface of R&D management and information science. These chapters are primarily interested in advanced techniques for revealing the content and structure of science and technology.

The remaining regions are areas that may provide new tools and techniques for technical intelligence. For purposes of discussion, these regions have been organized into three groups. The first group deals with pattern recognition. Traditional pattern recognition techniques draw primarily from mathematics and applied engineering (region 2828). The use of analogies is a pattern recognition technique that draws from cognitive psychology (region 1391). And the work by Tufte on the visual display of quantitative information deals with evoking and communicating patterns through visual means (region 2713).

The second group of regions deals with experts. Technical intelligence can be viewed as an extension of the way R&D managers access expert knowledge in their decision-making process. Reframing technical intelligence in this fashion raises some interesting questions. How have R&D managers traditionally accessed expert knowledge? Does technical intelligence differ in terms of content (the type of knowledge accessed, such as more knowledge about competitive intentions) or process (the way that technical information is gained, analyzed, and disseminated)?

ANALYSIS AND FINDINGS

Table 4 summarizes the degree of momentum (the percentage of the research communities that are science-, technology-, or dollar-driven) and the degree of disruption (the percentage of the research communities that are new to the 1994 model) for the six regions identified in Table 3.

The research that corresponds with Part I (purpose of technical intelligence) and Part IV (use of technical intelligence) provides a great deal of insight into the context from which technical intelligence is viewed. As mentioned previously, the context is technology strategy, innovation processes, learning processes, embedded

TABLE 4
Prioritizing research on technical intelligence

Part/Area	No. of Research Communities	High-Momentum Research (%)	Disruptive[(a)] Research (%)
Part I and Part IV	83	7.2	66
Part II (processes)	11	36.4	100
Part III (information)	48	4.2	52
Part III (scientometrics)	11	0.0	57
Analytical Methods	22	9.1	73
Use of Experts	42	16.7	61

(a) Percentage of research communities that are "new" to the 1994 Science Model knowledge, and computer-assisted cooperative work. The underlying science is, however, not of an exceptional nature. The amount of high-momentum work is below average, suggesting that fundamentally new ideas are not likely to appear; and the amount of disruptive research is slightly above average (but about average for social science research). This research is not likely to create fundamentally new insights into how R&D managers form technology strategies, innovation strategies, or knowledge strategies.

The research on process reengineering of information systems is the most exceptional area of research (highest momentum and highest amount of disruption). This research focuses primarily on managerial processes, not information processes, and is reported primarily in the operations management literature. This research corresponds with the chapters presented in Part II of this book. All four chapters provide practical insights into managerial processes associated with technical intelligence.

The research that corresponds with the chapters in Part III is, on average, the least exceptional. Some 48 communities provide a great deal of relevant research dealing with accessing information and system design, but, on average, this research has the second least amount of momentum and is least disruptive. The other part of Part III (research generally dealing with scientometrics) has fewer research communities (7), the least momentum, and the second least amount of disruption. The indicators used here suggest that the research underlying Part III is not remarkable. There is not a body of new science to form the infrastructure for new tools and techniques.

The research that deals with analytical techniques not addressed in this book (22 research communities in 3 regions) is much more exceptional. Although this research does correspond with the purpose of Part III (new analytical techniques), there were no chapters explicitly on pattern recognition, analogical thinking, or the visual display of quantitative data. These research topics are much more disruptive, but, on average, the amount of high-momentum work is below average.

The last group of regions in Table 4 is associated with the research on experts. This research is exceptional: both the amount of high-momentum research and the amount of disruptive research are above average.

EMERGING TOOLS AND TECHNIQUES

The purpose of this analysis was to anticipate the tools and techniques that are emerging from science. In the near term (1994 to 1998), one looks for research that is most related (for example, core regions) and published in practitioner journals (close to commercialization). The research dealing with scientometrics best fits this profile. This research corresponds to the last three chapters in Part III. But the indicators from CRP's 1994 Science Model suggest that there is not a new and exciting wave of scientometric approaches on the horizon. Existing research is now mature and reaching commercial application. The chapters in Part III discuss some of the first commercial applications of these tools.

Over the longer term (1999 and beyond), exciting new tools/techniques are likely to come from three sources:

- Process reengineering of information/intelligence systems
- Changes in R&D managers' use of experts
- New analytical tools/techniques.

Process reengineering of information/intelligence systems was the most exceptional area of research in the R&D/information research universe that was relevant to technical intelligence. Therefore, this area is the most likely to generate new and unusual tools/techniques. The chapters in Part II are just the beginning of what one can expect in the future. By 1999, process-related techniques for developing technology strategies, innovation strategies, knowledge-based strategies, and computer-assisted cooperative work could increase significantly.

R&D managers' use of experts was the second most exceptional area of research and the area most likely to change the way one views technical intelligence. At present, technical intelligence is perceived as an aspect of technology strategy specifically aimed at anticipating threats and seizing R&D opportunities. This research raises a different issue: technical intelligence might be viewed as an alternative way for R&D managers (or executives) to access technical expertise. The traditional method is to hire experts. An alternative method is to install a technical intelligence system. The following questions might be asked: What are the relative advantages of experts? What are the relative advantages of a technical intelligence system? How can one design a process that takes the best from both approaches?

New analytical tools/techniques may be emerging from some pockets of research in the R&D/information universe. These tools are not emerging from the traditional source of analytical methods (for example, scientometrics). They are from dispersed sources, such as the literature on pattern recognition, analogies, and visual display of quantitative data. These new tools and techniques are not likely to fundamentally change the way one collects, analyzes, or disseminates technical intelligence. They do, however, provide additional approaches with corresponding advantages.

Today's science is positioned to support the development of technical intelligence. The infrastructure is in place. Techniques for assessing opportunities and threats are most likely to become commercialized in the near term. Managerial processes for linking technical intelligence to decision-making are more likely to appear in the long term.

REFERENCE

Prescott, J.E. 1996. The Evolution of Competitive Intelligence. *International Review of Strategic Management* 6:71–90.

ENDNOTE

1. For a comprehensive analysis of this method for modeling science, see J. J. Franklin and R. Johnson, Co-citation Bibliometric Modeling as a Tool for S&T Policy and R&D Management: Issues, Applications, and Developments, *Handbook of Quantitative Studies of Science and Technology,* van Raan (ed.), Elsevier, Amsterdam.

Japan as a Model for a National Approach to Business Intelligence

JUSTIN L. BLOOM

The question is often raised how Japan has managed to achieve a preeminent position in world trade involving highly sophisticated manufactured products, while experiencing an apparently short history of technological competence. An important factor—but not the only one—in Japan's growth to an economic superpower has been its diligence and its success in acquiring industrially important technical information from other countries, as an adjunct to its indigenous development of industrial technology. It is this factor that will be analyzed here as typical of Japanese information gathering in general.

Many consider the Japanese information gathering and dissemination system to be the epitome of a successful national approach to technology acquisition (see, for example, Herring 1992, NRC 1992, Bonthous 1994). The purpose of this chapter is to explore the conditions under which the importation of technology and its successful application have flourished in Japan, thereby setting forth the principles by which other nations might emulate the Japanese success as a model, in whole or in part. The published literature, both in English and Japanese, is rich on the elements of this subject. Only a sample of available publications (and those only in English) is used as background for this chapter, and these are limited—with a few exceptions—to citations within the past five years.

It is fair to say at the outset that no nation can hope to (or would want to) reproduce in its entirety what will be shown to be a complex path, but certainly elements of that path are worthy of consideration by others.

EARLY TECHNOLOGICAL EVOLUTION IN JAPAN

Isolated geographically as it is from the other nations of Asia, Japan has created a culture that is both uniquely indigenous and, at the same time, has been heavily based upon the importation of knowledge of every description, ranging from religious practices to language to technology. A purely indigenous evolutionary process probably would have resulted in a culturally and economically backward nation with a relatively small population since the Japanese archipelago is too poor in natural resources to sustain by itself the 125 million or so people who now live there. The fact that a number of other island societies have evolved around the world without achieving economic success or advancing culturally indicates that conditions in Japan other than geographic isolation were participatory in the evolution of Japanese ethnicity (Sakaiya 1993).

Indeed geographic isolation was not so severe as to literally cut off the Japanese archipelago from the rest of the world. Casual inspection of a map of the area shows that the island of Kyushu is separated from the Korean Peninsula by the Tsushima Strait, only about 100-km wide at its narrowest point. Likewise, the northern end of the island of Hokkaido is separated from the tip of Siberia's Kamchatka Peninsula by an even smaller distance. In fact, it is commonly believed that the Japanese archipelago was populated by the migration of peoples from the Asian land mass across these two straits. The water barriers only modestly restricted easy intercourse with the rest of the world, but they did afford the archipelago protection from invasion.

The Japanese people became seafarers early in their history as they sought food supplies from the ocean and, thus, were able to explore the coastal regions of East Asia without difficulty. Ultimately, Japanese seafaring prowess, coupled with a highly competent industrial and technological structure, resulted in Japan's being able to invade and conquer Asian nations with much larger land masses and populations. Thus the water barriers acted as two-way valves, controlled by the Japanese. It is not usually recognized that another seafaring nation, now called the United Kingdom, evolved under similar geographic constraints, became a leading trading power, was technologically sophisticated, and vanquished a sizeable fraction of the less-developed world before the advancements made by other nations caused the British Empire to collapse.

CONDITIONS FOR THE ABSORPTION OF TECHNOLOGY

A large number of analysts have attempted to address the reasons for the apparently unique ability of Japan to acquire and absorb technology so effectively. Recent publications by Japanese authors are particularly illuminating.

Taichi Sakaiya has devoted most of an entire book to examining this subject (Sakaiya 1993). He claims that the conversion of Japan from a feudal, largely agrarian society to a modern, politically cohesive, industrial society took place in a remarkably short period of time: beginning with the downfall of the Tokugawa shogunate and its replacement by the Emperor Meiji and a centralized government in 1867-1868 and extending for about 40 years thereafter. Enormous efforts were made during this time to import manufacturing technology from abroad. However, 40 years was too short a period in which to set the conditions for the effective absorption of such technology, so these conditions must have evolved earlier.

An internationally known Japanese scientist who is currently the president of Tohoku University, Jun'ichi Nishizawa, recently addressed the relationship of Japanese culture to its scientific and technological status (Nishizawa 1994). He postulates that Japanese culture originally was one of frugality, asceticism, and self-renunciation. These attributes did not seem to interfere with the introduction of foreign technology into Japan, but they appear to have contributed to the generally held assertion that the Japanese people lack creativity (for example, in scientific research). Yet, Japanese scientists who have worked abroad have made many important advances in science, a few at the Nobel Prize level.

Nishizawa believes that the educational system U.S. authorities introduced after World War II turned Japan away from budding creativity in the sciences and toward ". . . mass education and teaching as opposed to research and to inadequate funding for basic research." He foresees a new era in which elements of Japanese culture will be adopted by other nations as the world moves toward the acceptance of "energy-conserving, ecology-friendly technology."

Masanori Moritani, an engineer and popular author, also agrees that the Japanese have not been creative in the Western sense and have relied heavily on the introduction of foreign technology (Moritani 1982). He points out the importance the Japanese place on learning foreign languages and how culturally based aptitudes such as skills in miniaturization and the integration of process and product have permitted Japan to excel at transferring and using foreign technology.

In Sakaiya's view, the most important condition ultimately affecting Japan's ability to import technology was the physical environment of the archipelago. The mountainous islands made animal husbandry difficult and forced the populace to engage in intensive farming on limited plots of flat land. Rice became the staple crop, requiring the intensive labor of a sizeable proportion of the people. Rice farming and the infrastructure supporting it (for example, building and maintaining complex water supplies, terracing land, etc.) required the pooling of human resources and thus led to the necessity for forming cooperative communities larger than the family unit.

Suppression of the individual's role in society and dependence on the group became the norm. Collectivization of thinking and labor in primitive society has extended to the modern milieu in Japan, where the position of the group at various levels of aggregation remains more important than the position of the individual.

This collaborative approach to problem-solving has had a heavy influence on the nature of research and development in Japan and on Japan's approaches to the transfer of technology internally and from foreign sources. An extensive treatment of this complex sociological phenomenon has been written by prominent Japanologists at the Massachusetts Institute of Technology (Levy and Samuels 1989).

Other nation states have shown a similar collective organization of society at one or more stages of their development and yet have not achieved economic prominence or technical sophistication. Therefore, other factors must have played important parts in setting Japan's course.

Undoubtedly, the degree of literacy and formal education attained is one of these. In this respect, Japan has demonstrated outstanding success, setting it apart from the rest of the nations of Asia and from most of the other nations of the world. Although centralized management of education by the national government in Japan and the dependence to a large extent on rote learning at the primary and secondary levels have been criticized both internally and externally, the fact remains that the Japanese people exhibit a literacy rate in excess of 99 percent (presumably excluding in the counting those who are physically and mentally incapable of learning to read and write), probably the highest in the world for a relatively large country. Likewise, the proportion of students who attend and graduate from secondary schools and the percentage of these graduates who go on to complete college educations rank among the highest in the world.

Statistics provided by the International Institute of Education (Chambers and Cummings 1990) indicate that over 94 percent of Japanese youths attend senior high schools, with 74 percent participating in academic curricula. In contrast to the situation in the United States, very few high school students in Japan drop out, so about 70 percent of Japanese high school graduates are academically qualified for college entrance. About 50 percent of high school graduates actually matriculate in post-secondary institutions—roughly the same proportion as in the United States. However, more American students than Japanese enter four-year programs. This entry rate is offset by a greater attrition rate in the United States, so ultimately, the two countries produce the same proportion of bachelor's degree graduates: one out of every five young people.

Although signs of this national commitment to education were apparent in the feudal era preceding the Meiji Restoration and were attributed to adherence to Confucian principles in Buddhist religious schools of the era, the real growth in education—particularly at the university level—did not occur until the Meiji era began and educational principles and practices were introduced from abroad (primarily from Germany). This transformation was neither simple nor free of controversy. It probably would not have occurred without a mandate from the central government, thereby overcoming opposition from religious quarters and from the ultra-nationalists who represented the vestiges of the warlords who had ruled Japan and had kept it free of major foreign influences for 300 years.

Furthermore, to carry out the transfer of information on educational processes required that large numbers of Japanese pedagogues learn foreign languages, travel to other countries to see firsthand how these processes were applied, and then return to their home country to adapt and apply what they had learned. While Japan was hardly unique in such an undertaking, what was remarkable was the rapidity and the thoroughness with which it was accomplished.

This massive undertaking was paralleled by similar missions to Europe, the United States, and elsewhere to learn about technology, manufacturing, finance, agriculture, the arts, and just about every other field of human endeavor. Aside from the political determination required to proceed in this direction, a heavy financial burden was imposed on the people to pay for missions which did not return dividends for many years to come. Japan was a very poor country in that period and burdened itself still further with a military buildup intended to make Japan a power in Asia. That the Japanese people did not reject these movements is another sign of the power of collectivism that existed there in the late 19th and early 20th centuries.

One particularly important effect of the effort to acquire and absorb foreign information was the recognition of the need for large numbers of people to learn foreign languages. It can be postulated that only a nation with a centralized educational system could make it mandatory that essentially all students learn at least one foreign language. Before World War II, German, French, and English all received priority attention, but after the War, English (primarily American English) became the language of choice and mandate.

Today, almost all Japanese have some knowledge of written English, although few can speak it with fluency. Until the past decade or so, the teaching of English had been the responsibility of native Japanese teachers, few of whom had any verbal fluency in

English. Now, native speakers of English can be found throughout Japan acting as language teachers, brought in by the Ministry of Education and the Ministry of Foreign Affairs from the United States, Canada, Australia, the United Kingdom, and other Anglophone countries.

Another reason for the relatively poor ability of the Japanese to speak English has been the retention of a special Japanese phonetic syllabary (*katakana*) for writing and printing foreign words in what can only be described as an approximation of their true pronunciation. Without going into elaborate detail, the problem can be easily understood when it is realized that all Japanese syllables (and hence words) end in the English vowel sounds a, i, u, e, and o, with the exception of some syllables and words that end in the English consonant n or a variant of the n sound, m. Thus syllables in English that end in consonants cannot be transposed directly into Japanese phonemes. With the advent of modern computerized wordprocessing and typesetting techniques in Japan, it is possible to print foreign words in their original form in Japanese texts without converting them to *katakana* symbols. When this capability is coupled with better training in the spoken language, verbal English in Japan should improve.

The purpose of this digression into the teaching of foreign languages in Japan is to illustrate that Japan has invested an enormous amount of its wealth and time to enable its citizens to understand English and other languages. This ability to use foreign languages has enabled Japan to transfer foreign information far more readily than would be the case otherwise. It must be remembered that English is a difficult language for those whose native tongue is Japanese, and thus, the attribute has not come easily. Most linguists say that a good idea of the complexity entailed is to examine how difficult it is for those whose native tongue is English to learn Japanese. The obstacles are equivalent.

Notwithstanding Japan's huge investment to teach its citizens foreign languages, the continuous thirst for knowledge from abroad is not satisfied by individual foreign language capabilities. Translation services are still in strong demand, some of which is met by commercial organizations. According to one recent report, interpretation and translation services constitute a burgeoning business in Japan (JETRO 1994). Translation services alone are said to produce more than ¥2 trillion ($18.2 billion) in revenues.

Interpretation services are smaller in volume but are growing steadily.

For most of the past 100 years, superficial foreign observation of technological development in Japan led to a widely accepted view that the Japanese were inherently incapable of innovation and invention and thus were forced to rely on obtaining technical information or knowledge from others. This flawed view was supported to some extent by Japanese exports of cheap, poorly manufactured toys and other consumer goods before World War II. Actually, Japan was developing a strong technical infrastructure, heavily emphasizing engineering rather than science. This approach was consistent with the cultural reliance on consensus and group action.

As a consequence that has extended to the present time, the "NIH" (Not-Invented-Here) Syndrome is notably (but not completely) lacking in Japan (Bloom 1990; Branscomb and Kodama 1993; Grimes 1993; Bonthous 1994). This syndrome has plagued other countries, including the United States, where information, technology, or hardware not developed indigenously was viewed as being inferior. The MIT Commission on Industrial Productivity examined an even broader aspect of this failing in the United States by pointing out that national parochialism had led to a great loss of markets both domestically and globally (Dertouzos et al. 1989).

The emergence of Japan as a world economic power required that the disparaging view of Japan as an imitator be reexamined. Professor Ezra Vogel of Harvard University was one of the first to publicly show the danger of believing that Japan could not compete with the West because of its innovative failings (Vogel 1979). An extensive and provocative examination of Japanese culture and creativity and Western misunderstandings of these values (Bolton 1991) indicates that in the right environment, "learning by watching"—often the Japanese approach—is more valuable than "learning by doing."

"Learning by watching" implies a rather passive approach to technology transfer. Just the opposite is true in Japan. A joint study panel composed of senior American and Japanese policy analysts under the auspices of the United States and Japanese governments recently has defined the technology acquisition process in Japan as being "receiver-active." Under this paradigm, ". . . aggressive receivers can obtain technology from passive senders, but passive receivers are unlikely to obtain technology from even the most aggressive senders." (Morin and Kodama 1993).

Thus the characteristics of Japan's historical approach to gathering information from abroad are seen in summary as

- Establishment of technological parity at the international level as a national goal, based on the absorption, adaptation, and exploitation of foreign technology to the extent necessary for maximum efficiency in time and cost.
- Use of a national consensus to commit resources toward obtaining information.
- Strong, long-term commitment to education, literacy, and universal teaching of foreign languages.
- Training of professionals to levels permitting the absorption and application of transferred information at various levels of sophistication.
- Culturally induced suppression of individualism or national chauvinism in the valuation of externally generated information.

MECHANISMS FOR TRANSFER AND ABSORPTION OF TECHNICAL INFORMATION

A relatively large number of pathways exist for moving technical information from outside of Japan to users within. Some of these paths are obvious and perhaps trite, while others are obscure and complex. Regardless, the Japanese approach to using them often is unusual and even unique. To enumerate the most important of them,

- Dispatch undergraduate and graduate students to universities abroad to improve foreign language capabilities, learn the status of foreign science and technology, adapt to foreign teaching and research methods, and establish personal and professional contacts as the basis for future relationships.
- Support and subsidize the assignment of employed graduate scientists and engineers to research establishments abroad operated by foreign governments, universities, or private entities,

with objectives similar to those above but with the understanding that information will be shared or jointly developed with the host organizations.

- Acquire foreign technical information or technology through private purchase from or by royalty payments to technically oriented firms, usually as part of a higher level business strategy; in the extreme, purchase the firms outright.
- Create private manufacturing, research, or sales subsidiaries in other countries, primarily staffed by the nationals of those countries, with the subordinate objective of following local advances in pertinent research and development.
- Send study missions abroad, sponsored by either the public or private sectors, to gain a current awareness of the status of particular technical developments.
- Enter into governmental-level agreements with other countries to jointly develop and share technical information, usually for public benefit rather than commercial value.
- Endow fellowships in foreign universities or establish advanced research facilities at these universities to facilitate access to academic research.
- Invite foreign scientists and engineers to work in Japanese universities, government laboratories, and private research facilities, subsidizing the costs through fellowships, grants, and salaries or living expenses.
- Hire consultants abroad to perform surveys or technical studies.
- Develop and operate information organizations in Japan, in both the public and private sectors, with responsibilities for obtaining, translating, and disseminating foreign technical journals and gray literature in both electronic and print forms.
- Use the presence of Japanese diplomats, businessmen, and academics working abroad to formally or informally monitor and report on a current awareness basis any technical advances, competitor strategies, government policies, or other information of value to their home offices.

None of these activities is surprising. In fact, all of them are practiced to one extent or another by every country. Japan, however, has demonstrated both persistence and diligence in these undertakings and has been willing to make the significant financial investment required to be effective. There is no apparent grand scheme in this direction orchestrated by the central government, but cooperation between the government and the private sector—as in so many endeavors in Japan—has ensured that at least public and private efforts are reasonably consistent with each other and often are mutually supportive. Strangely, competition between government ministries and agencies (a long-standing problem in Japan as in other countries) may actually serve to diminish the efficiency of the information system by creating duplicate channels of supply. Within the private sector, competition is expected, since much of the information-gathering process there is for proprietary purposes rather than to serve public policy.

GOVERNMENT ORGANIZATIONS

Ordinarily the first place to look for the creation and operation of a national business intelligence system would be within a national security intelligence network. Modern Japan does not have a formal intelligence agency of the type well known in other advanced nations, although a number of government organizations perform intelligence or counter-intelligence operations of a conventional nature. These include the Ministry of Foreign Affairs, the National Police Agency of the Ministry of Justice, and the Japan Defense Agency.

The amount of information in the open literature about the functioning of these organizations is limited and may be largely anecdotal, with the only extensive treatment of the subject being a recent book on the Japanese secret service by Richard Deacon, a British authority on the world's secret service agencies (Deacon 1990). In the last chapters of his book, Deacon characterizes the present Japanese intelligence system as follows:

> *Naturally some of the work associated with Japan's intelligence services is concerned with defence: it would be a rash nation which acted otherwise. But one can estimate that something like eighty-five per cent—possibly even ninety per cent—of Japan's*

intelligence gathering is directed towards making Japan more prosperous.

Deacon assigns to Japan's Ministry of International Trade and Industry (MITI) the role of masterminding the intelligence function, stating that MITI is ". . . at the pinnacle of this intelligence network. . . ." While some of Deacon's other conclusions are quite fanciful and probably erroneous, at least he has made a serious effort to link Japan's economic progress with its acquisition of foreign scientific and technological information. He describes many of the nongovernmental organizations in Japan that are involved in gathering, analyzing, and using business intelligence.

Comparatively little has been written about the Japanese information system as an element of business intelligence. One comprehensive paper that addressed this subject was given in 1989 at an international conference on access to Japanese information (Sigurdson and Nelson 1990). The paper contained only a few references to earlier studies. The authors portrayed the Japanese approach as being enormous in monetary terms, citing a figure of $3 billion per year or greater for collection of business intelligence in the United States alone.

Undoubtedly a figure of this magnitude implies that the purchase or licensing of technologies and the acquisition of companies fall within it and is not solely related to the costs of maintaining intelligence "operatives" in the United States. To put this figure into perspective, it is greater than the annual R&D budget of MITI. Actually, the figure may be in error, although it is widely quoted as the justification for increasing U.S. expenditures for obtaining information from Japan. According to another source,

> *In return for billions of dollars generated by the transfer and adaptation of foreign technology, Japanese companies paid a relatively modest cumulative sum of only $17 billion. Amortized over 33 years, Japanese industry paid, on average, only about $500 million per year, a fraction of what it undoubtedly would have cost to develop the technology at home, provided Japanese companies could have achieved the breakthroughs.* (NRC 1992)

Sigurdson and Nelson, citing a Japanese study, report that the top five intelligence sources used in Japan are business and trade newspapers, trade magazines, personal contacts, specialty books, and company reports, but other analysts are said to believe that the Japanese also rely on reports generated by outside think tanks and consultants. Other external sources mentioned are databases, information gained at exhibitions and conferences, and catalogs and brochures for production and R&D equipment. Mention is also made of the use of "diggers" to gather information on request, but it is difficult to differentiate between this appellation and the more common term of "consultant."

Another assessment of Japan's information acquisition policies and practices was contained within a broader study conducted in the United States by the private Council on Competitiveness. This study on Japanese technology policy was conducted at a time when the need for a formal technology policy—or indeed an industrial policy—was being debated (Cheney and Grimes 1991). This assessment acts as a good summary of Japanese business intelligence practices in the realm of technology, but its statistics should be updated by reference to more recent information.

In a different vein, Herring has made a study comparing business intelligence activities in Japan with those in Sweden (Herring 1992). He finds both countries superior to the United States in terms of applying business intelligence operations to enhancing economic competitiveness.

More recently, Bonthous (1994) has compared the cultural foundations of the intelligence networks that are operated by Germany, France, Sweden, Japan, and the United States. He devotes more of his analysis to Japan than to the other countries and reaches conclusions that are consistent with those independently arrived at here.

It is probably impossible to identify all Japanese organizations engaged in finding foreign technical information and seeing that it is placed in the hands of potential users. For example, every large multinational corporation of Japanese parentage engages in this practice (Herring 1992), just as do corporations with other national identities. Little value is added by simply listing all Japanese multilaterals; therefore, a more aggregated approach to identification of organizations is attempted here.

Although all government ministries or executive agencies with technical responsibilities have information collection and distribution processes, a relatively small number sponsor international collection efforts or have representatives abroad. The most prominent are discussed here.

MINISTRY OF FOREIGN AFFAIRS

The Ministry of Foreign Affairs acts as an indirect conduit for technical information since it has no appreciable technical staff or responsibilities of its own. At its embassies in selected foreign countries, it houses a science counselor and a small support staff. This official is engaged primarily in representing the Japanese government to the host country's government on policy matters with heavy technical content, such as energy, environment, and technical cooperation. The official is always seconded from another government organization, so far always the Science and Technology Agency (STA) (located administratively in the Office of the Prime Minister), and serves abroad for three years before returning to the parent organization. In larger embassies, such as in Washington, the science counselor is supported by a First Secretary, who is also seconded from STA, and a Second Secretary who is a nontechnical Foreign Service Officer.

This small staff, burdened by formal responsibilities and by housekeeping functions such as arranging for the arrival of delegations from Japan and accompanying them on their visits, has little time to collect technical information and does not appear to do so. On occasion, other officers in the Embassy have technical backgrounds, such as those representing MITI; the Ministry of Education, Science and Culture (MESC); the Environment Agency; or the Japan Defense Agency (JDA). But these officers also seem to be concerned with functions other than information gathering.

The role of the Japanese science counselor is markedly different from that of officers with similar titles in other embassies. For example, French and Swedish science officers are heavily engaged in collecting technical information for use by their industrial sector and have large support staffs for this purpose (Herring 1992). In fact, the Japanese counselor functions in much the same manner as his American counterpart—concentrating on policy matters, administering agreements, and handling the flow of official visitors.

SCIENCE AND TECHNOLOGY AGENCY

The Science and Technology Agency (STA) is nominally responsible for developing, coordinating, and implementing the Japanese government's science and technology policies and is located administratively in the Office of the Prime Minister for these purposes. In practice, however, STA shares responsibilities with other ministries and agencies, such as those mentioned above. Although STA is represented unofficially in Japanese embassies by the science counselors and first secretaries for policy matters under its jurisdiction, it must look to others for collection of technical information. It uses its own subordinate organizations for this purpose: a series of government-owned public corporations chartered to carry out R&D in the national interest or to support R&D through technical services. Each of these corporations operates information services of substantial competence and, in a number of instances, maintains small offices in important foreign cities for both liaison and information transfer purposes. The most significant of these corporations in terms of their foreign presence are

- Power Reactor and Nuclear Fuel Development Corporation
- Japan Atomic Energy Research Institute
- National Space Development Agency
- Japan Information Center of Science and Technology.

These organizations maintain foreign offices that appear to be completely independent of their embassies. It must be made clear, however, that there is nothing covert about them. They are well known and act as significant suppliers of Japanese technical and management information to host-country organizations. In the United States, the visa status of the Japanese staff members does not permit them to engage in business, and therefore they do not let study contracts or otherwise act officially for their parent organizations.

The Japanese Information Center of Science and Technology (JICST) deserves special mention because it is the principal government entity responsible for acquiring and translating foreign technical information. At the same time, JICST is one of the Japanese government's doors to its own technical information databases, albeit much of the information is in the Japanese language and therefore inaccessible to most foreigners. (A subset of JICST's information holdings is maintained in an English-language database called JICST-E). Offices are maintained in

Paris and Washington. The JICST Washington office holds a particularly close relationship with the National Technical Information Service (NTIS) of the Department of Commerce.

The JICST also has been a leader among Japanese government agencies in promoting the development of machine translation of English into Japanese and vice versa. Considering that it now collects more than 8500 foreign technical journals for absorption into its various databases, JICST believes that the ultimate application of machine translation will be cost-effective. Of total JICST periodical holdings, 54.4 percent originate in Japan, 17.5 percent in the United States, and 9.3 percent in the United Kingdom. Other advanced countries have smaller proportions. At present, large numbers of human translators are employed part-time to abstract foreign journals into Japanese and to prepare English-language abstracts of Japanese journal articles for foreign consumption. Machine translation is used to assist in the activity (Uchida 1991, JICST 1993a, JICST 1993b, STA 1992).

To provide a measure of the importance attached to the JICST role, its budget has doubled in the past eight years, reaching a level of ¥16.98 billion in 1993. Of this amount, approximately 37 percent was supplied by the central government in the form of subsidies or investments, with the remainder attributed to income from the sale of products and services. Converted to dollars ($1 = ¥105), the 1993 budget amounted to about $161 million. This budget can be contrasted with the NTIS budget for 1993 of $46.9 million, $7.6 million of which came from a government appropriation. The estimated 1994 budget for NTIS is $68.0 million, with no federal appropriation. There is some indication that NTIS will again be receiving government financial support in the FY 1995 budget (OMB 1994).

If all of the technical staff members in foreign offices of STA's public corporations are added together, they form a reasonably large body of scientists and engineers who acquire a good knowledge of their host countries' programs, policies, and technical information.

MINISTRY OF INTERNATIONAL TRADE AND INDUSTRY

The word "International" in the MITI's English-language title (the word does not appear in the Japanese-language version) would appear to indicate a strong presence of MITI technical personnel abroad. Although MITI maintains a significant complex of industrial R&D operations in Japan through 16 industrial research institutes and other research organizations and includes an Agency of Industrial Science and Technology (AIST) as part of its management structure, it relies on a separate, semi-independent network for technical representation in other countries.

One of MITI's adjunct agencies, the Japan External Trade Organization (JETRO), has offices throughout the world. The larger ones employ engineers who act as listening posts and who also contract for studies of foreign technological developments. This role has diminished somewhat as Japanese corporations have expanded their foreign operations over time and no longer depend as much on information provided by JETRO and MITI. Its formal mission is currently stated as follows (JETRO 1994):

- *Promoting exports to Japan;*
- *Collecting and analyzing information on local industry and trade;*
- *Helping local firms introduce their products to Japan through business shows and exhibitions;*
- *Facilitating cooperative ventures including technology transfer and investment;*
- *Conducting a wide range of activities to improve mutual understanding between the host country and Japan;*
- *Working as an intermediary in the dialogue between local industry and Japanese companies;*
- *Broadening the channels of communication with local government agencies;*
- *Providing for the exchange of trade missions and personnel.*

From this description, it is not surprising to find that today some JETRO offices (at least those in the United States) act more as a point of entry for those wishing to sell their products in Japan and that they provide financial sponsorship of bilateral conferences on business prospects and technology sharing. Regarding technology transfer specifically, JETRO even publishes a technology journal in English, *New Technology Japan*, to promote the licensing or sale of Japanese technology to the world.

Table 1 contains a list of a far-flung network of offices JETRO now has (JETRO 1993a, JETRO 1993b, JETRO 1994). It is clear from even a casual examination of this impressive network that neither the United States nor any other advanced nation can match Japan's efforts to promote its products and to facilitate imports into Japan, while at the same time monitoring foreign economic and technological developments. The U.S. Foreign Commercial Service, the diplomatic arm of the Department of Commerce, is JETRO's counterpart in the U.S. government. It does not have the financial resources, the experienced manpower, or the independence to match JETRO, and it does not appear to be heavily involved in acquiring foreign technical information.

JETRO is not omniscient or all-pervasive. For example, at the moment, it has no presence in the states formed from the former Soviet Union, although private Japanese firms actively pursue business prospects in them. Presumably, functions that JETRO might perform are conducted by private business interests to the extent possible. Of course, this situation can occur for the United States also. The United States has no formal representation in Iran or Vietnam, for example, but Japan does, and JETRO has offices there.

ORGANIZATIONS SPONSORED BY THE MINISTRY OF INTERNATIONAL TRADE AND INDUSTRY

The Ministry traditionally has not carried out its technical objectives by creating a system of public corporations of the type STA uses. However, it does sponsor a few of these, among them specifically (for the purposes of this analysis) the New Energy and Industrial Technology Development Organization, which also maintains offices in a few foreign countries (Washington, D.C.; Sydney, Australia; Paris, France). Other MITI agencies with foreign offices (mostly in Washington, D.C.) include the Japan Patent Office, the Manufactured Imports Promotion Organization, and the Japan National Oil Corporation (Kahaner 1994).

TABLE 1
JETRO overseas offices

NORTH AMERICA	CENTRAL & SO. AMERICA	EUROPE	
New York	Mexico	London	Zurich
Chicago	San Jose	Dublin	Geneva
Houston	Bogota	Paris	Vienna
Dallas	Caracas	Hamburg	Milan
Los Angeles	Lima	Dusseldorf	Rome
San Francisco	Santiago	Frankfurt	Athens
Atlanta	Sao Paulo	Munich	Madrid
Denver	Rio de Janeiro	Amsterdam	Lisbon
Toronto	Buenos Aires	Rotterdam	Warsaw
Montreal		Brussels	Belgrade
Vancouver		Copenhagen	Bucharest
		Stockholm	Sofia
		Oslo	Prague
		Budapest	
ASIA	**OCEANIA**	**MIDDLE EAST**	**AFRICA**
New Delhi	Sydney	Istanbul	Cairo
Karachi	Melbourne	Baghdad	Algiers
Dahka	Perth	Teheran	Nairobi
Colombo	Auckland	Dubai	Dar es Salaam
Singapore	Harare		
Jakarta	Johannesburg		
Kuala Lumpur	Douala		
Bangkok	Lagos		
Hong Kong	Abidjan		
Manila			
Seoul			
Beijing			
Shanghai			
Dalian			
Hanoi			

OTHER MINISTRIES WITH OVERSEAS REPRESENTATION

Through their subordinate organizations, MITI and STA dominate the Japanese government's technical representation abroad. A few other specialized ministries maintain foreign offices, again mostly in Washington, D.C. These include the Japan Society for the Promotion of Science (JSPS—an organ of MESC), with offices in Washington, Bonn, Nairobi, Cairo, Bangkok, and Sao Paulo (JSPS 1992); Nippon Telegraph and Telephone Corporation (partially owned by the Ministry of Posts and Telecommunications); and the Japan Transport Economics Research Center (under the Ministry of Transport). The proliferation of these and other similar offices, which do not have technical interests but which serve the same general purposes, is said to be of concern to the Ministry of Foreign Affairs as a dilution of the formal intelligence-gathering diplomatic function (Kahaner 1994).

GOVERNMENT/INDUSTRY ASSOCIATIONS

Both MITI and some other government ministries seem to prefer another type of structure for both internal and external functions involving large numbers of private industrial corporations: the industry association. This approach to government/industry interaction is highly developed in Japan and will be discussed below as an element of the private sector.

STRUCTURE OF THE PRIVATE SECTOR

As has been intimated earlier, most of Japan's business intelligence activity takes place within the private sector, often with government encouragement and, in some instances, with government subsidies. It is difficult to categorize the variations that occur in this regard, so an arbitrary differentiation has been made: industry associations chartered and partially funded by government agencies are classified as hybrid government/industry agencies and have been described above, all other private organizations are put into the "private" category. For the purposes of this discussion, Japanese universities are classified as "private," although the approximately 100 prestigious national universities are owned, operated, and staffed by the central government.

THE PRIVATE CORPORATION

By far the most important entity in the collection and, of course, use of technical information is the private corporation in Japan. Approximately 80 percent of all R&D in Japan is financed by private funds, and most of this investment is in private industry. The industry receives only about 2 percent of its R&D financing from government sources (Bloom 1990).

During the "catch-up" phase of the Japanese economy beginning after World War II and extending into the 1970s, during which reconstruction of the Japanese manufacturing industry took place and a commitment was made to production of goods with unparalleled quality, the public sector invested heavily in acquiring foreign technology. The government encouraged this practice and provided some financial assistance coupled with favorable tax breaks. The outright purchase or licensing of technology was the largest of several parallel approaches employed in the past, and these practices continue partially because of long-term agreements signed years earlier.

Today Japan has reached the state of "relative parity" in technology resources relative to the United States. Although its exports of technology to the United States have increased steadily, its technology deficit with the United States is still substantial. Table 2 depicts the trend (Dalton and Genther 1991). However, Japan's overall technology trade with the world is essentially in balance, according to the Japanese government's Management and Coordination Agency and as shown in Figure 1 (STA 1993). This conclusion depends heavily on the assumptions made in the nature of technology trade and in calculating the associated costs.

How Japan and other advanced nations relate to each other in technology trade is shown in Figure 2 (STA 1994). Admittedly, the purchase or licensing of technology has not been considered a conventional tool in the business intelligence arsenal, but in the case of Japan, its importance—both in magnitude and in impact on Japan's technological and economic growth—suggests that it be included. Once again, it is necessary to emphasize that the mere purchase of technology by a nation does not ensure that the

TABLE 2
Technology trade between the United States and Japan
(in millions of dollars)

Year	Outflows of Technology[(a)]	Inflows of Technology[(b)]	Net Outflow
1982	853	89	764
1983	930	121	809
1984	1008	173	835
1985	1004	168	836
1986	1360	295	1065
1987	1948	354	1594
1988	2451	388	2063
1989	2571	491	2080

(a) Receipts of royalties and license fees.
(b) Payments for royalties and license fees.

Source: Dalton and Genther 1991

technology will be applied for economic benefit and that highly sophisticated processes for adaptation and exploitation of the technology are required. Japanese corporations have met this condition.

According to Atsuro Kokubo, who is a senior staff member of Arthur D. Little (Japan), Inc., Japanese corporations have been forced to change their approach to gathering competitive technical information as they have emerged from being imitators to being innovators. He has written,

> *Competitive intelligence is fully developed as part of the R&D decision process in leading Japanese firms. In their corporate pep talks, top executives emphasize that CI activities—fully exploited beyond R&D considerations—will be a key to seizing the initiative in a complete range of business activities. These executives preach this gospel wisely, because they have learned that high-tech businesses decline when CI activities get lazy.* (Kokubo 1992).

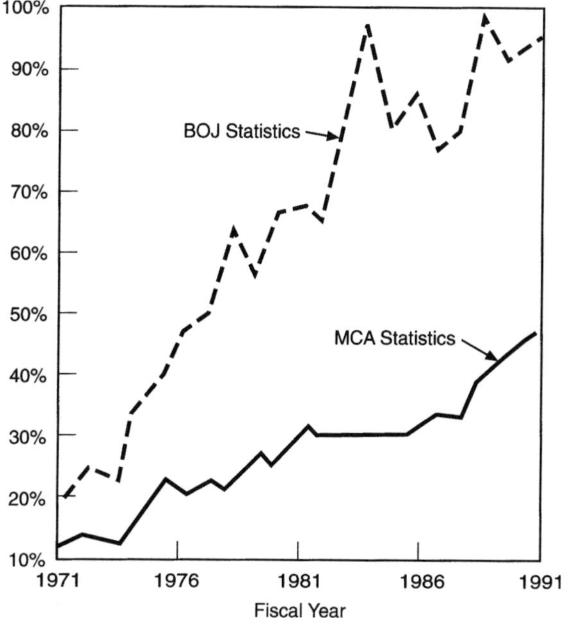

Notes:

- BOJ = Bank of Japan; MCA = Management and Coordination Agency
- BOJ data include wholesale, retail, and service businesses; MCA data do not.
- BOJ data include transfer of rights for trademarks and designs and the approval of license; MCA data include know-how and industrial technological instructions accompanying plant exports.

FIGURE 1. Export/import value ratios for Japanese high-technology trade

INDUSTRIAL CONSORTIA, THE *KEIRETSU*

One of the most efficient means for acquiring and digesting technology has been the characteristic Japanese industrial consortium called *keiretsu* (a simple Japanese word meaning "system" or "series"). Other countries have sometimes characterized it as an exclusive cartel, formed for the purposes of managing business, excluding imports, diminishing competition, and other nefarious reasons. The *keiretsu* concept has been studied extensively by economists (for example, Nanto 1990, 1991; USITC 1990; Ballon 1993). A full discussion of its principles and characteristics is beyond the scope of this chapter.

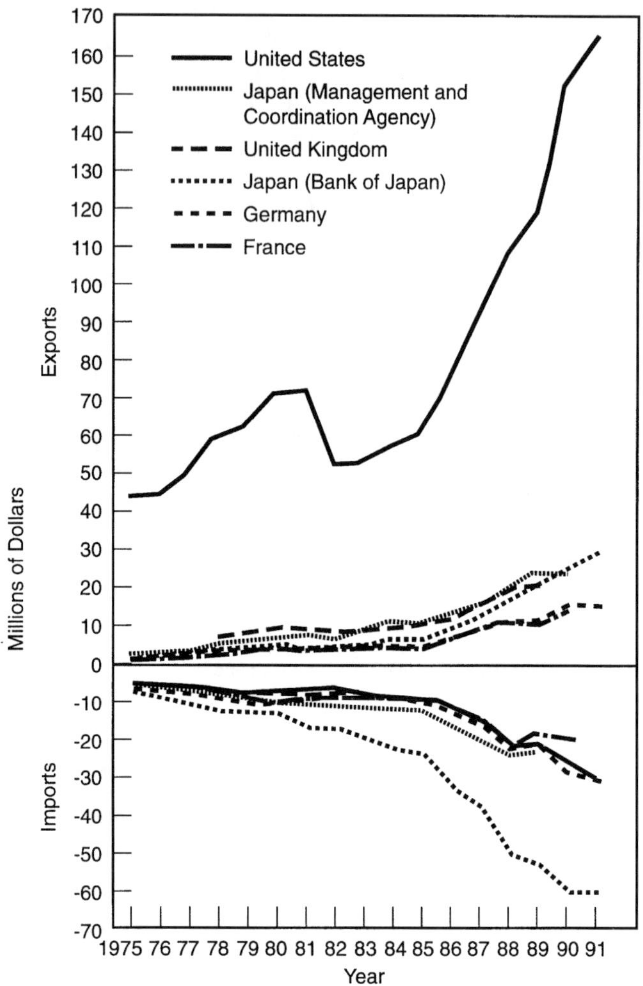

Note: There is considerable uncertainty in the two sets of data concerning Japan. For a discussion of the variables, see STA (1993 and 1994).

FIGURE 2. Comparison of technology trade balances among advanced nations

There are two general types of *keiretsu*: the horizontal and the vertical (the former is called the conglomerate type by some). The horizontal *keiretsu* extends across various types of industries and is usually centered on a commercial bank and/or a trading company. This type is found in limited numbers in Japan and is an outgrowth of the more notorious *zaibatsu* monopolies that existed until the end of World War II—at which time they were outlawed by the Occupation.

An example of the horizontal *keiretsu* is the Mitsubishi Group, which comprises at the center Mitsubishi Corporation (a trading company), Mitsubishi Bank, and Mitsubishi Heavy Industries (a large manufacturing organization with both defense and commercial product lines). Another 35 affiliated Mitsubishi companies are engaged in almost every aspect of Japanese industry and commerce. Figure 3 portrays the enormous complexity of interactions among the parts of the Group (USITC 1990).

The conglomerate *keiretsu* have many advantages and some distinct disadvantages. Among the former is their ability to amass large amounts of money for investment in R&D and to share the results of R&D among the members when useful or appropriate. The same goes for investing in technological intelligence.

The vertical *keiretsu* are not so easily defined since they may vary widely in size and function. Typically they consist of companies involved in only one industrial sector, led by a large manufacturer or distributor that is joined by its suppliers of parts, raw materials, or services. Vertical *keiretsu* are far more numerous than the conglomerates. By one counting, in 1987 there were 39 vertical keiretsu with annual sales greater than ¥1 trillion ($10 billion in 1994 dollars) (Nanto 1991), and, obviously, many more with lower sales.

Familiar examples of this type of *keiretsu* are the Japanese auto makers (except Mitsubishi), Sony, Hitachi, Toshiba, and Sharp. Again, this type of *keiretsu* is better able to develop, acquire, and exploit technology than its individual members, and the sharing and introduction of new technology occur more quickly than in the conglomerates. The Toyota Group is said to be the strongest of the vertical *keiretsu*; it consists of 13 member companies (Figure 4) (Ballon 1993).

Neither the vertical nor the horizontal *keiretsu* are exclusive domains. They interact with each other at various levels through banking, marketing, distribution, and other connections.

TRADING COMPANIES

Another important feature of the Japanese industrial and commercial economy is the trading company, found far more frequently and on a larger scale in Japan than elsewhere (USITC

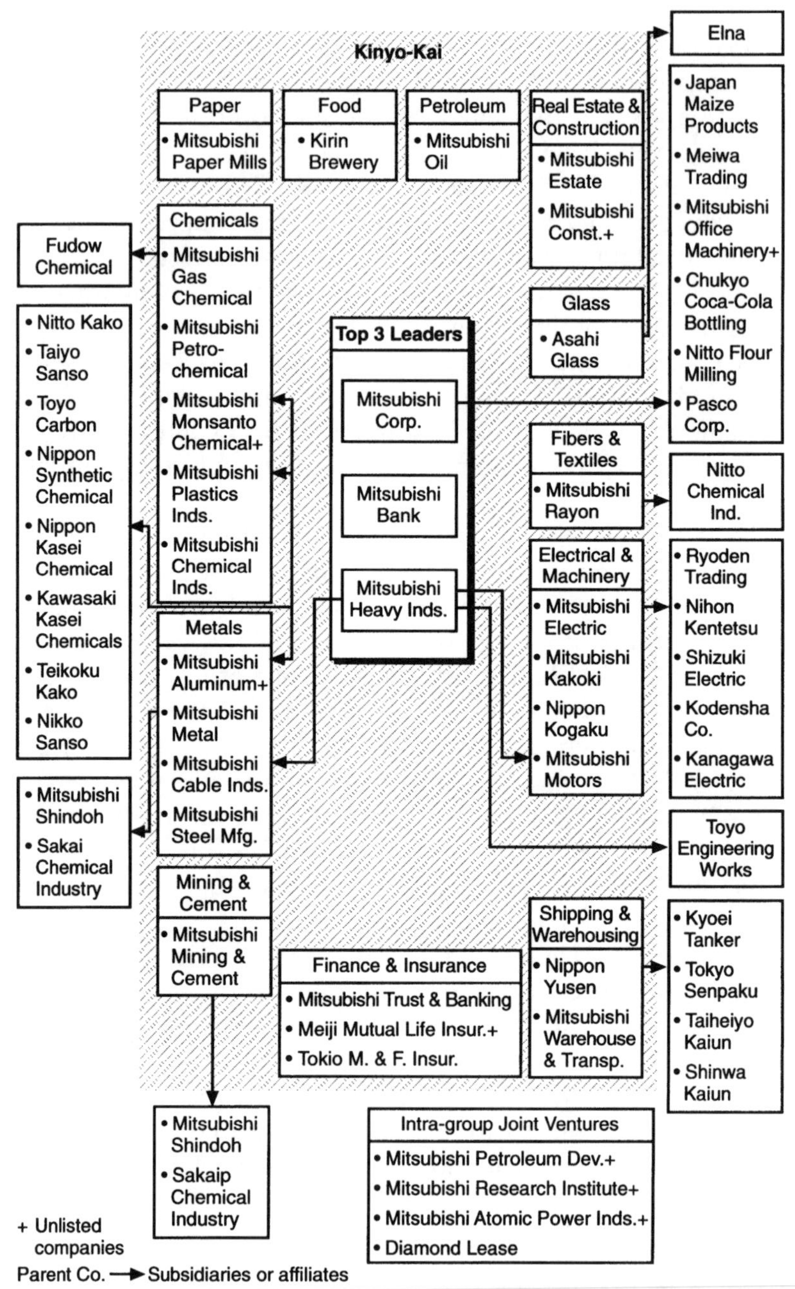

FIGURE 3. Conglomerate *keiretsu* structure of the Mitsubishi Group (USITC 1990)

Toyota Motor Corporation	
Toyoda Automatic Loom Works, Ltd.	Manufacture and sales of spinning and weaving machines, automobiles and industrial vehicles
Aichi Steel Works, Ltd.	Manufacture and sale of specialty steel and forged steel products
Toyoda Machine Works, Ltd.	Manufacture and sale of machine tools and auto parts
Toyota Auto Body Co., Ltd.	Manufacture of auto and special vehicle bodies and parts
Toyota Tsusho Corporation	Import, export and trading of raw materials and products
Aishin Seiki Co., Ltd.	Manufacture and sale of auto parts, household appliances and industrial equipment
Nippondenso Co., Ltd.	Manufacture and sale of electric auto components, air-conditioning equipment, household and other electric appliances
Toyoda Boshoku Corporation	Manufacture and sales of cotton thread, cotton cloth, synthetic products, auto parts and household appliances
Towa Real Estate Co., Ltd.	Real estate development, management, sales and rental
Toyota Central Research & Development Laboratories, Ltd.	Basic technical research for the Toyota Group
Kanto Auto Works, Ltd.	Manufacture of auto bodies, auto parts, equipment and materials for housing construction
Toyoda Gosei Co., Ltd.	Manufacture and sales of synthetic resin, rubber and cork products

FIGURE 4. The Toyota Group—a vertical *keiretsu* (Ballon 1993)

1990). About 10,000 trading companies are involved in foreign trade and in the distribution of products in Japan. The seventeen largest are known as general trading companies *(sogo shosha* in Japanese). Of the six leaders in this group, all are among the ten largest non-U.S. firms in the world. The global networks of these six firms handle 4 percent of the world's trade. Each has between 150 and 200 branches or affiliates in foreign countries, which gather trade, financial, technical, and general economic data in addition to arranging the purchase of goods and materials. Another source states that the top nine *sogo shosha* employ more than 60,000 people in 2200 overseas offices (Nakagawa 1992). Many of the smaller trading companies also maintain networks of overseas offices. These companies tend to specialize in relatively narrow subsectors of the total economy, such as electronic equipment or agricultural products.

The nine largest trading companies are

- Mitsui & Co., Ltd.
- Mitsubishi Corporation
- C. Itoh & Co., Ltd. (now called Itochu Ltd.)
- Sumitomo Corporation
- Marubeni Corporation
- Nissho Iwai Co., Ltd.
- Toyo Menka Kaisha Ltd.
- Kanematsu-Gosho, Ltd.
- Nichimen Corporation.

For the purposes of the discussion here, the trading companies act as passive collectors of business intelligence by astute and close observation of current events in the territories of their overseas offices. In addition, they often contract for studies of technical advances taking place abroad, using the nationals of the involved countries as consultants. Most overseas offices of the trading companies are staffed to a considerable extent by nationals of the host country, so no language barrier exists at the first point of interaction.

A number of the trading companies have close formal or informal relations with the *keiretsu*, who in fact may be the sponsors of the technical studies. (In some instances, the trading companies are the heads of their own *keiretsu*). Considering the close and pervasive personal ties that exist in Japan among professionals in government and industry, it is not out of the question to imagine that some studies contracted for by the trading companies are actually for the benefit of the government.

The trading companies also perform another function that results in the transfer of timely information to Japan. In many regions of foreign countries (including parts of the United States), a local trading company office may be the only contact immediately available for companies wishing to do business with Japan. These contacts are welcomed and often result in actual sales or, in the case of technology transfer, in the execution of R&D joint ventures or patent licensing agreements. Whether they do or not, it can be postulated that new information—either technical or economic—has been caused to flow to Japan since the local offices do not seem to have decision-making authority of their own.

Thus the trading companies are important conduits for the flow of information of all sorts from other countries to Japan. It is difficult to imagine that any other country could emulate on any large scale the Japanese trading company system, considering the enormous investment that has been made in that system and the time required for it to become effective.

DIRECT FOREIGN INVESTMENTS AND JOINT VENTURES

The huge foreign exchange earnings Japanese manufacturing companies have accumulated during the past several decades from their exports have led in a natural sequence of events to plowing back of these resources into all sorts of investments in other countries. Putting aside investments made strictly for direct financial return, such as in real estate, financial institutions, or commercial enterprises, many of the capital expenditures have been for the construction of wholly owned "green-field" manufacturing plants, the outright purchase of existing manufacturing facilities, or investment in joint ventures of various kinds with foreign companies seeking additional capital or technical know-how. All of these arrangements facilitate access to business intelligence information, although this objective probably is not a fundamental reason for making the investment.

All manufacturing facilities wholly owned by Japanese corporations in other countries are preponderantly staffed by the nationals of those countries, who can interact with their compatriots just as they would if employed by a domestic corporation. Consequently, they are well equipped to maintain a level of current awareness of technical and business developments of value to the parent corporation. Japanese corporations hold no special privilege in this respect. In the United States, for example, they are by no means the largest investors. U.S. corporate investors abroad enjoy the same privileges and exercise them.

Joint ventures are more complicated. They may be financial arrangements only, with no access to day-to-day intelligence by the foreign investor, or they may not permit employees of the foreign investor to work side by side with the domestic employees. That is, they may be more of an arm's length arrangement (Gamota 1992).

On the other hand, some joint ventures are based on the intimate sharing of technology and other forms of information and thus constitute a good channel for the flow of information—either unilaterally or bilaterally, depending on the nature of the venture. When they appear to be causing technology to flow disproportionately toward Japan, then warnings appear that the transfers will reappear as worldwide competition. Joint ventures are said to account for an estimated 40 percent of manufacturing affiliate assets held by Japanese companies in the United States (and over 70 percent of the assets of United States manufacturing affiliates in Japan) (Christelow 1990).

Foreign direct investment in R&D facilities (either wholly owned or through joint ventures) is an important subset of the direct investment picture in that the motivations for this kind of investment include monitoring technological developments in the host country as well as acquiring or generating new technology. The latter function relies heavily on the use of foreign scientists and engineers, who have the previously mentioned capability of interacting with their compatriots. Figure 5 depicts the extent of Japanese ownership of overseas R&D facilities (Serapio 1994).

While Japanese investment abroad has attracted much attention and adverse criticism in the countries affected, relatively little attention has been paid to counter-investments in Japan by foreign corporations. In the case of R&D facilities, two recent surveys—one conducted in Japan and one in the United States—indicate

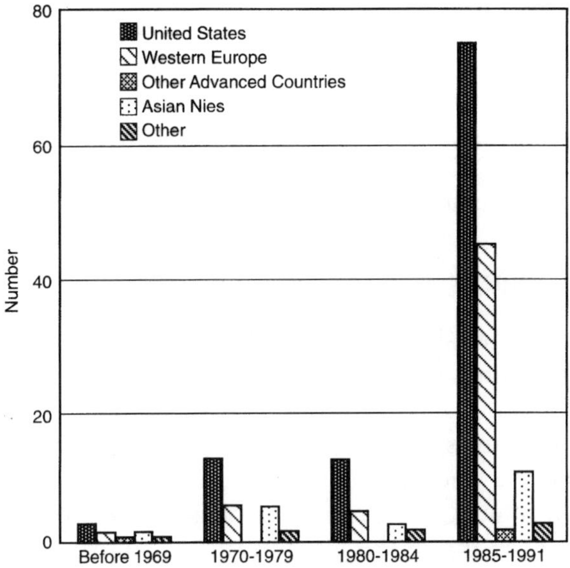

FIGURE 5. Trend in Japanese investment in R&D facilities abroad

that the United States and other foreign multinational corporations have been making substantial investments in such facilities in Japan and have included increasing their access to the Japanese scientific and technological scene as part of their rationale (Bloom and Rubinger 1991; Bloom 1992; Camargo 1992).

Wholly owned foreign R&D facilities offer one path to obtaining current information. Cross-investment in or joint ownership of R&D facilities by corporations of different national parentage also occurs and is just one more link in a very complex pattern of technical relationships now being called "strategic alliances" between or among private corporations across national boundaries (Mowery and Teece 1992). Such alliances provide enormous opportunities for the transfer of intelligence in all directions, since they involve considerable movement of people if they are to succeed.

It is becoming increasingly clear that characterizing a multinational corporation as "American" or "Japanese" has almost no meaning in terms of ownership of proprietary information, so historical concerns about restricting the flow of such information between or among nations for, say, competitive reasons are becoming less and less meaningful. Thorough analyses of the implications of this trend have been made by Edward Graham and Paul Krugman of the Institute for International Economics (Graham and Krugman 1991) and by Jon Choy of the Japan Economic Institute (Choy 1992). The case of Japanese investment in the United States is treated specifically and in depth in each study.

INDUSTRY ASSOCIATIONS

The consummate ability of the Japanese to work together harmoniously in settings not always conducive to harmony is demonstrated once again in the numerous industry associations that exist in Japan. Some are sponsored by government ministries, among which MITI is the leader, and others are able to function independently of government encouragement or financial support.

Probably at the top of the list in terms of political influence is the Federation of Economic Organizations, which is better known by its Japanese acronym, *Keidanren*. Roughly equivalent in character and scope to the U.S. Chamber of Commerce and to similar organizations in other countries, it also has a strong interest in science and technology and maintains a department on this subject to keep its membership informed of the latest in international technological developments. Its membership consists of the larger Japanese corporations, not the entire spectrum of Japanese commerce and industry. It receives no financial support from the central government and, in fact, had been a major contributor of campaign funds to members of the long-dominant Liberal Democratic Party, which is no longer in power.

Another horizontal association, *Nikkeiren*, represents smaller companies. It also has technical interests (Bloom 1990; Cheney and Grimes 1991).

Typically, the associations are product- or process-oriented, or they may be broader in scope so as to include an entire industrial sector. They number in the hundreds. Those that are chartered by MITI or other ministries have quasi-official status, but their cost of operation is borne largely by the member companies, with only relatively small financial subsidies being obtained from the government.

One of the most important functions of the industry associations is to collect, analyze, and distribute information obtained from other countries. Aside from assiduously following the foreign print media and gray literature, the associations also sponsor the dispatch of missions to other countries to investigate new trends in technology, potential markets, etc. Missions of this type would appear to be of special value to smaller companies that do not have subsidiaries abroad or that cannot afford to hire others to perform proprietary studies. Obviously, this kind of information cannot be considered proprietary in the sense that it benefits one company, but it certainly improves the technical competence of the industrial grouping involved. The industry association is another exemplar of the group approach to problem-solving so often found in Japan, whereby a contribution to the common good is often considered as valuable as self-interest—up to some limit.

The organized sharing of what has come to be called "pre-competitive" information is far more developed in Japan than in other advanced countries. No attempt is made here to enumerate all of the industry associations that exist in Japan; it is substantially more accurate to assume that in Japan, an industry association for any particular or general product/process line does exist rather than to assume that it does not exist. While the same might be said for industry in the United States, relatively few U.S. associations are actively engaged in ferreting out foreign technology advances, sending technical missions abroad, establishing industry standards, and disseminating information to their memberships as their Japanese counterparts do (Morin and Kodama 1993).

The Congressional Research Service (CRS) of the Library of Congress has studied the phenomenon of the Japanese high-technology industry association and has compared it in depth with its American counterpart (Nanto and McLoughlin 1991). The CRS study separates the Japanese associations into the following categories:

- Research Association. Formed to cooperate in performing R&D and to share information. Exempted from antitrust laws. Receives financial support from MITI. Focuses on specific R&D objective. Has limited lifetime and is disbanded at the end of the research program.

- Industrial Association. Formed to exchange information when a new industrial field has appeared or is about to appear. Funded primarily from member companies, although the government may furnish seed money or execute a research grant. Maintains liaison with central and prefectural governments. Collects information, stores it for retrieval by members, arranges study missions, etc. The predominant form of high-tech association, numbering in the hundreds.
- Policy or Deliberative Council. A committee drawn from all parts of the society to advise the government on policy issues, technical matters, and future needs. May identify R&D tasks, recommend methods of technology assessment, and propose international cooperation in research. Used primarily by MITI, which has about 30 such councils or committees.
- R&D Support Foundation. Relatively recent approach for interdisciplinary fields. Funded jointly by government (usually MITI) and industry. Makes R&D grants to private sector. May have in-house R&D capability.

MITI seemed to become so enamored of the industry association concept as a device for accelerating the inward flow of technology that it sponsored the creation of a broad-based, all-encompassing one, the Japan Technology Transfer Association (JTTAS). This organization boasts about 2000 corporate members, from whom it receives membership dues. MITI augments this financial base with an annual subsidy of unknown amount.

The primary function of JTTAS is to organize teams drawn from member companies, government agencies, and universities for the purpose of studying emerging technologies or new products appearing abroad (JTTAS 1990). As of 1990, 100 technical committees were meeting regularly. Appropriate assessments are written and disseminated to the membership. When necessary, groups of experts are sent to foreign countries known to be at the leading edge in given technical fields. As might be expected, detailed technical reports are written to summarize the findings of these missions. JTTAS has a staff of about 40 in its Tokyo office, where it maintains an excellent library of information collected in the past.

Through an arrangement that could probably be tolerated only in Japan, a private company, the Technology Transfer Institute

(TTI), was formed to provide support to JTTAS by making the complex arrangements for conducting tours abroad through offices located in the United States (New York and Los Angeles), Europe, and Asia. The Executive Director of JTTAS is also the President of TTI.

During the halcyon period of the 1980s, when Japanese corporations were reaping enormous profits and plowing large sums back into R&D, participation in JTTAS/TTI missions was high and the system flourished. TTI then reasoned that there should be a market for its services in the reverse direction, that is, for missions from foreign countries to Japan. Notwithstanding continuous complaints in those countries about difficulties in obtaining technical information from Japan, there was only a modest response to this service, apparently because of the high costs entailed in visiting Japan and because of the unattractiveness of the group approach to collecting information.

According to informal reports, the recession currently being suffered by Japan has caused a drop-off in interest in Japan as well, and the TTI overseas offices have been reduced in size or closed. However, a remnant of the New York office is engaged in a new activity that demonstrates vividly how creative the Japanese can be in searching for new technological developments. The organization is now known as High-Tech Shower International.[1] It interviews scientists and engineers in the United States who are engaged in leading-edge R&D and makes video tapes of the interviews for showing in the Far East. The tapes also show news about technology developments in the United States and display new product announcements.

As of June 1994, almost 700 recordings had been made. These have been seen in Japan, China, Hong Kong, and Taiwan. Efforts are being made to sell the recordings in the United States, Mexico, Canada, and Europe, but so far without success. Corporate subscribers in Japan pay an annual fee to receive the programs via satellite broadcasts. The programs are then distributed without cost to technical high schools and research laboratories. The technical content of the tapes is very high, although they are quite short (typically 20 minutes). They often contain information that has not been published in more conventional channels.

As far as is known, the High-Tech Shower video service is unique. It is remarkably representative of what can be done with modern information technology. The reluctance of potential users in Western nations to subscribe to the service is also instructive, again demonstrating that Japan and the newly emerging economic states of the Far East appear to be leading the world in their receptivity to new technical information and are willing to pay for it.

UNIVERSITIES

Students of Japanese innovation processes know that universities in Japan have a much different role than do universities in Europe and the United States, and this role is not for the better (Anderson 1992). Since most of the R&D performed in Japan is the responsibility of private industry and since the universities do not have the close ties to industry that would be found in the United States, for example, there tends to be a gap between the Japanese academic research community and the industrial research community. This gap does not extend to informal connections between members of the same discipline, and Japanese professors are known to act as consultants to counterparts in industry (NRC 1989).

Also, there are other venues for informal interaction, such as professional society conferences and government committees. Nonetheless, the well-developed mode for acquiring technical information by Western academics under contract to industrial sponsors is not seen to any extent in Japan.

One reason for this lack of interaction—in a society known for the intensity and breadth of its interpersonal relations—is that academic research in Japan has not been as innovative or creative as that in the West, and thus, there is a mismatch between university laboratories and industrial laboratories in the quality of their work. Another reason is that university professors traditionally have been more liberal politically than their industrial counterparts, leading to a measure of distrust between the two communities.

A consequence of these two factors is that private industry in Japan has looked upon the universities more as the source of entry-level scientists and engineers, with industry itself then taking the responsibility for the advanced education and training of the more promising employees. This set of conditions is not the result of some formal national policy and therefore should not be cast in black-and-white terms; there are many exceptions to the conditions, and caution is necessary in reaching conclusions based on them.

The relatively poor quality of Japanese research universities (primarily the government-operated national universities and their inter-university research institutes) has caused many Japanese to continue their academic studies abroad. This situation is particularly true at the Ph.D. and post-doctoral level. (Japanese universities graduate far smaller proportions of Ph.D.'s than do their Western counterparts). However, this situation is by no means as acute where Japan is concerned as it is with other countries of Asia who aspire to become leaders in science and technology.

Tables 3 and 4 demonstrate that the number of Japanese students studying natural science and engineering in the United States is not greater than the numbers from other leading countries of the area, either in absolute or per capita terms. The percentage of Japanese students enrolled in U.S. graduate schools is less than from the other countries, and the number of doctoral degrees awarded to Japanese students is far less than for other countries.

TABLE 3
Asian students in U.S. universities in natural sciences and engineering: 1989–1990 and 1990–1991

	No. of students		Percentage		Percentage	
Country	**1989-90**	**1990-91**	**Under-graduate**	**Graduate**	**Natural Science**	**Engineering**
China	33,390	39,600	12.9	82.7	44.0	20.1
India	26,240	28,860	21.1	75.5	40.9	52.5
Japan	29,840	36,610	61.7	19.5	31.0	14.0
Singapore	4,440	4,500	73.2	25.0	35.0	52.0
S. Korea	21,710	23,360	24.1	69.7	45.4	35.6
Taiwan	30,960	33,530	19.0	76.3	51.0	45.0

Notes: Percentages by level and field are estimated from Institute of International Education (1990). The percentages of undergraduate and graduate students do not add to 100; the balance have research appointments. The percentages of natural science and engineering fields do not add to 100; the balance are in non-S&E fields.

Source: Johnson 1993

TABLE 4
Doctoral degrees in natural science and engineering awarded domestically and in the United States for selected Asian countries: 1990

	Within Country		U.S. Universities	
Countries	Natural Science	Engineering	Natural Science	Engineering
China	772	1054	660 (46.1%)	280 (21.0%)
India	4600	250	311 (6.3%)	301 (54.6%)
Japan	937	948	56 (5.6%)	17 (1.8%)
S. Korea	399	439	343 (46.2%)	350 (44.4%)
Taiwan	104	165	446 (81.1%)	460 (73.6%)

Note: Figures in parentheses are U.S. doctoral awards as a percentage of the country's total doctoral degrees in that field.

Source: Johnson 1993

Hidden within the statistics of Table 4 is another indicator worthy of mention: almost 20 percent of Japanese students enrolled at U.S. universities have research appointments—a substantially higher proportion than is found for the other countries listed (Johnson 1993). To these might be added the significant number of Japanese post-doctoral researchers employed by the National Institutes of Health and other public institutions. (More recent statistics on overall foreign participation in U.S. academic science and engineering have been published recently by the National Science Foundation [Huckenpöhler 1993]).

A related and intentional device for obtaining current technical information is the dispatch of scientific personnel to study or research assignments for relatively short times. This approach is often preferred by governments, who can control the nature of the assignments through their funding of the visits.

In the case of Japan, the number of fellowships awarded to academic scientists by MESC's Japan Society for the Promotion of Science is quite small. The United States is the largest receiving country by far. In 1989, JSPS sent 352 scientists to the United States for cooperative research projects under a bilateral scientific agreement and also sent an additional 66 scientists to participate in seminars (JSPS 1990). If all exchanges of scientists through governmental channels are considered, 1989 saw 1574 visitors traveling from Japan to the United States and 657 going in the opposite direction (Anderson 1992).

Thus the presence of large numbers of Japanese scientists and engineers abroad in academic settings of one form or another provides a vehicle, planned or otherwise, for the timely transfer of information to Japan. The degree to which this path is effective in terms of supplying information of value to private industry is uncertain. As just noted, linkages between those in academe and those in industry are not particularly strong. Furthermore, networking among technical personnel through electronic means (that is, e-mail and its variants) is not as well developed in Japan as elsewhere, so the timeliness factor may be questionable as well.

What undoubtedly *is* important are the institutional and personal contacts made and the subsequent abilities to tap into current sources of information. In any objective treatment of this aspect of technology transfer, consideration also must be given to 1) Japanese technical information imparted to host personnel through the usual technical dialogues that occur (at the graduate or postdoctoral level), and 2) the contrary general lack of interest by foreigners in pursuing similar paths in Japan.

Further evidence of a lack of cooperation among Japanese government ministries can be found in the presence of the National Center for Science Information Systems (NACSIS), a scientific information collection and dissemination system for Japanese academia, sponsored and funded by MESC, more or less in competition with JICST. A number of observers have questioned the need for two separate entities with almost identical missions. Nonetheless, NACSIS exists to collect scientific information from many sources and make it available to Japanese universities through a modern database and printed publications. It does not appear to be engaged in information intelligence activities abroad and is not known to have offices in other countries. For a few years, it made available a terminal at the National Science Foundation in Washington, D.C., to permit American scientists to obtain access to its database (with the assistance of a bilingual operator) but the NSF suspended that function in 1993.

"THINK TANKS" AND CONSULTING FIRMS

Independent institutes performing contract R&D in the hard sciences and engineering are essentially unknown in Japan. Another class of independent research institution, engaged in research in the soft sciences such as economics, sociology, and the humanities, exists in large numbers and is given the Western appellation "think tank" in Japan (Itonaga and Ishida 1990).

A quasi-governmental organization, the National Institute of Research Advancement (NIRA), is a think tank itself, but it also sponsors research conducted by other research institutes, both domestic and foreign. In the latter sense, NIRA can be considered to be involved in the collection and analysis of foreign information.

The two largest think tanks, Mitsubishi Research Institute (MIRI) and Nomura Research Institute, are profit-making and are supported financially by their parent organizations, Mitsubishi Corporation and Nomura Securities, Ltd. MIRI deserves special mention because 1) it has overseas offices, 2) it is heavily involved in studies of information flow, and 3) it has significant technical staffing and missions. It contracts for studies conducted abroad by other organizations on behalf of private and government sponsors. It is clear, however, that the think tank concept, as exemplified by organizations in the United States and Europe, has not yet reached the same level of maturity in Japan and therefore is not yet a significant part of the information scene.

Consulting firms play a much more modest role in Japan than they do elsewhere (Morin and Kodama 1993). In fact, several of the more prominent consulting organizations in Japan are subsidiaries of foreign companies, such as Arthur D. Little, SRI International, and the Boston Consulting Group. Such firms can be very effective in obtaining business and technical intelligence from foreign sources, but must have Japanese employees to interact with clients in their local offices in Japan. Many consulting organizations in foreign countries that do not have offices in Japan provide advice to Japanese clients, but the extent of this flow apparently is not known in quantitative terms.

PROFESSIONAL SOCIETIES

Japanese professional societies perform the same functions as their counterparts in other countries, but in some aspects with different emphasis. Most notably, professional society meetings held in Japan are characterized by the large number of short papers given, the lack of refereeing, and often the lateness or failure to publish most of them (Shimizu et al. 1991). Thus attendance at these meetings becomes more important than would be the case in the United States, for example. The meetings act as strong vehicles for the exchange of timely information through personal networking, and there does not appear to be any opprobrium attached to the presentation of unsubstantiated or radical scientific ideas.

Although meetings of international societies are often held in Japan because of that nation's advanced status and are usually conducted in English, meetings of the Japanese societies are, of course, conducted in Japanese. Most foreigners are thereby effectively excluded, probably removing a constraint on free and open debate.

Journals published in Japanese by the professional societies are not widely read abroad, but increasingly are being abstracted in English by JICST, NACSIS, and commercial information services. Recognizing that Japanese science is not going to receive international recognition and acceptance under this condition, the leading professional societies have been converting their journals to English. There is at least the possibility that this trend, plus gradually wider use of the Internet and international e-mail communication, will cause an increase in English-language conference proceedings and other so-called gray literature.

CONCLUDING OBSERVATIONS

Although Japan's traditional approaches to the gathering of technological intelligence, as described above, have been very effective in the context of the objectives being pursued, these approaches will not remain in effect for the indefinite future. To the contrary, considerable change can be and should be expected.

One of the primary driving forces for the broad and intense Japanese commitment to technology acquisition has been the need, perceived or real, to catch up with the rest of the world economically. Japan has succeeded in this objective and now must face the challenges entailed in being a world leader in both economic and technological terms.

As a nation, it may not be able to continue to muster a national consensus on dedication to education and training; the submersion of the individual for the benefit of the group; or even more narrowly, the broad sharing of technical information at the precompetitive level. There are many signs that these and other characteristics of Japanese society are becoming frayed. Thus Japan may have reached the point where the high cost of purchasing or licensing new technologies may be offset by investment in indigenous R&D (which would include R&D performed in Japanese-owned research facilities located overseas)—an approach possible only when technological parity has been achieved. Japanese corporations already plow more of their earnings back into R&D than do their foreign competitors, although the current recession in Japan has forced cutbacks in industrial research. Presumably, this condition is transient.

At the more fundamental level, Japanese scientists are striving for individual recognition, just as are scientists in the West, and are demanding better research facilities in universities and related research institutes. Their competence and creativity in many fields are being acknowledged by their peers abroad; as a consequence, scientific information will be flowing between Japan and the rest of the advanced world in a more balanced manner.

Both the public and private sectors of other countries have become much more wary about giving the Japanese ready access to advanced technical information, sometimes flatly denying access even in unclassified fields or, in other instances, exacting very high prices. The practice of technological isolationism can be very effective when the technology provider is substantially ahead of the receiver, but the situation becomes much muddier when the two are on a par and the receiver may well become the future provider. How this situation will play out in the future will occupy the attention of many members of the business intelligence community.

When the U.S.-Japan Technology Transfer Joint Study Panel referred to earlier (Morin and Kodama 1993) published its findings, it drew conclusions that are consistent with the above and yet are framed in other terms. The final paragraph of the Panel's report is worth repeating here as the conclusion of this chapter:

> *While these very different systems* [the U.S. and Japanese technology transfer systems] *have served each country reasonably*

well over the past few decades, it is apparent that changes are already under way and likely to accelerate in the years ahead. Though different in each country, competitive pressures are the driving force behind these changes. The changes are sometimes subtle and sometimes obvious, but all are significant. We believe the result will be Japanese and U.S. technology transfer systems that more closely resemble each other. The two systems may never be the same, but they are converging.

REFERENCES

Anderson, A. 1992. Academics Bemoan the Cost of Years of Neglect. *Science* 258:564-569.

Ballon, R. J. December 1993/January 1994. Corporate Groups Japanese Style: The Concept and the Fact. *Journal of Japanese Trade & Industry* 12:12-16.

Bloom, J. L. 1990. *Japan as a Scientific and Technological Superpower*. PB90-234923, National Technical Information Service, Springfield, Virginia.

Bloom, J. L. 1992. American Corporate Investment in Japanese Research Facilities. *New Perspectives on Global Science and Technology Policy*. Proceedings of Third International Conference on Science and Technology Policy Research, eds. S. Okamura, F. Sakauchi, and I. Nonaka. National Institute of Science and Technology Policy, Tokyo, Japan.

Bloom, J. L., and B. Rubinger. 1991. *Survey of Direct U.S. Private Capital Investment in Research and Development Facilities in Japan*. NSF 91-312, National Science Foundation, Washington, D.C.

Bolton, M. K. 1991. U.S. and Japanese Approaches to Knowledge Production: Internal and External Information Cultures. *Preprints, 3rd International Conference on Japanese Information in Science, Technology and Commerce,* Vandoeuvre-les-Nancy, France, May 15-18, 1991, pp. 107-125. Institut de L'Information Scientifique et Technique, Paris, France

Bonthous, J-M. 1994. Understanding Intelligence Across Cultures. *International Journal of Intelligence and CounterIntelligence* 7(3):275-311.

Branscomb, L. M., and F. Kodama. 1993. *Japanese Innovation Strategy.* CSIA Occasional Paper No. 10, Center for Science and International Affairs, Harvard University, Cambridge, Massachusetts.

Camargo, Orlando. 1992. Foreign Affiliate R&D Activities in the Science and Technology System: — The Views of Local R&D Managers in Japan —"Who Can We Become?" *New Perspectives on Global Science and Technology Policy*. Proceedings of Third International Conference on Science and Technology Policy Research, eds. S. Okamura, F. Sakauchi, and I. Nonaka. National Institute of Science and Technology Policy, Tokyo, Japan.

Chambers, G. S., and W. K. Cummings. 1990. *Profiting from Education*. Institute of International Education, New York.

Cheney, D. W., and W. W. Grimes. 1991. *Japanese Technology Policy: What's the Secret?* Council on Competitiveness, Washington, D.C.

Choy, J. 1992. *Japan's Growing Role in U.S. Research: Bane or Boon?* Report No. 36A, Japan Economic Institute, Washington, D.C.

Christelow, D. B. 1990. Japan-U.S. Joint Manufacturing Ventures. *Japan's Economic Challenge*. Study Papers Submitted to the Joint Economic Committee, Congress of the United States. U.S. Government Printing Office, Washington, D.C.

Dalton, D. H., and P. A. Genther. March 1991. *The Role of Corporate Linkages in U.S.-Japan Technology Transfer*. PB91-165571, U.S. Department of Commerce, Washington, D.C.

Deacon, R. 1990. *Kempei Tai, The Japanese Secret Service Then and Now*. Charles E. Tuttle Co., Inc., Tokyo, Japan.

Dertouzos, M. L., R. K. Lester, and R. M. Solow. 1989. *Made in America*. The MIT Press, Cambridge, Massachusetts.

Gamota, G. 1992. Technology Assessment in the U.S.-Japan Context. *Japan's Growing Technological Capability*. National Research Council. National Academy Press, Washington, D.C.

Graham, E. M., and P. R. Krugman. 1991. *Foreign Direct Investment in the United States*. Institute for International Economics, Washington, D.C.

Grimes, W. W. 1993. *Refocusing U.S. Technology Policy. Monograph Series Number 3, Center of International Studies, Program on U.S.-Japan Relations*. Princeton University, Princeton, New Jersey.

Herring, J. P. March/April 1992. Business Intelligence in Japan and Sweden: Lessons for the U.S. *Journal of Business Strategy*, pp. 44-49.

Huckenpöhler, J. G. February 1993. *Foreign Participation in U.S. Academic Science and Engineering: 1991*. Special Report NSF 93-302, National Science Foundation, Washington, D.C.

Itonaga, S., and H. Ishida. 1990. Japanese Think Tanks and the National Institute for Research Advancement (NIRA): Think Tank Publications.

Proceedings of 2nd International Conference on Japanese Information in Science, Technology and Commerce, eds. D. Mönch, U. Wattenberg, T. Graf Brockdorff, R. Krempien, and H. Walravens. IOS Press, Amsterdam, Netherlands.

Japan External Trade Organization (JETRO) 1993a. JETRO Overseas Offices. *New Technology Japan* 20(12):46.

Japan External Trade Organization (JETRO). 1993b. *Introduction to JETRO's Industrial Cooperation Activities*. Tokyo, Japan.

Japan External Trade Organization (JETRO). 1994. JETRO Builds Stronger Overseas Presence. *Focus Japan* 21(1-2):12.

Japan Information Center of Science and Technology (JICST). 1993a. *The Japan Information Center of Science and Technology, 1993*. Tokyo, Japan.

Japan Information Center of Science and Technology (JICST). 1993b. *JICST 1993-94: The Japan Information Center of Science and Technology*. Tokyo, Japan.

Japan Society for the Promotion of Science (JSPS). September 1990. *JSPS Annual Report, 1989-1990.* Japan Society for the Promotion of Science. Tokyo, Japan.

Japan Society for the Promotion of Science (JSPS). October 1992. JSPS New Liaison Office Opened in Bonn. *JSPS Newsletter* 9:6.

Japan Technology Transfer Association (JTTAS). 1990. *Japan Technology Transfer Association*. Tokyo, Japan.

Johnson, J. M. 1993. *Human Resources for Science and Technology: The Asian Region*. Special Report NSF 93-303, National Science Foundation, Washington D.C.

Kahaner, D. K. April 26, 1994. Japanese Information Gathering Offices in Washington, D.C. Internet posting to "kahaner-dist." Translation of an article from *Nikkei Business*, November 15, 1993.

Kokubo, A. January/February 1992. Japanese Competitive Intelligence for R&D. *Research Technology Management* pp. 33-34.

Levy, J. D., and R. Samuels. 1989. *Institutions and Innovation: Research Collaboration as Technology Strategy in Japan*. Report MITJSTP 89-02, Massachusetts Institute of Technology, Department of Political Science, Cambridge, Massachusetts.

Morin, W. G., and F. Kodama. May 3, 1993. *Report of the U.S.-Japan Technology Transfer Joint Study Panel.* U.S. Department of Commerce, Technology Administration. PB93-182921, National Technical Information Service, Springfield, Virginia.

Moritani, M. 1982. *Japanese Technology*. Simul Press, Inc., Tokyo, Japan.

Mowery, D. C., and D. J. Teece. 1992. *The Changing Place of Japan in the Global Scientific and Technological Enterprise*. National Research Council, National Academy Press, Washington, D.C.

Nakagawa, J. 1992. Intelligence, Trade and Industry. *The Intelligent Corporation: The Privatization of Intelligence*, eds. J. Sigurdson and Y. Tagerud. Taylor Graham, London, England.

Nanto, D. K. October 1990. Japan's Industrial Groups, the *keiretsu*. *Japan's Economic Challenge*. Study papers submitted to the Joint Economic Committee, Congress of the United States, Washington, D.C.

Nanto, D. K. April 30, 1991. *Japan's Business Advantage in Commercializing Technology*. Hearing before the Subcommittee on Technology and Competitiveness of the Committee on Science, Space, and Technology, U.S. House of Representatives. Committee Print No. 30.

Nanto, D. K, and G. J. McLoughlin. June 6, 1991. *Japanese and U.S. Industrial Associations: Their Role in High-Technology Policymaking*. CRS Report for Congress 91-477 E, Congressional Research Service, Library of Congress, Washington, D.C.

Nishizawa, J. March 1994. Science and Technology and Japanese Culture. *The Japan Foundation Newsletter*, pp. 1-6.

National Research Council (NRC). 1989. *Learning the R&D System: University Research in Japan and the United States*. National Academy Press, Washington, D.C.

National Research Council (NRC). 1992. *U.S.-Japan Strategic Alliances in the Semiconductor Industry*. National Academy Press, Washington, D.C.

Office of Management and Budget (OMB). 1994. *Budget of the United States, 1994*. Washington, D.C.

Sakaiya, T. 1993. *What Is Japan?* Kodansha International, New York.

Science and Technology Agency (STA). 1992. JICST's Documents Collection and Depositing. *STA Today* 4(10):10.

Science and Technology Agency (STA). 1993. Analysis of Japan's Technology Trade Statistics. *STA Today* 5(3):9.

Science and Technology Agency (STA). 1994. The Status of Science and Technology in Japan and Other Nations. *STA Today* 6(11):12.

Serapio, M. G., Jr. 1994. *Japan-U.S. Direct R&D Investments in the Electronics Industries*. PB94-127974, National Technical Information Service, Springfield, Virginia.

Shimizu, S., Y. Kaneko, and S. Suda. 1991 Disclosing Process of Scientific and Technical Information in Japan. Role of Academic Societies as Publicizing Research and Development Outgrowth. *Preprints, 3rd International Conference on Japanese Information in Science, Technology and Commerce*, Vandoeuvre-les-Nancy, France, May 15-18, 1991, pp. 155-172. Institut de L'Information Scientifique et Technique, Paris, France.

Sigurdson, J., and P. Nelson. 1990. Intelligence Gathering and Japan: The Elusive Role of Grey Intelligence. *Japanese Information in Science, Technology and Commerce*. IOS Press, Amsterdam, The Netherlands.

Uchida, H. 1991. Recent Activities of JICST in Japanese STI Distribution and in International Cooperation. *Preprints, 3rd International Conference on Japanese Information in Science, Technology and Commerce*, Vandoeuvre-les-Nancy, France, May 15-18, 1991, pp. 77-85. Institut de L'Information Scientifique et Technique, Paris, France

U.S. International Trade Commission (USITC). 1990. *Phase I: Japan's Distribution System and Options for Improving U.S. Access.* USITC Publication 2291, Washington, D.C.

Vogel, E. F. 1979. *Japan As No. 1*. Harvard University Press, Cambridge, Massachusetts.

ENDNOTE

1. Personal communication with Hisa Watanabe, May 31, 1994.

PART II

Managing Technical Intelligence Organizations in Business

PART II
Editorial Introduction

Establishing and maintaining a CTI organization in business is often straightforward, but maintaining such a function over the long term has proved very difficult in many companies. Many competitive intelligence groups have been downsized, shuffled to different parts of a company or simply dropped, often for reasons that are not clear, given the contributions these groups have made to company success. The four chapters that follow describe current practices for successfully developing and maintaining technical intelligence organizations in business. Each chapter is written by professionals who have designed, managed, or worked in CTI groups.

The section begins with a chapter by Jan Herring, an international leader in business intelligence and a strong spokesman for intelligence activities, that focuses on science and technology. Herring draws on his experiences at Motorola, Inc., where he established one of the leading competitive intelligence organizations in the United States, and as a consultant helping to start similar organizations at many more U.S. companies. He presents an overview of basic principles, emphasizing the point that TI programs must be based on a strong sense of purpose. Herring outlines other major elements of a successful S&T intelligence program, pointing out that it should be led by someone with close professional and personal ties to the director of R&D, and it should involve senior management. S&T intelligence activities consist of information services, collection and reporting of data, analyis of data, and forecasting. The author points out the important characteristics of an effective intelligence analyst and draws attention to the importance of training and adequate resources.

In their chapter on establishing technology intelligence organizations, Bill McDonald and John Richardson report on experiences from the oil and gas industries. The chapter describes the general steps and functions to be addressed in development of a TI system. The design process for a TI system includes steps such as interviewing key personnel, assessing organizational needs, auditing past activities and resources, and developing an initial design. The authors emphasize the importance of major TI system building blocks such as management, monitoring/reporting, assessment, information acquisition/storage, and quality assurance. Important implementation activities such as staff training and growth planning are also covered. They stress the importance of senior management's involvement in the development of the TI program. They also offer insights as to what type of information will be useful and how it is best presented. The authors also emphasize the important role of the so-called gatekeepers: the key players in the company's TI program whose job it is to obtain, evaluate, and communicate technological information. Other groups within the corporation that can also contribute to the founding of a TI program include the library/information center, computer support services, regulatory affairs, and corporate communications offices.

Using their experiences in another highly successful CTI organization, Pat Bryant, Tom Krol, and Jim Coleman describe typical CTI operations at Marion Merrill Dow (now Hoechst Marion Roussel), a leading firm in the pharmaceutical industry. The authors describe the various processes found in a successful CTI unit, outlining key steps in the business intelligence-gathering process. Major considerations include developing a clear mission statement; identifying clients; clarifying user needs; identifying data sources; converting raw data into competitive information; converting information into intelligence; presenting and applying the findings; and measuring the results of the CTI operation. The authors recommend sources of data as well as information management techniques. They further describe the characteristics of a successful CTI analyst and explain how the information gathered can benefit the organization. Finally, they emphasize that the most successful CTI programs are those that are integrated into the ongoing operations of the corporation.

The final chapter discusses CTI organizations in French manufacturing companies. The authors, Thomas Durand, François Farhi, and Charles de Brabant, note that although many companies have competitive monitoring systems in place, most tend to use these systems as passive, information-gathering tools. They demonstrate how a systematic competitor-monitoring function can be used as an active strategic tool to enhance corporate decision-making and improve company performance. Methods for gathering, summarizing, analyzing, and communicating information to maximize its usefulness are discussed. The authors also present two case studies illustrating different methods of gathering and using strategic information. One company organized a large and successful monitoring effort, which enabled it to cut costs, better understand its competitors, and more effectively protect its own activities from competitors' monitoring efforts. Another company used patent monitoring techniques to analyze the technology strategies of its major competitors. Through systematic monitoring, the firm was able to identify changing areas of research as well as the potential impact of established and emerging competitors.

Creating Successful Scientific and Technical Intelligence Programs

JAN P. HERRING

Purpose is the essence of all effective intelligence operations. Among the basic forms of intelligence—that is, military, political, economic, etc.—scientific and technical (S&T) intelligence plays a very special role since it is often a component of each of the other forms. Military intelligence clearly requires good S&T intelligence to understand an enemy's future weapons capabilities. Political or diplomatic intelligence often uses S&T intelligence as a bargaining chip, as was done in the strategic arms limitation treaties. Economic or business intelligence is dependent on an understanding of a competitor's technological capabilities to create economic or competitive advantage.

The purpose of S&T intelligence therefore is to play two important roles: providing insight and foresight for other forms of intelligence and providing the basis upon which an organization's own research and development (R&D) activities are directed, measured, and executed. It must be clear from the onset which of these purposes or which combination of applications of S&T intelligence is needed. The resulting S&T intelligence program and organizational structure will depend highly on these purposes.

THE ORIGINS OF SCIENTIFIC AND TECHNICAL INTELLIGENCE

Scientific and technical intelligence as we know it today marks its beginning with Sir Francis Bacon in the 1600s. Bacon was the first person in recorded history to recognize scientific knowledge as the engine that drives technological and, hence, world change.

Interestingly, and quite likely purposefully, he describes, in his last and possibly most fascinating essay called *New Atlantis*, a small island country that creates a global intelligence organization to gather and assimilate worldwide scientific knowledge to be used in its developmental progress. The intelligence organization was called Salomon's House, and the intelligence operations it carried out were almost identical to those involved in the intelligence activities of today.

The intelligence collectors were called Merchants of Light. There were those who specialized in the collection of information in books, that is, published material. And others who collected information on experiments of "all mechanical devices." They were called Mystery Men. The analysts were those who organized the information that was collected and derived the lessons to be learned. They were called Compilers. The next step in the intelligence process was to apply the new knowledge that had been gathered and analyzed; those who did this were called the Dowry Men or Benefactors. This intelligence activity was solely for the benefit and future growth of the island state of Atlantis.

During the same time period, Galileo was developing the modern telescope, which has had long and lasting utility and value to the scientific community. Interestingly, one of the first applications of the telescope was military intelligence, providing Galileo's nation state the ability to spot and identify enemy ships at long distances so that defenses could be properly deployed. Many scientific developments have had almost simultaneous applications in the field of intelligence and military purpose, the most recent being microelectronics and space satellites.

One of the earliest uses of balloon technologies, in fact, was for military reconnaissance. This technology was perfected during the American Civil War when the combination of photography and the balloon provided the first modern aerial photography for military purposes.

The 1800s also saw some interesting developments in scientific and technical intelligence, which involved collection and assimilation of other's technology. The U.S. textile industry was created as a result of the gathering and transfer of technical intelligence to the United States from England. Andrew Carnegie is reported to have said that he could not have created his steel industry here in America without the technology intelligence he gathered in Europe. In each case, technical intelligence was involved, but the purpose was industrial development.

World War II saw major advances in the field of scientific and technical intelligence, both as a collection tool and as the object of intelligence gathering. R. V. Jones, Winston Churchill's young scientific intelligence officer, broke new ground when using electronic means to collect information and photographic interpretation to unravel Germany's secret weapon developments. Reading his book *The Most Secret War* (U.S. title: *The Wizard War*) is a must for students of S&T intelligence.

Jones' description of a "scientific intelligence service" clearly lays out both the premise and the operational approach for modern and scientific intelligence activities. He states, "The primary problem of a Scientific Intelligence Service is to obtain early warning of the adoption of new weapons and methods by potential or actual enemies." He goes on to examine the stages and basic objectives of the competition's R&D program and posits how one must develop intelligence operations almost in reverse to gather the intelligence and derive insight and, thus, the early warning needed to prevent the organization from being surprised. While many of the specific tasks and the words used are military in nature, their commercial counterparts are easily developed.

Today, U.S. government intelligence continues to make great use of scientific and technical intelligence. In addition to being a target of and a tool for intelligence operations, technology has greatly enhanced the analysis and support of intelligence operations themselves. From U2s to satellites, the collection of advanced scientific and technical information has grown. As mentioned earlier, S&T intelligence is also the basis for diplomatic initiatives and strategic arms limitation treaties.

SCIENTIFIC AND TECHNICAL INTELLIGENCE IN THE PRIVATE SECTOR

During the period since World War II, the U.S. private sector has made little progress in either the development or the use of scientific and technical intelligence. This situation is not surprising, in view of the fact that American corporations as a whole have done little to develop or use intelligence as a business tool. But, more important, foreign companies have significantly advanced in the development and use of competitive and business intelligence programs.

Japanese companies are without doubt the most advanced in the development and use of S&T intelligence in today's modern business world. Their advancement began when the government of Japan recognized that Japanese industry needed Western technology to modernize its industry after World War II (Herring 1989). The establishment of a joint enterprise, the Scientific Information Center, was a major step in this process. Initially, the government gathered much of the foreign scientific and technical information, with the Center providing the means for broadly disseminating the information throughout various Japanese industries.

By 1963, all Japanese multinational companies had created dedicated S&T intelligence units. One of the principal tasks for these units was to assimilate and disseminate throughout the company the S&T information collected by the Scientific Information Center. A survey conducted in 1963 by the Ministry of International Trade and Industry identified the scientific and technical collection means most used by the companies (Tsurumi 1980). The methods ran the gamut from the company's overseas offices to the use of foreign consulting/collection services and included the government's Scientific Information Center.

Today, Japanese companies involved in international business and trade use their own intelligence unit, typically located in their planning department, to gather both business and S&T intelligence. Manufacturing companies often use what is referred to as listening posts, i.e., offices located in their competitors' local regions with the specific mission of gathering competitor and technical intelligence. These companies use the technical intelligence to improve their own product performance.

Since the mid-1980s, Japanese firms have established overseas entities that are referred to as R&D centers. These centers are foreign-based laboratories whose basic mission is to hire foreign researchers to develop new and old technologies, often based on what they had created for previous employers. These technologies are transferred back to Japan and, as they refer to it, "Japanized" to avoid any potential conflict with the original firm's patents and copyrights. The number of Japanese R&D centers in the United States now exceeds 300, indicating they are both popular and successful (Serapio and Dalton 1994). A number of leading U.S. firms are now doing the same thing in Japan.

German companies probably have created some of the more organized S&T intelligence functions, referred to as Competitor Technology Intelligence. A survey conducted in 1991 entitled "Competitor Technology Intelligence in German Companies" (Brockhoff 1991) provides a good look at the state of S&T intelligence within German firms. Of some 80 companies surveyed, 45, or over one half, have institutionalized their S&T intelligence programs. About one third have centralized the competitor intelligence technology activity in separate departments including the patent department. One such firm, Henkel, was cited for having actually computerized its early warning intelligence process to trigger specific countermeasures and actions to be taken as a function of the various early warning indicators. As in studies by the U.S. Conference Board and the Society of Competitive Intelligence Professionals, the German study found that human sources such as the customers and the sales force provide the most valuable competitor intelligence.

The German survey concluded that S&T intelligence provides three primary benefits:

- Enhanced decision-making, resulting from more knowledge of the competitive situation
- A greater understanding of the total competitive environment, permitting identification of a greater variety of competitive actions the company may take
- Increased warning times, over an organization that does not have a Competitor Technology Intelligence function: in the chemical and pharmaceutical industries, about six months of additional warning—from 31 months to 37 months; in other industries, including electrical equipment, the early warning time almost doubled—from 17 to 33 months

A study conducted by Arthur D. Little in 1989 provided some interesting insights into the state of competitive intelligence among American, Japanese, and European companies' R&D functions. The survey of 35 major corporations—20 U.S., 8 European, 7 Japanese—found that while management considered the value of the intelligence high, only 10 of the 35 made it a budgeted activity; most of the rest cited concern about the risk of establishing a new internal bureaucracy as the principal inhibiting factor. Managers interviewed during the Arthur D. Little survey expressed similar concerns about starting and operating such activities, including "How do we establish one?" "Who does it?" and "Should it be centralized or decentralized?" Most of the companies surveyed opted for less capability, budgeting for one or two full-time people to serve as the core team for the S&T intelligence activity companywide (Esposito and Gilmont 1991).

In an excellent article in the *Harvard Business Review*, "Technology Fusion and the New R&D," the Japanese use of technical intelligence is described by Fumio Kodama (1992). Kodama, a professor at several universities, headed Japan's National Institute of Science and Technology Policy from 1988 to 1991. His book on the same subject won a prestigious Japanese literary award and had a major impact on Japanese corporate thinking.

Kodama identifies three basic principles essential to the modern harnessing of technology, somewhat reminiscent of Bacon's views some 300 years earlier. The second of his three R&D principles is intelligence-gathering, designed to monitor technological developments inside and outside an organization's own industry. He states that all employees, from senior managers to front-line workers, must play a part in collecting and disseminating intelligence.

Kodama goes on to state that most Japanese companies have **elaborate** intelligence-gathering networks, both formal and informal, that can be traced back to post-World War II reconstruction. He states that from the 1950s through the 1970s, Japanese R&D efforts were directed primarily at absorbing foreign technologies; the Japanese Ministry of International Trade and Industry estimated that, during the 1960s and 1970s, Japanese manufacturers devoted over 25 percent of all R&D investments to digesting imported technologies.

Kodama makes an important point that companies have both visible and invisible competitors: visible being those who are easily recognized as competing companies; invisible being those who possess technological capabilities that could threaten a company but that lie outside the company's familiar industrial framework. He sees the identification and analysis of such potential competitors based on technological potential as a major objective of a company's S&T intelligence activities. He also views gathering information on the technologies of such companies as a way of acquiring new technologies for a company's own purposes, a form of S&T intelligence operations known as "scouting."

The primary objective of this intelligence-based activity is to provide Japanese firms with scientific and technical intelligence that will assist them in accomplishing what Kodama refers to as the "techno-paradigm shift." He believes that future competitive success will depend strongly on integrating or fusing technology and intelligence into the product development process.

So, from Francis Bacon's earliest identification of the role of science and technology in achieving a nation's or state's objectives to the industrial revolution in the United States to its military applications during World War II and the Cold War to the present recognition that future business competition will be based on the fusion of technology and intelligence, S&T intelligence plays a very critical role.

The gathering, analysis, and production of S&T intelligence is both a necessary and legitimate activity in modern-day business. It behooves companies and R&D organizations alike to do this professionally and proficiently. The purposes of such activities must be clearly defined if the intelligence function is to help the organization accomplish its goals and thus benefit from such activities.

THE CONTEMPORARY NATURE OF COMPETITIVENESS

In the past, competitiveness has been based mainly on manufacturing competencies, namely, cost, quality, and the timeliness of product and service delivery. However, leading U.S., Japanese, and European firms are increasingly moving their manufacturing and design centers to low-cost overseas locations to achieve further cost and efficiency advantages. As they do this, they are further diffusing this technologically based advantage worldwide.

Whether a company is in manufacturing or services, today's competition is increasingly conducted on the **use** of advanced technologies. Global competition is becoming more dependent on advanced product and production technologies for competitive advantage. Whether it is communications technology in the financial services industry or advanced diagnostics in pharmaceutical or automotive companies, technology is the primary factor in winning today's competition. Knowing where that technology is and being the first to acquire and apply it in an industry provide the competitive advantage.

Thus, future competitive advantage will be derived from obtaining superior knowledge and foreknowledge of the world in which companies compete—for technologies as well as markets. Companies that accomplish this task the most efficiently and the quickest will be the winners. Intelligence systems are the most effective means for accomplishing this learning objective, and S&T intelligence is the most appropriate intelligence discipline for this task. **The competitive advantage goes to companies that know where the future technologies are being created today.**

THE NATURE AND UTILITY OF BUSINESS S&T INTELLIGENCE

The most valued and salient feature of S&T intelligence is that it provides the best long-range look at the future competitive environment. Both political and economic intelligence have rather volatile components based on human frailties and whims; as a result, predicting future economic or political events is very uncertain. However, when an organization commits millions of dollars to an R&D program, it is telling much about its future aspirations as well as its intentions. And, once such resources are put in place, such efforts are much more inclined to continue.

Good S&T intelligence provides an objective measure of one's current and future technological position. An assessment of the technological state of one's industry, along with an objective view of the status of competitor technologies, provides not only a current assessment of one's competitive position, it also provides the basis from which to forecast one's future competitive situation—and to evaluate current technology decisions and plans (Herring 1992a).

Experience has shown us that technological forecasts provide the longest view of future opportunities and threats. Political and economic forecasts are more short term and volatile. Good technological forecasting also provides the best measure of a competitor's current intention to change direction.

Identification and analysis of technological trends in one's business often presage major structural changes in that industry. Assessment of technology trends that looks both at how technology is changing and at the rate of that change provides valuable insights into the identification of future success factors in one's business.

S&T intelligence concerning a competitor's commitment to its future technological objectives is without a doubt the best way to assess that competitor's future capabilities and, more important, his intentions regarding one's business and customers. S&T intelligence, properly analyzed and forecasted, provides the best early warning intelligence that can be produced. As in government intelligence, the primary objective is to prevent technological surprise. Corporations, like governments, do not respond well to Sputnik-like intelligence surprises. Better that we identify such possibilities early on, so that management does not overreact.

S&T intelligence by itself, however, is a rather naked policy or strategy tool. For S&T intelligence to be used effectively, it must be combined with military intelligence or, in the business world, the competitor's intentions to provide the appropriate insights and have the desired impact on the company's planning, decision-making, and operations. A good S&T intelligence program incorporates this feature into both its design and production program.

THE KEY ELEMENTS IN A SUCCESSFUL S&T INTELLIGENCE PROGRAM

The first and most important element in any intelligence program is purpose. Senior management provides that purpose and focus. While specific intelligence needs vary from company to company and from business to business, the basic types of intelligence needs do not. First and foremost is early warning—of both opportunities and threats. Since Biblical times, intelligence organizations have been solely responsible for providing early warning of pending threats or dangers. While threats are important, the identification of opportunities is of prime importance in today's business environment. Alerting management to new and future business opportunities is the primary responsibility of the intelligence system.

While early warning is the *primary objective*, enhanced decision-making is an intelligence organization's *primary function*. Each company is faced with a few major decisions each year, decisions that clearly will affect the company's current and future success. Decisions that are affected by external forces in some major way are those that require intelligence support. Among such decisions are

- Entering new markets and businesses
- Investing in and acquiring new technologies
- Making major capital investments, particularly those involving foreign entities
- Selecting strategic partners, forging alliances, and making wise acquisitions
- Implementing trade and public policy initiatives.

Intelligence also provides the basis for more comprehensive and perceptive *long-range plans and strategies*. The intelligence department should be called on to provide inputs for such planning activities. One such assignment would be to assess future competitors as well as the total competitive environment in which one's company and its competitors will likely compete. Depending on a company's planning process, the intelligence department also can be called on to provide objective assessments of the underlying assumptions associated with such planning, since the departments typically have no conflicting program or budgetary bias (Herring 1992b).

For technology managers, a strong scientific S&T intelligence function will provide very valuable and unique information for the department's technology planning and decision-making processes. Intelligence operations focused on the external environment, including future competitive developments, will provide not only time-sensitive inputs, but also objective inputs for comparing one's own technology development programs with those of others in the industry.

Because S&T development today is both an international and an interdependent enterprise, a company must regularly monitor and assess those foreign developments that have the greatest impact on the company. Identifying and assessing the potential or unexpected impact of such external technology developments is very important. Monitoring and assessing competitor research is one such input. Similarly, using the S&T intelligence department to regularly monitor alternative and substitute products and processes can provide sources of new technology as well as competitive early warning. Knowing what is happening in those related technology areas outside one's direct business is also helpful, and something not typically done by companies R&D personnel.

The most serious competitors that companies will be facing are those that operate globally, acquiring technologies worldwide from the most advanced sources of R&D, as well as creating those technologies themselves in foreign laboratories and through international joint ventures. Most governments—and I think most companies—recognize that the future threats they will be facing are actually being created today in someone's laboratory or development program. Having an organization devoted to identifying and monitoring such future threats today is the only way to prevent being surprised tomorrow.

SPECIAL REQUIREMENTS FOR THE S&T UNIT: INTELLIGENCE FOR R&D MANAGERS

It behooves corporate R&D and technology managers to be fully informed about the development of new technologies outside their company. Senior management expects these managers to be totally knowledgeable about the technology needed to develop and produce new products and services for their own company. Equally important, they must be aware of relevant competitor activities if they are to optimize their own technology planning and make wise budgetary decisions (Herring 1993).

Intelligence about the competitor is essential if one is to compete effectively. A good intelligence program should keep the organization informed of the status of its major competitors' R&D

capabilities. Such a program should also keep the organization abreast of its competitors' new product developments, providing estimates of those products' future performance. Such estimates are critical in designing a product's future capabilities as well as making adjustments during the product's R&D program.

Some competitors are more aggressive than others, collecting intelligence that goes beyond the boundaries of propriety. The Hitachi-IBM case in the early 1980s is a case in point. The temptation to take a look at IBM's next generation of software was just too much for the Japanese competitor. The U.S. government's sting operation exposed the illegal and unethical practices of Hitachi and several other Japanese firms in gathering S&T intelligence in this country. Good competitive intelligence programs provide the basis for enhancing a company's security to better protect its intellectual property.

An S&T intelligence program can provide R&D managers with a continuous and objective source of S&T information on technology developments outside the company. Such efforts are in addition to the department's regular activities, including analytical research by its own R&D personnel. Such technology intelligence efforts facilitate a manager's ability to supplement his or her own R&D efforts. Identifying alternative sources of technology on a continuous basis means that a company will know where the technology is when and if it is needed.

Being better informed about external S&T developments as well as competitor R&D will help a company better plan and manage its R&D programs. Knowing where external technologies stand and when one's own programs might need them is very valuable management information. During periods of tight corporate budgets, S&T intelligence will also help a company make better use of external sources and provide the basis for justifying its own R&D projects. Technology development programs that are sensitive to competitors' product developments are more likely to meet the program schedules, cost, and performance goals and to create a sense of overall urgency within a company to develop and introduce new products.

S&T intelligence on competitors' technology capabilities and customer needs provides the basis for some rather sophisticated corporate strategies. Such technology-based strategies are becoming more popular with both Japanese and European firms.

Strategic R&D partnerships with customers and suppliers provide a means of maintaining strong customer relationships by building interdependencies. Selecting the right partners also permits companies to supplement their own R&D funds—knowing which partners to select is the intelligence task.

Companies that form alliance strategies to gain necessary technology also require good S&T intelligence. The task is to identify the industry leaders and those most interested in alliances. Such intelligence permits companies to implement vertical integration strategies to achieve totally new products and service goals, as well as to support rapid product introduction strategies.

Rapid product introduction strategies, ironically, have resulted in technology half-lives growing shorter by the month. This development puts a premium on knowing the state of technology among the various competitors and companies in one's industry—not only for competitive purposes, but for the purpose of knowing when it is the "right time" to trade a technology for market access or capital gain, a very difficult but important function in R&D management.

R&D plans that incorporate S&T intelligence about the competition are more likely to impact the company's long-range planning since they describe future opportunities and threats, not just the internal plans and goals of the company itself.

ESTABLISHING AN S&T INTELLIGENCE PROGRAM

Purpose is the essence of all effective intelligence operations. Begin by identifying key users of the intelligence and, in particular, how they would actually use the intelligence that is produced. Identifying key users and their key intelligence topics provides focus and purpose to all subsequent intelligence operations, including collection and analysis. Linking management decisions, plans, and operations directly to intelligence activities is the underlying secret of success for any intelligence program (Herring 1991).

An intelligence unit should be led by a director of intelligence with close professional and personal ties to the head of R&D. The actual use of S&T intelligence by R&D and by business managers will be critical to the success of the activity. Having a director whom management respects and includes in its inner circle of planners and decision-makers is a necessary element in an effective intelligence program.

The critical element for success for any intelligence operation is the direct involvement of senior management. The intelligence process begins with management needs and ends with delivery of intelligence to those in the company who have the authority and responsibility to act on it. Begin the intelligence operation with a clear understanding not only of who will use the intelligence but, most important, how they will use it. Thus, the intelligence operation becomes focused on those decisions and strategic issues that are important to manage the R&D activity and/or meet the business objectives of the company.

Next, establish the three basic intelligence operations *simultaneously*:

- Information services—timely, comprehensive, and proactive
- Collection and reporting—systematic, on-going, and focused
- Analysis and forecasting—dedicated and professionally trained.

The basic responsibilities of the three operations are identified in Figure 1. The size and makeup of each intelligence unit will depend on the size and scope of the R&D or business organization they support. Combining all three operations into one unit is the most effective organizationally. The two basic configurations are 1) a self-contained unit consisting of library services, collection management, and intelligence analysts or 2) a center concept where people and space are shared with other business functions, but all are dedicated to the production of intelligence. A third, much less effective, concept is the assignment of a single intelligence practitioner whose role is to organize and lead ad hoc intelligence tasks. Regardless of the unit's organization, its primary function is to produce the intelligence needed by the company's management.

Creating an effective S&T intelligence unit begins with selection of the right people. Experience tells us that the right people typically are those with broad technical backgrounds and many years of business experience. In particular, the intelligence analyst should be selected from employees who have been in the company and industry for a minimum of five years and who possess what intelligence professionals refer to as a "pattern-thinking" mind.

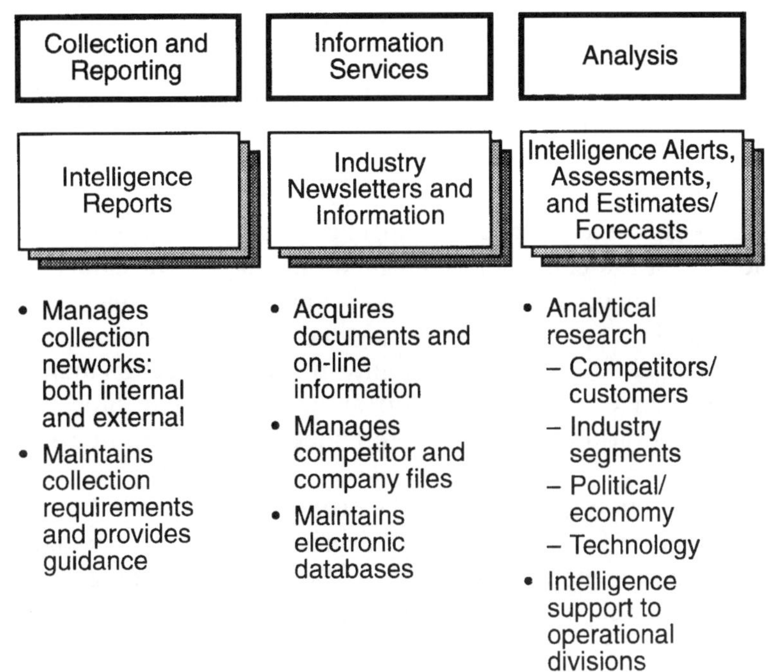

FIGURE 1. Intelligence department operations

For the most part, these individuals must be sought out and identified based on recognized attributes. We have found no way to train the mind in this form of analytical thinking.

All members of the intelligence department must be professionally trained in their particular function, that is, collection and reporting, analysis, and information services. It is advisable to rotate the S&T personnel from the laboratories and business functions into the intelligence department as analysts. Japanese companies often use assignments to their intelligence functions as rewards for engineers and scientists who have been on the line for extended periods of time. After spending one to two years in such intelligence activities, these engineers and scientists are full of new ideas and, upon returning to operations, often become very productive.

The S&T intelligence unit will require several professionally trained intelligence analysts. These analysts will often serve as "lead" analysts for ad hoc intelligence tasks. They will organize, plan, and lead both technical and multidisciplinary intelligence assessment teams, combining business and S&T intelligence to produce appropriate results.

Intelligence collection should be managed by a full-time, professionally trained practitioner. In addition to guiding collection and reporting the required intelligence back to management and other users, the collection manager's ongoing responsibility is to set up and maintain both external and internal human source networks. This task in itself is a full-time job. In addition to strong interpersonal skills and writing ability, the S&T collection manager will need an experienced understanding of such technical collection operations as reverse engineering and photographic interpretation.

The collection function should be centrally coordinated, serving all aspects of R&D as well as business activities. It should be responsible for monitoring all related external technology developments, as well as technology-intensive competitors. S&T intelligence reporting can serve both the R&D and business intelligence departments. The S&T unit should have responsibility for providing counterintelligence in support of the company's security program, a function associated with gathering S&T intelligence.

Achieving early warning requires attention not only to collection of intelligence but also to its analytical interpretation. Combining these two functions in a single operational unit is the key to providing early warning intelligence. As stated earlier, S&T intelligence produces a rather naked form of intelligence but, when combined with business or marketing intelligence, it often adds the future dimension and the insight required to make the combined intelligence product a more prescient and useful one.

The library or information service operation provides the foundation for both intelligence collection and analysis. Staff must be trained properly to be proactive. An existing library can provide the service, but the trained resource must then be dedicated to supporting the intelligence unit. In addition to providing operational support, the library should also be responsible for producing an intelligence newsletter.

Many companies have created advanced information systems to store all sorts of information and have called this their intelligence system. This is a serious mistake, often raising high expectations that are never met by searching through one's information files. Good intelligence is produced by the proactive intelligence collection of current information and is analytically developed by human beings, not computers.

Nevertheless, because of the large amount of information generated by intelligence collection and analysis, it is important to have some form of information management system. An S&T intelligence information system should be established, but only after the basic human intelligence process has been developed and proved. This system should be compatible with the company's existing information management system and e-mail operation and should probably be one of the last developmental activities in establishing the intelligence program—not the first.

Last, but certainly not least, the establishment of explicit legal and ethical guidelines early in the program is highly recommended. The company's law department is a good partner to have in an intelligence program and is oftentimes an excellent source of intelligence. Also, as the S&T intelligence program begins to gather counterintelligence on competitors, assistance from the legal department will become necessary to protect the proprietary property of one's company.

THE SUCCESSFUL S&T INTELLIGENCE PROGRAM

The successful intelligence program is the one that best meets the needs of its users. Identification of those user needs at the beginning of a *new* S&T intelligence program or a new task for an *established* intelligence unit is the *first* critical success element. This is the primary role and responsibility of the intelligence unit's director.

The *second* critical success factor is provision of adequate resources, particularly professionally trained and dedicated staff. This staff must be capable of carrying out a variety of basic intelligence activities in a professional and proficient manner. Figure 2 depicts the range of S&T intelligence activities that should be possible by an effective intelligence unit.

Third, no matter how it is organized, the intelligence unit must possess the three basic intelligence operations and be capable of providing the five primary intelligence functions shown in Figure 3.

Type of Activity	Intelligence Function	Application
Literature search	Collection/scanning	Influence own R&D
Patent research	Scanning/search	Warning and protection
S&T conferences	Focused search/ scouting	R&D, plans, strategies
Field collection – Human – Photography – Emissions	 – Proactive search – Targeted/ measurements – Scanning/ search	 – Decision-making, scouting – Analysis, credibility – Analysis, verification
Reverse engineering	Investigative research	Performance and cost
Competitive benchmarking	Comparative research	Cost and performance
Competitor assessments – Competitor analysis – R&D projects – R&D program – Alliances and acquisitions	 – Capability/ strategy/intent – Threat assessment – Future plans and strategy – Strategy and threat assessment	 – Strategies and security – Product performance and timing – Long-range plans and strategy – Strategies and acquisitions
Competitive environment – Technology assessment and forecast – Industry trends and structure	 – Assessing threats and alternatives – Future threats and opportunities	 – Technology plans and budgets – Long-range plans and strategy

FIGURE 2. S&T intelligence activities

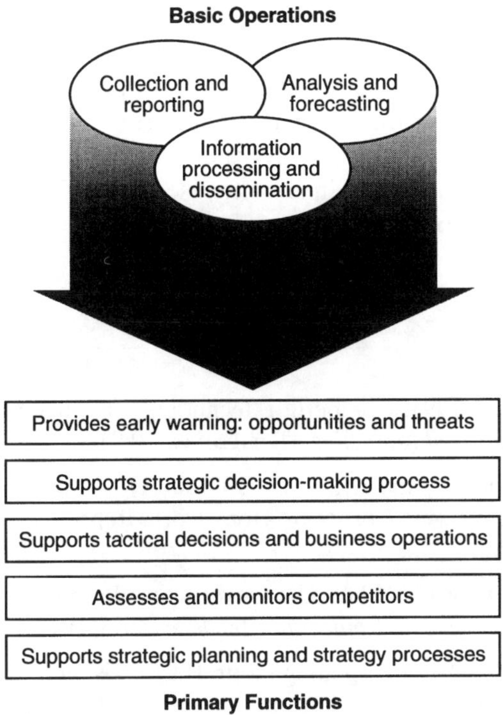

FIGURE 3. Business intelligence system operations and functions

In addition, the S&T intelligence unit must be capable of providing the R&D manager the S&T intelligence to

- Support the R&D planning and technology acquisition programs
- Scout external technology worldwide to speed up product development
- Conduct R&D that is relative to and motivated by the competition's capability and intentions.

And, finally, the unit must gather the counterintelligence upon which to base a contemporary security program to protect the company's own intellectual property.

In the final analysis, the program's success will depend directly on the quality of the intelligence the program produces. And that, in turn, will depend on the quality and skills of the practitioners running the operation. Understanding the intelligence organization and operation is a necessary condition for creating an effective S&T program, but a successful program requires professionally trained personnel to manage and run it.

Basically, find good people, give them the appropriate resources and tools, and train them in how to use them. But management must provide the purpose for these operations.

REFERENCES

Brockhoff, Klaus. 1991. Competitor Technology Intelligence in German Companies. *Industrial Marketing Management* 20:91-98.

Esposito, Michael A., and Ernest R. Gilmont. December 1991. Competitive Intelligence: Doing Corporate Homework. Reprinted from *Pharmaceutical Executive*.

Herring, Jan P. February 1989. The Government Role in Japanese Competitive Intelligence. *The Competitive Intelligencer* 3(4):11-13.

Herring, Jan P. 1991. Sharpening Your R&D Vision Through Intelligence. Presentation at the IRI Annual Meeting, Chicago, Illinois, October 14, 1991. The Futures Group, 80 Glastonbury Blvd., Glastonbury, CT 06033-4409.

Herring, Jan P. 1992a. The Unique Role of the Future in Intelligence. *The Intelligence Corporation: The Privatisation of Intelligence,* eds. Jon Sigurdson and Yael Tagerud. Taylor Graham Publishing, Los Angeles, California.

Herring, Jan P. September/October 1992b. The Role of Intelligence in Formulating Strategy. *Journal of Business Strategy* 13(5):54-60.

Herring, Jan P. May/June 1993. Scientific and Technical Intelligence: The Key to R&D. *Journal of Business Strategy* 15(3):10-12.

Kodama, Fumio. July/August 1992. Technology Fusion and the New R&D. *Harvard Business Review*.

Serapio, Manuel G., Jr., and Donald H. Dalton. November 1994. Foreign R&D in the United States. *IEEE Spectrum*, pp. 26-30.

Tsurumi, Yoshihiro. June 1980. *Technology Transfer and Foreign Trade: The Case of Japan, 1950-1966*. Arno Press, New York.

Designing and Implementing Technology Intelligence Systems

D. WILLIAM McDONALD and JOHN L. RICHARDSON

Almost all organizations that develop and/or apply technology to a significant extent have what might be described as a "technology intelligence" system. That is, personnel in the organization acquire information about new technological developments from various sources, such as vendors, trade publications, personal contacts, and so on. Frequently, this information is reported and used. A common example is the acquisition and dissemination of information on computer hardware and software.

NEED FOR FORMAL TECHNOLOGY INTELLIGENCE SYSTEMS

The current focus in both industry and government on global competitiveness, innovation, and increased productivity in all operations requires that information on technological developments and competitors' activities be obtained and assessed in a timely and effective manner. Rather than carrying such "intelligence" activities out on an *ad hoc* or "do-it-yourself" basis, businesses and other organizations are to an increasing extent establishing formal intelligence programs or systems. The organization and management of these systems may vary widely in different organizations, but the common intent is to provide information that management can use in making key decisions on strategies and the tactics to implement the selected strategies.

In organizations where technology is a major driving force, formal technology intelligence (TI) systems have been implemented. These TI systems often interface with other intelligence operations that may be titled "business intelligence," "competitive intelligence," or similar terms. As will be discussed later, the scope of TI systems may include tracking and assessing market trends, regulatory changes, competitors' activities, and other subjects that may significantly affect the technological decisions the organization makes.

The most effective TI systems have formal networks of employees (often called "gatekeepers") who obtain, evaluate, and communicate technological and related information on a part-time basis. This network is usually managed by a relatively small, core group of full-time intelligence personnel who help ensure that the intelligence activities are focused on areas of current or potential importance to management and that the quality of the effort is appropriately high. Both the information networks and the management function will be discussed in more depth later in this chapter.

MISSION AND MAJOR OBJECTIVES OF EFFECTIVE TECHNOLOGY INTELLIGENCE SYSTEMS

As indicated above, the primary mission of TI systems or programs is to provide information that supports business decisions—normally those decisions that relate to the allocation of technological or other resources. Systems that are effective in fulfilling this mission are

- Focused on major business opportunities and competitive threats
- Customized to meets the needs of specific "clients"
- Timely, objective, and appropriately rigorous.

This mission is most effectively accomplished by having all major functions (for example, marketing, operations, planning, etc.) involved, rather than just the major technological functions such as research, development, engineering, etc. This multifunctional involvement is particularly important when a special assessment is made to respond to a significant management inquiry or to support an important business decision.

Some common objectives of TI systems are to

- Provide more lead time for responding to opportunities and threats
- Keep business and technological management personnel better informed on relevant technological developments
- Introduce technological issues into strategic discussions more effectively
- Make senior management more comfortable with decisions involving technology
- Have an impact on important resource allocation decisions.

Other important objectives for TI systems are to help guide the planning of research and development (R&D) programs, to provide information to assist in the purchase or license of technology, and to support the selection of potential partners in strategic alliances or joint ventures.

SCOPE AND OVERVIEW OF AN EFFECTIVE TECHNOLOGY INTELLIGENCE SYSTEM

The scope of an effective TI system should be relatively broad, rather than being limited to developments in science and technology only. A typical scope would cover the following areas:

- Technology monitoring/tracking
- Technology assessment and forecasting
- Assessments of competitors, vendors/suppliers, and potential partners
- Tracking and analysis of market, societal and regulatory trends.

The primary guidance for the directions to pursue in acquiring and communicating intelligence from these areas should be the objectives and strategies of the business or other organization.

Before it is provided to management, the intelligence from all of the above areas must be integrated into a unified "story." Further, the intelligence communicated should include both the ambiguities and potential implications of the findings and, if appropriate, recommendations on what should be done as a result of this information.

From a conceptual viewpoint, the TI process consists of five steps: defining needs, acquiring data, converting data into information, refining the information into actionable intelligence, and communicating the intelligence to management for support of decisions. Figure 1 shows these steps as a linear process (although there are multiple feedback loops) and provides a brief explanation of the key elements of each step.

The functions or activities required for a TI system, such as that shown in Figure 1, include a monitoring capability (often performed by a gatekeeper network), a system for storing and retrieving data/information, a means of assessing information provided by monitoring and other sources, and mechanisms to

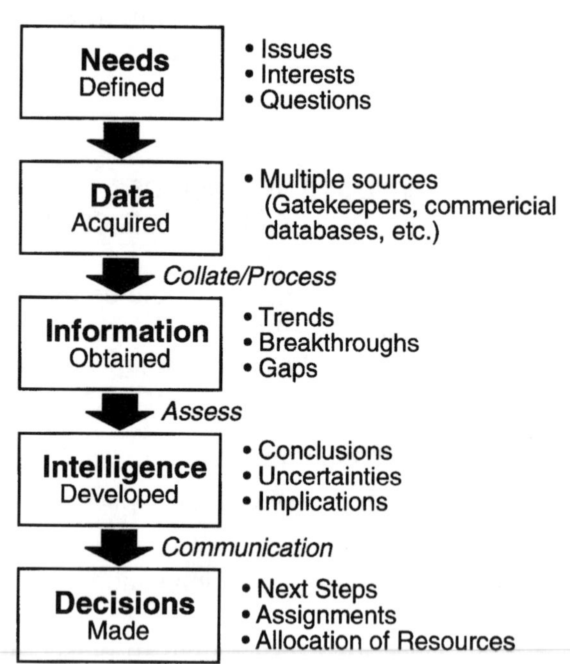

FIGURE 1. Overview of the technology intelligence process

communicate the findings to management. A flowchart illustrating how these functions fit together is shown in Figure 2. These major functions or activities will be discussed in more detail later. As in the prior chart, the multiple feedback loops that exist in practice have been omitted.

In keeping with the mission and objectives of TI systems noted above, the design of a system must start with the bottom of the diagram, that is, the clients and the decisions to which the intelligence will be applied. Intelligence systems that have failed have often focused on gathering and disseminating copious amounts of information that was not tailored and refined to meet the needs of business decision-makers.

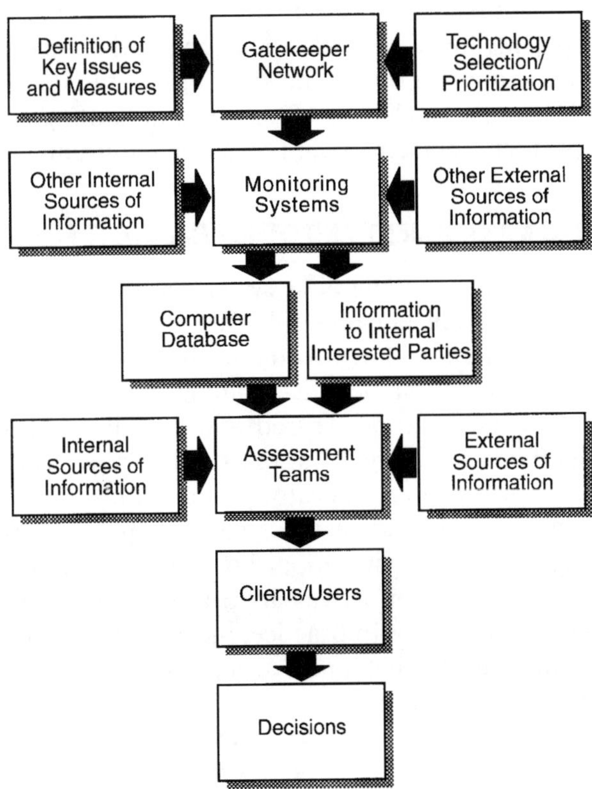

FIGURE 2. Flow chart for a technology intelligence system

DESIGNING A TECHNOLOGY INTELLIGENCE SYSTEM TO MEET ORGANIZATIONAL NEEDS

The major tasks that must be accomplished in designing a formal TI system or process are discussed below. The discussion assumes that there is no successful TI system in place and that management is interested in changing this situation.

In the first task, key management and other personnel are interviewed to define their interests/needs and the relevant technologies. Next, the needs and associated technologies are prioritized and reviewed with appropriate management personnel. The third task is the selection of gatekeepers to track and report on the technologies judged to have sufficient priority to warrant a continuing monitoring effort. Approaches for accomplishing this and criteria for selecting the gatekeepers are discussed. The fourth task area includes audits of past TI-type activities and of the capabilities of needed supporting functions such as the technical library and database software support groups. The final task is the design of the proposed TI system, including structure and staffing, reporting relationships, focus, objectives, and resource requirements.

INTERVIEWING MANAGEMENT AND OTHER RELEVANT PERSONNEL

The first step in designing a TI system is to interview several high-level management personnel, both to get their opinions on the proposed system and to acquaint them with the possible options and their potential benefits. Among the key inputs sought are the types of information desired and the intended uses, the preferred methods of communication, the technological areas of most interest, and favored indicators that would be used in the future to judge the success of the system. If possible, the most senior managers in the organization should be interviewed so that their suggestions and their active support, including commitment of resources, are obtained. In practice, most successful TI systems have a very high-level "champion" whose support is well known throughout the organization.

Subsequently, a number of lower-level managers and senior technical personnel are interviewed to get similar inputs, as well as suggestions on staff who are believed to have the qualifications to be effective gatekeepers, for example, in-depth knowledge of the field and the ability to communicate. In these interviews, the key technologies that should be covered and their supporting sciences and technologies are usually discussed in detail; a suggested approach for prioritizing the technological and related areas is discussed below. These interviews are also used to determine the types of ongoing or past intelligence activities and their relative effectiveness. In addition, the willingness of the interviewees to commit resources is probed.

PRIORITIZING ORGANIZATIONAL NEEDS AND TECHNOLOGICAL AREAS

The information obtained from the interviews should be analyzed and reviewed with the key sponsors of the proposed TI system to obtain agreement on the system design premises—such as the scope, primary intended clients or users, preferred methods of communicating with these clients, and so forth. The design premises should be recorded and circulated appropriately.

Next, the suggested technological and related areas should be prioritized based on criteria such as the following:

- Current and forecasted impact of the technology on the organization
- Probability and timing of future impact
- Degree of change occurring in the technology (a key indicator of its maturity)
- Potential opportunities and threats from competing technologies
- Interest senior management personnel have shown in particular technologies.

In a new TI system, only a relatively few technologies should be actively monitored and assessed. For example, out of 80 to 100 suggested technologies, 10 to 20 might be considered as top priority. The remainder either would be given less attention or not considered at all until the system is more fully developed.

SELECTING GATEKEEPERS TO MONITOR IMPORTANT TECHNOLOGICAL AREAS

As noted above, one important objective of the interviews is to obtain suggestions on possible gatekeepers or monitors. The characteristics of effective gatekeepers have been described by Allen (1984), Nochur and Allen (1992), and others. These characteristics can be summarized as the five C's: competent, connected, current, communicative, and committed.

"Competent" means having well-recognized background/experience in the technological field or related area, including knowledge of how the technology is currently or potentially applicable to products, processes, or services of interest to the company or other organization. "Connected" implies having effective sources of information both within and outside the organization. "Current" means staying up-to-date on developments worldwide that may be relevant to the company/organization. "Communicative" means having the ability to communicate both with various sources and with the persons in the organization who should receive the information. Last but not least, having gatekeepers who are "committed" is crucial, because they usually serve in this role on a part-time basis, often with conflicting demands on their time.

Another important factor that may not be within the control of the gatekeeper candidate is the person's availability to serve. Thus, if high-level management does not fully support the TI effort, many of the best gatekeeper candidates may not be considered to be available by their managers/supervisors.

The screening process usually involves personal interviews with the gatekeeper candidates, as well as interviews with others in the organization about how well the candidates fit the characteristics described above. The tentative selections are reviewed with appropriate managers and agreement is reached on who will be the primary gatekeepers and who will be the support. A given area of technology may have a number of subsets of technological disciplines that are best handled by persons who have specialized skills, but are neither fully qualified nor available to be the primary gatekeepers.

Next, the selected gatekeepers are briefed on the justification for and objectives of the planned TI program and provided specific information on what is expected of them, including a commitment to appropriate training. Recommendations on training will be given in a later section of this chapter.

AUDITING CURRENT OR PAST TECHNOLOGY INTELLIGENCE ACTIVITIES AND SUPPORTING RESOURCES

The interviews described above will normally provide useful information on current or past TI-type activities. In addition, it is often helpful to review relevant documents and to talk to other individuals who have been involved in intelligence activities both within and outside of the technology organization(s). The inputs obtained may prevent duplication of past ineffective practices or of intelligence activities in progress in other parts of the organization.

A necessary step in developing a design for a TI system is to evaluate key supporting functions, particularly the library/information center and the computer operations support staff. Both the corporate library and the technical center library normally play key roles in doing searches of computerized databases, assisting in searches of in-house sources, and obtaining documents not available internally from external sources such as university or governmental agency libraries. Some libraries/information centers also help in the ongoing monitoring efforts by screening information sources such as trade publications and journals and directing pertinent items to those involved in the TI effort.

The key elements of a typical computerized information or database system needed to support the TI effort will be discussed later. Existing database systems and the capabilities of the computer operations staff to support the design and maintenance of the planned TI information system should be evaluated relatively early in the design process. The cost and time of developing and implementing a new database system, if required, could have a major influence on the planning premises of the TI system.

Other functional groups within the organization, such as those responsible for regulatory affairs, corporate communications, and university relationships, may be needed to support the TI system. If so, information on the resources of these functions and their willingness to help should be obtained early in the design phase.

DESIGNING THE PROPOSED TECHNOLOGY INTELLIGENCE SYSTEM

The organizational structures for TI systems generally fit the following three options:

- Centralized—having a self-contained function, usually corporately managed, which collects, assesses, and disseminates intelligence information to management and to the technical staff.
- Distributed—having subject matter experts (gatekeepers) throughout the organization who collect information from various sources and communicate it to others, primarily technical personnel; the operation is often managed by a part-time "coordinator."
- Hybrid—a combination of a core TI group and a distributed network of gatekeepers, with the core group providing guidance and training, maintaining contact with clients, and ensuring that the system operates effectively.

For most relatively large companies or other organizations, the hybrid approach appears to provide the best results. Having a trained, clearly designated TI function provides a continuing focus on meeting management's needs and the appropriate quality control. In addition, having a distributed network of gatekeepers to monitor and assess new developments gives better coverage of sources than a core group alone and brings more people into the consideration of strategic issues. The long-term goal should be to have all professionals in the technical functions (and in other key functions such as marketing and planning) cognizant of and contributing to the intelligence needs of the organization.

Aligning the design with organizational needs, culture, and resources is essential. As noted previously, TI or intelligence functions must provide value to management if they are to remain viable. At times, management may not be clear about its needs in a given area, or these needs may change frequently. Thus, the management of the TI function must stay in touch with its clients and be prepared for rapid shifts in priorities. Understanding the culture of the organization is crucial, both in dealing with senior management and with the lower-level personnel who will be involved in the gatekeeper network, the supporting functions discussed above, and the separate assessment teams when these are formed to study specific issues.

The time focus of the organization is a key element of culture; for example, if the focus is on the very short term, designing a TI system that emphasizes long-term trends and developments would not be appropriate (unless senior management was deliberately trying to change the focus). Similarly, if business units have a great deal of autonomy, attempting to install a central system that makes large resource commitment demands on these units would probably prove to be counterproductive.

Another key factor is the availability of resources. In most organizations the staff feels that it is already fully loaded; hence the introduction of another system that will make demands on some of the key people requires the full backing of senior management and usually a lot of "salesmanship." Further, if vital resources (gatekeepers in important areas or primary supporting functions such as literature searchers) are not available, the design of the TI system obviously must take these limitations into account.

MAJOR BUILDING BLOCKS OF TECHNOLOGY INTELLIGENCE SYSTEMS

The major elements or "building blocks" of effective TI systems include a management function with a number of key responsibilities, a monitoring and reporting function based on gatekeepers and information networks, and an assessment function capable of producing analyses and other information to meet management's needs. Also required are a "user friendly" information acquisition, storage, and retrieval capability and quality assurance/client feedback to help ensure that the intelligence generated and reported fully meets the needs of management and other clients.

MANAGEMENT FUNCTION

As noted earlier, the optimum organizational structure for a TI system appears to be a hybrid of a core group and a distributed network of gatekeepers. Depending on the size of the company and the scope of its technological efforts, this core group may vary from one part-time person to several full-time staff members and one or more managers. Preferably, the management of this core group will report to a senior-level person to give the group the visibility and clout needed to function effectively. Some primary responsibilities of the management of the TI system are to

- Build and maintain effective interfaces with senior management
- Establish priorities and objectives
- Define the organizational structure of the TI system
- Obtain funding and prepare and administer budgets
- Recruit, train, and manage system personnel, both full- and part-time participants
- Enhance client relationships
- Negotiate with other managers for assistance
- Communicate.

These responsibilities place a heavy emphasis on building relationships throughout the organization. Thus, the TI management personnel must have high credibility and strong communications skills.

If the core TI group has several members, there is the opportunity to have specialists in intelligence gathering and assessment and also in some very high-priority technology areas. The latter may be staff who serve as full-time monitors in certain fields or who focus on maintaining contacts with important outside sources of information such as universities, government agencies, or major industry consortia technology development organizations (for example, the Electric Power Research Institute, Bell Communications Research [Bellcore], the Institute of Paper Chemistry), and so forth. Some TI groups have staff members who are skilled in strategic planning and who maintain close contacts with business planning functions.

MONITORING/REPORTING FUNCTION

The word "reporting" is in the title of this function to emphasize its importance in the intelligence process. If the gatekeepers do not take the time to evaluate, summarize, and report their findings on a predefined basis, much of the value of the effort is lost. This problem is accentuated when the monitoring network covers multiple locations, especially if it includes company facilities in foreign countries. The timeliness and completeness in reporting will be improved if the TI core group provides guidance on reporting formats and makes these formats as "user friendly" as possible.

Another key element in the success of monitoring/tracking programs is an emphasis on selectivity in what is monitored or tracked. A useful approach for achieving selectivity is to get the gatekeeper(s) for a given area to define the issues that are most important (such as cost and quality trends, new applications, etc.) and the indicators or measures for defining significant changes in these issues. If possible, these measures should be quantitative, but in some cases only qualitative indicators are available or reliable.

Once the measures have been defined and accepted by all concerned, the gatekeepers focus their monitoring efforts on changes in technology that affect these key issues either directly or indirectly (as in a competing technology) and pay minimum attention to other information. This focusing may increase the risk of missing early detection of some new development that eventually becomes important. The primary loss will probably only be time because the change will be picked up later if it becomes significant.

The network of monitors or gatekeepers is normally composed of staff who perform this role in addition to their major assignments. As indicated above, however, some organizations have full-time gatekeepers who cover areas of very high priority, such as relatively new technologies that may have a major impact on the organization in the future. These full-time gatekeepers usually reside in the TI management group, but may be located in other functions that work closely with the TI group. The TI group may also have some external gatekeepers, such as university professors, consultants, or vendor or industry association personnel.

Keeping the part-time monitors/gatekeepers sufficiently motivated to perform this role well when the bulk of their time is committed to regular work assignments is an ongoing challenge to those responsible for the management of the TI program. Some senior and functional management actions that have proved effective are

- Recognizing the contribution of the monitoring/gatekeeping effort, both publicly and when appraising and rewarding the performance of those involved
- Keeping participants in the network up to date on business unit/organizational goals

- Providing tangible evidence that the monitors/gatekeepers' inputs are being used by management and are influencing decisions
- Allowing gatekeepers to attend external meetings and conferences more often than normal
- Providing opportunities for the gatekeepers to interact with management, various personnel in other functions, vendors, consultants, other visitors, and so forth
- Making access to internal and external databases as "hassle-free" as possible
- Providing at least adequate facilities, equipment and staff support.

A directory giving the names, backgrounds, areas of current interest, and other pertinent information about the gatekeepers can be a useful means of providing recognition and acquainting the entire organization with the gatekeeper network. In large organizations, it is particularly helpful to provide information on whom to contact about an area of technology or a related field.

Staff who are not in the monitoring network should also be encouraged to contribute to the TI program by reporting information obtained at external meetings or conferences or from contacts with vendors or contractors. TI management can facilitate this process by briefing staff on issues of importance and by ensuring that appropriate debriefings are held and/or reports prepared. Some firms require a written report summarizing what was learned in specific areas of interest before the expense account for the trip is approved.

ASSESSMENT FUNCTION

An effective TI system must be able to make more detailed assessments than those normally done by gatekeepers in their monitoring/reporting activities. Such assessments may range from a brief review to answer a simple inquiry to an in-depth assessment to provide crucial information to those making important resource allocation decisions. The timeliness and quality of these assessments are key factors in keeping the support of management for the TI system

Assessments may be carried out by members of the TI core group; but unless the assignment is relatively straightforward and the expertise exists in the group, the most effective approach is to use a multifunctional team. The assessment team should be chaired by someone who has both the technical and managerial skills to lead the effort. One or more members of the TI core group usually serve as facilitators and internal consultants on assessment procedures and tools and may also have specific assignments comparable to others on the team.

Before undertaking a significant assessment, the management of the TI function or group must ensure that the scope, objectives, timing, and resource requirements are clearly understood and recorded. A useful approach is to execute a formal contract or agreement with the client(s) for the assessment. Experience has shown that several weeks may be required to negotiate a sound agreement, but this is usually time well spent. In some situations, however, the timing requirements may preclude having a carefully drawn agreement before the assessment is started. In any case, the management of the TI function and/or the chair of the assessment team must stay in close contact with representatives of the client to ensure that changes, internal or external, which might alter the desired output of the assessment are promptly recognized and acted on.

Another important responsibility of the management of the TI function is to recruit the best-qualified persons for the team handling each significant assessment. Often, the most attractive candidates are already assigned to high-priority projects; such situations require strong skills in negotiating with the candidates' managers to get them to agree to the assessment assignments.

Before any major assessment begins, a plan similar to technical project plans should be developed and circulated to team members and others as needed. During the course of any assignment that lasts several weeks or months, the assessment team should hold regular meetings that result in specific action plans for the future. Periodic progress reports to both the client and others as appropriate should also be prepared. The TI core group representative(s) on the team must exercise a "quality control" role to ensure that team working procedures and meetings are productive and that appropriate reports are issued on a timely basis.

In complex assessments that take significant time to complete, the assessment team leaders and facilitators should meet periodically with the client, or client representatives if the client is a very senior manager. The frequency of these meetings will probably depend on the availability of the client. Experience has shown that going too long between face-to-face meetings with the client may result in project delays or even failures to meet the clients' needs, which may change during the course of the assessment.

The style and quality of reporting the results of the completed assessment are usually crucial to achieving client satisfaction; a poor presentation may undermine a well-executed assessment. The methods of transmitting the results vary widely, but most high-level clients prefer an oral briefing based on slides or charts, supplemented if appropriate with videos, photographs, models, prototypes, or demonstrations. Gib and Walraven (1993) reported that presentations to executives and their direct reports were the most effective means of communicating assessment findings, whereas company newsletters, computer network notes, and official written reports were among the least effective.

Preparation of a high-quality presentation often requires a significant amount of time and effort that should be planned for in establishing the schedule and budget for the assessment. In some situations, a detailed written report is also needed; if so, preparation of such a report must also be in the assessment plan and budget. The time and human resources required to communicate effectively both during and at the end of the assessment are often greatly underestimated.

INFORMATION ACQUISITION, STORAGE AND RETRIEVAL SYSTEMS

TI systems usually process a great deal of information. To do this efficiently and effectively requires a computerized system that permits users to acquire, store, and readily retrieve information from electronic databases and to communicate electronically a wide variety of information from an in-house database. The key elements of this type of system are

- A central library/information center

- An electronic capability for searching internal and external databases
- A TI information storage and retrieval system for exclusive use of designated participants
- An electronic mail system for communicating with internal and external colleagues.

The TI database system should be kept as simple as possible, especially in the early stages of the TI program. Preferably, the database would be limited to internally developed information, with the balance being useful references. The TI system should not try to emulate the library, but instead use the library resources to the fullest extent. Likewise, if a suitable database already exists in the business unit or other organization, it should be tried and modified as needed rather than developing an entirely new system. If the latter is necessary, software that has been proved and "debugged" should be chosen over new programs.

The internally developed information that should go into the database would include the following:

- The most current list of technologies being monitored and their priorities
- The key issues for each technology or related topic and the relevant indicators or measures/metrics that should be watched
- The gatekeepers and supporting gatekeepers assigned to the technologies
- A directory of information on both internal and external gatekeepers
- Reports generated by the gatekeepers and by others (for example, from outside contacts and meetings)
- TI assessment reports, presentations, and backup information.

A suggested high-level architecture for a TI database with the above features is shown in Figure 3. The TI system database should

- Be relatively inexpensive to install and maintain
- Be "user friendly"

- Be capable of handling a wide range of formats, such as documents, photographs, and ultimately, video clips
- Allow users to format and print out selected information or to transfer it electronically
- Provide variable levels of information at the user's option
- Give a record of who used the system at what time and what was added or deleted
- Be capable of ready expansion as the TI system grows.

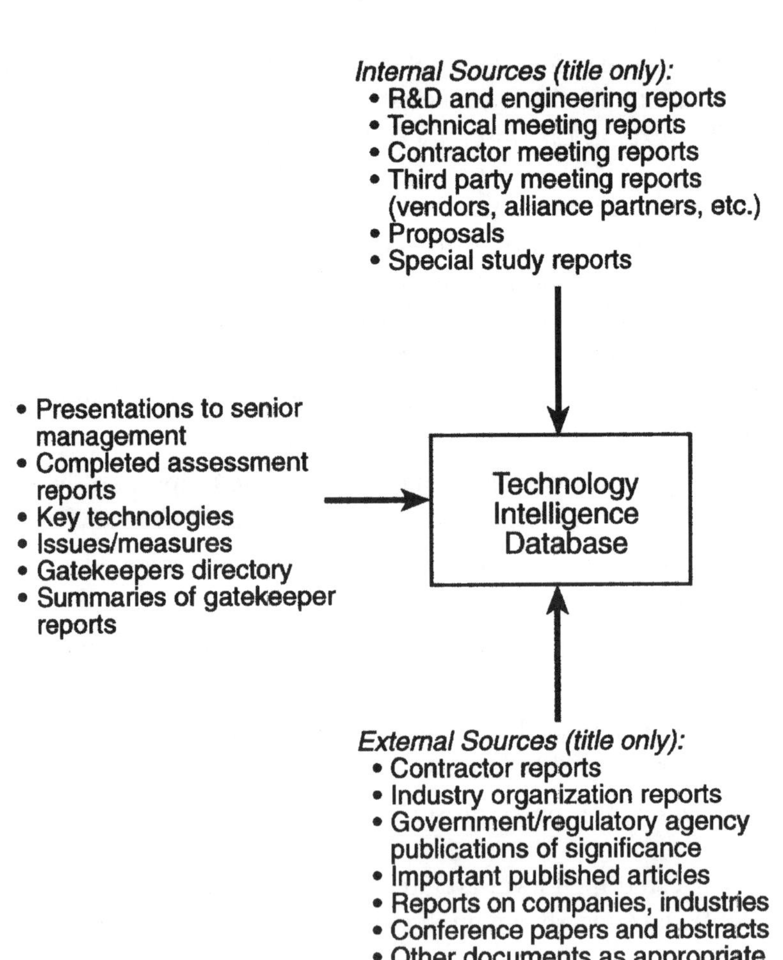

FIGURE 3. High-level architecture for a technology intelligence database

TI database systems should have appropriate security features depending on the size of the system, the number and origin of users, and existing protocols. In general, the system should provide for different levels of security for different types of information; for example, presentations to senior management on sensitive topics might be available only to a small group of users while gatekeeper reports might be broadly available. A well-designed system should allow for changes in passwords and for temporary clearances based on approvals by the TI manager or a designee.

The number and location of interfaces with the database is another key issue. For example, should it be accessible from all desktop or smaller computers or only from designated computers in locations such as the library or the TI office area? These and other issues must be considered over different time frames, such as starting with only a few interfaces and broadening as the TI system grows and, we hope, prospers.

Any TI database system is likely to change over time as the organization's needs change. Further, rapid advances in computer hardware and software may make a given system obsolete in a few years. Thus, TI management should plan for some continuing level of system design and programming support to keep the database viable.

QUALITY ASSURANCE/CLIENT FEEDBACK SYSTEM

The key elements of an effective quality assurance system are

- Multiple sources of information
- Effective monitoring and assessment methodologies and tools
- Client and internal review group critiques
- Total quality management (TQM) approaches.

The use of multiple sources is a basic tenet of intelligence gathering. At least two, and preferably more, sources should be sought to help ensure that a piece of information has credibility. Persons skilled in obtaining information from various external sources can usually find a way to confirm important information. If only one source is available, this limitation should be noted when the information is presented to clients or others.

The employment of effective monitoring and assessment tools by staff with at least some basic training in their use is crucial to the success of a TI system. The management of the TI system must ensure that both the tools and the training are kept up to date. Periodic reviews will be useful in identifying what appears to be working and what is not. Core group staff should keep up with the growing literature on TI and other types of intelligence and, if possible, attend some of the meetings sponsored by organizations such as the Society of Competitive Intelligence Professionals. The use of consultants is another well-known method of obtaining expertise, as well an outside viewpoint on the strengths and weaknesses of the current TI effort.

Critiques by clients are the most important indicators of the effectiveness of the TI program. At the conclusion of all formal assessments or other projects done at the request of a client, feedback on the content and the presentation of the information should be obtained. A useful approach is to get some oral feedback at the time of the presentation, followed by a written critique based on a simple form. Sometimes, it is difficult to get a high-level manager to provide the written critique, but the TI manager must pursue this diligently. Others, such as experienced functional managers, can also provide helpful reviews, especially of "dry runs" of important presentations to senior managers. Periodic workshops for the gatekeepers and assessment team members (if different from the gatekeepers) to discuss problems and successes are also recommended.

Finally, most organizations now have "quality" programs such as TQM. These programs can be very helpful in ensuring that the TI program is delivering value to its customers. TQM approaches are also useful in examining whether the TI activities are being carried out in the most cost-effective manner. The currently popular concepts of "reengineering" organizations can be used in evaluating how a TI system can be improved.

IMPLEMENTATION OF A COMPREHENSIVE TECHNOLOGY INTELLIGENCE SYSTEM

Once the focus, objectives, and design have been approved, a formal TI system can be implemented. Several steps are involved, the first of which is training the active participants. Concurrently, one or more pilot monitoring and assessment projects should be carried out, both to provide hands-on training and to check at least some of the design premises. After the pilots are completed and critiqued, some modifications to the system may be appropriate. The next phase is the ramp-up to full-scale operation and the consideration of possible expansions. In the final part of this section, we summarize the key issues that must be addressed in establishing an effective TI system and the expected benefits of such a system.

TRAINING

Training of the core TI group and the monitors/gatekeepers should begin as soon as the scope and conceptual design of the system are approved. Some of the members of the core group may have enough background in intelligence activities to prepare training materials and to provide the appropriate training. If not, the assistance of consultants will be needed. The initial training can be accomplished either through formal classes or by on-the-job coaching; in most cases, a combination of these approaches is needed.

Experience has shown that a typical large business will see a significant turnover of gatekeepers and core TI personnel because of changes in assignment, transfers, promotions, resignations, etc. Their replacements need training, requiring an ongoing effort. In addition, staff members who are not gatekeepers but are asked to do in-depth assessments because of their technical or other expertise also need training in assessment methodologies and tools.

Because of time pressures on most staff members, formal training sessions should be brief, for example, less than one day, and should be scheduled well in advance. In some instances, enticing the managers of the gatekeepers or other personnel involved to also attend the training meetings has proved to be helpful to the TI effort. The relevance of the training will be enhanced if examples from the industry involved or, preferably, from the company/organization itself are used. Outside speakers who are experts in intelligence or related fields can liven up the training meetings and improve attendance and subsequent performance.

Each person who participates in training sessions, either formal or informal, should be given a copy of a manual containing the material covered, plus other relevant background materials and references. The manual will be easier to keep up to date if a loose-leaf format is used.

PILOT MONITORING AND ASSESSMENT EFFORTS

To help keep the initial TI efforts from encountering problems as a result of taking on too much too fast, a pilot project is strongly recommended. For the monitoring program, a small number of technologies (for example, 10 to 12) of high interest could be tracked for several months while the "bugs" in the system are identified and removed and the monitors are trained. Before this pilot effort is begun, the key issues and their measures or indicators discussed previously should have been defined with the active participation of the monitors/gatekeepers. Doing this well gives each gatekeeper a head start on carrying out the desired focused effort and preparing reports on pertinent findings.

At least one pilot assessment should also be completed, preferably on a medium-priority topic that can be completed in two to three months. In practice, however, an assessment of a "hot" area that management wants studied is usually needed. This demand places a heavy burden on the new assessment team, but ensures that the results of their efforts will be eagerly awaited. Doing an urgent assessment also results in a higher priority for the human resources needed.

One or more members of the TI core group (and of the consulting team, if involved) should have active roles as facilitators and coaches; if some of the core group are inexperienced in formal assessments, they will gain needed training. The process being employed, as well as the results being obtained, should be critiqued frequently to help ensure that the maximum amount of learning is achieved in these pilot assessments.

SYSTEM MODIFICATIONS BASED ON PILOTS AND FURTHER MANAGEMENT INPUT

After several months of pilot monitoring and assessment activities and initial tests of the database, the preliminary design of the system should be formally reviewed and appropriate changes made. Fine tuning of the system should be ongoing, since the organization and its priorities are likely to change over time.

Periodically, for example, annually, a review should be held with the management function(s) funding the TI effort and with other sponsors or champions. Such reviews can provide useful feedback, as well as an opportunity to discuss longer range goals and the possibility of making the TI effort more valuable and visible to senior management. Staff activities such as intelligence gathering and dissemination can be particularly vulnerable to budget cutbacks; hence, there is a continuing need not only to increase the contributions of the activity, but to "sell" these contributions.

RAMP-UP TO FULL OPERATIONS AND POSSIBLE EXPANSION OPPORTUNITIES

After the pilot operations described above are completed, the system can be expanded to accomplish its major objectives. This expansion would obviously be constrained by budget and human resource limitations, but achieving one or preferably two or more successes in the first year of operations makes it much easier to get the needed resources.

Staffing of the core TI group to obtain the appropriate balance of skills is a significant challenge for the management of the group. One approach is to select staff who are specialists in specific areas of interest, such as assessment and forecasting techniques, information acquisition, database operations, and so forth. Another approach is to bring in relatively young, high-potential employees who can rapidly learn enough of the specific skills to function effectively and then replace them with other "fast trackers" every 18 to 24 months. This latter type of staff member can help the TI effort longer term in subsequent assignments because of their backgrounds and presumably their awareness of the contributions that the TI group can make. In practice, a combination of specialists and high-potential "generalists" who may have pertinent technological skills appears to offer the optimum mix of core group personnel.

Expansion of the TI function can take several paths. One is to broaden its scope into business or commercial intelligence if there is not already an adequate effort in this area. Another possible expansion route is to become more involved in technology and business planning activities by providing needed skills and taking on specific assignments. The latter could include detailed analyses of industries or major players in selected industries, assessments of expansion opportunities in foreign countries, heavy involvement in trade association activities, and participation in planning task groups.

SUMMARY OF KEY ISSUES IN ESTABLISHING AN EFFECTIVE TECHNOLOGY INTELLIGENCE FUNCTION

A number of key issues or tasks in building a TI function have been mentioned previously. These and other important concerns are summarized below:

- Secure and maintain strong support from senior management (particularly, have at least one very high-level "godfather").
- Have the core TI group report at a sufficiently high level to obtain appropriate attention.
- Define the scope and size of the TI effort and obtain adequate and predictable funding.
- Establish an organizational structure that can deal with the growth of the system over time.
- Get a clear definition of clients' needs and set priorities.
- Secure the optimum mix of skills and experience in the core group.
- Get capable people in other organizations to serve as monitors/gatekeepers and/or members of assessment teams.
- Keep all participants trained in spite of the significant turnover of staff most large organizations experience.
- Maintain a balance between "fire fighting" and longer term projects.

Other important issues are related to communicating with different constituents, obtaining adequate support from the library and computer operations functions, working with other intelligence groups, and staying abreast of changing industry and company priorities.

EXPECTED BENEFITS FROM TECHNOLOGY INTELLIGENCE PROGRAMS

Listed below are several major benefits expected from well-managed TI programs. Some of these benefits are content-type results, while others may be defined as process-type payoffs.

- Technology "alerts" and periodic status reports on selected sciences and technologies, applications, developers and users.
- More rapid identification of opportunities and threats, for example:
  - "best" sources of different technologies
  - potential alliance partners
  - possible commercialization approaches for our company and for competitors
- Assessments of key issues raised by senior management, covering areas such as the following:
  - forecasts of technology developments including cost and performance trends and growth of applications
  - assessments of the strengths and weaknesses of competitors, vendors/suppliers, and potential strategic partners
  - benchmarking studies on selected topics
  - definition and assessment of the business and technological strategies of competitors or other organizations of interest
- Intangible benefits, such as increased understanding of technology issues by senior management, more effective technology and business planning, improved interfunctional communications and teamwork, and reduced need for externally done assessments.

The "bottom line" is the influence that the TI effort has on resource allocation decisions. If there is little impact, the TI program is not likely to survive.

DEVELOPMENT AND APPLICATION OF OPERATING TECHNOLOGY INTELLIGENCE SYSTEMS

Case studies on TI systems provide valuable insights into successful systems operated by industrial and government organization.

The following discussion highlights several published studies. In addition, it includes two unpublished case studies covering the design, startup, and operation of TI systems in which the authors were involved as consultants. Based on the learnings from these various experiences, a summary of key success factors for effective TI systems is presented.

PUBLISHED CASE STUDIES

Studies on the characteristics and practices of successful research and development (R&D) organizations have shown that most of them have active TI functions. Krause and Liu (1993) reported that 15 well-known R&D organizations were benchmarked to define their "best practices." Included in the 13 best practices selected was having formal programs to monitor and assess external technological developments. The best companies also had effective approaches for communicating the findings from the TI activities.

Similarly, Perrino and Tipping (1989) noted that among the "best practices" needed to manage technology on a global scale were 1) "a proactive program to track 'pockets of expertise' and identify leading-edge technologies is a high priority," and 2) "an early warning system for identifying evolving technology, followed quickly by an informed decision on the merits of acquiring it."

Ashton et al. (1991) described an approach developed by Pacific Northwest National Laboratory and the U. S. Department of Energy for monitoring and analyzing advances in science and technology and the activities of specific organizations involved. Ashton et al. also provide a case study of a monitoring program of the U. S. Department of Energy. This monitoring program affected decisions by the DOE Office of Conservation relative to R&D project selection and task content. In some cases, the program has played a key role in major shifts in R&D program direction; for example, the problem of chlorofluorocarbons emissions was given increased attention. The monitoring program has also improved DOE's interface with U. S. industry by providing increased understanding of industry's technical needs related to energy.

Gilmont (1991) reported the results of a survey of several U. S. and European companies that have active TI efforts. Some of the "best in class" practices and results were the following:

- A major international chemical company, European headquarters—In this large company, TI occurs at all levels including continuous monitoring of external events in technology. Many business units have proprietary TI practices. TI information on markets, production, and R&D is a major input to strategic planning, whose methodologies engender an awareness of the importance of TI.
- A major manufacturing company, U. S. headquarters—This company has a unique TI process based on a corporate policy of continuous improvement. It gets inputs through numerous sources, including direct contacts with competitors. TI helps the company decide whether to be a technology leader or a middle-of-pack player or a follower. The sharing of TI information in various forums and media has greatly improved technology communications within the company.
- Japanese pharmaceutical company—This company has an intense TI effort in the R&D planning organization. Information is obtained from a wide variety of international sources, including satellite offices worldwide, through a primary technology transfer function. TI is an important element in all R&D decisions. The company stated that "in our business, TI is indispensable."
- Multinational consumer products company—TI is collected and analyzed globally. The intelligence generated is a key input to business planning and drives R&D and strategic planning decisions.
- Pharmaceutical division of a multinational corporation—Each business unit in this organization has an active TI program that is responsible for the planning function. In numerous cases TI has led to directional changes in R&D programs. A quote was, "You can never have enough TI."

UNPUBLISHED CASE STUDIES

Two case studies, drawn from our consulting work with a telecommunications company and an energy company, provide some insight into the successful design and implementation of TI systems.

Telecommunications Company

The corporate technology function of a major telecommunications company installed a TI system in 1991-92. The impetus for undertaking this project was senior management's concern that the company might not be adequately informed in a timely manner about the potential impacts, both threats and opportunities, of rapidly changing technologies affecting the telecommunications field. An executive vice president with corporate responsibility for technology and strategic planning assumed the role of sponsor or "godfather" of the TI program. He and other senior managers expressed the desire that TI become a corporate "core competence."

Within the corporation, responsibility for the TI project was assigned to a staff group in the technology function that managed external research funded by the corporation (such as university grants and cooperative programs and work done at a telecommunications technology organization sponsored by several companies in the industry). Our consulting group was retained to help design and implement the envisioned TI system.

The initial focus was to define the mission, scope and objectives of the planned TI system. To help ensure that the system would meet the needs of the corporation, over 30 senior-level business and technology managers across the corporation were interviewed. Each interview lasted approximately one hour and was conducted by a team of two interviewers, who used a carefully constructed interview guide. An observer provided an overview of the goals of the interview and a subsequent critique. A summary of each interview was prepared and the responses to key questions collated and analyzed.

Concurrent with the interviews, a potential TI system design and implementation plan was developed by a core group using the "storyboard" approach. This technique proved to be effective in obtaining a wide range of inputs and classifying and prioritizing them. Each element of the system was designed with a focus on providing outputs that would meet the needs of its clients or customers.

At the conclusion of the interviews, the objectives and design were completed. At that time, a decision was made to give priority to assessing potentially important technologies and their applications, with less emphasis on developing a monitoring system involving a significant number of gatekeepers. The first three assessments to be done by multifunctional teams were considered to be prototypes or pilots. Considerable attention was given to critiquing and polishing the assessment processes the teams employed, while making sure that the processes would provide content that would meet clients' needs.

Some early problems in dealing with changes in clients' interests and priorities over the course of several months of assessments led to the development of a formal client agreement that defined the scope, objectives, deliverables, timing, resources needed, and other key information. This agreement was reviewed in briefings of the client(s) during the assessment period and modified as needed.

An approach for obtaining oral and written feedback from the client at the conclusion of each assessment was developed and used routinely. This feedback was used to help improve the performance of future assessment teams. Total quality management principles were routinely applied throughout the development and implementation of the TI system.

Considerable effort was spent on formal and on-the-job training of the core TI group staff, key gatekeepers, and members of the assessment teams. The consultants prepared manuals covering the assessment and monitoring processes and provided them to all training participants. Because of normal changes in job assignments and locations, training sessions were offered periodically to cover new participants in the TI process and to reinforce the skills of "veterans."

Another major thrust in implementing the TI system was the development of an information storage and acquisition system. The design premises for the system were defined jointly with specialists in database systems; software was subsequently developed and implemented. The guiding principle in this effort was to keep the system as simple as possible without sacrificing adequate capability and flexibility for future growth.

After the initial prototype or pilot assessments were completed, new technological and commercial developments in telecommunications and related fields prompted senior management to request a number of assessments. The core TI group was expanded to include some full-time monitors for very "hot" areas, a person to manage the monitoring effort and its supporting gatekeeper network, and a competitive intelligence information specialist. Subsequently, the TI group became more involved in joint efforts with strategic planning functions, and a staff member to help handle this responsibility was added.

The TI system has made a significant impact on corporate strategy and resource allocation in the company. For example, the decision to make a major investment in a large cable television company with the intent of subsequently offering interactive multimedia services grew out of early TI monitoring and assessment studies. The goal of making TI a corporate core competence appears to be on track.

Energy Company

Faced with the threat of new competitors, increasingly stringent environmental regulations, and rapidly changing technologies, a large energy production and distribution company, decided in 1992 to install a formal TI system. The company wanted this system in order to track new developments in relevant technologies and their applications and to assess those technologies to the depth required to support resource allocation and other business and technology management decisions.

An experienced project manager from the R&D function was appointed to manage the effort, and our consulting group was retained to assist in designing and implementing the TI system. A committee consisting of department managers from the R&D, engineering, marketing, and planning functions was designated to oversee the project and to provide progress reports to the corporate technology committee, the top-level group charged with technology policy, direction, and resource allocations.

The first step was to interview senior and other managers who were expected to be the primary clients of the system to define their interests and priorities. The latter included several vice presidents who were members of the corporate technology committee, functional department managers and their direct reports, and some technical specialists. These interviews provided crucial information needed to define the scope and objectives of the planned system, the technologies and related areas of interest, and the names of persons believed to qualified to be effective gatekeepers/monitors.

The technologies suggested in the interviews as being worthy of monitoring were collated and further reviewed with various managers and specialists to help ensure that all relevant areas were being considered. The relative current and potential future impact of these technologies was evaluated using a set of criteria, and each technology was assigned to one of three levels of priority for monitoring and reporting efforts.

Concurrently, the qualifications of staff recommended as gatekeepers were reviewed with appropriate managers, and those with the optimum combinations of skills and job assignments were selected to be primary or lead gatekeepers. Others were designated to be supporting gatekeepers who would cover a more restricted area and have fewer responsibilities.

The next phase of the project was focused on training the gatekeepers and other personnel in monitoring and assessment methodologies and tools. This training consisted of one-day workshops, informal coaching, and the execution of an assessment of a developing technology of strong interest to the company. Results from this assessment were subsequently used in the workshops to provide additional concrete examples. A comprehensive training manual and supplementary materials were provided to all gatekeepers and relevant managerial personnel.

To help achieve a highly focused and effective monitoring effort, a list of key issues and measures or metrics to describe the status of these issues was defined for each high-priority technology. The list was developed by having the lead and supporting gatekeepers for these technologies do a "mini-assessment" of their areas with the assistance of the project manager and the consultants. These issues and measures allow the focused tracking of new developments that could lead to the achievement of important milestones or threshold advances (such as cost and/or performance targets, acceptance by standards or regulatory groups, etc.). Definition of the key issues and measures for the important technologies has proved to be an effective approach for communicating to managerial and technical specialist personnel what is happening in these technologies and related areas. For example, in their periodic reports on technologies, the gatekeepers have used the issues/measures approach to present changes of interest in a concise manner.

The successful start-up of the TI system has increased the interest of senior management in having a more effective business/commercial intelligence effort to complement the technology intelligence thrust. The executive who chairs the corporate technology committee has become an active supporter for and sponsor of both types of intelligence, which in practice have considerable overlap. Important resource allocation decisions are now being influenced by the intelligence generated by the monitoring and assessment activities.

KEY SUCCESS FACTORS FOR EFFECTIVE TECHNOLOGY INTELLIGENCE SYSTEMS

Following are a number of common elements or practices in TI systems considered to be effective by their users or clients:

- Early development of a realistic TI system implementation plan that includes achievable goals, clear assignments, and appropriate quality control measures
- Use of an iterative process to ensure that monitoring and assessment goals are linked to client needs, with the focus on influencing resource allocation decisions
- Ongoing evaluation of information sources, monitoring and assessment methodologies, and operating practices
- Regular interactions between monitors/gatekeepers, assessment team members, and clients or other interested parties
- Effective integration of different skills, viewpoints, and information sources to give a total story that includes the implications of the intelligence and its ambiguities and limitations
- Effective mechanisms for communicating with different audiences or stakeholders
- A quality assurance program based on client/user feedback
- At least one very senior sponsor
- An early success (or two) to build credibility.

The managers of intelligence systems can never "rest on their laurels"; they must continually demonstrate the value of what they do to senior management. It is important to serve the technical community as fully as possible; but the ultimate customer is senior management—a relationship that places a premium on good communications and close cross-functional teamwork to provide the total story noted above.

REFERENCES

Allen, T. J. 1984. *Managing the Flow of Technology*. MIT Press, Cambridge, Massachusetts.

Ashton, W. B., B. R. Kinzey, and M. C. Gunn Jr. 1991. A Structured Approach for Monitoring Science and Technology Developments. *International Journal of Technology Management* 6(1/2):91-111.

Gib, A., and E. Walraven. 1993. Teaming Data Management and CI Professionals: An Approach that Provides a Competitive Advantage. *Proceedings of the Eighth Annual Conference, Society of Competitive Intelligence Professionals*, pp 111-157. Society of Competitive Intelligence Professionals, Alexandria, Virginia 22314.

Gilmont, E. 1991. Technology Intelligence: A Powerful Tool for Decisions and Actions Involving Technology. *Proceedings of the Fall Meeting, Society of Competitive Intelligence Professionals, New York*. Society of Competitive Intelligence Professionals, Alexandria, Virginia 22314.

Krause, I., and J. Liu. Jan.-Feb. 1993. Benchmarking R&D Productivity. *Planning Review*, pp. 16-21, 52-53.

Nochur, K. S., and T. J. Allen. 1992. Do Nominated Boundary Spanners Become Effective Technological Gatekeepers? *IEEE Transactions on Engineering Management* 39(3):265-269.

Perrino, A. C., and J. W. Tipping. May-June 1989. Global Management of Technology. *Research-Technology Management* 32(3):12-20.

Organizing a Competitive Technical Intelligence Group

PATRICK J. BRYANT,
JAMES C. COLEMAN, and THOMAS F. KROL

The discipline of competitive technical intelligence (CTI) is relatively new. More and more, technology has become an inescapable element of the competition (Link and Tassey 1987). Groups dedicated to supplying this type of intelligence have been evolving over the last few years (Prescott and Gibbons 1993).

This development is, in part, due to the increasing difficulty associated with gaining valuable information on the technology efforts of others. The result has been a more focused approach to formal techniques for gathering and analyzing technology (Paap 1994).

Those CTI units in existence have evolved by expanding their services to a point that a dedicated unit could be justified. Successful units have been able to garner management support, obtain sufficient resources, maintain flexible analyzing processes, control data overload, and integrate CTI into ongoing operations within the organization (Ashton et al. 1994).

The first part of this chapter describes the evolution of the CTI unit at Marion Merrell Dow Inc. The remainder of the chapter describes the "how to's" associated with organizing a CTI group. Much of the insight shared in the how-to part of this chapter was obtained from the experience of organizing the CTI unit at Marion Merrell Dow Inc.

EVOLUTION OF A COMPETITIVE TECHNICAL INTELLIGENCE UNIT

The CTI unit at Marion Merrell Dow Inc. evolved from an informal process used to identify/evaluate potential in-licensing candidate products. This informal process was initiated approximately 10 years ago within Marion Laboratories Inc., about 5 years before the merger with Merrell Dow Inc.

Marion Laboratories was well known for its ability to stock the pipeline with in-licensed products, as opposed to discovering compounds through internal research. For this reason, sophisticated processes for identifying and evaluating the potential of in-licensing candidates evolved within the organization.

One such process was to identify candidate products by analyzing all compounds within a specific pharmacological class. For example, diltiazem was considered a very attractive calcium channel blocker for in-licensing because of its multiple positive effects on the cardiovascular system with minimum incidence of side effects compared with other calcium channel blockers.

A customized database was designed and implemented to track emerging products within several pharmacological classes that were under development for various disease states of special interest to the corporation. This database also provided a means to compare the potential in-licensing candidate with other compounds in its class. A thorough comparison of the positive and negative attributes of the candidate with those of other similar products assisted in the overall technical recommendation to license or not to license the products.

Following the merger between Marion Laboratories Inc. and Merrell Dow Inc., which resulted in the formation of Marion Merrell Dow Inc., less emphasis was placed on the in-licensing process as the only source of new compounds. This decision was primarily due to the large discovery research effort brought to the new company. At the time of the merger, the database contained well over 12,000 compounds, with a considerable amount of information on each. It was determined that a concerted effort should be made to convert this information into competitive intelligence with a technical emphasis.

The emphasis on CTI was in contrast to the more traditional business intelligence units being formed in the pharmaceutical industry at that time. A tremendous amount of literature was available on techniques other industries used to gather business competitive intelligence. Key concepts were extrapolated from this literature base and implemented as the foundation for the new CTI process.

One key concept provided a working model that, when modified, helps to illustrate where CTI comes from and how it can be differentiated from business competitive intelligence (Fuld 1992). This concept is illustrated in Figure 1. The working model shows that data are organized into information which can then be analyzed to create intelligence. The working definition of intelligence is information which has been analyzed to the extent that decisions can be made.

Two major points illustrate the differences between scientific or CTI and business competitive intelligence (Bryant et al. 1994). The first difference is that the data being organized are from technical rather than business sources. Once this technical information is analyzed, it becomes CTI. The second difference involves the educational background and experience of the CTI analyst who initially organizes the data into information and then analyzes the information to a point where a decision can be made. With CTI, the most qualified person has a strong technical background and some additional experience in research and development.

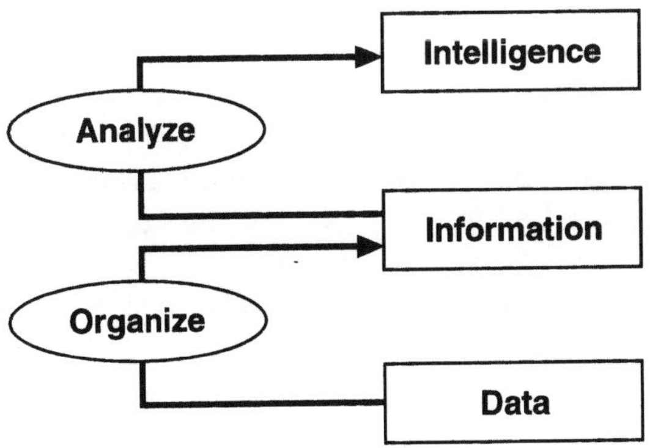

FIGURE 1. Competitive intelligence model (Bryant et al. 1994)

The model which explains the differences between CTI and business competitive intelligence can be used in initial awareness presentations to help all facets of the organization. This model can also be used to explain the differences between existing competitive intelligence efforts of a business nature and the proposed new function which adds a new service not being performed by any other group. The remainder of this chapter describes the processes which can be used to expand a competitive technology intelligence group into a full-service CTI unit.

CLARIFYING USER NEEDS

The first step in clarifying user needs is to define the client(s) (Ashton et al. 1994). This step requires a thorough understanding of the company's business. From this understanding comes the identification of key decision-makers within the organization. Those key decision-makers are the primary clients.

In addition, one or more of these clients could become champion(s) for the CTI process. A champion is key to the overall success of the CTI unit (Fuld 1988). The champion provides support for the unit when questions about its value to the corporation arise. It is important that the champion have influence with upper management because that group determines whether the services provided by the CTI unit should be continued.

The intent of the CTI unit is to have a significant impact on the success of the company (Matteo and Dykman 1994). Interacting with and providing CTI to key decision-makers will ensure high impact because they are the ones who can take action (Barber 1991).

Key decision-makers can be individuals, committees, or departments/divisions. These key individuals should depend on CTI to assist them in making decisions. In addition, CTI analysts should serve on and provide CTI to various committees to ensure that the most informed decisions are being made.

Once the clients have been identified, the next step is to conduct one-on-one or small group interviews to better understand their needs for CTI. Initial awareness presentations which define CTI and its potential role in the decision-making processes may be necessary to engage the client in discussion. This open discussion provides the greatest understanding of each client's particular expected uses and, therefore, needs for CTI on both an ad hoc and a proactive basis. The CTI unit should strive to anticipate the client's needs and provide CTI in a proactive manner.

The concept of CTI may be new to a client, and examples of how this type of intelligence might assist the client in making decisions are essential. The CTI unit should determine what those decisions are during the discussion and incorporate CTI into the conversation to illustrate the elevated, informed decision-making process.

A start-up CTI unit should never leave one of these awareness interviews without obtaining a request from the client. Such a request will provide a real-life example and an opportunity to follow up with the client for more assignments at a future date. Salesmanship is key to the future success of the unit, especially in its initial stages.

After identifying and working with a nucleus of clients, a decision should be made to expand to a broader client base. The time and resources available to the CTI unit will drive this decision. Getting the required resources is often easier after the value of the service has been established for this expanded group of clients.

The process of identifying new clients may be assisted by use of a formal survey of employees throughout the organization. Questions used in such a survey might include the following:

- What specific functions are carried out by this position that would require competitive information/intelligence?
- What percentage of your time do you spend performing the above functions?
- What impact do these functions have on the success of the corporation?
- In what ways would competitive information/intelligence improve/maximize the quality of the work product?
- What would be the maximum increase (percentage) in quality of the work product if competitive information/intelligence was provided?
- If competitive information/intelligence is not provided, what impact will this have on the success of the corporation?

Categorizing potential clients based on the questionnaire results provides a step-by-step strategy for the future roll-out of services. Clients can be categorized into various tiers as follows:

- Tier 1—clients who can use CTI currently being gathered and analyzed for existing core clients.
- Tier 2—clients who require different CTI than that currently being gathered and analyzed.
- Tier 3—clients who require additional CTI that is more highly labor-intensive than that currently being gathered and analyzed. For example, new clients who request large, time-consuming CTI projects such as management profiling for the top ten pharmaceutical companies in the United States.
- Tier 4—clients who have little direct impact on the success of the corporation. For example, new clients asking for CTI that will help them personally, but will have little, if any, impact on the success of the corporation.

Figure 2 illustrates the categorization/prioritization of potential clients. Tier 1 clients can generally be immediately incorporated into the current client group. Available time and resources will drive the decision of how and when to incorporate Tier 2 and Tier 3 clients into the client group. Tier 4 clients will probably never be seriously considered.

Once a thorough needs analysis is completed, constructing a mission statement for the CTI unit is necessary. The purpose of

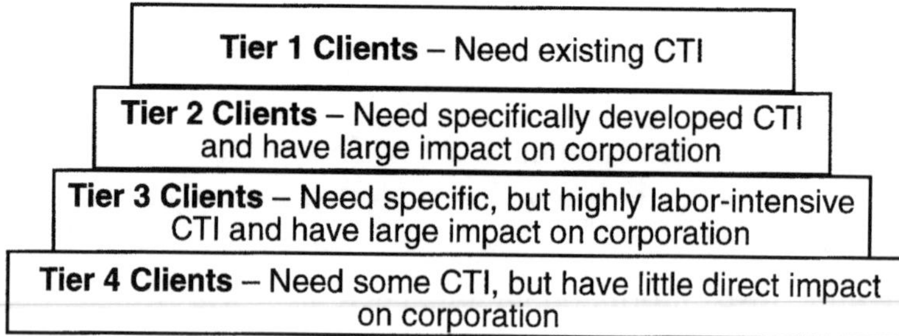

FIGURE 2. Categorizing and prioritizing potential clients

the mission statement is to focus the members of the unit and provide clear direction as to what is important for the corporation. In addition, a well-written mission statement serves as a quick description to others as to why the CTI unit exists. It should be a clear, action-oriented statement similar to the one that follows:

> *The Mission is to provide to a focused group of clients accurate, comprehensive and timely CTI which will have a direct effect on the success of the corporation.*

This example can be distilled down to the simple understanding that the group will provide an accurate, comprehensive, and timely product (CTI) to make the company successful. The value of the product is reduced if any one of the three characteristics (accuracy, comprehensiveness, or timeliness) is missing.

This mission statement is powerful because the three key characteristics are clear and easily remembered and can be reviewed quickly to ensure that they are in the product. In addition, anyone reading this mission statement understands that this unit exists in order to have a positive impact on the success of the company.

Clients and their needs change over time. A continual examination of clients' needs is required to ensure the long-term success of the CTI unit. It is a dynamic process. This evaluation can be accomplished by ongoing monitoring activities, periodic one-on-one formal follow-up interviews, or formal follow-up questionnaires. The culture of the particular organization will determine the most appropriate method.

IDENTIFYING DATA SOURCES

The CTI analyst can draw from essentially two general types of data sources: published and unpublished. Both sources contain valuable data that, when organized into technical competitive information, will supply the CTI analyst with a good foundation for beginning the analysis process (Keiser 1994). Choosing source materials depends on several factors, including the technical area involved, client needs, available funding, and CTI resources (Ashton et al. 1994).

PUBLISHED SOURCES

Published sources provide data that have been printed and that are available in the public domain. These data tend to be relatively easy to acquire. In fact, the CTI analyst is constantly at risk of data overload. Scientific knowledge is currently doubling every thirteen to fifteen years (Roukis 1990). There may be more readily available data on a subject in the public domain than the CTI analyst can deal with in a realistic manner and time frame (Krol et al. 1994; Paap 1994).

Typical published sources include the following

- Commercially available databases
- Patent literature
- Trade and industry journals
- News wires
- Technical literature
- Abstracts from technical meetings
- Funded research grants
- Annual reports
- 10-K SEC annual reports
- Quarterly reports
- Multi-client technical trend studies
- Newspapers (especially local)
- Analysts' reports
- Press releases from companies in your industry
- Directories
- Classified ads in trade/technical publications (hiring practices).

It is critical that the CTI analyst continually evaluate the usefulness of published sources. Several questions should be perpetually asked. Are those sources proving to be useful for meeting client needs? Which sources are the best for a given request? How can the most accurate answer or the truth be found in the most expedient manner? How is conflicting information resolved? How is the validity of existing information confirmed? How much does it cost?

As previously stated, client needs may change over time. The CTI analyst must continuously monitor these changes and respond appropriately, which often requires the addition of new published sources. This monitoring activity requires continuous interaction with the clients.

During that interaction, the CTI analyst should also determine if the client's future responsibilities are changing or expanding. This information allows the CTI analyst to proactively seek potential new published sources and become familiar with the strengths and weaknesses of each source.

Identifying and obtaining the published source can take time. Therefore, predicting the need for these sources early can ensure that they will be available when the CTI analyst needs them.

New sources of published data can be identified in several ways. One way is to publicize the existence of the CTI unit by joining a professional organization such as the Society of Competitive Intelligence Professionals. Membership is an easy way to get on mailing lists for several of these sources.[1]

Depending on the size of the company, the corporate library may provide a large amount of published information. Library searchers are often the first to receive notices of new commercially available databases. In addition, the publishers regularly provide corporate libraries with advertisements of new publications.

It is good practice to keep key members of the library aware of specific needs for published sources. A good rapport with this key group can save tremendous time and effort in identifying potential new sources of published data (Chitwood 1993).

Many other sources of published competitive information exist throughout a corporation. Examples of these sources include special reports purchased by corporate departments such as marketing, research and development, government relations/regulatory, legal, human resources, operations, public relations, or purchasing. Often these groups purchase reports for their department only. A comprehensive competitive information audit of the corporation is key to uncovering these reports (Fuld 1988).

When several published sources have been identified, it is critical to evaluate the value of those sources over time. The analyst must know the key characteristics and value of each source for a given competitive intelligence request (Krol et al. 1994). This knowledge allows the CTI analyst to derive a more accurate, complete, and timely depiction of the truth. In addition, it eliminates or helps resolve conflicting information. This evaluation is a two-step process.

1. The *source identification phase* involves locating the originating source of the information. Once identified, all details available from the originating source should be requested. These details could include dates, people contacted, places, and surrounding circumstances. In many cases, one telephone call to the originator is all that is required to clarify, validate, or invalidate a source. These additional details are important for analytical purposes. In addition, they become invaluable in performing the next step.
2. The *validation phase* can become quite complex when the number of sources and the amount of potentially conflicting information increase. Decision matrixes and/or timelines have been used in these cases to bring clarity. Weighting sources based on accuracy, validity, and historical reliability is the key. The CTI analyst must document this process. Assigning the appropriate weight to each source is dependent on the CTI analyst's experience with each source; however, over time, experience is gained, and this information becomes invaluable to the CTI unit.

UNPUBLISHED SOURCES

Unpublished sources provide data not always available in the published domain. Acquiring data from unpublished sources tends to be more difficult and time-consuming than from published sources. These sources can be difficult to identify; however, once identified, they may become the most valuable data-gathering tool. For example, in addition to routine interviews with previous employers, customers, and competitors, the Japanese acquire useful unpublished data by socializing (Moffat 1991).

Unpublished sources primarily include internal technical experts and external consultants and their networks. The internal technical experts can usually be identified through informal networking processes. More formal processes such as questionnaires and the development of a directory by area of expertise can also prove effective.

These internal technical experts often attend external technical conventions. They can keep the CTI analysts abreast of any new research results discussed at the meetings. In addition, each internal technical expert has a network of external contacts who may possess critical unpublished information concerning the competition.

External consultants are either experts in the particular technical area of interest or professional competitive intelligence practitioners. Generally, the process to identify technical consultants focuses on academic centers or government agencies such as the National Institutes of Health. These experts usually publish prolifically in journals associated with the technical area of interest and are well respected in their area of expertise.

Various approaches should be used to establish a base of external experts in the area of interest. Literature searches focused on the technical area may be helpful in identifying potential technical consultants. Editorial boards of technical journals can also be a means to identify the experts in a particular area. Research grant listings from various government agencies can also provide names of possible candidates who have been awarded research dollars based on the credibility of the research and reputation of the expert. Networking with researchers in the area can help identify the various theories being explored and the leaders of each of those "schools of thought."

External consultants or information brokers who specialize in the competitive intelligence area serve as a tremendous source of unpublished data (Lesky 1994). One primary benefit of adding competitive intelligence consultants to a CTI unit's armamentarium is an extended network.

Not all competitive intelligence consultants are appropriate for CTI projects. Krol et al. (1993) propose a method which involves the use of a survey questionnaire to help identify the most useful consultants for CTI. The following are the main points identified in the questionnaire:

- Does the consultant prepare "ad hoc" (as needed) reports (oral and/or written)?
- Does the consultant have written ethical guidelines?
- What is the expertise of the consultant's staff (that is, technical)?

- What differentiates this consultant from everyone else?
- Does the consultant have a global presence?
- What is the consultant's fee structure?
- Does the consultant have a list of clients who can be contacted?

The questions are derived from careful analysis of the type of consulting needed. For instance, if the technology involves pharmaceuticals, the consultant should have a scientific background in that area with some experience working with the pharmaceutical industry.

Ethical issues such as whether or not the consultant observes ethical guidelines should be considered. Not all consultants are willing to provide brief, ad hoc consulting services. Some consulting groups will only accept large, long-term projects.

The results of a questionnaire can be organized for easy evaluation (see Table 1). Organizing the results this way allows the CTI analyst to compare the various consulting groups to the required consultant characteristics.

Secondary characteristics can assist in prioritizing those consultants that have the required characteristics. Examples of secondary characteristics include average turnaround time; unique sources used; and key differentiating characteristics such as experience level, global presence, and fee structure. This table can be continuously updated for quick reference to consultants based on the type of competitive intelligence request received.

Finally, a CTI analyst should not limit sources of unpublished data to internal experts and external consultants only. Any personal contact can be considered a source for unpublished competitive data. The telephone is a valuable tool, and learning appropriate interview techniques is critical. For more on these techniques, the reader is referred to the interview techniques section of Fuld (1985), McGonagle and Vella (1990a), and Kight (1995).

CONVERTING DATA TO COMPETITIVE INFORMATION

As mentioned earlier, data are the raw material from which competitive information is derived. The process of organizing the

TABLE 1
Results of consultant survey (Krol et al. 1993)

Consultant	Ad Hoc Reports	Ethics	Pharm. Expert.	Science Expert.	Differentiating Characteristics	Comments	Recommend
Consultant A (name, phone)	Minimal	Yes. Institute of Management Consultants guidelines	Some	Minimal	None given	Good presence in US/Europe, weak in Japan; primary orientation to large projects >$5000	No
Consultant B (name, phone)	Yes $150/hr	Yes. Willing to send written guidelines	Yes	Some	Rapid response	Global presence	Yes
Consultant C (name, phone)	Yes Limited	Yes. Willing to send written guidelines	Some	Minimal	Experience	Prefers larger projects as opposed to ad hocs; 18 yrs experience with pharmaceutical industry but primarily market/business; other clients claim high priced; limited to US/Japan.	Maybe

continued

TABLE 1 (continued)
Results of consultant survey (Krol et al. 1993)

Consultant	Ad Hoc Reports	Ethics	Pharm. Expert.	Science Expert.	Differentiating Characteristics	Comments	Recommend
Consultant D (name, phone)	Yes $175/hr	Yes. Willing to send written guidelines	Yes	Yes	Technology focus	High presence in Japan and Europe; large company with more than 60 associates worldwide	Yes
Consultant E (name, phone)	Yes Negotiable	Yes. Unwritten	Yes	Minimal	Willing to try anything	Small company; appears easy to work with	Maybe
Consultant F (name, phone)	Yes $115/hr	Yes. Institute of Management Consultants guidelines	Yes	None	Experience	Good connections with US government	Yes
Consultant G (name, phone)	Yes	Yes. Unwritten	Some	None	None given	Primary focus is market analysis	Yes
Consultant H (name, phone)	Yes Negotiable	Yes. Unwritten	Yes	Some	Quick turnaround	Covers US and Europe, very weak in Japan	Yes

data into competitive information can occur several ways and primarily depends on the outcome desired.

For example, storing the information in a computerized database provides a means to organize the data into competitive information and allows easy access. In the digital domain, competitive information lends itself to quantitative analyses through the use of a wide variety of commercially available mathematical and graphic software programs. Mathematical and graphic illustrations can often provide additional insights into the interpretation of the competitive information; that is, a picture is worth a thousand words.

DATABASE DESIGN

Database design begins with the understanding that a decision has already been made to use this form of storage as opposed to a manual filing system. There are numerous manual filing index systems; however, the intent of this section is to focus on a computerized database approach. The reader is also directed to chapters by Hohhof and by McDonald and Richardson in this book.

Several "off the shelf" database software packages that may serve to store technical data are available in computer stores. Table 2 lists some of these software programs. In most cases, these programs will satisfy the needs of the CTI analyst.

Other services will not only provide software for the database function, but will also automate the process of searching and identifying commercially available data sources. In most cases, these services involve monitoring of commercially available databases, from technical databases to press releases. The user selects key words to be used as search criteria. Any publication containing these key words is pulled into the database and stored in the appropriate section based on a hierarchy determined by the CTI analyst. For example, a publication containing the key search words "Alzheimer's Disease" would be pulled into the database and stored under the section entitled "disease states." A sample listing of these types of services is presented in Table 3.

Special requirements unique to a given industry or technology may require the design of a custom-made database software program. In this case, it is best to solicit the assistance of a professional information systems programmer. A current-state analysis

TABLE 2
Selected examples of database software programs

Product	Developer and Address	Contact
askSAM	askSAM Systems P.O. Box 1428, Perry FL 32347	(800) 800-1997 (904) 584-6590
ISYS	Odyssey Development 650 S. Cerry St. #220, Denver CO 80222	(800) 992-4797 (303) 394-0091 (fax)
GoFer	Microlytics, Inc. Two Tobey Village Office Park Pittsford NY 14534	(716) 248-9150
KnowledgeSet	KnowledgeSet Corp. 555 Ellis St. Mountain View CA 94043	(415) 254-5400 (800) 456-0469 (415) 254-5451 (fax)
Marco Polo	Mainstay 591-A Constitution Ave., Camarillo CA 93012	(805) 484-9400 (805) 484-9428 (fax)
On Location	On Technology Inc. One Cambridge Center Cambridge MA 02142	(800) 767-6683 (617) 374-1400 (617) 374-1433 (fax)
Personal Librarian	Personal Librarian Software 2400 Research Blvd. #350, Rockville MD 20850	(301) 990-1155
Power!Search	Horizons Technology, Inc. 3990 Ruffin Rd., San Diego CA 92123-1826	(619) 292-8320 (619) 565-1175 (fax)
Recollect	MindWorks Corp. 735 N. Pastoria Ave., Sunnyvale CA 94086	(408) 730-2100 (408) 730-2143 (fax)
Retrieve It	Claris Corporation P.O. Box 58168, Santa Clara CA 95052-8168	(800) 3CLARIS
Sonar	Virginia Systems 5509 West Bay Court, Midlothian VA 23112	(804) 739-3200 (804) 739-8376 (fax)
ZyIndex	ZyLab 100 Lexington Dr., Buffalo Grove IL 60089	(708) 459-8000
BIN	Expressway Technologies 100 Fifth Ave., Waltham MA 02154-7527	(617) 890-8670
ConQuest	ConQuest Software Inc. 9700 Patuxent Woods Dr. #140 Columbia MD 21046	(410) 290-7150

Source: Competitive Information System Development Futures Group (1994)

TABLE 3
Selected examples of online consolidator software

Product	Developer and Address	Contact
First!	Individual Inc. 84 Sherman St., Cambridge MA 02140	(800) 766-4224 (617) 864-4066 (fax)
Hoover	Sandpoint Corporation 124 Mount Auburn St. Cambridge MA 02138	(617) 868-4442
Journalist	PED Software 1340 Saratoga-Sunnyvale Rd. #203 San Jose CA 95129	(800) 548-2203
Newscast	Mainstream Data 420 Chipeta Way #200 Salt Lake City UT 84108	(801) 584-2800
NewsEDGE	Desktop Data 1601 Trapelo Rd., Waltham MA 02154	(617) 890-0042 (617) 890-1565 (fax)
Newsline	Market Analysis & Information Database Inc. 352 Park Ave. South New York City NY 10010-1709	(212) 447-6900 (212) 447-0060 (fax)
OmniNews	Comtex Scientific Corp 4900 Seminary Rd. #800 Alexandria VA 22311	(703) 820-2000 (703) 820-2005 (fax)
OneSource	OneSource Information Services Inc. 150 Cambridge Park Dr. Cambridge MA 02140	(800) 554-5501 (617) 441-7058
SmartStream	Dun & Bradstreet Software 550 Cochituate Rd. Framingham MA 01701	(508) 370-5000

Source: Competitive Intelligence System Development Futures Group (1994)

should be performed and all requirements for the new system should be identified (Hohhof 1991). To accomplish this, interviews with the CTI unit's clients may be required to ensure that their needs will be met in the future.

The CTI analyst should remain close to the information systems programmer throughout the development of the software program. Frequent reviews of report formats will ensure that the program will meet the requirements identified.

The CTI analyst can also serve as a test subject to determine how user friendly the system is. The programmer will have many questions during the development process, and the availability of the CTI analyst to answer these questions will ensure that the end software product meets expectations.

There usually are some hurdles to jump over when a new database is brought into full production. Initially, it is best to limit the number of end users in an attempt to minimize the difficulty associated with implementing the new database system. The number of end users can be expanded at a later date.

Initial training of end users is vital. The information systems group can assist in this training process. If this resource is not available, the CTI analyst can accept the role of trainer. Successful methods used in the past to teach new software programs include formal presentations, one-on-one instruction, and self-instruct manuals.

Databases are not static. A key factor to remember is that every database implemented must be maintained over time. Maintenance includes adding additional data continuously, as well as revising programs.

The maintenance function can be a drain on resources. For this reason, it is important to weigh the benefits of such a system and how it contributes to the success of the corporation against the requirements for manpower to maintain the system.

Some commercially available systems have automated maintenance functions. For example, the Sandpoint system (see Table 3) provides a real-time search capability which scans commercially available databases and news wires. Key-word search terms are used to scan, and full text documents are extracted and placed into the database for subsequent searching.

DATABASE ELEMENTS

Database elements are those pieces of information which are considered key to monitor and retrieve rapidly; for example, the following:

- Product/research
- Indications for use
- Pharmacological class
- Developer(s)
- Status of development
- Description.

With the exception of full text databases that can be searched by key words, all other databases must have elements defined up-front. These definitions allow the programmer to design a system which rapidly retrieves the key information.

CONTINUOUS MONITORING

Continuous monitoring is the process of maintaining a constant vigil on primary competitor products (Bryant et al. 1993). Available resources usually limit the number of competitor products and companies that can be monitored on a continuous basis. Primary competitor products can be categorized into two groups: critical and noncritical.

Critical competitors are those whose products have the potential to create a significant negative impact on a company's future market share for a particular product. A noncritical competitor may have the potential to create a significant negative impact on future market share; however, such an occurrence is either less likely or not known for sure at the moment and therefore requires periodic monitoring. Noncritical competitors are those who may become critical in the future and, thus, must be monitored periodically over time. There is no need to monitor noncritical competitors continuously.

The changes noted as a result of continuous monitoring of critical competitors provides valuable insight into the strategy and decision-making processes of a competing company. This insight, in turn, can assist with the strategic/tactical planning efforts within the corporation (Vella and McGonagle 1988; Bille 1993). The analogy is a routinely updated chart of hazardous coastal waters. Knowing where hidden reefs are located allows the ship's captain to plan the next landfall and monitor that passage using landmarks to avoid hazards and prevent running the ship aground.

Competitors can be continuously monitored in various ways. The effort may involve scanning published literature. As mentioned earlier, some services such as the Sandpoint system can do this automatically once the pertinent search terms are identified. One drawback to relying totally on an automated system is that not all published data are available in electronic form to be searched. For this reason, a comprehensive continuous monitoring effort combines both manual and automated processes.

Maintaining contact with internal and external networks to capture unpublished competitive information pertaining to the critical competitors is important. Unpublished competitive information is often difficult to confirm, but it is also the most timely. Over time, the reliability of specific persons within the networks can be determined. Electronic bulletin boards are another excellent way of maintaining a constant communication with the internal network. External networks require more time and are limited only by current technology such as modems, facsimiles, and bulletin board networks.

It is important to capture the competitive information the CTI group is gathering during the continuous monitoring process. Later reference to this information will allow broader interpretation of individual events over time. This interpretation is what gives the CTI analyst insight into the competition's strategy and decision-making processes (Vajk 1992). Automated databases are ideally suited for storing and subsequently retrieving this competitive information.

Competitive intelligence resulting from competitive information obtained from continuous monitoring is also extremely valuable to tactical decision-makers. These people are responsible for the day-to-day implementation of tactics that will ultimately achieve long-term goals.

A process may be put in place to immediately notify key clients of important changes in a competitive profile. Such notification can take the form of a simple handwritten note, a facsimile, an electronic-mail message, or a telephone call. The important point is the timeliness of the notification. Any additional interpretation or prediction of the implications associated with the CTI can be included.

Competitive intelligence resulting from continuous monitoring efforts is valuable to the strategic planners within the corporation, but possibly to a lesser degree. They should be kept abreast of any developing situations which might have an effect on the assumptions they are currently using in their planning process. Timeliness is not as critical an issue with these clients.

CONVERTING COMPETITIVE INFORMATION TO COMPETITIVE INTELLIGENCE

Converting competitive information to competitive intelligence is essential when a more in-depth study of a complex situation is required in order to make decisions or recommendations. A working definition of competitive intelligence is competitive information that has been analyzed to the point that an action or recommendation can be made (Fuld 1992). Therefore, the conversion process involves analysis of the competitive information.

Competitive information, in itself, can often meet the needs of a client. In such instances, any additional effort to analyze this competitive information would be a waste of time and resources. The CTI analyst must always remember—if clients are just asking for the time of day, do not tell them how to build a clock.

Determining what clients really need is sometimes a subjective call and experience with the client on previous requests is helpful. A successful CTI group, however, must provide more than just competitive information (McGonagle 1992).

REQUIREMENT FOR ANALYSIS

The most important initial task of the CTI analyst is to determine and then confirm the necessity of the analysis with the client. Converting competitive information into competitive intelligence is a resource-intensive analysis process.

The key is a good understanding of the client's question. As mentioned before, the question often requires nothing more than competitive information to allow the client to progress with the planning/decision-making process. However, if the question requires consideration of multifactorial competitive information to allow for an action/recommendation, then a more sophisticated analysis may be necessary.

TYPES OF ANALYSES

The depth and complexity of the analysis is entirely dependent upon the client's needs. The CTI analyst has the responsibility to determine these needs upfront.

The CTI analyst should have a clear understanding of the question. This requirement may appear to be obvious. But, experience has shown that in too many instances the specific question is missed, and as a result, the CTI unit completely fails to provide value to a corporation. If this problem recurs, the result may not be favorable to the longevity of that unit.

The analyst needs to know the ultimate use of the competitive intelligence. Is this just a check to confirm a rumor of little impact or will this intelligence be used to determine a future merger candidate?

In addition, the analyst needs to know the audience that will receive this competitive intelligence. Knowing the audience will help determine the format and level of technical terminology and jargon to be used.

Competitive intelligence should provide an action/recommendation to the end user. The clearer this message is, the more likely an action/recommendation will be considered. A presentation to upper business management involving volumes of graphs and tables written in highly technical terminology may not be the best vehicle to provide a clear message. Know the audience.

A planned method of distribution or communication is essential to the CTI analyst who is compiling the competitive intelligence. Has the client requested a report or presentation? The key here is to know upfront what the client wants the final deliverable to be and to meet or exceed those needs.

Finally, the CTI analyst should find out from the client about any concerns or sensitivities associated with the question being asked. The CTI analyst should never compromise integrity to avoid sensitive issues; however, a clear understanding of any sensitivities can assist in the appropriate choice of words. Careful wordsmithing can ensure that the competitive intelligence will be read and used appropriately. For example, CTI that shows negative impact on a project sponsored by upper management should be carefully worded, but the issue should not be avoided.

Numerous specific techniques are being used to analyze competitive technical information, and the number continues to multiply (Mathey 1990; Paap 1994). The focus of this section will be on the broader scope of qualitative and quantitative analyses.

Qualitative analyses usually involve piecing together bits of competitive information to form an overview of what the competition is doing. Quantitative analyses are more specific and usually involve compilation of assumptions and model development.

Qualitative analysis requires the collection of as many bits of competitive information as time will allow. During this collection, the analyst may need to speculate, depending on the competitive information gained. As the picture begins to take shape, new questions will arise, requiring the use of additional competitive information.

Qualitative analysis is like a jigsaw puzzle that pictures a tree. As the puzzle is assembled and the top of a tree takes shape, we can speculate that the tree has a trunk; however, the pieces of the puzzle for this section are missing. Careful examination of the area around the puzzle produces the missing pieces which can then be put into place to form the trunk of the tree and finish the puzzle. Time constraints will usually prevent the completion of the picture, and it may be necessary to speculate what the entire picture looks like. This analogy holds true with qualitative analyses, where the CTI analyst must rely upon speculation to provide the final action/recommendation.

Quantitative analysis involves compilation of assumptions and model development and is relatively more complex. Very little has been published in the CTI literature concerning model development. For this reason, standardized, validated models are not available in the public domain. Therefore, the CTI analyst is required to develop models pertinent to a specific situation.

Model development is a multi-step process. First, pertinent assumptions need to be identified and retained in a list. Assumptions are required since it may be impossible for any single model to predict every possible situation. For example, an assumption could be that all competitors possess the same technology; however, if an assumption is proved invalid, the model as developed would no longer contain the factors that are required for accurate analysis of the new situation. A comprehensive list of assumptions should be kept. The CTI analyst is encouraged to interview experts in various disciplines, all of which relate to the situation being modeled. The CTI analyst should refer back to this list of assumptions throughout the model development process.

Next, all pertinent factors to be considered in the model must be identified; for example, the analysis of a competitor's product pipeline. Factors to be considered would include the innovativeness of the technology within the pipeline, the ability to produce and reproduce this technology on a commercial scale, the relative timing to market for the various technologies in the pipeline, and regulatory hurdles associated with the development of each technology.

Once quantitative measurements have been identified, a mathematical expression to represent the relationship among the multiple factors may be derived. The assistance of statistical experts either from an internal statistics/mathematics department or external consultants who specialize in modeling may be helpful. These experts may be indispensable in validating the model, the final step before applying the model.

CHARACTERISTICS OF THE COMPETITIVE TECHNICAL INTELLIGENCE ANALYST

The ideal CTI analyst should be expected to have formal technical training pertinent to the specific industry. A CTI analyst within the pharmaceutical industry, for example, should have significant background which includes pharmacy or medical training in the laboratory or a clinical setting, or both. Thorough knowledge of and extensive experience in research activities is required. In addition, the ideal CTI analyst should have some business training or savvy. At the very least, the CTI analyst should understand the basic business principles of the specific industry involved.

A CTI analyst within the pharmaceutical industry should understand commercialization processes for pharmaceutical products, which include marketing and sales, licensing of technology, strategic planning, business analysis, and business development. Experience in product development, preferably broad-based, is also essential. A generalist who can apply specific technical skills in a broad fashion is needed for this position.

The CTI analyst should also possess many of the same personal characteristics seen in analysts of business competitive intelligence: outstanding interpersonal, communication, interviewing, writing, and presentation skills.

In addition, the CTI analyst should possess an inherent persistence characterized by a relentless pursuit for the answer to a question. That drive from within which will not allow the CTI analyst to rest until every rock and stone have been turned to find the answer to the question is critical (McGonagle and Vella 1990b; Porter et al. 1991).

PRESENTING THE FINDINGS

Distribution of CTI is dependent upon client needs. This determination requires communication with the client similar to that conducted during the analysis determination phase. A clear understanding of the bottom-line message the client desires and the CTI analyst wishes to convey is essential.

Nontechnical people should be able to understand the action/recommendation. If the final decision-maker cannot understand the action/recommendation being proposed, CTI runs a high risk of not being used. This risk can be minimized by using less technical terminology.

Remaining sections of the report or presentation can be constructed around the "take home" message to emphasize its importance. Repeating the crucial message in different ways is often good.

The CTI can be distributed through traditional routes such as paper reports or untraditional routes such as voice mail; electronic mail; and bulletin boards, both poster board and electronic (Fuld 1994). If the report must stand alone, more details are probably required. This additional information may be handled as appendices to allow the reader the opportunity to use it as needed but, at the same time, maintain the conciseness of the report. For example, R&D scientists may wish to examine the detailed data which are provided in the appendices.

A concise, accurate executive summary presented at the beginning of a written report maximizes the communication of the final action/recommendation. Time is a valuable resource to everyone in the current environment of corporate America. Presenting the key findings of the CTI, along with the proposed action/recommendations in a concise, easy-to-read section of the report, ensures that the greatest number of people on the distribution list will read at least this section.

The executive summary is followed by the analysis methodology and results of the analysis in greater detail. Readers who have questions or want more detail on a particular point of the executive summary can go to these sections or appendices. This format puts readers in control and provides them with various options and tiers of detail.

Similar formats can be used for oral presentations. A more concise manner may be required. Proposed actions/recommendations resulting from the CTI analysis should be stated upfront in the presentation. The rest of the presentation is used to support how these actions/recommendations were formulated.

Tables, graphs, and illustrations are effective tools for presenting supportive data (Hayward 1991; Holcombe and Stein 1993). Slides should be concise and simple. Handouts with adequate space for the listener to make notes are recommended. Handouts containing the same material as that being presented allow the listener to focus on the message as opposed to frantically writing down the information from the slides.

APPLYING THE FINDINGS

The CTI analysis has been completed; results have been successfully distributed; a presentation has been provided to the key planners and decision-makers. Now what happens? A measurement of impact would be a logical followup.

RANGE OF IMPACT

"You can lead a horse to water but you can't make it drink." There is probably no better way to describe the helpless situation a CTI analyst faces after completing a project. The message is that the range of impact CTI will have at any given time depends directly upon the client and the situation. Making the "water" more attractive to drink is not the solution.

Clients realize and appreciate the value of CTI because it helps them make more informed decisions (Ashton et al. 1994). The CTI analyst earns credibility by the quality and usefulness of the product provided to the client.

Quality can be ensured with accurate, timely, and comprehensive CTI. Disclaimers may be added to CTI to accurately describe the analyst's comfort level with the validity of the report. Usefulness of the CTI is directly related to how well the analyst determined the client's needs upfront and to what extent those needs were met.

A particular situation may also dictate the impact CTI will have on the planning/decision-making process. CTI is often just one of the many tools that planning/decision-makers have to use. For example, CTI that describes a potential acquisition target's product pipeline, technical capabilities, and how well that pipeline fits current objectives will be only one of many things considered in making a decision to buy that company. Other factors such as financial health, global presence, and infrastructure will be weighed before a final decision is made.

IMPACT MEASUREMENT

The actual measurement of the impact a competitive intelligence unit has on the overall planning/decision-making process is currently an active topic of discussion within corporate America (Jaworski and Wee 1993). Impact measurement data could be most helpful in the justification to maintain such a unit.

Support from the top down would be ideal. Robert Flynn, Chairman and CEO of The NutraSweet Company, places a value of $50 million dollars a year on his competitive intelligence unit (Flynn 1994). This value was based on the impact competitive intelligence had on revenues gained and revenues not lost. In reality, not all CTI units have this kind of direct access to the CEO of the company. To get top-down recognition and support of this kind requires bottom-up appreciation and impact measurements.

IMPACT MEASUREMENT PROCESS

Impact measurement for CTI is in its infancy. Very little is published on the impact measurement processes within the competitive intelligence discipline.

Processes that will fit the culture of a particular company need to be developed. Different companies will have different methods of obtaining client impact or responses, and therefore, the process will need to be customized. The human resources department may be a valuable resource to assist in this situation because they may be able to share successful approaches used in the past to obtain feedback from clients concerning a particular group's performance. Some approaches used include formal telephone interviews, formal surveys, and/or informal one-on-one discussions with the clients.

Impact measurement for a CTI unit focuses on two key questions:

- What did the client do differently based solely upon the CTI supplied?
- How can the results of this change be directly related to revenues gained or revenues not lost.

The answers to these two questions need to be presented in an easy-to-understand format. Actual case studies should be cited to support overall findings.

USES FOR RESULTS

The CTI unit can use these favorable impact measurements in several different ways. Positive results need to be effectively communicated. The CTI analysts should develop a strategy to fully exploit these positive impact assessments. One strategy might be to use the results to justify adding more CTI analysts to the unit. Another strategy might be to use the results to support a proposal to focus CTI efforts on high-impact clients.

The audience for the impact measurement results should be considered in the CTI analyst's strategy. This audience should be people who will dramatically influence the future of the CTI unit. For example, the CEO of the company should have a general understanding of the value of the unit, while the person who supports the unit financially should be convinced of the value, based on clear impact measurements.

Other individuals within the corporation may be strong champions. In some instances, the person who supports the group financially is not the primary champion for the CTI unit. For example, the unit may reside within the corporate side of the business, but a primary champion may be in R&D management. Do not forget this person when it comes time to present the results of the impact measurement. This person will convince the corporate leaders of the unit's true value. Make sure this champion has all the ammunition that can be provided with impact measurements.

Understand that primary champions move on in corporate America. It is important, therefore, to continually identify and nurture additional champions within the corporation. Think diversification when identifying these new champions. If the CTI unit resides as a corporate function, it is wise to recruit new champions from both the R&D and commercial side of the business. Impact measurement results are key to garnering support and convincing skeptics of the value offered by the CTI unit.

REFERENCES

Ashton, W. B., A. K. Johnson, and G. S. Stacey. Spring 1994. Monitoring Science and Technology for Competitive Advantage. *Competitive Intelligence Review* 5(1):5-16.

Barber, D. Fall 1991. Competitor Intelligence—The Essential Challenge. *Competitive Intelligence Review* 2(2):23-24.

Bille, T. J. Fall 1992/Winter 1993. Competitive Intelligence System: A Time-based Strategic Method. *Competitive Intelligence Review* 3(3/4):19-22.

Bryant, P. J., J. C. Coleman, and T. F. Krol. 1993. Scientific Competitive Intelligence as a Decisionmaking Tool. *Proceedings of the Eighth Annual International Conference of The Society of Competitive Intelligence Professionals*, pp. 29-45. Society of Competitive Intelligence Professionals, Alexandria, Virginia 22314

Bryant, P. J., J. C. Coleman, and T. F. Krol. Summer 1994. Scientific Competitive Intelligence: A Tool for R&D Decisionmaking. *Competitive Intelligence Review* 5(2):48-50.

Chitwood, L. Spring 1993. The View—A Survey of SCIP's VIPS. *Competitive Intelligence Review* 4(1):33-37.

Flynn, R. E. April 1994. NutraSweet Faces Competition: The Critical Role of Competitive Intelligence. *Proceedings of the Ninth Annual Conference of The Society of Competitive Intelligence Professionals*, pp. 208-209. Society of Competitive Intelligence Professionals, Alexandria, Virginia 22314.

Fuld, L. M. 1985. Getting Started: The Basic Techniques for Collecting Competitor Intelligence. *Competitor Intelligence: How To Get It; How To Use It*. John Wiley & Sons, New York.

Fuld, L. M. 1988. Super-Monitoring: Motivating Your Entire Organization to Monitor Your Competition. *Monitoring the Competition*. John Wiley & Sons, New York.

Fuld, L. M. March 1992. The U.N. Question: Can You Export Intelligence? A Parallel Lesson for U.S. Industry. *Proceedings of the Seventh Annual Conference of The Society of Competitive Intelligence Professionals*, pp 57-87. Society of Competitive Intelligence Professionals, Alexandria, Virginia 22314.

Fuld, L. M. Summer 1994. Talk It, Show It, Write It. *Competitive Intelligence Review* 5(2):56-57.

Hayward, M. G. Fall 1991. Graphically Illustrated. *Competitive Intelligence Review* 2(2):14-17.

Hohhof, B. March 1991. Technology's Role in Producing Intelligence. *Proceedings of the Sixth Annual Conference of The Society of Competitive Intelligence Professionals*, pp. 1-27. Society of Competitive Intelligence Professionals, Alexandria, Virginia 22314

Holcombe, M. W., and J. Stein. Fall 1992/Winter 1993. Creating Powerful Visuals—Less Is More. *Competitive Intelligence Review* 3(3/4):43-46.

Jaworski, B., and L. C. Wee. Fall 1992/Winter 1993. Competitive Intelligence and Bottom-Line Performance. *Competitive Intelligence Review* 3(3/4):43-46.

Keiser, B. E. Summer 1994. Using R&D to Turn Competitors into Allies. *Competitive Intelligence Review* 5(4):35-39.

Kight, L. May 1995. Make Your Telephone Your Hotline to CI. *Proceedings of the Tenth Annual Conference of The Society of Competitive Intelli-*

gence Professionals. Society of Competitive Intelligence Professionals, Alexandria, Virginia 22314.

Krol, T. F., J. C. Coleman, and P. J. Bryant. Fall 1992/Winter 1993. Consultant Evaluation for Scientific Competitive Intelligence in the Pharmaceutical Industry. *Competitive Intelligence Review* 3(3/4):43-46.

Krol, T. F., J. C. Coleman, and P. J. Bryant. Winter 1994. Sources, Sources, Sources: Making the Most of Them. *Competitive Intelligence Review* 5(4):19-22.

Lesky, C. Summer 1994. The Role of Information Brokers in Competitive Intelligence. *Competitive Intelligence Review* 5(2):22-25.

Link, A. N., and G. Tassey. 1987. The Competitive Challenge. *Strategies for Technology-based Competition*. Lexington Books, Lexington, Massachusetts.

Mathey, C. J. Fall 1990. Competitive Analysis Mapping. *Competitive Intelligence Review* 1(2):16-17.

Matteo, M. R., and E. K. Dykman. Summer 1994. Building Credibility, Champions and a Mandate for Competitive Assessment. *Competitive Intelligence Review* 5(2):26-30.

McGonagle Jr., J. J., and C. M. Vella. 1990a. Evaluating and Analyzing Data. *Outsmarting the Competition*. Sourcebooks, Inc., Naperville, Illinois.

McGonagle Jr., J. J., and C. M. Vella. 1990b. Beyond the Obvious: More Sophisticated Applications for CI. *Outsmarting the Competition*. Sourcebooks, Inc., Naperville, Illinois.

McGonagle Jr., J. J. Spring 1992. Patterns of Development in CI Units. *Competitive Intelligence Review* 3(1):11-12.

Moffat, S. March 25, 1991. Picking Japan's Research Brains. *Fortune* 123(6):84-89.

Paap, J. E. Spring 1994. Technology Management and Competitive Intelligence: New Techniques for a Changing World. *Competitive Intelligence Review* 5(1):2-4.

Porter, A., A. Roper, T. Mason, F. Rossini, J. Banks, and B. Widerholt. 1991. *Forecasting and Management of Technology*. John Wiley & Sons, New York.

Prescott J. E., and P. T. Gibbons. Summer/Fall 1993. The Seven Seas of Global Competitive Intelligence. *Competitive Intelligence Review* 4(2/3): 4-11.

Roukis, G. S. 1990. Global Opportunity and Analytical Framework. *Global Corporate Intelligence*, eds. G. S. Roukis, H. Conway, and B. H. Charnov. Quorum Books, Westport, Connecticut.

Vajk, H. Spring 1992. Business Intelligence and the Corporate Director. *Competitive Intelligence Review* 3(1):13-15.

Vella, C. M., and J. J. McGonagle, Jr. 1988. Integrating CI into Business Plans and Planning. *Improved Business Planning Using Competitive Intelligence*. Quorum Books, New York.

ENDNOTE

1. An application for membership can be obtained from the Society of Competitive Intelligence Professionals, 1700 Diagonal Road, Suite 520, Alexandria, VA 22314, (703) 739-0696; fax (703) 739-2524.

Organizing for Competitive Intelligence: The Technology and Manufacturing Perspective

THOMAS DURAND, FRANÇOIS FARHI, and CHARLES DE BRABANT

Costs, process flexibility, and technological innovation are believed to be the key success factors for the 1990s. Therefore, information on the competition is indispensable in today's increasingly competitive markets. Having precise and comprehensive information on competitors presents a competitive advantage for the better-informed company.

But gathering information on the competition is obviously not an end in itself. One may note that we live in a world with an overabundance of information. Thus, information on competition must be summarized, analyzed, and communicated to the right people in the company to develop, implement, and adapt competition-oriented strategies and actions.

This chapter is devoted to both the technology and the manufacturing side of competitive intelligence because technological innovation takes place on the shop floor as well as in the research laboratory.

Different ways can be followed to use technological information to a competitive advantage. After a discussion on the nature of competitive intelligence activities, in which we show how technology is just one part, we will present two case studies of relevant ways to gather and use strategically different types of information. The first case study emphasizes the interest in analyzing a competitor's manufacturing capabilities, whereas the second shows how to map a competitor's technology strategies.

Following the case studies, we sum up our experience and discuss the main features of an efficient organization to monitor competitors, that is, a method to systematically collect and exploit publicly available data and information about competitors' technological capabilities and manufacturing plants. We emphasize the need to define the goals and questions to be answered before launching the project, as well as the importance of the process of selecting people who will carry out the work. Finally, we discuss the different ways to collect data from a variety of external and internal sources.

Let us first deal with some definitions and segmentation of the whole concept of competitive intelligence.

DEFINING COMPETITIVE INTELLIGENCE

Several key words related to our theme are often used indiscriminately to describe what we mean by competitive intelligence: economic intelligence, strategic monitoring of competitors, industry analysis, environment scouting, etc. In our opinion, all of these are equivalent. **Please note that we do not accept the word "industrial spying." We regard this perspective as unethical. Indeed, all the activities we refer to in this chapter require only legally available information. Nonlegal activities fall outside the scope of our work and practice**. Let us define and clarify what, in our view, the various terms mean.

Under the generic term "competitive intelligence," we include any activity designed to collect, analyze, and organize "strategic" information about competitors. Inasmuch as any information may *ex post* turn out to be strategic, it is difficult to assess *ex ante* what information should be regarded as relevant and what information should be disregarded. In addition, redundancy is better than voids because it enables one to cross-check bits and pieces of information. As a result, competitive intelligence turns out to be an endless quest for any information about competitors.

We also need to clarify the concept of competition. Behind this word, we include not only direct competitors but also Porter's competitive pressures, that is, potential new entrants, new technologies/products/services, suppliers, and clients (Porter 1980). Thus, in a broad sense, competitive intelligence covers the monitoring of information about the entire industry at hand.

SEGMENTING COMPETITIVE INTELLIGENCE

Competitive intelligence activities can be segmented into subcategories. In fact, most competitive intelligence activities turn out to be organized functionally, with different processes adapted to the specificities of each category. Figure 1 summarizes the classical subcategories of competitive intelligence encountered in practice.

Market intelligence covers traditional marketing activities such as market surveys; analysis of market share; evaluation of competitors' products by committees; characterization of market segments; and upstream marketing and analysis of latent, implicit needs yet to be satisfied. These activities are usually well taken care of by marketing departments.

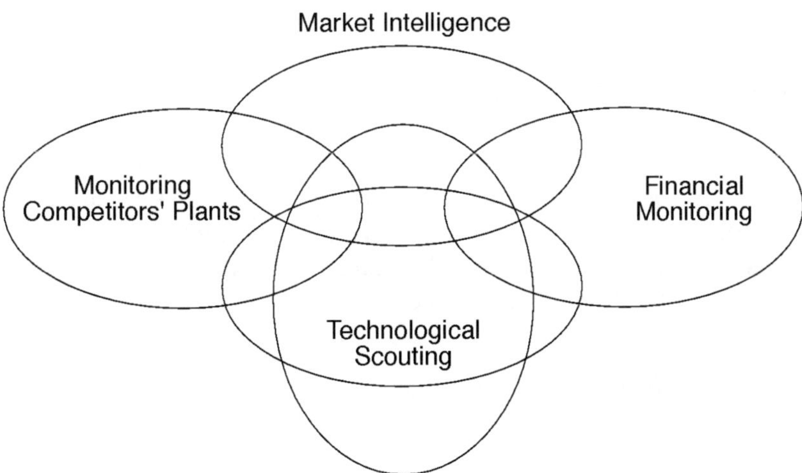

FIGURE 1. Classical subcategories of competitive intelligence

Technological scouting is quite a different matter, focusing on new technical developments, newly available technologies, improved product designs, or more efficient manufacturing processes. Several typical questions surround a given target (technology): What technologies are the competitors adopting? What technologies have been dropped and why? What are competitors doing in terms of new technological developments? What are their R&D priorities? What are they patenting on? What external competencies are they tapping through R&D cooperations and subcontracting? What new technological options are suppliers developing? What new ideas are stemming from universities, public research centers, or R&D laboratories in other industries? Technological scouting usually falls under R&D responsibilities and, in one form or another, relates to the activities of technical librarians.

Less commonly encountered is the term *monitoring competitors' plants*, that is, "manufacturing scouting." This activity is devoted to understanding the manufacturing performance of a competitor's plant or of a set of plants. It typically aims at reconstructing the cost structure for the corresponding products, evaluating the production capacity of the plant(s), and learning about future plans and manufacturing priorities and strategy. This activity is not conducted as often as the others. The responsibility for this activity falls to the manufacturing department. Plant managers and their staff, however, are not well prepared for the task because they tend to act internally more than externally.

Another classical component of competitive intelligence is *financial monitoring* where competitors' yearly or quarterly accounts are analyzed when available. More specifically, financial statements and reports are systematically compared in order to assess each firm's performance with respect to specific issues, for example, stock rotation, return on fixed assets, interest payments, investments, borrowing capability, etc. Such activity is usually carried out by the finance department.

FROM FUNCTIONAL ACTIVITIES TO COMPETITIVE INTELLIGENCE

Beyond these activities, several other aspects of competitive intelligence may be identified in some organizations, for example, human resources management, logistics, purchasing, etc. All in all, these functional activities, each monitoring some specific aspect of the competition, compose what may be regarded more globally as "competitive intelligence." However, we have rarely seen a complex process combining these different facets of competitive monitoring into an integrated competitive intelligence system. Instead, our experience is more that of duplication of effort, lack of coordination and communication, or even the absence of any such real activity.

When a firm has a global competitive intelligence approach, it has usually been organized directly by top management. A team of librarians is usually in charge of gathering any accessible information without significant interaction with functional departments. Analysis and the systematic exploitation of the information is then usually the weak part of the process.

BENCHMARKING

Benchmarking has a wider scope than competitive intelligence. Indeed, while competitive intelligence focuses on direct competition, benchmarking aims at learning from best observable practices wherever they come from, especially when they come from other sectors.

For instance, a chemical company needing to find the best way to transport quantities of powdered material may find it a good idea to ask a cement company how to do so. No direct competition comes into the picture, no conflict of interest appears, thus yielding a potentially productive exchange. Benchmarking in this sense usually turns out to be a much easier task than gathering competitive intelligence.

Many practitioners, however, tend to use the word benchmarking when they compare their firm's performance to that of competitors. In our opinion, this use of the word benchmarking is narrow and inappropriate. We believe that in such instances, competitive intelligence or any equivalent should be used instead.

STRATEGIZING OR IMPROVING PRACTICES

Another useful categorization of competitive intelligence stems from what the firm conducting such activities is trying to achieve.

One may identify two major objectives behind monitoring activities:

- Strategizing, that is, making decisions as a consequence of the moves, practices, or performance of competitors
- Finding ways to improve performance by imitating/adapting/learning from competitors or other firms.

Using this distinction, as well as a categorization of the targets under scrutiny, Figure 2 summarizes how competitive intelligence and benchmarking relate to one another.

All in all, when a firm starts looking outside—be it to strategize or to find better ways—the firm really looks at its own organization, as in a mirror. What managers really view when monitoring competitors or comparing their firm with other organizations in other sectors is an image of their own organization, its practices, its strategy.

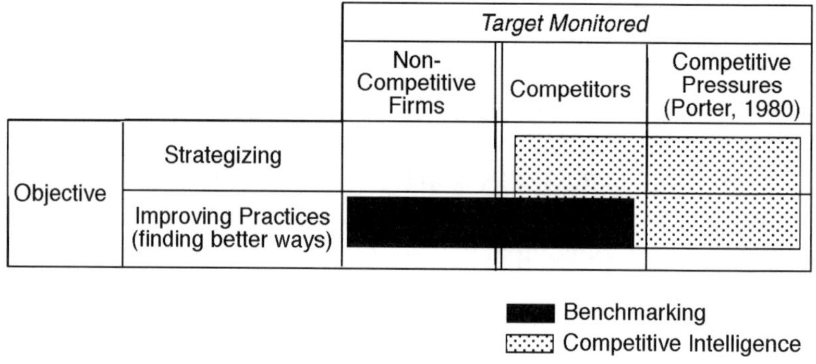

FIGURE 2. The relationship between competitive intelligence and benchmarking

COMPETITIVE INTELLIGENCE: TWO CASE STUDIES

Following are two case studies illustrating the different ways in which competitive intelligence can provide the competitive edge. In the first case study, a company analyzes a competitor's manufacturing capabilities; in the second, a company maps a competitor's technology strategies.

ANALYZING COMPETITORS TO CUT COSTS

In the late 1980s and early 1990s, Company F, a large multinational Europe-based company, was confronted with a serious competitive threat. The sector saw the successful emergence of new, small and aggressive competitors each of whom individually focused on a particular segment of Company F's product range, offering quality products at significantly lower prices. Some products were sold under their own brand names, but the majority were sold under distributor brand names. These products were gaining increasing market share, up to 25 percent in some segments.

This transformation in the marketplace had broken down some old business rules, namely those of economies of scale in manufacturing and in distribution. As a result, competitors were no longer only the very large conglomerates, but now also included a slew of small, incredibly active competitors all over Europe.

In early 1992, the Executive Vice President of Manufacturing in Company F was increasingly worried about this evolution. He wanted to organize a thorough competitive watch system throughout the company.

Lack of Strategic View on Information

This is not to say that competitive information did not exist in the company. It did, but in a very diffuse and often "ad hoc" form. Many departments collected information about competitors. The marketing departments of most subsidiaries continually collected market information on products in their respective segments. Oftentimes through suppliers, the buyers received and sometimes collected information on the manufacturing capabilities of their competitors. Moreover, a technological surveillance unit had been created to monitor technologies and patents.

However, very rarely was this information compiled, analyzed, summarized, transmitted, and, thus, used to its full potential. For instance, each month, the technological surveillance unit, staffed with technicians and librarians, would send out a listing and a summary of all patents published in the sector. No attempt was made to condense and analyze the information. All subsidiaries would receive the same 300 to 400 pages of unreadable patent jargon. A quick survey of 25 technical managers showed that only 20 percent of them would glance through it; the other 80 percent, overwhelmed by the amount of paper they received, would never look at it.

Developing an Active, Companywide System

Faced with this situation and an increasingly competitive environment, the company decided to put in place an active, companywide system for monitoring the competition. The principle of the operation was to involve people from all departments, get them to collect and share information on competitors, analyze the information, and build an action plan.

As a first phase, the manufacturing capabilities of approximately 40 competitors were targeted: their plants, their organization, their equipment, their manufacturing costs on key products. To achieve this objective, Company F established an organization with three tiers: a steering committee, operational teams, and a team of consultants.

The Executive Vice President of Manufacturing headed the steering committee. Its tasks included identifying the competitors/products to be analyzed, explaining why they were targets, defining the organization and the budget required, and monitoring the work in progress. A key reason for the creation of the steering committee was to guarantee that the work undertaken would receive approval and support from top management.

At the operational level, eight teams of four to five people were created, each covering a geographical area and including people from manufacturing, R&D, marketing, and finance. Their objective was to collect, analyze, summarize, and communicate information on a given number of competitors, generally not more than four per team. All employees in the company were expected to assist the working team by transmitting available information on the competitors to the appropriate group.

As the third tier, our team of consultants assisted the whole process. Our role included advising the steering committee, training the operational members, helping gather information in the field, as well as helping to analyze and summarize the information so as to communicate the results.

For three to four months, the groups gathered information on competitors and spent time analyzing the data collected. As noted earlier, only legally available information was collected and used.

Company F wanted to be a good corporate citizen throughout the process.

Long-Term Results

The results were many and durable. Among them, one may note the following:

- Cost savings of $17 million per year through the adoption of practices and techniques used by some competitors. The accumulated incremental innovations on one product alone were enough to recoup the costs of the whole project.
- A thorough understanding of some 40 key competitors, both large and small. This included knowledge of
  - –their manufacturing capabilities and their plants
  - –the cost structure of key products manufactured in these plants
  - –the anticipation of several product launches
  - –the manufacturing strategies and development plans of some of the competitors.
- The mobilization of a core of some 40 to 50 people who were trained and able to thoroughly monitor competitors and the indirect mobilization of another 200 to 250 people who quickly realized the importance of this process. Moreover, the managers of the various subsidiaries were positioned to react to incoming results.
- Appreciation of the importance of counterintelligence measures and the ability to better protect its own activities from the monitoring efforts of competitors.

For Company F, this project was so successful that the system was later expanded to include other competitors, to go beyond monitoring manufacturing capabilities to include other dimensions (marketing, finance, purchasing, etc.). Moreover, a similar process has been put into place with R&D and technical staff to monitor technologies.

Most European companies for whom we have worked have put into place a system to monitor competitors, but have tended to use it as a passive tool, essentially collecting information. Rare are those who use the system as an active strategic tool, with a long-term impact on their competitive positioning. Through the process described, Company F became one of the latter.

ANALYZING COMPETITORS TO DEFINE A TECHNOLOGY STRATEGY

Most main industrial companies usually follow the incoming flux of new patents. Their objective is always the same: to make sure that they are aware of key patents issued around their own lines of business/technology. Such an approach is essential to keeping an eye on important developments by potential or existing competitors.

But this "nugget-hunting" approach ignores the fact that patents are only the top of an iceberg. For a company or a research center, a patent is not only a means of protection, it is also a sign of interest for a specific thema, as well as an indicator of spending and, thus, of accumulated competencies around the corresponding technological path. In other words, as companies file patents, thus claiming property rights on specific technologies, they send signals, revealing at least part of their own technology strategy. Patent databases thus contain strategic information available for the analysis. Some of that information may have been intentionally distorted, yet some of it is worth the analysis.

Hence, analyzing *all* the patents submitted by a company in a technological field may help draw a picture of the technological paths explored over the years and thus evaluate their potential value. It may also help identify new technological developments as they unfold and the technology strategy a company has followed.

To gain a clearer understanding of these concepts, let us look at what Company X did. Company X was envisioning the launch of an important research effort which could lead to a major breakthrough. Before doing so, Company X decided to look at the technological strategies of its main potential competitors. Company X believed that such an analysis would not only provide a tentative map of the technological routes others had followed, but would also identify potential entrants and newly envisioned avenues.

For the project, Company X assembled and systematically analyzed a database of relevant patents issued within North America, the European Union, and Japan—approximately 4,000 patents.

Identifying Competitors' Research Strategies

Competitors adopt various research approaches. Through the International Patent Classification, one can identify whether research activities are more concerned with new product concepts, new applications, or the development of process equipment. Our experience shows that each company tends to emphasize one type of activity.

- A company files patents centered mainly around the product concept and the manufacturing process.
- Competitor 1 is mainly concerned with new applications for each product concept, leaving to others the task of developing new product concepts and the manufacturing process.
- Competitor 2 aims to protect a potential competitive advantage gained through the development of its own process equipment.

Along the same line, two radically different strategies can be pursued: a win/lose strategy that gambles on specific technological paths or an assurance strategy that covers more or less all known technological alternatives (see Figure 3).

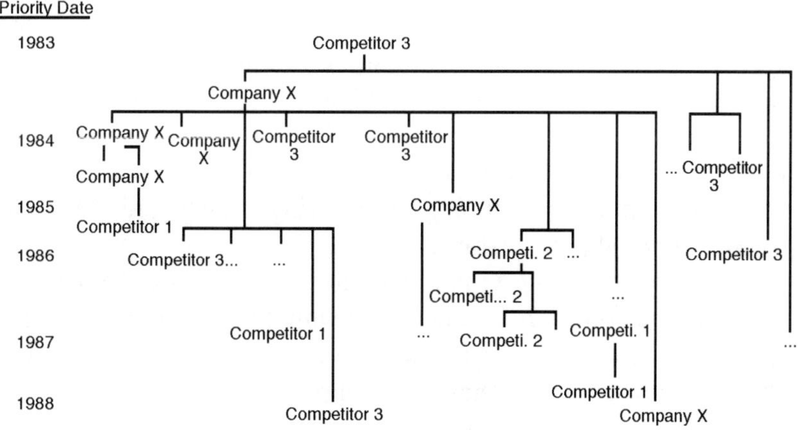

FIGURE 3. Win/lose strategy versus assurance strategy

Because each new patent has to cite previous patents on which the innovation has been based, one can identify families of patents, that is, technological routes, easily reading each competitor's strategy. For instance, Company X has chosen two or three alternatives and has developed them; competitor 1 has tried to be present in the main routes, covering multiple alternatives; competitor 2 has gambled on a particular route.

For Company X, there are therefore two issues: 1) monitoring the route followed by competitor 2 and 2) identifying new routes not yet covered (apparently) by competitor 1.

Identifying Competitors' New Technological Areas

Company X needs to identify changing areas of research pursued by competitors or emerging competitors and measure their potential interest and impact. Several criteria can be used: the appearance of new key words in their patents; co-patenting, which shows their willingness to develop new technologies more quickly through alliances; and development of niches that can be identified by a new product concept followed shortly by patents on applications.

Using these criteria, one can characterize the innovativeness of each competitor's patents portfolio and can measure the potential threat to one's company (see Figure 4). Company X's share of innovative patents is quite high. Competitor 1 is very close to Company X's markets, but has a low share of innovative patents, preferring a time-to-market strategy. Competitor 2 is very innovative, but is not really in Company X's markets. Still, Competitor 2 is a potential entrant and should be monitored. This competitor seems to do a minimum of technology monitoring, reducing its R&D cost by using several partnerships.

Concepts appearing in patents only during the last four to five years can be considered to be new technological routes (the time span may vary from one industry to another). Figure 5 shows a shift in the research emphasis in Company X's area. Development on "noise," "fluid entrance," and "waterproofness" is replacing research on "corrugation," "plastic," "turbulences." Company X has also identified the main competitors on these new routes.

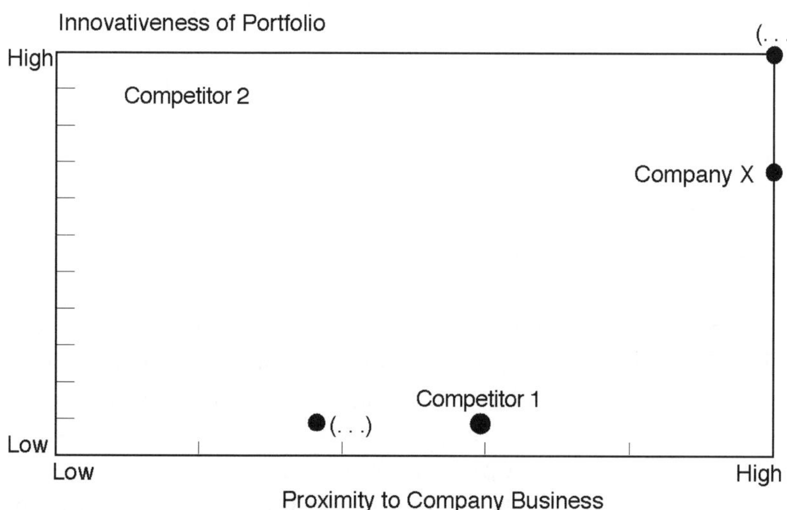

FIGURE 4. Characterizing the competition and measuring the threat

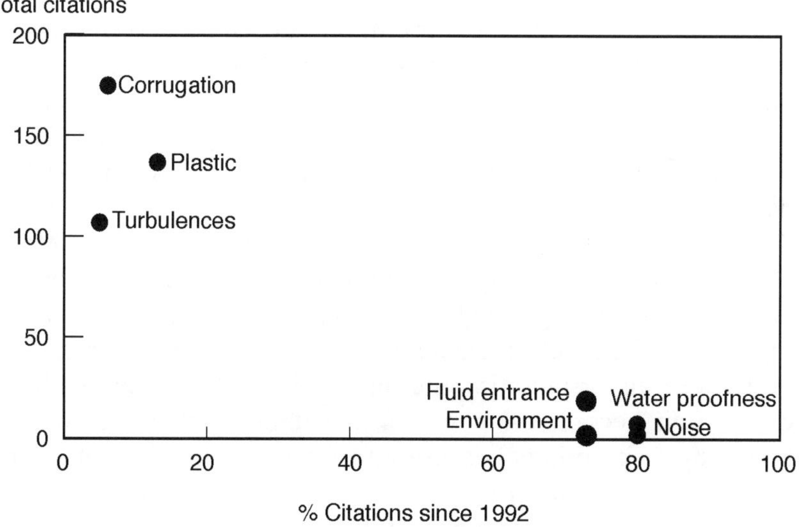

FIGURE 5. Shift in research emphasis

ORGANIZING TO MONITOR COMPETITORS

To monitor competitors, a company has many options. Among them, three stand out:

- Hire a consultant
- Create a monitoring unit
- Mobilize an important part of the company.

We believe that the first two are options, the third is a necessity.

Hiring a consultant may get the analysis you want very quickly. It may also be essential when compiling confidential information on a competitor for a specific purpose, such as for an acquisition dossier. However, this option mobilizes and teaches few people about the company's interest in and the importance of gathering and analyzing information on the competition.

Creating a monitoring unit is the most frequently used option within firms we have surveyed. It has the substantial advantage that information can be centralized around one core group of individuals. A monitoring unit is created, usually headed by an information specialist or a librarian. In most cases that we have analyzed, this type of unit is useful for certain aspects of technological surveillance, such as monitoring and analyzing patents and publications. Case study 2 above (where the in-depth analysis of information contained in patents helped Company X develop a technology strategy) is the perfect example of the eventual usefulness of such a unit.

Beyond that, it more often than not loses its effectiveness. Many such units have limited or no power in the organization. The librarians in these units passively collect information, communicating the results of their efforts in a raw format which very few read and even fewer understand. In other instances, we have seen the head of the unit become all powerful, unwilling to share his or her knowledge with others because information is a source of power within many organizations.

Mobilizing an important part of the company is essential. Everybody in an organization receives or needs information on the competition. The competition is and should be everybody's business. Hence, we feel it is important to get as many as possible involved in an organized process. But to do so, everybody must be integrated in an intelligent and constructive manner.

FOUR-TIER ORGANIZATION

Our experience has shown that a major program lasting many months is essential to make people aware. As illustrated in the first case study presented above, we suggest a four-tier organization (see Figure 6).

Steering Committee

A steering committee should be created to oversee the operation. It should be headed by a strong personality within the organization who can act as the godfather of the operation. In the case study above, the head of the steering committee was the Executive Vice-President of Manufacturing. A strong personality within the

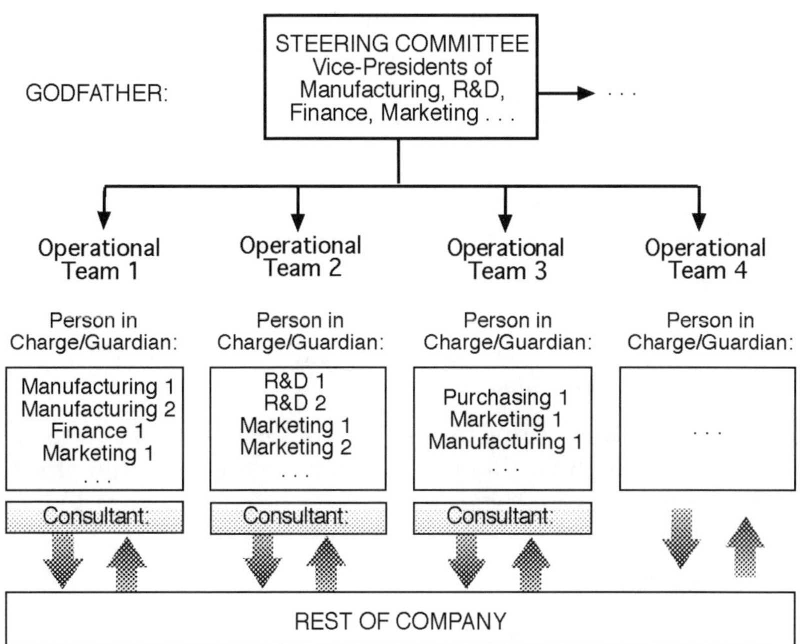

FIGURE 6. Four-tier organization

company, he continually pushed the operation forward with both upper and lower management.

The steering committee's membership should be wide, covering as many functions/geographic areas as possible. Competitive information is like a puzzle with little pieces coming from all sides and sources. Hence, people from marketing, finance, purchasing, R&D, manufacturing, human resources, and so on should all be included no matter what the objectives of the project are.

The steering committee's tasks include

- Defining the objectives. As noted previously, one can monitor competitors for a number of reasons, including distribution strategies, manufacturing costs on key products, technologies used. Hence, it is important to identify clearly what one is intending to achieve from this project.
- Identifying target competitors/products/technologies to monitor. The idea here is not to be exhaustive, but to have a representative sample to get the monitoring effort under way.
- Setting up the organization. This may entail naming an operational person to follow the project on a day-to-day basis. It will certainly involve creating a number of operational groups and selecting the people who belong to each group. Operational groups can be set up by geographic region, major competitive groups, or technologies to be monitored.
- Establishing a timetable. An example is discussed below. One should not underestimate the time required to collect information on competitors, analyze it, and summarize it for future action plans.
- Assigning a budget. Monitoring the competition is a time-consuming and, hence, expensive, endeavor. A budget should therefore be set aside.
- Continually monitoring the progress of the project. To do so, the steering committee should meet every two to three months to review the work undertaken.

Operational Groups

Operational groups should be set up to undertake the work at hand. Like the steering committee, these groups should be multifunctional, calling on people with different, but complementary skills. Membership to one group should not exceed five or six people.

Their role would include

- Identifying in more detail the competitors/products/technologies to be monitored. This process should involve a clear understanding of why one is interested in a competitor or a technology, the types of results expected, the kind of information required, and the available sources.
- Collecting the information. This step is time-consuming and may take months.
- Analyzing and summarizing the information. With the vast amount of information to be collected, it will be essential to analyze, to make intelligent hypotheses, and to summarize the information on each competitor.
- Communicating the results. The results on each competitor should be communicated to the right people in the right format.
- Being the institutional memory for the company. Information on competitors should be stored by those who need and use it daily. The operational groups are the most likely to fill this role; thus, it may be useful to store the information centrally.

A strong personality should be named to head each group. His or her role is to make sure that the work is advancing according to schedule, to be the link with the steering committee, and to communicate the results to the steering committee and the rest of the company. The head of each group should also become the guardian of the information collected and analyzed under his or her supervision.

One of the key success factors of such a system is that the members of the operational teams spend the necessary amount of time gathering and analyzing information on competitors. It is a time-consuming task, demanding many months at least, several days a month from each member.

Rest of the Company

The rest of the company needs to participate in the process. Many studies on the subject have shown that 60 percent of the information one wants on a given competitor already exists within the company or is easily available. However, the information exists in a diluted and diffuse form, with each person and/or department using it to its own ends and often forgetting to pass the information on to other interested parties.

Mobilizing the rest of the company involves

- Informing them. People in all departments need to be informed that a system is being put in place to monitor competition. Departmental/divisional meetings may be ideal settings for this. Staff must be told that **legally** collecting information on the competition is vital to the survival of the company and is everybody's business.
- Passing the right information on to the key operational groups. Because the rest of the company will be called upon to pass on information about competitors, staff need to know to whom the information should go. A "who's who" of the various operational groups may be a useful guide.
- Communicating results. It is important that the rest of the company be systematically and appropriately informed about the results of the monitoring effort (top management may not want to divulge all the findings).

Consultants

Hiring outside consultants may be useful in animating the process of collecting competitive technical intelligence. Their role could entail

- Assisting the steering committee in its various tasks.
- Training the operational groups on the various aspects of monitoring competitors. Such training might include a session on the objectives, the set-up, and the timetable of the system; a second session might be on what information is required and the potential sources of information; and a third might be on analyzing the information and communicating the results.
- Assisting the operational groups. Each group may be assigned a consultant to assist in collecting the information, analyzing it, and summarizing the results.

- Being the timekeeper. Consultants may act as the timekeepers, making sure that the project sticks to the pre-established timetable.

TIMETABLE

The process of collecting information is a time-consuming one. It involves an introductory phase, a start-up phase, and a permanent phase.

During the *introductory phase*, the steering committee is created and meets to establish the objectives, the organization, the budget, and the timetable of the project. The operational groups are put in place and trained; they have identified in detail the competitors/products/technologies to target, as well as the information required and the sources to tap. The rest of the company is informed that a monitoring system is being put into place, told that they are an essential part of it, and asked to seek information on competitors and transmit it to the appropriate groups. Depending on the urgency and the size of the company, this step can last from two to three months.

The *start-up phase* is to test the system put in place. The operational groups gather information on a given number of competitors/products/technologies from an extensive list of sources. They meet regularly to discuss their findings. After collecting the majority of the information, they analyze and summarize their findings, knowing that they may have to go and get more information to fill the gaps. At the end, they communicate their results to all interested parties.

The steering committee supervises the work in progress and solves major problems. The rest of the company transmits all information to interested groups and is progressively informed of key results. Our experience shows that this step takes from six to twelve months.

Collecting information on the competition is an on-going business. Hence, once the monitoring system is up and running, it should become a *permanent aspect* of the company's activities. This phase can include continuing to monitor existing competitors/products/technologies, expanding to others, and/or expanding the scope of what is to be analyzed on a given topic (finance, marketing, purchasing, R&D, logistics, etc.)

EXTERNAL SOURCES OF INFORMATION

Outside sources of competitive information are many and varied. Depending on what the objectives are for the company, the information and, hence, the sources may differ. In general, legal outside sources of information include the following:

- Clients
- Sales force/distribution channels
- Suppliers
- Bankers
- Consultants
- Technical research centers
- General and specialized publications
- Exhibits
- Databases, patents
- Publicly available administrative documents
- Recruitment
- Analysis of competitive products (reverse engineering)
- Alliances, mergers, acquisitions.

Competitive intelligence is like a puzzle. Different sources provide pieces on a given competitor. However, note that on a given topic, many sources exist (more or less reliable and more or less useful) and that one source may be the most useful for one competitor, another source for another competitor. For instance, equipment suppliers may be the most useful source for information on one competitor, whereas an in-depth article in a technical magazine may be the most informative source on another competitor. Hence, it is vital that all sources be tapped because they may have information to help solve the puzzle.

ANALYZING, COMMUNICATING, AND STORING INFORMATION

If a competitive intelligence system is to work, information must be structured to create a corporate memory and to prepare for the future. Information can be treated and analyzed in four increasingly time-consuming forms:

Raw data/brut information is often unreadable (for example, patents), dispersed, and voluminous. It is helpful (but not sufficient) to store information on a competitor/product/technology in a given place or with a guardian.

The *memory of analysts* is the worst form of institutional memory. The information has been analyzed, but it is volatile and not always communicated to the interested parties. Information stored in this form is also more likely to be forgotten by the analyst in question or to leave when he or she leaves the company.

Summary sheets/slides for presentations are essential to communicate the results of the analyses to upper management and to other departments within the firm. However, these documents are often too brief and incomplete.

Reports on competitors/technologies is the ideal tool to serve as a corporate memory. Properly structured, the report will be exhaustive and analytical. It states the hypotheses explicitly and identifies the missing gaps. The report can be easily updated by a guardian, whose principal task is to systematically update the report. The principal drawback of the report is that it is an extremely time-consuming task.

CONCLUSION

Competitive intelligence cannot be seen simply as a collection process. Over and above gathering information, one must analyze and exploit it, as well as transmit useful and pertinent summaries to key decision-makers. There is a value chain in a competitive intelligence process—gathering information is only one step among several.

Our experience shows that a great deal of the needed strategic information is already within the company; a little bit of organization enables one to legally collect the remaining share.

But even more than an effective process for monitoring competitors, competitive intelligence is a good way to reopen the learning capabilities of an organization. Companionship to gather and analyze information leads to positive forms of interfunctional work. People find evidence that "better ways" exist elsewhere. This discovery unleashes creativity to reach past the achievements of competitors.

REFERENCE

Porter, Michael E. 1980. *Competitive Strategy: Techniques for Analyzing Industries and Competitors*. The Free Press, New York.

PART III

Producing Competitive Technical Intelligence: Approaches and Tools

PART III
Editorial Introduction

Many activities and skills are essential in producing effective technical intelligence, and simple prescriptions for success are difficult to define. Experienced intelligence professionals believe that a proven track record (that is, professionals who have spent time in the "school of hard knocks") is one of the most important assets for creating intelligence that makes a difference. Of course, producing effective intelligence is no guarantee that it will have an impact; however, intelligence rarely has an impact unless it has been produced and delivered effectively.

In this section, several experienced professionals describe three aspects of the intelligence creation or production process: information gathering, information storage, and intelligence analysis. Information gathering is covered in chapters addressing technology scouting and use of external databases as information sources. Information storage and retrieval is discussed in a chapter on computer support systems. Finally, intelligence analysis is illustrated in one chapter discussing scientometrics and two chapters describing patent analysis.

The first chapter describes the emerging field of technology scouting, which is the practice of searching a variety of sources to answer specific information requests on technologies or technology experts anywhere in the world. Jean Tibbetts is a experienced technology scout, and she describes several aspects of scouting in her chapter—the purposes, methods, and impacts. Both the targeted (very focused) and the reconnaissance (broad surveillance scouting) investigations are covered. A number of scouting information sources (for example, computer/electronic, literature, people, organizations, networking) are described, and examples of scouting successes are summarized. Tibbetts provides suggestions regarding potential sources of information, including many that are often overlooked. She discusses the merits of various human, paper, and electronic resources and describes the most effective way of using each. Tibbetts also calls attention to the importance of the human element in scouting. She describes some of the characteristics of a successful scout, emphasizing that technical expertise is not necessarily a prerequisite; certain personal attributes often prove more important.

A widely recognized expert in computer information systems for competitive intelligence, Bonnie Hohhof discusses internally developed computer intelligence systems for storing, retrieving, and processing CTI data. Her chapter emphasizes the importance of careful planning and evaluation of options before purchasing software. She discusses the need for system designers to understand existing information flows and resources in the organization and to carefully assess the customer's information and system design requirements. Ms. Hohhof also covers several success factors—organizational culture, managers' attitudes, and the importance of strong links between database elements and specific uses such as technology investment decisions. According to Hohhof, the single most important factor in influencing the success of a CTI system is the system's compatibility with the organization's culture. She also notes the importance of implementing the system in phases, starting with the simplest and most effective components.

Bruce Kinzey and Anne Johnson provide a overview of computerized databases as sources of technical information in intelligence studies. They discuss the nature and types of databases available, methods of searching, and benefits of using databases. They emphasize the importance of establishing the depth and breadth of the search by first understanding the user's needs and resources, then formulating a well-defined question for the search. Another important consideration highlighted in this chapter is the reliability of data. The authors discuss potential pitfalls arising when sources of documents found in databases are not easily recognizable. A case study of a technology search covering advanced concepts and methods for handling toxic chemicals is also included to illustrate the process of interaction between analyst and customer in conducting a database search.

An experienced patent researcher, Mary Ellen Mogee describes the basics of analyzing patents to provide information and intelligence for technology management and strategy. Mogee's approach uses patent data to construct indicators of a firm's technological strengths or of a technology's development status. She begins with a discussion of patent systems, types and sources of patent data, and methods of patent analysis. She discusses thoroughly the use of patent citation data as a cornerstone of patent analysis. Also, the strengths and weaknesses of using patent data as technology indicators are also covered, along with many ideas regarding use of patent data in CTI applications.

Jean-Pierre Courtial, Anne Sigogneau, and Michel Callon introduce the discipline called scientometrics and show its application to technical intelligence problem-solving. Scientometrics uses bibliometric techniques to analyze scientific and technological literature. The goal of the analysis is to identify technological events, trends, and themes of interest to users. Scientometric methods enable specialists to identify emerging scientific fields through analysis of trends in published literature. Because publications in a given field tend to appear in predictable patterns, statistical analysis of these patterns may indicate the relative importance of a given patent or technology. Data sources such as technical literature and patent databases are discussed. Techniques such as co-word analysis using the LEXIMAPPE software are also described. An example analysis of chemical purification of residual gases is presented, and ways to model the dynamic nature of technology change are discussed.

Françoise Perdrieu-Maudière and Christine Leboulanger demonstrate how patent analysis can be used to help firms understand emerging trends in their fields of interest. Drawing upon the scientometric methods described by Courtial, Sigogneau, and Callon, Perdrieu-Maudière and Leboulanger analyze superconducting technologies, which are important in transmitting electric power. The authors show that patent analysis can enable companies to identify other organizations and countries that lead in the development of a given technology or product. This method can also help identify emerging markets and can provide insights into the activities, business strategies, and strengths of potential competitors, as well as their relative positions. Further, it can suggest rates of change within the industry. A network characterization of firms in the superconductivity technology area is presented to describe relationships among the various players. Patent citation analysis is used to characterize the relative positions of competitors, and changes in the structure of the competition (for example, nature of technical specialization) are studied over time. Finally, the chapter discusses the nature of relationships among the patenting firms, including potential strategic alliances, and draws attention to patterns of concentration and specialization among firms as an important determinant of future market growth.

Technology Scouting

JEAN TIBBETTS

Historically, of course, necessity hasn't always been the mother of invention. Invention proliferates; some technologies are ahead of their time, others are beside the point. Most technologies need a nudge in the direction of usefulness or must be championed by someone with a vision

—L. Alberthal

We live in an era of technological implosion. Rapidly radiating waves of change are sweeping the industrial world. Although innovations and breakthroughs have occurred in almost all fields, the most dramatic effects have probably been seen in information technology and in communications. The advances in these two fields alone have impelled a dynamic rush forward that has impacted on industries around the globe.

While this dramatic leap has opened international markets, it has also increased competition. These increasing competitive pressures have forced corporate decision-makers to seek intelligence on which to base dependable strategic planning.

Organizations must be informed on what is happening in their fields and potential markets. They must also be adept at forecasting future courses of action and be sensitively aware of emerging developments that may affect their particular industry or niche. If you are the manufacturer of an old line medical product or therapeutic and a new surgical technique that will eliminate the need for your product is being developed, you need to know about this breakthrough almost before it happens to prepare for the future. The discovery of a cheap new energy source could affect the industrial world today even more profoundly than the advent of electrical power affected industrial development earlier in this century. It pays to be alert to progress.

Technology scouting is a form of information-gathering that can provide an organization with a competitive edge. A scout serves as the eyes and ears of an organization striving to meet goals, to stay ahead of competition, and to achieve growth in a fast-paced industrial economy. Just as pioneer scouts set out to explore new territories and provide intelligence on unknown terrain in the adventurous days of our country's early development, corporate technology scouts today chart the marketplace and prepare the way for growth in new industries and markets.

Scouting can be patient and persistent surveillance, or it can be a focused and intensive action designed to obtain specific data as rapidly as possible. The pages that follow will describe grounded procedures, some general, some specific

FORCES DRIVING THE QUEST

Typically, one of three major forces drives a scouting project to help companies achieve a competitive advantage. These forces are the need to know, the need to lead, and the need to improve productivity.

THE NEED TO KNOW

What you do not know can be disastrous to your business. Firms should, of course, be aware of technological and scientific developments within their fields, but they should also know what their competitors are doing. Competitive intelligence is more than a management tool; it is survival training. Knowing the competition's strengths and weaknesses can give a company a significant edge.

It is also important for a company to know itself. Benchmarking is the process of comparing one's own company with the state of the art in the field or comparing present performance with past performance. This activity can provide important, objective information on company strengths and weaknesses. The company that knows its position relative to competitors can avoid unpleasant surprises and move forward to exploit its strengths.

In addition to uncovering information on competitors, searches can also lead to the discovery of

- New technologies
- Technology trends
- Research in progress
- Emerging or advanced technology
- Improved processes and production methods
- Outsourcing possibilities and expertise
- Technology breakthroughs
- Proven products
- Potential strategic alliances
- Organizations doing research in targeted fields
- Potential mergers or acquisitions
- New markets, new applications
- Regulations, standards, and laws
- Solutions to technological problems.

All of these objectives can help companies enhance their business potential. In some cases, lack of access to information can result in lost opportunities and even lost revenues.

THE NEED TO LEAD

The need to stay ahead is one of a company's strongest driving forces. Companies that lead in their field are usually innovators and, typically, the innovative tendencies firing that leadership extend well beyond product lines into all corporate areas, from marketing to management.

Keeping up today involves looking ahead, identifying trends, and forecasting where today's markets are headed. Well-managed technology scouting projects will provide information on trends as well as on opportunities. Recognizing the trends influencing a technological field is extremely cost-effective. It can save the devastating expense of going down the wrong path while the rest of the world is marching off in a different direction. No one wants to repeat the Beta/VHS experience that rocked the video cassette recorder world a few years ago.

While few dispute the value of knowing about new products and technologies as they emerge or advance through commercialization, few of us have felt as driven to understand the science that shapes the technology. Companies on the cutting edge, however, are aware of the need to know advanced science if they are going to integrate advanced products successfully. Progress involves assimilating knowledge on many levels. Keeping up with relevant scientific developments has become increasingly necessary as processes become more complex, standards more important, federal regulations more demanding, and environmental constraints more stringent. Often, access to experts and to scientific information is vital to growth. Scouting for technology today requires highly sophisticated radar.

The need to lead can drive inspired scouting operations down unusual paths in the search for unique or distinctive technology. Creative projects may initiate parallel projects in cross-fertilization. Crossover projects require considerable imagination, as they involve exploring unrelated fields to locate technology that can be adapted to dissimilar applications. A good example of cross-fertilization is cryology, where similar techniques can apply to freezing both fish and blood products. A clever scout will brainstorm to identify potential fields to scan for dual-use technology.

Faced with a rapidly changing and technologically sophisticated scientific environment, technology scouting has taken new directions in serving industries and industrial development. In addition to providing information on new technologies and tracking what is already on the market, a scout may also need to compile information on how to manage the technologies located in the search. This activity can range from gathering intelligence for briefings to obtaining the materials, instructors, or expert consultants needed to set up training programs.

THE NEED TO IMPROVE PRODUCTIVITY

Productivity, quality assurance, and competitive pricing are all part of the formula for achieving competitive advantage. Updating production with new technology, automation, information systems, equipment, and training systems may be vital to increased productivity and/or enhanced product quality. Finding the best technologies at the least cost and highest assurance of service is a basic operation for the experienced technology scouting team.

THE LOGISTICS OF THE HUNT

Technology scouting may be conducted in-house, that is, within the company itself, or it may be outsourced, that is, contracted to another organization. Before taking on an in-house scouting mission, however, companies should consider such factors as their knowledge of the markets, the technologies in question, and the scouting techniques that will be required. They may also need to ask whether they will be able to free their staff to find the time necessary to undertake what can be a very demanding task. If not, it may be wiser to outsource the project or to work with consultants or brokers.

IN-HOUSE SCOUTING

Depending on the size and needs of a company, in-house technology scouting can be done satisfactorily by one or two full-time staff, or it can be the work of a whole department staffed by a number of employees involved with gathering, compiling, analyzing, processing, and distributing information.

Such departments are generally molded by a firm's organizational structure. Corporate culture is more than a buzzword when it comes to in-house scouting: it underlies and colors the entire operation.

Scouting is more likely to be directed by the needs of top management, R&D, and/or product planning teams than by the interests of those in the engineering, production, or finance departments. The scouting approach of one company, Air Products, has been a notable exception. The company has developed a scouting operation known as APTECH (Air Products' Technology Clearing House). APTECH's customers are the 900 or more people in engineering, commercial development, and R&D at Air Products. Scouting concentrates on technological developments outside the company; however, these activities are focused by internal needs.

Writing about APTECH, Merrill Brenner (1992) states,

> *APTECH's emphasis is generating opportunities rather than solving problems. If one of our internal customers wants to know "everything in the world" on a particular topic, Air Products' Information Services Department would be the primary source of information. APTECH would supply far less, but complementary information. We seek extensions and improvements for technology areas in which Air Products is already involved, rather than major diversifications or totally new businesses. These scope definitions are some of the key decisions that any technology transfer service must take.*

Since APTECH workers assume that the company's technology developers routinely monitor the literature pertinent to their specific technological interests, they direct their scouting efforts to reviewing and providing information from a broad, worldwide spectrum of technology information that is not readily available on-line or in known periodicals. These sources include university catalogues of technologies available for licensing, foreign journals, and newsletters from esoteric research centers. They also include bulletins and newsletters from the National Technical Information Service, reports from government laboratories, as well as information from conferences and professional societies and associations.

Brenner believes some of APTECH's best sources originate through verbal contacts. Ultimately, all of their incoming information is organized and distributed to their in-house "clients" on a customized basis. Much of the printed material gathered during the course of scouting efforts is scanned and put into a full-text searchable database maintained to serve retrospective studies or to provide background for users whose interests may be taking new directions.

Generally, individual scouting projects conducted in-house in larger companies like Air Products are more apt to be clearly circumscribed than those farmed out to consultants. Project planning for in-house scouting, for instance, necessarily goes beyond simply locating and accessing technology or information on technology. The overall activity involves education, evaluation/analysis, and acquisition. Eventual integration of a prospective innovation or product is also a consideration. Integrating new technologies into any organization may require delicate maneuvering at best, since successful integration takes considerable time, patience, and effort.

Frequently, the in-house scouting team must be agile advocates in selling their technology discoveries to management. Writing about Sylvia Ruffo, a former manager in Baxter Travenol's technology scouting department, Michael Wolff states that Ms. Ruffo stresses

> *I don't want to send a memo to the decision maker telling him to look at this interesting technology. I don't want the decision maker to know simply that there's a competitor out there who is trying to do the same thing we are doing in a different way. Rather, I'm going to put my career on the line and tell him I think this competitor has a better technology and I think he should stop what he's doing and adopt this instead. That is radically different from competitive intelligence. It's a very risky business—for me and for the decision maker* (Wolff 1992).

In their article on science and technology scouting at Elf Aquitaine, Jacques Bodelle and Claude Jablon (1993) note that

> *the integration of new technologies is most often closely linked with good access to science. Often, new technologies are born in the academic world before they are transplanted into industry for development. At a time when everyone is looking for advanced information, close relationships with university laboratories bring us in direct contact with emerging technologies that may have a relevance for our markets in the medium to long term . . . educational institutions and, to a lesser extent, government research centers are training grounds for industry staff, especially in R&D. Although the employment picture is generally bleak nowadays, it appears that industry may face some shortage of scientists and engineers in the future; thus, competition for scientifically trained personnel is a real concern for our company,*

and a continuous interaction with the best universities is an excellent support for our recruiting.

To sum up, we are convinced that industry must include science as one of its strategic tools, and we ensure that our R&D organization provides access to it in an efficient way.

OUTSOURCING SCOUTING PROJECTS

Outsourcing a technology scouting project may be an expedient solution if a company is faced with staff limitations and a lack of know-how or resources for conducting such tasks. Typically, smaller companies depend more on outsourcing to meet their information scouting needs than do large firms. Large firms tend to have internal information resources staffed by full-time personnel and call on outside specialists or consultants as the need arises.

Finding the right partner to work with in setting up scouting projects can be challenging. Few firms specialize in providing the requisite information for scouting technology. Those that do work in the field generally do so in a highly individualized manner—each consultant bringing to the project his or her own experience, knowledge, resources, and, occasionally, bias.

Firms scouting technology usually offer services on a variety of levels. There are firms that broker technology and firms that provide matchmaking services. Some firms only provide information on which to base decisions or to take action. These companies may locate technology available for transfer, but take no further part in evaluating the worth of the innovations located or in expediting a successful transfer.

Other consulting firms not only locate the technology, but also provide market or technical evaluation and analysis or regulatory advice and/or assistance. Many organizations involved in licensing and technology transfer participate in the negotiation of agreements and even help integrate the technology into a product line, thereby assisting the licensee throughout the entire commercialization process. Most of the firms offering technology transfer services will provide the technology, but not all engage in comprehensive searches.

Technology brokers typically promote their own portfolio of available products or innovations. They often obtain patents and manage the marketing and licensing of many university-developed inventions. A few companies also run comprehensive computerized databases for accessing technology available for licensing. One such company offers a database listing more than 30,000 technologies grouped in 56 categories. Another company offers 12 databases on available technologies drawn from universities; the government, including the National Aeronautics and Space Administration, the Environmental Protection Agency, the Department of Energy, the National Institute of Standards and Technology, the National Technology Transfer Center; and, most important, technology from the small research and development (R&D) firms granted awards under the federal Small Business Innovation Research (SBIR) program.

The SBIR is a highly competitive government program which funds high-risk/high-pay R&D on federal agency needs with commercial potential. It supports R&D in applied research to underwrite technological development and spur job creation. The program provides risk funding to small firms (those with fewer than 500 employees) and has been instrumental in commercializing new technologies in almost all fields.

PROJECT PLANNING

Technology scouts should design a detailed plan before commencing the search. The most efficient and productive search plans require the scout to clearly define the mission, clarify the technological objectives, and set the search parameters.

DEFINING THE SCOUTING MISSION

The "scouting mission" refers to the purpose of the search; it determines which strategies will be employed in conducting the survey. If the purpose is to monitor a field or technological developments in a specific area, for example, the mission will be conducted differently than if the goal is to address a specific problem or to locate technologies that can be developed into a clearly defined product line. Once the scouting team understands the mission, it can plan how it will accomplish its goals.

CLARIFYING THE TECHNOLOGICAL OBJECTIVE

Clear objectives are essential to implementing the search. It is trite but only too true that unless you know clearly what you are looking for, you probably will not recognize it when you find it. Specific, clearly stated criteria delineating the technology, product, or information needed are crucial to any scouting endeavor.

Where to look depends to a great extent on what is sought. Technologies can be initially categorized under a few broad but qualifying terms, including high technology, low technology, emerging, or advanced technology. Products or processes considered high technology usually result from intensive research and engineering efforts. Most information on these types of technologies will be found in scientific or professional literature, although the lay press may cover dramatic breakthroughs or new product introductions. Applications evolving from an area with strong emphasis on basic research will be more prevalent in university settings. Primary networking interviews would be a likely source of information on these developments.

Once the scout has determined the nature of the technology sought, further refinement is required to sharpen the focus of the search. For example, is the development to be found related to a mature technological field known for "classic" products, such as oatmeal or electric can openers? Should the technology preferred be breakthrough or concept stage research? Does the technology require clinical or other types of testing to meet regulatory approval acceptable? Do we look for near-term or earlier stage research? Do we need to know whether patents been filed or issued? If products are sought, are new products or proven products the object? Does the client want prototypes? Answering these basic questions will help the scout know how to proceed with the search.

SETTING THE SEARCH PARAMETERS

As we have seen, some of the search parameters are set by defining the technology. But other parameters may also limit the search and should be considered in designing strategies. Is location an issue? Should a particular country, region, state, or area be targeted? Is the field to be limited to a particular industry or discipline? Is the object of the search really new technology, or can innovations from other fields be creatively applied?

Other factors also play a role in determining the nature of the search. These include the extent to which the selected field is to be covered and the amount of time available. Will the project require a comprehensive review, or will a field survey or overview suffice? Should the activity be intense, leaving no stone unturned? Should the review be open-ended or time-limited? What are the budget constraints?

Cost is a most important consideration. What type of resources are available for the search, and how can one maximize one's research budget? On-line searches, for example, can be expensive and can produce gluts of stale or useless information along with nuggets of pure gold.

It is good to know that there are alternatives to the commercial on-line search that offer comparable or better results for less. Public libraries across the country now provide patrons with extensive computer services—usually at no cost, or, when necessary, at a nominal fee. In addition, Internet searching has become an increasingly valuable low-cost resource; it is indeed worth the effort to learn to navigate the "Net."

SEARCH STYLES: THE TARGETED INVESTIGATION VERSUS THE RECONNAISSANCE SEARCH

There are two primary types of scouting strategies: the *targeted investigation*, which is a highly focused, intensive search undertaken to locate specific technological information, and the *reconnaissance search*, which is aimed at providing general or comprehensive awareness of developments in a given field. The reconnaissance search usually involves monitoring the objective on an ongoing basis.

Mission definition will determine which type of search will be most effective. Both styles require that goals be defined, objectives clarified, and parameters set.

THE TARGETED INVESTIGATION

The targeted search is usually intensive, time-limited, and highly focused. It hinges on a precise definition of the technological target; all activity focuses on uncovering very specific information.

This type of scouting is most effective when there is an immediate need for very specific knowledge. Sometimes conducted like investigative reporting, targeted scouting is the preferred method for locating information needed to resolve problems and to develop new products rapidly.

Planning the Targeted Investigation

Because a targeted search is so highly focused, it must be based on a solid understanding of the objective. Planning plays an especially important role. Plunging in without a plan results in the frustration of charging down too many blind alleys and a fruitless pursuit of "will-o-the-wisp" leads. In many cases, a brief on-line search of the targeted technological field can provide direction.

Determining which databases to scan depends on the initial planning and, certainly, on the objective. If the objective is to locate research in progress, for example, the search will entail scanning abstracts from articles in professional journals, such as those found in the MEDLINE or BIOSIS databases. New product announcements will probably be found in a review of trade journals or a database oriented toward marketing. In either case, information obtained in this initial search will point the way to the journals most likely to contain useful information or to universities or companies most apt to be involved in the field. An initial on-line search can also provide U.S. patent abstracts around which to organize further research.

Implementing the Targeted Investigation

A targeted search comprises five major steps: 1) an on-line database search; 2) a literature review; 3) interviews with experts; 4) a patent search, and 5) networking with selected contacts and sources.

The *on-line search* is only the first step in the targeted investigation; information uncovered will need to be carefully followed up. This preliminary search will help the scout "get smart" on the subject and develop leads for further investigation. On-line reviews can provide the following: names of periodicals, newspapers, universities, and manufacturers active in the field; market and patent information; names of related associations, experts, and consultants; and information on conferences, research in progress, and trends in the field.

There are literally thousands of databases, each having a slightly different focus. On-line keyword searches of various newspaper databases and market research databases such as DIALOG's PTS PROMPT or ABI/Inform can provide valuable leads. ABI Business Periodicals database on compact disk can provide information on corporate activities and market research. DIALOG also has a New Product Announcement database that may offer useful information. An on-line search should also disclose projects under way in university laboratories. One can often find company references by running an author search through a technological database, such as MEDLINE. A listing of some major science-related databases can be found in the Appendix of this book.

An on-line search will usually uncover useful *literature* that can provide more detail on the topic and leads as to who is active in the field. It is helpful to review the past one to three years of relevant publications; many useful articles may turn up.

Scouts should also become familiar with the universities specializing in the particular technology of interest. Many of these produce research reports. For example, early stage research that may not yet be in publication may be described in annual reports from university laboratories. The Massachusetts Institute of Technology (MIT), for instance, publishes an excellent "Progress Report" on its Research Laboratory of Electronics. MIT also puts out a newsletter for the same laboratory and publishes an annual report for its Department of Biology. Documents such as these can be exceedingly useful.

A scout should also contact and *interview* experts whose names appear in the on-line search or in the literature. These individuals may be journal editors, librarians, directors of federal programs, authors of articles, scientists, staff of associations, or consultants. Often these people can answer questions directly or can point out other useful information sources. Many scouts have found that developing a personal relationship with the research staff at certain university laboratories can likewise bear fruit.

Depending on the type of information sought, a *patent search* can produce a gold mine of information. Clearly, the most effective type of patent search is a hands-on search at the U.S. Patent

Office in Washington, D.C., where most of this information is housed.

Not only do patent searches provide information on the technology in question, they can also uncover information on the technology's subclasses, which may lead to other valuable finds. Patent searches further provide names of people to interview for primary source information. Assignees and inventors' names and addresses are always listed on the documents. Sometimes a patent is the only clue to finding small companies who are developing interesting technology or large firms who have technology interests in unexpected fields.

In some cases, it may not be possible to locate the inventors because they have moved or because their company has been acquired by another firm. In these situations, it is still possible to contact the lawyer who represented the inventor when he or she filed the patent. Much can be learned from direct contact with these people. Should all else fail, the application files (with examiner's notes and correspondence) for issued patents are available for review in the U.S. Patent Office. These files not only may offer leads to the whereabouts of elusive inventors or assignees, but they also may contain useful and perhaps surprising information.

Finally, the technology scout should be *networking* with others at all times. Indeed, the value of networking cannot be overemphasized. It involves everything from simply conversing with acquaintances in the field to phoning the experts; it begins with the information gleaned in the initial on-line search and continues throughout the project. One should never conclude a networking call without having asked for names of other possible contacts. The additional leads obtained from each interview help move the project forward.

THE RECONNAISSANCE SEARCH OR STUDY

Reconnaissance studies typically entail monitoring technological developments in a field, the activities of a competitor or competitors, or both. Reconnaissance scouting is usually a protracted process directed at providing a general or comprehensive awareness of developments or activities within a field. The level of effort devoted to such projects depends on budgets and informational needs. They can run the gamut from a simple scan or overview of a field to meticulous data collection over a long period of time. Project strategies are usually determined by clear mission definitions, just as they are in targeted projects. The study parameters and economics are also similarly determined.

Reconnaissance operations may be open-ended or finite, although the most effective reconnaissance projects are likely to be ongoing. The majority simply monitor technology on a continuing basis.

Planning the Reconnaissance Search

Strategies for reconnaissance search projects depend on mission goals and search parameters. Activities should take into account the nature of the information desired, since it is more likely to be general than specific and more open to creative association than are targeted searches.

Because these studies are usually ongoing, reconnaissance searches may employ more scanning or monitoring techniques than are used in targeted searches. Sometimes a scout can cover a field fairly well with a regular review of related trade and research journals. The depth of routine field explorations varies according to the mission and the search parameters. A determined probe for information may take persistent and serious effort. Like the artifacts in an archaeological dig, technological information seems to run in layers. The deeper probes tend to retrieve fewer hits, but the information unearthed is probably of greater value.

In reconnaissance scouting much depends on the field. Scouts seeking biological innovations available for license may find that current announcements of biological breakthroughs may proclaim technologies that are no longer available. Even though the product may have years to go before it can appear on the market, enterprising licensees have discovered it, acquired the rights, and locked it in with exclusive agreements. Locating early stage research may require creative reconnaissance work in many fields. Once it has been found, it may require an act of faith to make use of it.

Implementing the Reconnaissance Search

The steps for undertaking a reconnaissance search are the same as for the targeted investigation: on-line search, literature review, interviews, patent search, and networking operations. Because this is a long-term, ongoing investigation, however, the five procedures need not be followed in order. Rather, the emphasis is on maintaining, expanding, and refining existing leads. Information should be periodically reviewed and updated.

A comprehensive search plan for monitoring developments in a specific field would also include regularly surveying new product introductions, research in progress, and recent patents issued. New products can be reviewed at trade shows, in trade journals, in newspapers and product literature. Research papers will be found in professional journals devoted to the field, and patents may be found in a regular review of the *Weekly Gazette* or through an online database search. There are also commercial compact disks now available with full-text U.S. patents issued monthly. One should also check university departmental reports, newsletters, or technology transfer catalogues; reports from securities dealers; reports and journals from venture capital companies; initial product offerings (IPOs) at the Securities and Exchange Commission; government reports (especially national level); off-the-shelf market research reports; congressional reports (hearings transcripts); and computer bulletin board messages. Trend tracking is another important tool, which will be described in greater detail later in this chapter.

With all these sources, it is important not only to scan and update, but also to analyze new data for emerging trends and new directions in research. In the reconnaissance search, it is the analysis which gives the information value.

Again, to obtain useful information, nothing beats networking and talking with people involved in the field. More so than in a targeted investigation, attendance at trade shows and conferences is important. Attendance at such gatherings is an excellent means of following the latest developments in a field of interest. Usually these gatherings are sponsored by trade associations.

But no matter who the host, a useful scouting technique is to request whatever promotional material is available. Most sponsors will be happy to send a program from their last meeting, or they may be able to supply a promotional brochure for a future event. These programs can also sometimes be found in an association's trade journal.

The speakers and panel members contributing to the program are experts who may be able to provide up-to-date information on their technology or field. Many will also provide a copy of their presentation on request. Moreover, if the project budget permits, a scout can also purchase the meeting proceedings from the sponsoring agency.

Of course, one should not overlook the enormous potential of simply chatting with other conference or trade show attendees. A scout's eyes and ears need to be attuned to bits and pieces of information that may be picked up along the way during the course of casual conversation. Strong interpersonal skills are definitely a plus.

Finally, in a reconnaissance search, organization of data is highly important. If a scout cannot find the data he or she has uncovered, it is of little value. Notes should be carefully catalogued, indexed, and kept on a database or in file folders for analysis and evaluation. Some scouts rely on a computer notebook; others are sensitive to security issues and prefer to work with paper. Either system is only as useful as it allows for easy sorting, manipulation, and analysis of the data. Too many scouts skilled at collecting information end up suffocated by a data dump!

TREND TRACKING

Good decision-making in today's competitive environment requires the development of reliable technological and/or industrial forecasts. Trend tracking is a highly structured scanning of commerce aimed at providing an awareness of what is going on in the world outside a particular niche or field.

Trend tracking involves tracking federal regulations, consumer trends, economic pressures, political pressures, emerging technology, wars and revolutions, attitudes and philosophies, and the interests of futurists that may affect, either positively or negatively, the development and commercialization of technology.

Trends may be discovered accidentally during the course of a project devoted to monitoring a known technological field. Or they may be discovered intentionally in unfamiliar fields by charting events, noting activity, and cataloguing the evidence that indicates trends may have been gathering force. Depending on the project mission, the discovery of a trend may be merely noted and reported as a subset of a number of observations made in a survey overview, or the field may be closely monitored for significant new developments that could affect the direction and implications of the evolving trends.

Trends rarely occur in isolation. They almost always develop within the flow of stronger, more universal movements. Their significance is determined by relating them to the social, economic, or political forces from which they emerged. Collecting trend data should therefore include basic contextual data that support or explain the actual trend data observations. The parameters of time, as well as of those of the field, are usually much broader when one is looking for trends in general than they are in the more straightforward methods used in tracking the status of known trends.

An example of how trend patterns are shaped by a variety of forces can be found in the major changes that occurred in the U.S. food packaging industry during the 1980s. Aaron Brody, a well-known packaging consultant with Rubbright-Brody, Inc., notes that a walk through a local supermarket provides quick insight into significant shifts in American food shopping habits over the past ten to twenty years. There is now far more activity in the fresh or chilled food areas—fresh produce, meats, the delicatessens, and the salad bars—than in the aisles displaying canned or packaged food staples (Brody et al. 1993).

These developments relate to changing life styles and social patterns American families have experienced in the current economy. The trends observed in supermarket shopping today are significant, and they affect a wide range of directly and indirectly related industries. A good scout is always alert to the emergence of trends and is prepared to report when they may affect a client's field of interest.

TECHNOLOGY SCOUTING SOURCES

The choice of sources depends on the mission goals, the search definition, and the search parameters. The list outlines where to look, but each source must be approached and searched according to project definitions and needs. Learning how to best access a resource enables efficient and productive exploitation.

It is difficult to convince today's on-line information experts of the importance of paper, but nonetheless, a hands-on literature search is still definitely worth the effort. Society may eventually go "paperless," but for now, hands-on research is often substantially more productive and usually less costly than on-line searches.

ELECTRONIC RESOURCES

Electronic resources include computer databases, the Internet, and compact disks, all of which can yield large amounts of useful information.

Databases

An on-line search is usually the first step in the technology scouting process. Such a search can provide a springboard for action in planning a broader search strategy. Information derived from this type of initial inquiry should reveal further sources and contacts that may be useful in obtaining more detailed data.

Results of an on-line search need to be carefully listed and sorted for orderly follow-up. What depths should be plumbed in pursuing these leads depend on the level of detail required; there is no need to pursue an exhaustive search when a superficial overview is all that is required.

With this in mind, we can look to an on-line search to provide such leads as the names of periodicals and newsletters devoted to the field; names of universities, associations, and manufacturers active in the field; market information; conference information; patent numbers and related information; research in progress; names of consultancies, consultants, and other experts; and an overview of field status, as well as trends and experts' predictions.

New databases are added daily to what has become an almost overwhelming field of choices. Federal and state government agencies are now making huge amounts of information available on-line, as are many societies and trade associations. Many publishers have contributed to this electronic information flow, as have various corporations.

Access to data is now easier and faster than ever. The information available on-line is timely and comprehensive. Full-text articles are frequently found now, along with abstracts and citations.

Contents pages from many more periodicals are also now available for review.

Fortunately, excellent database guides and directories are available; a prudent searcher will keep them at hand. If you plan to make frequent dips into this information ocean, you may want to occasionally review one or two publications, such as *Online*, devoted to monitoring the database field.[1]

The Internet

The Internet is a present-day phenomenon that is exploding into, onto, around, under, above, and about the industrial, economic, business, academic, social, and everywhere/everything scene. The Internet is growing so fast that it is difficult to describe the type and extent of information available on it. We may report some of the major resources available to date only to find that by tomorrow the landscape has changed, and the Internet has gone well beyond our sense of what is going on now.

Although access had improved remarkably with the advent of such applications as Mosaic and Netscape, the Internet is still somewhat difficult to navigate.[2] Nonetheless, it is a veritable treasure trove of information and should not be overlooked as a resource. For example, a recent search for entomologists uncovered a dedicated database on ants that contained 18,000 references for a large portion of the world's ant literature. This database could be queried by keyword or author right on the Internet.

Doubtless, many such specialized databases are on the Internet awaiting discovery. One needs only to search. For example, technology transfer professionals should, at a minimum, check the sites listed below and set aside a good amount of time to dig for the specific sources that will be productive:

- *http://town.hal.org* or *gopher town.hall.org* to look at corporate annual reports filed with the SEC or text of 1994 patents at the U.S. Patent and Trademark Office
- *http://riceinfo.rice.edu/RiceInfo/Subject.html* or *gopher riceinfo.rice.edu* to search for information by subject area, such as Agriculture and Forestry
- *http://www.loc.gov/* or *telnet locis.loc.gov* to access the Library of Congress card catalogue

http:// www.nsf.gov/ or *FTP stis.nsf.gov* to search the National Science Foundation's Science and Technology Information System

- *http://www.carl.org/* or *telnet pac.carl.org* to search more than 14,000 magazines (including technical and trade journals) articles. The user can also have selected articles faxed for an additional charge, which includes copyright fees
- Newsgroups: There is a newsgroup—a discussion group on Usenet devoted to talking about a specific topic—on virtually every imaginable subject. If you want to read posts relating to polymers, for example, check out the newsgroup "sci.polymers."

Bulletin Boards

Bulletin boards are computer sites where users can participate in on-line discussions.[3] Participants range from the dedicated expert to the interested amateur. These boards can be a useful resource for locating elusive or esoteric information. Access requires a modem, a telephone access number, and a connection configured to the host computer.

Sponsors of bulletin board systems are varied. Federal, state and local governments host boards offering information specific to their agencies. Vendors also sponsor bulletin board systems to provide technical support, tips, specifications, and contacts for user groups. Universities likewise provide bulletin board services and/or systems. Similarly, the Internet hosts a wide variety of newsgroups.

After you have gained access to a user group, it may be a good idea to spend some time becoming familiar with the group and its interests before posting a message or an inquiry. People are often surprised at the useful information they can glean from a bulletin board query.

Compact Disks

The era of the silver platter has arrived. Disks proliferate in all technological fields and are able to store vast amounts of data. This media is not just "read only"—more and more hardware is being introduced to facilitate writing to these disks. CDs are a natural medium for catalogues and directories. They will probably soon be the routine source for this kind of information.

The federal government, as well as a number of state and county governments, has found CDs an especially effective means of disseminating information. New disks are made available to the public daily. Most of the better known catalogues and directories are now on disk, as is export information from the International Trade Administration's Trade Databank. Other agencies, such as the Department of Agriculture, the Environmental Protection Agency, the Department of Energy, and the Food and Drug Administration, to name a few, also have information available on CD. Likewise, U.S. patents are available on disk, as is information on initial public offerings (IPOs).

Many commercial information brokers offer both abstracts and full text articles from newspapers and general and business periodicals. Everything from statistics to market information will be available on disk soon.

LITERATURE REVIEWS

A comprehensive literature review is typically the second step undertaken in a well-planned scouting project. The literature search is an invaluable source of most secondary information; it can also provide direction on where to get the necessary primary source information. In most cases, the periodicals to review can be determined fairly readily from an initial on-line search.

While more and more full-text articles highlighting a project's focus can be found only on-line, a hands-on literature search is still the best way to obtain the bits and pieces of peripheral information that will complete the background, texture, and color of a well-integrated technology scouting assignment. The literature search should be included in the strategies outlined for any well-planned project.

A productive literature survey will involve reviewing at least the past year's issues of each relevant journal. If a journal seems to offer the kinds of information sought, a review of the last two years' issues is probably worthwhile.

Periodicals and newsletters reviewed in a literature survey should be scanned with great attention to detail. Meticulous review includes collecting information from advertisements, notices, new product announcements, association news, news and commentary on people in the field, reports on federal regulations, editorials, and subject-relevant excerpts, along with background and data found in articles that are of interest. It is often helpful to keep mastheads of publications reviewed, since the names, addresses, and telephone numbers of the editorial staff and authors found on mastheads will make it easier for the scout to conduct telephone interviews with these sources.

Examples of useful print sources include *Periodicals in Print* and other directories; professional journals; trade journals; new product periodicals; association journals; newsletters; newspapers; books; clipping services; and technology-oriented U.S. patents reviews.

In some cases, it is helpful to consult special libraries, which focus on particular fields. The National Library of Medicine, as its name implies, is a national—even a world—resource for medical information. Similarly, the regional libraries established by the Department of Commerce to enable nationwide access to U.S. patent documents exemplify special libraries that provide specific information.

INTERVIEWS

Think in terms of follow-up while doing a literature review. A good scout will note the names of relevant individuals mentioned in the literature and on-line searches. Sourcing the names of conference speakers or panelists can also lead to productive interviews. Authors of relevant articles and editors of related journals are always important sources of valued information. Sometimes a scout can obtain specific information by interviewing agency staff who developed cogent ads for products or technologies of interest. Market research reports may bring information already gathered from the field. Interviews with expert professionals in associations; state and federal government agencies; universities; consulting firms; and other organizations may contribute essential background or detail. Personal contacts should not be overlooked, as these often prove to be extremely valuable resources.

TRADE SHOWS AND CONFERENCES: PROGRAMS AND PROCEEDINGS

Many researchers seeking information on products or technology obtain useful information from the trade shows or conferences sponsored by associations, government agencies, or other groups devoted to specific fields. Often new products are kept under wraps until they can be dramatically introduced to the market during these events. Sometimes a scout can capture an immediate grasp of the market for certain technologies by attending a relevant trade show.

Product literature can be secured from major and minor companies involved in the market. Exhibitors demonstrating their wares are usually quite voluble in describing the virtues of their technologies. The intelligence data a scout can pick up at trade shows may range from privileged gossip overheard on the floor to unexpected details prompted by the camaraderie of interested consumers talking with enthusiastic salespeople. These opportunities frequently produce informal data that is very illuminating and usually not accessible from other sources. Most scouts do not go to trade shows just to pick up the literature!

Meetings, conferences, conventions, and workshops are also good sources of information. Even if a scout is unable to attend or participate in a meeting devoted to the field of interest, the meeting's proceedings can offer much useful information. Full text articles of presentations, panel discussions, or workshops can usually be purchased from the sponsors of most of these events. Even if the material published after-the-fact includes presentation abstracts only, they still will indicate whom to contact to obtain more detailed information. Often the promotional material for meetings held in years past can prove an invaluable resource for the names and addresses of knowledgeable or expert contacts for interviews. Contacting these speakers can be especially good for obtaining current information—even information that has been under wraps or that has not yet been released to the general public. Meeting promotions frequently include a list of exhibitor firms that can be used to identify major companies involved in the field.

PATENT SEARCH

A hands-on patent search of the classes and subclasses related to the objective can be an extremely productive means of obtaining information on technology that originated from a large corporation. In many cases, a firm develops a new technology and files a patent, but for one reason or another, the innovation is not commercialized and is left "on the shelf." The corporation's patent counsel can usually indicate the status of this technology. It may be available for license, or the rights may have been assigned to another firm. Sometimes one can locate spin-off firms or firms set up as management buy-outs that have been established with the rights to such patents. Occasionally, in an effort to downsize, a large firm may eliminate an entire R&D project or an entire engineering department involved in the development of a technology. The move may create a start-up firm that takes the technology with it.

GOVERNMENT SOURCES

So much information is available from federal sources that it would take many volumes to list and describe even a portion of what is available. The bulk of this information is provided as published text, but it is increasingly available in all kinds of information formats, from on-line resources to compact disks, videos and films, graphics, and lectures.

Government sources also transfer technology developed in national laboratories. Much of the advanced technology R&D under way today is either conducted in government laboratories or financed by federal funds, and all federal agencies are increasing efforts to bring these innovations to the private sector for commercialization.

Examples of important federal government sources include SBIR abstracts; data from the National Technical Information Service; the Departments of Commerce, Energy, Defense, Agriculture; the Environmental Protection Agency; the National Institutes of Health; national laboratories; congressional offices; the U.S. Patent Office; and others.

Examples of major state and county sources include the Office of the Secretary of State and the Department of Industrial Development, which often keeps directories of companies and technology involved in state SBIR programs. The state and county record offices (Registry of Deeds, corporate records, litigation, partnerships, etc.) are also important sources of technology and/or corporate information.

LOCAL SOURCES

Another useful means of tracking down an individual or firm in a distant location is to contact the public library in that city. Almost all cities and large towns have public libraries; the telephone company's directory assistance should be able to give you the library telephone number.

In most instances, a librarian can locate people, organizations, and companies in his or her area. City directory information can also provide the names, addresses, and telephone numbers of the nearest neighbors (businesses or residents). Sometimes these contacts are able to refer you to the new location of their former neighbors if that organization has moved. If the library does not hold local directories, you may be able to obtain the telephone number for the nearest library that does maintain such directories.

Once a firm's location has been established, a scout can learn much about it by making inquiries in the community. For example, it is often helpful to check court records (and interview clerks); review county or state deeds registry; check local newspapers (including editors and reporters); and contact local chambers of commerce. These sources often yield valuable information.

COMPANY DIRECTORIES

The best way to locate and/or obtain basic information on companies, regardless of size, is through a directory. This information is basic to scouting, and most scouts will have access to at least a small collection of directories, whether on-line, on disk, or in bound volumes. Depending on the need for such access, investment in these tools can run from modest to substantial. For the occasional search, most of the popular directories can be found in public libraries; others are accessible via on-line services.

Most directories are indexed by technology and, therefore, are a good place to start in monitoring specific fields. Such directory lists will provide some idea of company size and operations, along with location and contact information.

Directories focusing on special technologies are ideal. They seemed to proliferate about ten years ago, but these useful little niche industry publications have decreased in number in recent years. Evidently, the effort required to compile, publish, and update this information, especially in emerging technological fields, proved too costly. Hence, we see very few niche technology directories on library shelves nowadays.

Most of the trade periodicals devoted to particular fields still publish buyers' guides or product source directories as subscription supplements. More and more of the popular general business or manufacturers directories are being made available both on compact disk and in bound volumes.

Despite the downtrend in niche technology directories, the publication of directory information in general areas has surged. There are directories of on-line services information, directories of compact disks, directories of Internet resources, directories of computer software and hardware, directories of newsletters and statistical sources, and directories of reports in publication and of books and periodicals in print. There are directories of directories. Undoubtedly, there is a directory somewhere that lists who publishes the directories to consult in most technology scouting projects.

Pushed to make a choice of the six directories most useful in technology scouting, most scouts would probably list

- *The Federal Yellow Book* and *The Corporate Yellow Book* (Monitor Leadership)
- *Corporate Technology Directory* (CorpTech)
- *Register of American Manufacturers* (Thomas Publishing Company)
- *The Higher Education Directory* (Higher Education Publications, Inc.)
- *National Trade and Professional Associations of the United States* (Columbia Books).

LARGE CORPORATIONS

Large corporations are very useful sources of information on themselves, on their industries, and on various other industries that use their products.

In addition to financial data, the annual report of a publicly owned firm often contains considerable detail on the firm's goals, planning strategies, and philosophical and cultural climate. These reports also frequently include overview information on the company's technology and products, as well as occasional insights on the industry as a whole. Annual reports of many of our larger companies are worth the time taken to review in detail, particularly when the scouting project involves monitoring a field to obtain intelligence on how the industry is evolving.

A public company's quarterly reports (10-Q) and the annual 10-K report likewise provide specific information on a firm's financial condition and will describe its products or services, markets, distribution, parents, subsidiaries, properties, as well as provide names of executive officers and its directors.

Aside from the corporate information they provide in their annual reports, many large corporations are a huge resource for general or technical information. Most of these companies have technical support departments that will offer advice or information on their products or on the fields served by their products. Corning Science Products, for example, publishes general guides used in certain fields involving the use of their products. One of these, *General Guide for Cryogenically Storing Animal Cell Culture*, while somewhat out of date, offers valuable information on cryopreservation.

Quite a number of the large companies publish similar materials, either regularly or in comprehensive reports. Raytheon, for instance, publishes *Reliability Analysis News*, an excellent newsletter devoted to component analysis and materials evaluation. Information on such corporate technological publications and on related incidental data may be located by contacting a company's technical support centers, their publications division, or their public relations department (advisably in that order!).

Another example of large company information that may be a "hidden" source is *Dun & Bradstreet Looks at Business* and *Dun & Bradstreet Comments on the Economy*. These newsletters, which D&B Information Services used to publish with their now defunct *D&B Reports*, are now found monthly in the National Association of Credit Management's publication, *Business Credit*.

The knowledge and experience of many plant engineers at large firms should not be overlooked. Sometimes an engineer who has worked in the field with the technology in question can provide candid information that simply is not available from any published source. Similarly, laboratory technicians, purchasing directors, marketing directors, and sales representatives can also provide good information. Bear in mind, however, that such contributions usually cannot be attributed or documented. Nonetheless, these views have merit, and they can provide background, context, and direction for a search.

Another source of information on a field and/or a company may be found in the in-house newsletters many large corporations publish. These publications, especially past issues, can be somewhat more difficult to obtain, but a review of a past year or two may help reveal the corporate culture and suggest both corporate and technological trends.

SMALL COMPANIES

Small firms, too often overlooked in the past, are an enormous resource for new technology. Not only do they develop new technologies themselves, but they are also excellent sources of information about other small firms. Most keep up with their field and usually know about other organizations involved in similar or related technologies. If a small firm has gone public, the information presented in its prospectus can provide invaluable background on its primary technologies and markets.

Investment analysts' reports on small firms, as well as venture capitalists' reports, are also a good source of technological, company, and market information. CorpTech provides one of the best directories of high-technology firms, including a great many small firms that are producing widely diverse technologies.

UNIVERSITIES

University research often brings forth new technologies. One should bear in mind, however, that a university's primary role is to educate; therefore, much of the research conducted in universities is done for the purpose of educating. Because of the academic community's strong emphasis on publishing, many university research scientists prefer to publish rather than to patent. Also, it is not unusual for academic researchers to lose interest in a technology once the project has been completed and feasibility has been established.

The applied technology that is typically an outgrowth of university research is usually not fully developed or proven—more often than not, it is "embryonic." Prototypes are rare, and seldom is much thought given to how to apply research concepts commercially. Considerable investment is required to bring most university technology to market. Ora Smith, president and CEO of Illinois Superconductor Corporation is quoted as saying, "For every dollar spent on research, ten dollars need to be spent on development, and $100 on design and building" (Solomon 1993).

In spite of the nascent quality of university research, it must be emphasized that important concepts do evolve in this setting. For fast-changing fields, such as the life sciences, it is important to find technology at the early stage to make use of it at all. Although the pressure to develop new products is especially strong in the pharmaceutical industry, the average product development time is ten years. For many of the firms seeking new products, the time to begin looking at concept-stage research is now.

The pharmaceutical industry, more than most other industries, relies heavily on the basic research done in universities. Many pharmaceutical companies collaborate with universities on R&D, and this trend is on the upswing.

A Stanford University study, "American Universities and Technical Advance in Industry," reported universities and corporations complemented each other very well, with the universities contributing the "R" and the companies contributing the "D." (Rosenberg and Nelson 1993). The Industrial Research Institute also found in its study of industry-supported university research that such collaborations increased from $10.7 billion in 1989 to $81.3 billion in 1993. Such collaborations represented around 4 percent of academic research that was supported by industry in 1980. That support grew to almost 7 percent by 1993. Although a significant increase, this level of support still does not compare with the nearly 90 percent support of university research the U.S. government provides (Solomon 1993).

Under the University-Small Business Patent Act of 1980, universities obtained the right to patent inventions that result from federally funded research. This right brought with it, however, an obligation to promote commercialization of the patented innovations (Jenks 1993). The right to patent their research inspired many universities to quickly increase their patent filings and to investigate ways of stepping up their technology transfer activities. Some promoted commercialization of their research through technology transfer offices or departments within the university administration. Others chose to work with patent management groups, such as Research Technologies Corporation in Tucson, Arizona.

For technology scouting, university technology transfer departments serve as an organized information resource for university inventions. Most such departments publish catalogues of their holdings and will place the names of those interested in receiving them on their mailing lists. Reviewing these catalogues often proves rewarding. Some scouts may find it useful to join the Association of University Technology Managers (AUTM), which holds annual meetings, publishes its membership lists, and provides other member services.

Finding university research technologies that can be commercialized is becoming easier than ever before. On-line services and databases, such as Best America's Carter Mill and Knowledge Express, provide ready access to university and government research in progress, as well as profiles of researchers. Such access has its costs, however, and for scouts on a budget, more traditional means of locating information may have to suffice.

Access to university research can best be gained through a thorough literature review, followed by a targeted patent search of the field. An on-line search will indicate what is available and which journals should be surveyed. The review will also indicate the universities most likely to be involved in the research focus. University newsletters should be included in the literature review, as they often report developments in their field and their news is usually quite timely. Newspapers may also provide announcements of scientific breakthroughs. Background on research in progress and on those involved can often be found in the annual reports published by the departments or laboratories of most universities and research centers. These reports are usually available upon request at no charge.

Many of the scientists and/or students involved in university research are usually willing to share their knowledge and experience in an interview. Such interviews can provide useful data, guidance, or referrals available from no other source. Many professors are also available for consultation. Good scouting never underestimates the contribution these experts can make in setting up, rounding out, or moving forward a technology scouting project.

NETWORKING

Technology scouting projects, especially targeted projects, often involve creative prospecting in the field of interest. For information that is difficult to access, a good way to start is simply to talk with people working in the field.

Contact companies, university professors, consumers, or professionals. If the technology is animal-related, for example, talk to a veterinarian; if drug-related, to a pharmacist or physician. A scout who is looking for a small company in a specific field should talk with another small company working with similar technology, and so forth. Small companies are like a fraternity. Most are well aware of others in their field; they know which firms are newcomers and which are well established. They may even know which professor at which university is thinking of setting up a company based on his research.

Informal leads often yield the best results. For example, some time ago, in seeking the technology to produce a specific flavor, the author happened to talk to a young woman who was just starting an academic career in a southwestern university. The young woman mentioned that her previous mentor had been working on developing the desired flavor and referred the searcher to him at his New Jersey university. A call to the New Jersey professor paid off: the technology he had been working on was near-term, available, and exactly what was needed.

MISCELLANEOUS SOURCES

Other sources that should not be overlooked include technology transfer associations and groups; venture capital sources; initial public offerings; and incubators and incubator associations. Many associations conduct market research, collect statistics, provide membership directories, publish journals and newsletters, and will refer inquiries to member experts within the organization. Relevant associations can be located through the use of various association directories.

TECHNOLOGY SCOUTING IN THE FUTURE

> *"We must source the world, because the world is on fire with new technology!"*
>
> —Anonymous

As the world gets smaller and the pace of technological development advances at warp speed, it is clear that the future is now. We can perceive the impact of advancing technology on our lives just by reading the morning newspaper.

It seems as if all human knowledge has been captured electronically and disseminated across a wide spectrum of populations. The digital revolution is under way, forever changing the way we live. From now on, it is sink or swim in the information ocean. Given the explosion of new information technologies, then, what will technology scouting be like in the future?

THE SCOUTING ENVIRONMENT

Despite rapid changes in the information industry, the forces driving future technological scouting expeditions are not likely to change because firms will still be driven by the same need to stay abreast of developments in their fields. However, the future may see greater emphasis on competitive intelligence. Indeed, the inevitable explosion of new technology should make the need to achieve competitive advantage even more pronounced. Because the workplace will be redefined, strategies used to pursue information must also inevitably be redefined.

Scouts will travel less in thc future. Business travel can be very expensive and time-consuming, and many corporations are trying to reduce the number of meetings in distant locations. The obvious benefits of face-to-face encounters will continue, but such meetings will likely take place via desktop video. Future corporate conferring will rely more on electronic communications than on face-to-face contact. Tomorrow's telecommunications promise to be more efficient, more cost-effective, and more widely linked to the home/office computer. A universal surge in teleconferencing should bring with it a decrease in worker mobility; as a result, scouting will become more homebound.

Whether the advent of easy access to visual communications and a plethora of multimedia will bring about the demise of trade shows and related technology marketing events remains to be seen. Certainly many of today's seminars and workshops could be effectively captured on disk and disseminated through the media, which would provide an efficient and fairly dramatic landscape for future scouts to review.

While large electronic catalogues of available new technology would offer access to much more secondary information more efficiently and at far less cost than trade shows, many scouts would doubtless regret losing the opportunity for personal interaction that trade shows provide. This is especially true since much of the real intelligence gained at some of today's shows is obtained through "informal" means, such as overheard conversations and imprudent remarks made by enthusiastic sales and marketing representatives at various exhibits. It will be hard to pick up such inadvertent disclosures on a compact disk.

As technology advances, the hardware for accessing information will become smaller, more compact, and more affordable. Such improvements in electronic access to information could mean a shift in emphasis on the importance of primary data over secondary source information, although both sources will continue to play important roles in the foreseeable future. There may be so much secondary information available, in fact, that special agencies may be needed to sort and analyze large volumes of information.

Despite the many advances in technology that will facilitate future technology scouting endeavors, the fundamental methods used now to obtain information will probably not change significantly. Secondary source information will still lead to primary source contacts and to networking opportunities. Advanced technology will simply make it easier to access rapidly increasing volumes of information. Eventually, desk research done in special libraries today will be virtually eliminated.

In time, "hands on" research may refer to the keyboard or the touch screen. Even that may become dated, and we will find ourselves in a world of voice command or perhaps even the virtual experience of links we have yet to imagine.

The emergence of the *"virtual corporation"* has implications for technology scouting. In the virtual corporation, several companies specializing in different aspects of product development or commercialization unite to produce and market a single product. For example, a virtual corporation may consist of a design firm, a contract manufacturer, a sales and marketing firm, and perhaps a firm handling warehousing and delivery. All of the companies remain separate entities; their united activity need not be formalized to operate under a corporate link or umbrella.

This phenomenon is largely a result of the home offices and cottage industries which have proliferated since the early 1990s. The next several years will see an increase in the number of virtual corporations and "anywhere" offices. Undoubtedly, the informal nature of these enterprises will present a challenge to scouts seeking information on them. If the practice takes hold, virtual corporations will constitute a new direction in competitive and technological intelligence gathering.

Outsourcing, or the contracting out of jobs, projects, administrative functions, and even whole departments, has evolved from a mere phenomenon in the early 1990s to a full-fledged trend in the mid-1990s. By the turn of the century (if not before), outsourcing of many corporate operations will likely be the norm. When this happens, scouting may be conducted by smaller, specialized firms reporting to corporate clients more frequently than is currently the case.

ACCESSING INFORMATION

Access to information will increase, but so will the challenges of targeting the intelligence sought. A scout's skill may be ultimately distilled to a consummate ability to mastermind games. Technology to efficiently access information on tomorrow's technology will be crucial. With the tremendous amount of data that will be available to us globally, Boolean logic may prove too cumbersome to be useful. New techniques or algorithms may be needed to handle the search. Perhaps robotic searchers can be programmed to roam future neuronets, constantly seeking and retrieving data.

The challenge will be equally great for handling the data once it is retrieved. Even now, there is a critical gap in the amount of data we can collect and the amount we can use. For example, throughout the 1970s and 1980s, NASA collected an enormous amount of satellite data, some of which appeared to indicate the existence of a hole in the ozone layer above Antarctica. As this event seemed rather unlikely, NASA discounted the data, attributing the apparent hole to the angle of the sun. Eventually, however, a team of British scientists, looking up from their camp on the Antarctic ice, confirmed the validity of the satellite data (Achenbach 1994). In the future, we may well build understanding on information fractals and base decisions on neural net software.

Virtual reality, now in its infancy, may someday replace the actual experience of reality. As graphic images stimulate visual senses, other electronic impulses may be able to stimulate our senses of touch, taste, and smell. When this technology matures, the way we learn about everything will be greatly changed. Scientists in Tokyo and Seattle recently met at a virtual conference table somewhere in cyberspace between the two cities to manipulate electronic objects in a point-to-point virtual reality exercise. James Boudreux, program manager in simulation-based design for General Dynamics Corporation's Electric Boat Division was quoted as saying, "What they are doing is not trivial" (Richards 1994).

Owing to the recent advances in virtual reality, we can expect this medium will not only change the way we design and build aircraft and ships, but will also enhance training of workers in almost any discipline or trade. Everyone, from surgeons and pilots to chefs and machinists will benefit from virtual training. Virtual reality will bring the world to our desktop.

Cyberspace conferencing in time will become the norm. Trade shows and meetings that draw crowds for sales, social, and academic purposes today may go the way of the 18th century market days and county fairs, eventually disappearing. Future technology scouts may find information on technology introduced in trade shows held in near-time on compact disks and later on-line in cyberspace.

Compact disks and the whole world of multimedia are quite new. But, as with the VCR, these information gems will soon be everywhere, bringing the world's libraries, museums, and information repositories to our fingertips. CDs will soon teach, inform, diagnose, and entertain us in ways we never dreamed possible. Everything from maps to training manuals will be available on disk.

In effect, CDs represent storage technology. For now, they enable us to quickly transport large amounts of data that can be accessed repeatedly over a period of time. As such, they are ideal for storing certain kinds of information, such as art collections and encyclopedias.

The problem with CDs is that the information they contain becomes quickly outdated, and the disk must be replaced with a newer version. Data used by stock analysts, database information, newspaper and periodical abstracts, for example, all require regular updating. Perhaps future updates will be done through on-line downloads, rewriting the disks, the way some software is updated through the Internet now.

Despite the drawback of providing dated information, CDs provide an invaluable means of information-sharing, and use is skyrocketing. Federal and state governments are finding CDs particularly useful for getting information to the public. Everything that has been compiled over the years in federal and state agencies and archives—from vital records to deed registries to site maps, street maps and GIS data—soon will be available to the public on CDs in libraries or on home personal computers.

The government is not alone in its drive to publish large amounts of information. Medical and health care publishers will soon put their books on CDs. Similarly, corporate publishers are putting training manuals, catalogues, and documentaries of all kinds on disk.

The decline of CDs will probably begin when huge repositories of centralized databanks become accessible to everyone at the flick of the wrist or at a voice command. When all the information on CDs becomes available to the home television/computer screen with a simple command, interest in purchasing CDs for information or entertainment will most likely decline. Until this occurs, however, CDs will remain a significant source of information for the technology scout.

The *fax-on-demand* is still with us, although more and more of the information that was available through this source is now found on the Internet. Until the world really does go paperless, however, fax-on-demand technology will probably continue to provide some information to scouts. Both federal and state government information, however, is increasingly headed toward the Internet. Indeed, so much information is now Internet-focused that the future of this resource has become a question to most forecasters. Until the Internet takes over, however, information of many kinds will yet be found on the remarkably efficient "fax-on-demand" systems.

SOME FINAL THOUGHTS ABOUT TECHNOLOGY SCOUTING

Successful technology transfer involves people as well as technology. Initially, even the most improved mousetraps often need champions to convince skeptical or frugal managers of the worth of technology developed off-site. And supervision is still essential to production once the technology has been accepted. Knowledgeable people will be needed to train personnel to work with the innovation or to produce the product. In many instances, the licensor will probably require consultation or assistance in the eventual commercialization or marketing of the new product.

It is also vitally important to consider objectively how well the scout and/or the project coordinator can communicate with the user—often the department head who initiated the search—in order to bring back the needed data. There are arrogant scouts who do not know how to listen, and unfocused users who cannot articulate their needs. A scout has to earn the trust of the user. He or she can best do this by bringing useful information back in a friendly, manageable, and timely way.

A common misconception is that a person needs to be an expert in a specific field in order to become a successful scout. A scout needs only to be expert in the field of scouting, but scouting skills must be acquired. A would-be scout must have an innate curiosity, an interest in what he or she is doing, and great determination and tenacity. Although plenty of tools are available to facilitate the research, scouting takes energy and commitment. A scout needs to enjoy the challenge of finding information. If a person possesses this drive, he or she will excel in the field.

Sometimes a scout must take the information found and use judgment in submitting a report. For example, in seeking insect control technology, one soon learns that some pheromones attract ticks. Pesticide dips have been developed using this technology. But using the dips in developing countries may not be wise, since workers in these countries may not be knowledgeable enough to handle mixing the bath. Should a company put more money into this? The main issue here is not whether the technology itself is effective, but rather, is it appropriate for the intended situation? This is a good example of the need to develop clear definitions and parameters for a scouting project before plunging in.

More information is available today than has ever been available in recorded history. Even so, unless the technology scout knows how to retrieve the information and the user can interpret the data and champion its use, the information is worthless, the effort in vain.

In a report on a study his firm conducted to assess the value of competitive intelligence, Myles Kelly, of the *Marketing Audit,* observed that "a diversified chemicals respondent once said, 'for CI to have value, it must be linked to business decisions or strategic planning. Without the linkage, nothing would have any monetary value.'" He went on to say, "initially, CI seemed expensive, but historically, the CI function has enhanced decisions that were made three years prior and are profitable now. We are involved with long term opportunity decision-making" (Kelly 1993).

While *Marketing Audit*'s study was not quantitative, its interviews of 21 corporations ranging in size from $2 million to $65 billion in revenues did shed some light on an area many have questioned, especially since all respondents reported at least a 100 percent return on investment with an average payback for all projects being 310 percent of cost. Again, Kelly maintains that CI "recommendations must be integrated into a decision in order to attempt assigning a value or payback" (Kelly 1993).

Does tomorrow's explosion of new technologies mean that scouts will have to specialize in a limited number of fields and become trained in the technical and linguistic aspects associated with their specialties? Probably not. Scouting is a very specialized skill that, once mastered, enables a capable scout to access any field—new or old.

Perhaps the greatest challenge future technology scouts will face is not how to find information, but how to chart a trail through vast amounts of it. Future scouts may need to develop a sixth sense that will enable them to track, target, and hone in on the intelligence defined by the mission. And, as scouts become more dependent on expert systems and neural nets to analyze data and focus a search, users will become more reliant on sophisticated decision science techniques to use the intelligence tomorrow's scouts return.

The benefits of the information revolution are clear; but there are risks that must be considered by those who scout information and those who use it. "Net surfing" as Internet exploring has been called, may become a veritable addiction for some. No doubt, there are those who are seriously concerned with this possibility.

Perhaps it is a risk, but the greater risk may be that the coming information revolution will put some cherished civil liberties at risk: our right to privacy may be sacrificed to our stronger need to know. Data security risks are already becoming a paramount concern for many companies or people involved with the future of the Internet. Will the need for corporate security ultimately be sacrificed to a stronger need to access information?

REFERENCES

Achenbach, J. October 26, 1994. What on earth is NASA up to? *The Washington Post*, p. C1.

Alberthal, L. 1992. The Black Box Paradox. *Chief Executive*, pp. 24-27.

Bodelle, J. and C. Jablon. 1993. Science and Technology Scouting at Elf Aquitaine. *Research-Technology Management* 36(5):24-28.

Brenner, M. S. 1992. Technology Scouting at Air Products. *les Nouvelles* 27(4):185-189.

Brody, A. L., T. C. Cook, R. Lawrence, and R. Luciano. March 31, 1993. Four Forces Driving Food Packaging: Packaging by the Numbers. *Packaging* 38(4):10-16.

Jenks, A. Summer 1993. Bringing University Research to the Corporate Desktop. *Technology Transfer Business*, pp. 57, 58.

Kelly, M. P. November 1993. Assessing the Value of Competitive Intelligence. *The Journal of the Association for Global Strategic Information* 2(3):104-112. Published by Infonortics, Ltd., 9A High Street Calne, Wiltshire, S.N. 11 OBS, United Kingdom.

Richards, B. November 16, 1994. Test of Virtual Reality Spans the Pacific. *The Wall Street Journal*, p. B1.

Rosenberg, N., and R. Nelson. 1993. *American Universities and Technical Advance in Industry*. Stanford University Center for Economic Policy Research, Palo Alto, California.

Solomon, A. K. Fall 1993. R&D Also Means Reconcilable Differences. *Technology Transfer Business*, pp. 31-33.

Wolff, M. F. 1992. Scouting for Technology. *Research-Technology Management* 35(2):10-22.

ENDNOTES

1. For additional information on on-line services, see Andrew Kantor, Making On-Line Services Work for You, *PC Magazine*, March 15, 1994, and Joanna Pearlstein, Macworld's Guide to Online Services, *Macworld*, August 1994.
2. See also G.B. Newby. 1994. *Directory of Directories on the Internet*. Meckler Publishing, Westport, Connecticut.
3. Two excellent references on bulletin boards are *Online Users' Encyclopedia, Bulletin Boards and Beyond* (Addison Wesley, New York, 1994) and Washington Online, How to Access the Government's Electronic Bulletin Boards, *Congressional Quarterly*, Washington, D.C., 1995.

Computer Support Systems for Scientific and Technical Intelligence

BONNIE HOHHOF

With the widespread availability and (relative) cost-effectiveness of computers, competitive intelligence functions have significantly increased their use of this tool to handle and distribute information. This activity is especially prevalent in the scientific and technical fields, where most of the participants are already information- and technology-literate. In addition, the current management practices of forming teams, reengineering, and flattening the organization have emphasized the need to quickly move information from where it exists to where it is needed.

Virtually all information is now produced in computer readable formats somewhere along its production process. The use of faxes, videos, voicemail, teleconferencing, imaging, optical character readers, and other technologies are becoming increasingly sophisticated in business organizations with a corresponding need to capture this information and place it in one integrated system. Worldwide networks such as the Internet also encourage information transfer.

Even with this technological advancement, the issues and problems facing effective information transfer in the competitive technological environment still focus on the basic problem of getting the right information to the right person at the right time.

AN INTELLIGENCE SYSTEM

Competitive technical intelligence is a subset of a competitive intelligence (CI) system, the organizational process for systematically collecting, processing, analyzing and distributing information about an organization's external environment to the people who need it. Such a process organizes the flow of critical information and focuses it on issues and decisions.

The CI system may track

- Competitor capabilities, plans, and intentions
- Markets and customers
- Industry structure and trends
- Political, economic, and social forces
- Technological developments and sources (the focus of this book).

The essence of any CI system is its contribution to better and more timely decisions. Its primary objectives are to help decision-makers avoid surprises from the competitive environment and identify current and potential threats and opportunities. In the technical area, this system often supports project and scientific funding decisions and helps scientific decision-makers calculate the relative strengths of a competitor's research and technology.

The CI system is built upon three separate, yet interdependent activities: analysis, collection (primary information), and information sources (secondary or print information). The broader and most basic activity is information services, which focuses on identifying, retrieving, and distributing information (primarily published information).

This service is often provided by an individual with an information background who is either on the CI staff or in the organization's library. For competitive technical intelligence systems, this person also has a technical background complementary or equal to the group he or she serves.

The collection activity obtains information from primary sources, usually an individual. This individual may be an employee of the company or a specialist in another company, consulting group, university, or government agency. Primary information collection requires an extensive knowledge of interviewing techniques and the ability to develop and maintain a personal information network. Effective collectors in the technological intelligence area usually have technical backgrounds tempered with experience in journalistic or investigative areas.

INTELLIGENCE INFORMATION

Intelligence information is data about an organization's external environment compiled through a focused, continuous collection process. This information comes from both internal and external information sources and is analyzed in concert with the organization's internal data. In most situations, both primary (person) and secondary (print) information is collected. After analysis, this intelligence information provides as complete and accurate an understanding of the external environment as possible.

In the competitive technology areas, pairing of the primary and secondary information sources is particularly crucial. On one hand, the scientific and technical literature has a long shelf life, particularly when compared with other areas such as marketing, pricing, and other competitive actions. Also, scientists and technologists have a cultural bias toward sharing information through the published literature. Many scientific and technology trends can be tracked effectively over time, and their appearance can be readily identified and verified. However, there is an inherent time delay with published information, often measured in months and even years.

On the other hand, much technological information never appears in the published literature or trade press. Top individuals often are too busy to publish, or their technology changes so quickly that anything appearing in the established journals is out of date by the time it appears. In addition, much technological information falls into the area of trade or competitive secrets, and companies spend considerable time and effort blocking distribution of that information outside the company.

COMPETITIVE INFORMATION SYSTEMS

The key to a successful implementation of competitive information systems is facilitating the systematic collection and distribution of intelligence information. This function is often defined as computerizing the process. Computer support systems play several roles in the intelligence function:

- Provide access to secondary (print) competitive information for both intelligence systems analysts and intelligence system users
- Identify and distribute primary (person-sourced) information
- Organize competitive information for retrospective retrieval and provide access to other internal information sources
- Facilitate the intelligence analysis process
- Distribute competitive intelligence products to system users.

Before an effective computerized competitive information system (CIS) can be developed, several key areas must be understood. The two areas most overlooked in system development are understanding the existing information flow and adequately defining key customers' information requirements.

UNDERSTANDING THE EXISTING INFORMATION FLOW

A good CIS works with the existing information systems in an organization wherever they may be—the executive suite, the marketing department, regional sales offices, research and development, legal, etc. Many of these systems were designed largely to produce paper reports and support a differing set of management decisions needs. Thus, they are often difficult to work with. Early in the CIS design process, the designer must spend enough time to learn about these systems and to factor their capabilities and information into the final system design.

An organization's structure (or changing structure) often makes it difficult to identify all relevant systems, particularly across divisional or geographical lines. However, because the CIS requires access to all available competitive information, the designer must know where this business-critical information exists; where it travels; and, most important, who creates, controls, and uses it.

Before starting the CIS design, many organizations first complete an information audit. This audit identifies where information is created, modified, and transferred throughout the organization. It provides a "roadmap" of the current information infrastructure and information distribution. In addition, it often discovers how information use is affected by organizational and cultural hierarchies. Frequently the roadmap will help recognize the "information gatekeepers" of the organization, who are the primary information distributors among their peer group. These gatekeepers can provide invaluable help in identifying existing information sources.

DEFINING KEY CUSTOMERS' INFORMATION REQUIREMENTS

Because managers' decisions involve problems that are unstructured, complex, and influenced by other people, it is impossible to anticipate all their information needs. The more technical individuals also have highly specific and varied information needs and often rely on serendipity to identify important information unrelated to their primary research areas. As a result, most CIS include highly personalized search and browsing capabilities that extract information from a wide variety of sources. They allow users to filter the information they want through a set of criteria based on their individualized (and ever-changing) requirements.

System designers often attempt to identify and meet the information needs of all potential system users. They arrange system users into categories and rank the requirements of all the groups, then design a system. This process overlooks the political and organizational reality that some users are more equal than others and the functional reality that no new system can be all things to all people. A CIS that seeks to be effective initially must meet the information requirements of a select group of key users, then gradually expand its capabilities.

Most target CIS customers already consider themselves to be effective decision-makers using their own system of information gathering and analysis. Expect many to resist the idea of devoting their limited time and resources to learning a new system, even when they recognize the advantages the CIS could provide. The system must provide them with immediate and obvious advantages that justify their time expenditure. They will not use a system that offers only incremental advantages.

SYSTEM SUCCESS FACTORS

Many factors affect the design and ultimate success of a competitive information system. Several are obvious to those individuals versed in system design methodology, yet ignoring these factors frequently results in systems that are rejected by their target users. The following success factors were gleaned from research and analysis of the success and failure of numerous corporate systems.

- **The main factor affecting CIS design and operation is the organization's culture.**

  A competitive information system must support the operational and cultural changes taking place within a company, but it cannot force changes not already in progress. Many CIS failures are traced directly back to the conflict between the way the information is used and the way it is shared. This conflict sets up a culture that affects the success of the CIS.

  The organization's culture not only affects how the CIS is used, but how people contribute information to it. For example, a culture that allows information hoarding and does not reward information sharing cannot support a CIS. If information is valued only on its ability to support an individual's personal view or reinforce an existing decision, a CIS will not be effective.

  Individuals must already be making maximum use of the information currently available to them in various forms, including paper. Simply transferring that same information into an automated delivery system will not increase its use. If anything, changing the delivery vehicle will inhibit information transfer as its customers struggle with learning a new procedure. For example, if an organization is not making effective use of information obtained from current awareness searches on commercial databases, merely presenting that same information through a computer screen will not increase its use.

- **The project manager's attitude, efforts, and skills ultimately determine system success.**

  The CIS project manager bridges the worlds of competitive analysts, information processors, computer support, technical specialists, and decision-makers. He or she must understand the organization's key success factors, possess sound communications skills, and understand how information is used in the organization. Although CIS development often involves individuals from the company's information management groups, many innovative and comprehensive systems are created by non-information technology people. A competitive technical information system will often benefit from a project manager who has a technical background that is compatible with most of the system's users, but this is not an absolute requirement.

A successful project manager must

–Understand competitive analysis, information processing, and how decisions are made in the organization

–Have a personal commitment to the project's mission and vision

–Be able to determine what is important, why it is important, and to whom it is important.

- **High-level support, while essential, does not guarantee success.**

A developing CIS must have a senior management sponsor, usually at the vice-president level. Optimally all target users for the system should report to this person. He or she confers the high-level visibility, promotion, and patronage required to develop and maintain the project's focus and drive. This sponsor also supplies the support and resources necessary to successfully integrate the CIS into the organization's decision-making processes.

However, initial high-level support does not guarantee the system will succeed. Although no CIS will prosper without it, high-level sponsorship cannot compensate for deficiencies in planning, implementation, and end-user acceptance. For example, in one company, the CIS project had the visible and verbal support of the senior vice-president at the project's beginning. However, the vice-president assumed that his direct reports would also support this project and so did not require them to publicly promote the CIS within their own groups. As a result, the project did not receive adequate participation from several key user groups, and one vice-president actually disparaged the project to his staff. In retrospect, the CIS project manager felt that if he had urged the senior person to maintain continued active support after the project's inception, the CIS would have been significantly more successful.

The CIS project must also have sponsorship from a senior manager in the company's information services (or information systems) group. This person's support can make the entire project significantly simpler and more effective by ensuring the cooperation of his or her technical staff. The CIS project can be easily derailed by the lack of specific knowledge about the functioning of existing communication and computer systems and by ignorance of future information technology plans. In addition, because the CIS project (or at least interfaces with e-mail and groupware systems) will eventually be maintained by the organization's information systems staff, ensuring their participation early in the project will result in a more effective CIS.

- **A CIS delivers information relating to a decision, not merely more information.**

  A successful CIS project contains unique information relating to decisions facing the groups it supports. It must combine information gleaned from uncommon print sources and information obtained from knowledgeable individuals both within and without the organization. If it simply functions as a conduit for publicly available information, it will not be effective.

  Because information from commercial online text services is the simplest to obtain and distribute, many systems bring in external print information and simply redistribute it without any value-added organization, screening, or commentary. Often this creates the electronic equivalent of junk mail, particularly if newswires are included.

  Rarely, if ever, can an internal information system compete effectively with commercial services in providing cost-effective text information access. Frequently, a company will try to cost-justify a CIS by predicting significant reduction of their commercial online searching charges. If all system costs—including the personnel time for writing programs, information transfer, uploading, downloading, review and storage costs—are considered, an internal system is inevitably more costly. Often, a significant portion of these costs results from search efforts that duplicate each other; such costs can be reduced simply with better tracking of search topics and communication between individuals interested in the same topic.

External print information, however, does not cover all competitive information needs. For instance, much existing information about future technological possibilities is simply not published or appears in very specialized consulting reports. The people developing that technology are at the leading edge of their fields and do not have the time or motivation to publish. Also, many individuals and their companies do not want to publish their technological research because this could provide competitors with insight into their business strategies. This type of information is best obtained from knowledgeable individuals who have direct contact with these researchers.

- **Software is rarely the root cause of system failure.**

  The software on which the CIS was based usually receives the blame for system failure, even when it functions exactly as specified. More likely, the fault rests with the way in which the system was defined: the information flow the organization requires has not been accurately translated into a system.

  During the system design, the project team can easily become enamored with the software's capabilities, especially since the emphasis at that point in the project is to work with the technology to create a system. However, developers must resist the temptation to add functions simply because the software can support it. Otherwise, the final CIS will do a better job of showcasing the software's power than of meeting specific customer requirements.

  For a new CIS, the tendency is to develop a flawless system or at least a system that meets all the user requirements. An implicit assumption is that the system, once built, will not be altered. As a result, the design team spends much energy identifying all possible customer needs and evaluating all the options. Not only does this consume considerable time, but it can delay the delivery of any part of the project so long that the project team's enthusiasm is dulled and key clients loose interest.

  Most successful systems implement their capabilities in phases, starting with the simplest and most effective part. If basic customer needs have been defined, focus groups listened to, and environmental restrictions identified, the system will meet its key objectives.

CIS goals must be objectively ranked based on the users affected and on the relative importance of the goals to the business. The system then delivers on the top goals of the top users and phases in remaining requests. In some cases, the lower-ranked goals may never be implemented.

- **The system's value-added contributions must be defined in terms of the target audience's goals.**

  "The system passed all acceptance tests, but they (the users) will not use it." This statement often rings true when, after initial interviews with system customers, the project team creates its own assumptions on how the users will react to specific system design and capabilities. Worse, the project team begins to assume that the target customer goals and requirements coincide with their own views and experiences.

  The success of any new system depends heavily on how well the system developers understand their key customers and how well these customers understand the best way to use intelligence information. The system's primary and secondary customers—who may or may not be the end users of the information or intelligence provided through the system—need to be precisely identified and their individual requirements specified. The composition and demands of this group will also change over the life of the system, as the intelligence function becomes enmeshed in the normal decision-making processes of the organization.

  Although the CIS supports better and more informed decisions, it competes with other demands on the target audience's time and resources. Many will find it difficult to set aside the time needed to learn a new system. Often they are also being forced to learn several new computer systems (e-mail, groupware, Windows, etc.) and are suffering from the computer equivalent of jet lag. The CIS must provide a substantial and short-term return on their investment in time and effort; otherwise, the target audience simply will not use it.

- **A realistic budget includes system maintenance and information-gathering costs.**

  The ultimate value of a CIS should be measured against the total system cost. When the project is being funded, reasonable estimates should be included for all the system's development, maintenance, and information-gathering costs. System maintenance costs will continue to increase after the CIS is released—all systems (if they are used) will be expanded and enhanced over their lifetime. At a minimum, any computerized system requires at least one full-time equivalent to maintain it. In many cases, this responsibility is divided between a systems person and an information person.

At the onset of a project, it is tempting to minimize the expense, and the easiest way to do this is to ignore ongoing information and maintenance costs. However, this approach is certain to cause significant problems, even leading to cancellation of the project's rollout. For example, one company spent considerable time and expense to develop a comprehensive competitive information system for both their marketing and research groups. When it was time to roll out the system, there was no budget for "stocking" the system with information, and no department was willing to fund a person to maintain it.

TECHNICAL DEVELOPMENTS

The rising sophistication of computer software and the falling cost of computer hardware has fueled the use of automated information retrieval systems to support many management support processes, including competitive intelligence. The increased sophistication of end users and the burgeoning availability of information has also increased the acceptance of competitive information systems.

BACKGROUND

Prior to the early 1980s, mainframe computers dominated all corporate and information computing. In a company, all data were collected, analyzed, and distributed from a mainframe network managed by a centralized information technology or information services department. These groups were the gatekeepers of information. They determined what information would be collected and how; how the information would appear to the user; where the information would be distributed; and who would have access to it.

A major benefit of this system was that everyone worked from the same files, which were gathered and organized under the same processes and procedures. If individuals had access to the centralized mainframes, they had access to all the organization's computerized information.

When personal computers (PCs) began appearing in the early 1980s, electronic information gathering, analyzing, and distribution became decentralized. Critical information was now stored on PCs. More sophisticated and powerful PCs eroded the mainframe's advantages of memory capacity, speed, storage, and available software.

Advances in the late 1980s centered on networking and communications tools, primary local area networks, modems, and client-server architecture. Information technology groups began linking individual PCs and reconnecting them into the corporate mainframe structure. This development permits analysts to use the information as they wish and simplifies data collection throughout the organization. Client-server architecture is being promoted as the solution to the earlier fragmentation and decentralization of corporate data. Many organizations are implementing client-server networks to "reconnect" users.

However, in many instances the client-server hardware development has outpaced available software. Now that companies have determined what can be done, they are wrestling with how to do it. One recent outcome is the emerging popularity of groupware, whose central purpose is to inform or coordinate people. Currently, groupware has many different definitions and can include variations on group-scheduling programs, workflow automation, e-mail, conferencing, and shared-knowledge systems.

TEXT SYSTEMS

The original text-handling systems that historically formed the basis of many CIS programs arose from government-funded research in the late 1970s. Unlike the prevalent structured databases where all data were placed in rigid files, text was placed in unstructured records. Retrieval was by directly matching words and phrases through Boolean logic (and/or). Large text files could be quickly searched by using inverted word indexes (alphabetical list of individual words that included pointers to the specific records containing these words). Most of the software for large commercial online information systems such as DIALOG, Dow Jones, NEXIS, etc., are based on this inverted file search software.

Few major advances in search software have been made since then. Many of the current text search softwares used for CIS include enhancements that promote particular capabilities, often by developing specific terms and definitions. Retrieval speed has increased, and searching can be linked to custom thesauri or topic trees. Several systems allow searchers to "relevance rank" search output by the frequency of the searched terms in the text or to "weigh" certain search terms as being more important than others. "Fuzzy" or fault-tolerant searching, an outgrowth of optical character recognition software, allows information to be retrieved even when the search terms are misspelled.

Natural language processing principles are also being supported by several software systems. These systems provide

- Morphological analysis—the ability to match terms such as "mouse" and "mice"
- Syntactic analysis—giving insight into the relationship between words and, thus, their meaning
- Semantic analysis—resolving the different meanings of a single word such as "plant."

FILTERING AND AGENT SOFTWARE

With the increased availability of electronic information, automatic filtering of information becomes more important and feasible. Science and technology organizations generate large amounts of information internally in addition to the external printed sources such as journals, proceedings, and technical reports. The sheer volume makes it difficult to identify the small fraction of information actually relevant to any particular person. Filtering and intelligent agent software is one response to the problem of winnowing valuable information while minimizing time spent searching through irrelevant information.

Automatic filtering of information is based on a user-defined model of interests. This model is based on a set of descriptive words, but can also include input from past or current articles the person has found valuable. Complicating the matching of personal interests is the effect of factors such as familiarity, novelty, or urgency in predicting the usefulness of the retrieved information. Conventional text information retrieval is very closely related to filtering in that they both have the goal of retrieving what the searcher wants. In fact, filtering may simply be an application of the more sophisticated text search capabilities (such as ranking, topic trees, and query by example) applied to streams of incoming data rather than to an existing database.

Intelligent agent or personal agent software is being touted as the next wave of dealing with information overload. It automatically searches large databases and alerts users to variations that can affect their business. The programs look for patterns and focus on reporting exceptions to patterns, or "monitoring by exception."

Intelligent agent software applications appear in their purest form when monitoring large numerical databases. When applied to searching text, "agent software" is often no more than sophisticated current awareness or customized, profile-based information delivery. For example, a common definition of personal agent software is "delivery of personalized information from electronic mail systems and commercial services."

THE NEXT SOFTWARE PARADIGM

New technology will also be derived from government-funded research. Government intelligence agencies are facing increased pressure to provide information to help U.S. companies become more competitive.

The demand to provide more information to more people has also fueled the growth of more sophisticated retrieval systems. Ongoing software development focuses on providing information users with more complex tools to sharpen search results and allowing them direct information access.

One new technology area is context vectors. Context vectors represent text and queries as vectors in a multidimensional space, the dimensions being the words in the text. Queries and text vectors are compared; the more similar a text vector is to the query vector, the more relevant that text is to the query. Vectors for words with similar meanings will point in the same direction. Terms or dimensions of a query can be weighted by their importance, computed by the statistical distribution of terms in the database and text. This system can learn relationships between words in a specific discipline from a training text, then exploit these relationships for better precision and recall in text processing.

Another technology area being researched by the TIPSTER program (sponsored by the Defense Advanced Research Projects Agency) is text extraction or message understanding software. Developed from finite state automata research, this software analyzes the content of a document, extracts lists of information from it, and places that information into a structured database. It is effective for scanning text where only a fraction of the textual information is relevant. Information is mapped into a predetermined, relatively simple, rigid file—the subtle nuances of meaning and the writer's goals are of no interest. Message extraction applications include tracking joint ventures, keeping managers current with a minimal investment of their time. This type of system could also be applied to technology transfer agreements and technological developments.

THE INTERNET

Any current review of competitive information systems must make mention of the impact of the Internet development. Aside from the potential expansion of information sources, the Internet has had the major effect of stimulating research and software programs to make information searching and handling easier and more effective. Companies can make money on this development—rather than sales being limited to a select few information searchers or companies, they now have the large potential audience of all Internet users.

Individuals, who have either avoided the complexities of searching large databases by relying on intermediary searches or have not been aware of the depth and breath of knowledge existing in these text systems, are now plunging directly into information databases available on the Internet. They are demanding simpler graphical interfaces and the ability to quickly search across many information sources. In addition, developing increasingly sophisticated search programs and distributing them at low or no cost has almost become a issue of honor for graduate programming students at the leading universities.

In many cases, initial Internet exploration has elevated demand for access to more sophisticated text information within companies and has increased the need for personalized search support. After the first flush of exploration and discovery, many Internet users find it is a more efficient use of their time to support the development of in-house information search intermediaries, often sophisticated "cybrarians."

TYPES OF SOFTWARE SYSTEMS

The text-handling software to support competitive information needs falls into several overlapping categories. Most of these systems were originally developed to serve the specific software requirements first defined by government intelligence agencies and company information technology departments. Over time, they have evolved into applications to meet the basic text needs of the business end user.

Text-handling software can be grouped into six general categories, loosely defined by the environment in which they were designed to operate:

- Information routers
- PC-based software
- Document managers
- Analytical support
- Full text managers
- Imaging systems.

Each type serves specific competitive information interests. In any given situation, these software programs can be applied individually or linked into a common system to support the organization's competitive information needs.

INFORMATION ROUTERS

This wildly expanding service group supplies "filters" that extract pre-defined information from a continuous information feed or a time-defined set of new information sources. Based on a self-defined user profile, these systems sift out a word-restricted set of information documents from newswire feeds, online text sources derived from print publications, and original research papers. The programs differ in the breadth of information sources scanned, the design complexity of the profile, and the way the information is delivered and displayed to the user. Two of the better known services are Hoover (Sandpoint Corporation) and NewsEDGE (Desktop Data).

One of the first information router programs, Hoover, eliminates the need to learn the individual search interfaces of all the different information vendors, such as NEXIS, DIALOG, and Dow Jones. Once a simple search statement form is filled out, it is automatically run against specified commercial databases. The principal customer for this program is any person whose job is to analyze and synthesize information.

NewsEDGE monitors and organizes into a local database stories from as many as 20 live-feed newswires delivered by X.25 line, FM broadcast, or satellite transmission. When incoming stories match word- and phrase-based profiles, they are tagged and downloaded to the user's PC. NewsEDGE organizes news for use throughout an organization and is particularly useful for individuals who require up-to-the minute coverage of events.

Over the last two years more than six additional services have entered the market. Several focus on specific types or sources of information such as newspapers (Dow Jones) or individual information files (Dun & Bradstreet). All provide personalized information summaries based on information profiles and are delivered by fax, e-mail, and PC-download.

Few information router services cover technical information sources exclusively, but can be effectively used to supplement the analyst's own information-scanning processes. They often provide an information feed for internally maintained text databases, developed on other text-handling software such as TOPIC (Verity, Inc.).

PC-BASED SOFTWARE

The largest group of full text-handling software provides both stand-alone PC and networked access to information. Fueled by the increased processing power and exponential growth in low-cost large disk storage, the PC-based software primarily manages the text information resident on an individual's or department's computers. This information may have been downloaded from commercial information sources, created by the competitive intelligence group, or distributed by the organization's e-mail system.

Over 14 text-handling programs are currently available for the PC, and a quick scan of the popular PC magazines will probably turn up more. All have basic Boolean text-searching capabilities and most include proximity, relevancy ranking, and query-by-example searching. Several of the more popular programs are askSAM (askSAM Systems), Personal Librarian (Personal Librarian Software) and ZyIndex (ZyLab). These programs effectively organize and locate text information in a desktop or department environment and can be a simple way to handle the internal information-handling needs of a competitive analysis group.

DOCUMENT MANAGERS

Document management software has been a mainstay of publishing groups in an organization, such as specifications, legal, product literature, proposal and contract development, and technical documentation. First developed to handle large blocks of internally generated information, document management software focused on providing document integrity, publishing capabilities, and security, as well as handling document revisions and archiving.

These system have gradually developed and integrated the text processing and searching capabilities that make them appropriate for handling competitive information. Document managers are particularly suited for integrating internal and external information and often are supported by capable internal staff. FolioViews (Folio Corporation), Keyfile (Keyfile Corporation), and WorldView (Interleaf, Inc.) are some of the leading programs in this field.

ANALYTICAL SUPPORT

Several software programs provide varying degrees of support for the competitive analytical function. Some are applications originally designed for benchmarking, strategic planning, and military analysis. All use information feeds from other text programs and integrate closely with additional software packages. Selecting analytical support packages is a very personalized choice and most closely reflects the background and training of the individual analysts. Virtually all major strategy and planning consulting firms offer their own analytical support packages. WINCITE and Business Insight are two of the many widely available systems.

WINCITE (Braun Technologies Inc.) focuses on providing structured information and text in a format that directly supports the competitive analysis activities of a company. It supports both structured and text information and has a wide following of business analysts and benchmarking personnel. WINCITE is often used in conjunction with other text and specialized data software packages.

Business Insight is a rules-based system that allows the user to make a qualitative evaluation of multiple scenarios. Its primary purpose is to help business managers evaluate their own businesses by providing a model of the competitive marketplace. Through its ability to display the logic that created specific market conclusions, the product allows the user to understand how those conclusions were generated and how different interpretations of competitor capabilities will affect market outcomes.

FULL TEXT MANAGERS

The full text manager software products provide an integrated approach to handling and retrieving textual information throughout an organization. These packages are often complete systems whose capabilities can be applied to any department that has a need to effectively handle text information files. They all support the searching functionalities commonly available through the online text databases (Boolean logic, proximity searching, relevancy ranking, query-by-example) and operate over a wide range of computer platforms and networks.

These systems often provide the underlying text information repository databases that are filled by the information routers and extracted from by the analytical software programs. They can provide full document manager functions and often are used by the entire organization to handle all of the text information, regardless of its origin. These systems are usually integrated with available e-mail systems and have extensive internal and external programming support. Some of the more widely known full text information managers are BASISPlus (Information Dimensions Inc.), Search-Tools (Fulcrum Technologies Inc.), and TOPIC (Verity Inc.).

BASISPlus is a full feature system which runs on a wide variety of software and hardware systems, from a low-end PC server to Unix systems and to IBM and VAX mainframes. It provides full interactive searching, thesaurus and image linking, and maintains native word-processing formats. One of the original text processing software systems, BASISPlus has made an effort to keep its technology current and to improve system flexibility.

SearchTools, a suite of text-retrieval tools based on structured query language (SQL), enables users to search structured and unstructured textual information across the corporate enterprise. It provides a unified approach to integrating text into the standard data-management environment and operates in an open, client-server, multi-platform computing environment. The intuitive search capability provides exceptionally flexible searching.

TOPIC is specifically designed to work in a heterogeneous distributed network—multi-vendor networked environments such as DOS, OS/2, Unix, VMS, and Macintosh. Its distributed architecture supports databases from workgroups in local area networks to corporate-wide systems in wide area networks (WAN). TOPIC treats words and phrases as concepts, using a Topic Tree structure to define the hierarchical relationship between subtopics, words, and phrases. TOPIC provides the full text-searching capability in Lotus Notes.

A relatively new addition to the full text information software packages is ConQuest (ConQuest Software), a natural language-based system that uses published dictionaries to index data automatically. Its lexicographical base reduces or eliminates the effort and cost to build and maintain topics or knowledge bases for effective searching. ConQuest is now integrated into the image processing and optical character recognition capabilities of Excalibur Technologies.

IMAGING SYSTEMS

The development of fast, (relatively) inexpensive, accurate optical character recognition (OCR) systems and the increased ability of text search software to tolerate spelling errors has moved several of the traditional imaging software systems into the realm of competitive information support. More effective data compression techniques, less expensive data storage, and faster, wide-band networks in companies have increased the connection of text and images. These systems, with their built-in advantage of effective imaging-handling, are increasingly providing support for the storage and retrieval of text information. Several effective image/text systems are Excalibur (Excalibur Technologies) and FreeForm (MicroDynamics Ltd.).

Excalibur employs a unique pattern-recognition technology that supports flexible "fuzzy" searching capabilities on Unix platforms in a client-server environment. By indexing to the binary representations of the text, the software provides flexible options for retrieving text. Its ability to tolerate OCR input errors saves significant amounts of time by eliminating the need to edit and correct the inevitable OCR errors. Both the text and images of the document can be displayed on the same screen.

Developed to provide full-text searching of OCR documents, FreeForm is part of a turnkey imaging and OCR system, functioning in a Macintosh environment. It supports fuzzy searching and provides a high level of retrieval performance. FreeForm also offers a "breadcrumb" search through a series of documents. The software commonly supports application search files of more than 500,000 pages.

CONCLUSION

Technological change has provided both the need for science and technology competitive intelligence and the means to meet much of its information demands. The rising sophistication of text-information retrieval software and of information end users and the falling cost of hardware and electronic information makes developing a computerized system for competitive intelligence support significantly more cost-effective.

However, the critical factors in effective system design are a thorough understanding of the organization's existing information flow, cultural changes in information transfer, and target customer goals. The system's focus must be on delivering information relating to a decision at hand, not merely delivering more documents to more people, faster. The key is delivering the right information to the right person at the right time.

Using Databases to Gather Competitive Intelligence

BRUCE KINZEY and ANNE JOHNSON

Use of electronic databases for reviewing literature and locating relevant contacts has become common in all fields of study. Because the database is becoming increasingly valuable in the acquisition of competitive intelligence, no book on this topic would be complete without at least a brief treatment on the use of databases.

WHAT IS A DATABASE?

Fuld (1985) provides as simple and direct a definition of a database as can be found in the literature:

> *. . . a data base is simply a collection or pool of information that is recorded, indexed, and stored on a computer. In other words, it is nothing more than a computerized reference book.*

Perhaps the phrase reference library is more descriptive of the databases referred to in the context of this book. Databases identify and often provide access to millions of potential information sources. Such sources may take the form of published technical, news, or business articles; patent filings; company reports; company assessments or ratings (such as Standard & Poors); principal investigators or other points of contact; and numerous others.

As more and more information sources continue to be digitized (that is, recorded in electronic form), we may anticipate a day when virtually all of the world's libraries and reference centers will be on-line and accessible to the information researcher.

The power of the database lies in the computer's ability to scan it for items of interest at astoundingly fast speeds. Depending on issues such as the current number of users on-line, systems such as Mead Data Central's LEXIS-NEXIS system may scan through hundreds of thousands of newspaper articles looking for a key phrase in a matter of a few seconds. Articles found containing the phrase (so-called "hits") may then be read, stored, and/or printed at the user's request.

Databases are assembled by and accessed through vendors, who often combine digitized information from several outside sources. Virtually all information published today, if not originating on the computer, is input to the computer before it is published and, hence, exists somewhere in an electronic form. This information can be accessed via a database if the author or publisher simply provides it to a willing vendor for this purpose. The LEXIS-NEXIS system, for example, obtains full text electronic versions of published magazines, newspapers, newsletters, etc., and copies these into their huge database, instantly making the contents available for access.

Many publications are thus made available for searching as soon as the vendor receives the electronic file from the publisher. Publications may become available minute by minute, as in the case of Associated Press or United Press International newswire releases, or may be available periodically in the case of less frequently published sources such as translated materials or industry newsletters.

Databases may be intended for either a broad or a specific audience. For example, news-oriented services such as the PAPERS database in DIALOG, which covers a large number of U.S. and international newspapers, would typically be viewed by a wider audience than would a more narrowly focused database such as the Chemical Abstracts Service.

As might be expected, the types of information one would expect to find in these two very different databases would determine their primary user community. Although coverage can overlap to some extent, one would not generally turn to a news-oriented database to find a technically detailed description of a newly discovered chemical compound—except for information the *Wall Street Journal* or similar publication might provide. The databases in existence today are as numerous and varied as the user communities that produce them.

Data "banks" such as DIALOG provide a single pathway or interface to a host of individual databases. With these systems, a user connects the computer to one phone number and learns one set of commands (accessing, searching, indexing, printing, etc.) for all of the databases resident on that system. The data bank relieves the user of the need to be familiar with the potentially unique commands and idiosyncracies of each database. In addition, data banks allow the user to search multiple databases simultaneously, saving both search time and funds.

Because many different databases overlap, there are typically several options for accessing a particular piece of information. For example, a researcher might run across the same article from *Business Week* in several different databases. Different databases have different characteristics pertaining to costs, command procedures, and functions. Information researchers typically tend to center on one or a few databases to their individual liking and use them for most searches.

THE ADVANTAGES AND DISADVANTAGES OF DATABASES

Aside from the obvious time advantage, a primary value of databases is the ease with which crosslinks are investigated. For example, several articles may mention a second key phrase that may be of interest to the researcher or that may suggest an alternative method of obtaining relevant information. By conducting a new search, the researcher may uncover entirely new avenues to valuable information that could have been neglected because of the time constraints associated with non-electronic resources.

The advent of CD-ROM-based information takes the ease of crosslinking one step further. Many CD-ROMs are word-indexed so that words or phrases of interest are identified wherever they appear. Use of CD-ROMs can also be very cost-effective. Once the CD has been purchased, the researcher's time is the only additional cost. The researcher is thus free to follow up any secondary leads. A comprehensive set of relevant background information is thereby retrieved in a fraction of the time required for more conventional search (that is, hard copy) procedures.

A limitation of database sources is that they obviously depend on written materials, in other words, material that has been judged suitable for publication somewhere. A second judgment is then required as to whether a particular published resource is worth accessing electronically. Potentially valuable information related to a topic may be omitted for editorial, business, or philosophical reasons. For example, Roger Karraker (as quoted in Basch 1993) decries the lack of alternative political viewpoints available on-line through the conventional vendors.

Moreover, some of the most valuable information never makes it into a published form, and personal contact may be the only possible means of retrieving it. The "grey literature" phenomenon in Japan—where much of the best information is photocopied and passed around in technical meetings and conferences but never officially published—illustrates this point. This limitation applies whether the information is in electronic or hard copy form.

An additional disadvantage of databases, though one that is becoming less so as vendors become more proficient at updating their libraries, is the timeliness of information. An article may not be published for many months after it has been submitted; similarly, considerable time may elapse between the date of publication and the date it is available through a database. Although the latter delay has been considerably shortened in recent years, the former can still be significant. Timeliness of information is a particular limitation of CD-ROMs, where the information is "fixed" once the CD is cast. Information contained in a database may be months or even years old by the time a researcher retrieves it. For this reason, only information being carried through major news channels can generally be retrieved while it is still current.

Databases are therefore limited by the constraints common to all written materials. Their strength lies in the tremendous speed of searching, wide potential breadth of search, and the ability to establish and follow up crosslinked information that might have been previously neglected.

THE HOW TO'S OF SEARCHING

One of the most important steps in conducting a successful database search is formulating an effective search profile. The search profile includes defining the questions or topics to be investigated, defining the intended audience, and determining the level of effort required (or desired) to carry out the search.

Formulating the search profile is a necessary component of preparing to go on-line. Without it, the time spent on-line can often be frustrating, expensive, and, worse, unproductive. Sometimes individual situations will preclude development of an adequate profile and the researcher will have to improvise, but such situations can generally be avoided through planning.

DEFINING A MANAGEABLE QUERY

Ill-defined questions can have two negative results: either they return nothing of interest or they return a plethora of information through which the user must wade to find the desired nuggets. A search on the term "new ceramic materials," for example, will return enough information to fill a database of its own. The researcher would be greatly aided by focusing the topic, for example, "ceramic engine research in Japan." Or, taking it a step further, "ceramic adiabatic diesel research at Toyota or Isuzu."

Depending on the amount of time available, an over-wide search topic may be desirable at first to ensure that the largest number of relevant resources is retrieved. Subsequent searches can then be used to pare the retrieved file to the more specific topics of interest. In the preceding example, the term "engine" is broader than the term "diesel" and so might be expected to retrieve a larger number of articles.

Such word choices underscore an important aspect of defining the query. How many different ways might the information be presented in the literature? What different descriptors might be used?

Compiling a list of synonyms and alternative locations for the desired information before going on-line is invaluable; for example, recent ceramic diesel breakthroughs might be discussed in business publications as well as in automotive journals and trade publications from the materials industry.

Most databases have a unique set of operating commands that are invoked by function keys on the keyboard or specific words typed into a command sequence. However, most also use Boolean operators to construct search phrases. A Boolean construction of the above example might be “ceramic AND adiabatic AND diesel AND (Toyota OR Isuzu).” This phrase would only return articles with all of the first three terms and either (or both) of the corporations mentioned.

Occasionally, longer articles of a more general nature may contain all of the terms specified, but in unrelated sections. To avoid such hits, the searcher must modify the above phrase to something like “ceramic AND adiabatic diesel AND W/5 (Toyota OR Isuzu).” This phrase would return only articles with the specific phrase “adiabatic diesel,” and only when either “Toyota” or “Isuzu” appeared within five words of it. In contrast, the previous search would have returned any article containing those words, in any order, regardless of the context.

DEFINING THE AUDIENCE

Defining the intended audience will further narrow the search. The previous diesel engine example will return both financial and technical information, intended future directions of research, research participants, etc. Perhaps the audience for the information is primarily interested in only one of these topics, and the researcher can save time by filtering the extraneous information before analyzing it. Is this search for one specific person with a specific focus, is it for a group with a defined range of focuses, or is it for the general consumption of the overall organization?

User’s needs are largely determined by their responsibilities within the organization. Executives, for example, generally have less need for technically detailed descriptions of competitors’ R&D programs than for information on the future directions and expenditures of those programs. Technically detailed descriptions are of more interest to scientific and engineering staff who are involved with work at that level. Efforts to obtain information must focus on the specific needs of the people who will use it, or much of that effort will have been wasted.

Table 1 lists some different clients within an organization and the types of information each might typically find of most value.

TABLE 1
Information needs of different users

User	Typical Information Needs
Scientists/engineers and technical managers	Detailed technical data Technical objectives and approaches Technical results or progress Contacts/researchers
Marketing personnel	Competitive product features Product sales Cost/price data
Senior executives	Technical news New S&T directions Contacts/researchers
Policy makers/regulators	Science/technology policy National S&T goals and funding New S&T directions

The information needs shown are not absolute. Generally, the level of overlap increases as the size of the firm decreases and the corresponding responsibilities of individuals increase.

DETERMINING THE LEVEL OF EFFORT

The amounts of money and/or time available to conduct the search are primary drivers of its depth, breadth, and focus and must be understood and communicated up front. Searches are rarely exhaustive. More often, the timeframe within which the information is needed or the money available to conduct the search runs out or a level of diminishing returns is noted and the search is halted. Much confusion can be avoided if all involved parties understand both these aspects before setting off on the search.

What level of effort is appropriate for the available resources? A cursory search and delivery across a narrowly defined set of information, or a broad, intensive effort involving hours of follow-up analysis and packaging? The audience/client may not need to know everything ever published on the topic; perhaps a few representative articles will suffice.

Clipping services provide a useful alternative for users who need to search a particular phrase or set of phrases on a regular basis. With these services, the user automatically receives periodic updates of new articles. The vendor conducts the search and places into a file articles or abstracts that meet the user's criteria. This file may in turn be placed in an electronic mailbox for the user, may be electronically mailed to an Internet address, or may even be printed and mailed in hard copy form.

POTENTIAL PITFALLS

Despite their extreme utility, databases are not without problems or potential pitfalls that can trap unsuspecting users. Even experienced users can (and occasionally do) fall prey to a variety of hazards.

The adage "don't believe everything you read" is just as applicable in databases as anywhere else. Information appearing in print gains a measure of authority which may or may not be fully deserved. While materials presented in peer-reviewed journals such as *Nature* or *Science* may reflect the state of the art in the scientific community and be widely regarded, publications offering a less rigorous editorial review process may also be retrieved in a typical scan.

A potential pitfall with information obtained through a database is that the source of the information is less obvious than when one is reviewing original documents. Aside from a few lines indicating the source (frequently located on the first page), an article from one publication looks identical to one retrieved from another.

The researcher scanning through a large set of articles may lose sight of the relative reliability of sources when they appear side by side. By association with more reliable sources, less reliable sources may gain an undeserved credibility. This problem is exacerbated by the researcher who synthesizes an aggregate report from multiple sources.

Problems particularly arise when materials have been translated from their original language. Subtle but very important differences in words can greatly affect the meaning of a translated sentence. For instance, a translation of numbers that slips a digit on the decimal point significantly affects information on technical performance or cost. In other cases, an enthusiastic reporter may allow optimism to override objectivity. Combs et al. (1992) point out that single sources of information are unreliable and must be treated as rumors until they can be independently corroborated.

The researcher who is familiar with the topic can filter unreliable information and avoid lost effort down unproductive pathways. Furthermore, the researcher is much more able to discern the items of particular interest to the audience if he or she at least partially understands the topic. A little background research will pay significant dividends.

Even though the information may be retrieved, insufficient analysis may render it virtually useless to the audience. Aside from the excess of codes, identifier headings, and other extraneous verbiage typically accompanying a retrieved record, longer articles may cover additional topics outside those of interest. Or, because all of the major news sources will cover a story of significant merit, many hits may contain essentially the same information with only minor variations. The range of hits might number in the thousands. Similar results may occur from use of an overly broad search topic. Time is at a premium for the audience, so a typical part of the researcher's job is to clean up and consolidate the information into an understandable, concise story that clearly and quickly provides the topics of interest.

An essential component of any successful database effort is interaction between the researcher and the audience. It is generally worthwhile to communicate with the audience while the search effort is ongoing to determine if the search is producing valuable results. If it is not, the search should be stopped or redirected. If the audience receives communications it considers to be of no value, it may soon view the entire search in the same light. Moreover, communications perceived to have no value are ignored and, hence, are self-fulfilling. Two-way, open communication between the researcher and the audience helps focus the effort on topics of interest and steer the search into the most productive areas.

Finally, as mentioned previously, there is the issue of cost. Prices for connect time and document retrieval and delivery vary, but a single hour on-line can easily cost hundreds of dollars. Additional cost is incurred if the researcher needs time for post-processing and analysis.

On first consideration, the total costs may appear exorbitant, particularly during the early stages of the researcher's learning curve when the information retrieved is not yet as useful as desired. However, this cost must be viewed relative to the corresponding cost to obtain the same information through hard copy documents or through other avenues. Without a formal effort, several staff may perform the latter procedure, meaning that embedded staff costs are duplicated several times over. Although largely hidden to the organization, these costs can be quite substantial. The organization must be prepared to support the sometimes sizable invoices coming from a database vendor in the context that they more than offset hidden costs elsewhere.

IMPORTANT ASPECTS OF AN ONGOING EFFORT

To summarize, then, several aspects of a database monitoring effort contribute to its success:

- Integration—combining with a larger monitoring effort to cover information not found in on-line sources
- Analysis—adding value rather than simple retrieving documents
- Feedback—focusing the search effort and increasing value to the audience
- Support—obtaining sufficient funding for a thorough effort.

The following case study illustrates the use of databases in locating technical information needed for a specific research effort.

CASE STUDY: A DATABASE SEARCH FOR RADIOACTIVE WASTE CLEANUP TECHNOLOGIES

The leader of the nuclear chemistry group at Pacific Northwest National Laboratory in Richland, Washington, needed to find out what procedures were available for analyzing different types of low-level radioactive waste. In particular, he needed to be able to characterize approximately seven or eight long-lived, hard-to-measure, neutron-activated metals, including certain radioactive isotopes of nickel, silver, cadmium, and indium. These metals are found in various components of nuclear power plants, such as in reactor pressure vessels and/or control rod assemblies. Before these components can be disposed of, scientists must first identify radionuclides in the waste streams that might have long-term negative effects on the environment.

The group leader asked an information specialist at the Hanford Technical Library to conduct a search aimed at uncovering alternative state-of-the-art procedures used for analyzing various low-level radioactive waste compounds. Specifically, he wanted to ensure that his technology development group was using the most current and effective procedures and technologies.

FORMULATING THE SEARCH OBJECTIVES

The primary objective of the literature review was to identify measurement and instrumentation techniques that could be used for characterizing low-level radioactive waste. The group leader needed to know

- What kinds of procedures were currently being used to characterize radioactive waste
- How effective those procedures were
- Who had developed the procedures
- How the technologies could be obtained.

DESIGNING AND CONDUCTING THE SEARCH

In consultation with the engineer client, the information specialist identified a series of key words or phrases she would use to query the on-line databases. These included

low-level waste	LLW
nickel	nickel isotopes
class C waste	greater than class C waste.

The next step was to identify databases appropriate for the information she sought. The information specialist decided to use the following:

- National Technical Information Service (NTIS) database
- Energy Science and Technology Database (Department of Energy)
- Office of Research and Development Bulletin Board Service (ORDS BBS) (Environmental Protection Agency)
- Remote Access Chemical Hazards Electronic Library (RACHEL) database (Environmental Research Foundation)
- Hazardous Waste Database
- Vendor Information System for Innovative Treatment and Technologies (VISITT) (Environmental Research Foundation)
- Alternative Treatment Technology Information Center (ATTIC) (Environmental Research Foundation)
- Computer-aided Environmental Legislative Data System (CELDS) (University of Illinois)
- Nuclear Science Abstracts (Department of Energy)
- Selected company databases available through the Knight-Ridder (formerly DIALOG) service.

Each database has a slightly different focus; the information specialist and her client hoped to maximize the number of hits by scanning a wide variety of sources.

To obtain data, the information specialist used truncated forms of the words "technology" and "low-level waste." The only important caution was that the key words needed to be descriptive of the article rather than simply words mentioned in an unrelated context.

The information specialist conducted the search twice. The first search, which required about two hours, was a general query to find out whether the key words being used would actually yield the type of data needed. Once the information specialist had ascertained that the selected databases could indeed produce information she wanted, she began a more specific ongoing search whose purpose was to monitor developments in the field and identify new analytical procedures.

The information specialist devoted about one hour a month to these monitoring activities over the course of several months. During this time, she met with her client three or four times to discuss her findings and to broaden or modify the search as needed.

USING THE SEARCH RESULTS

In some cases, information specialists may be able to analyze the data obtained. The subject matter in this case was so specific and highly technical, however, that the information specialist did not feel qualified to assess the results. She eliminated data that were obviously of little use to the client and also reported to him on the degree to which she felt the search was successful. Since her primary responsibility was to retrieve the relevant information, she downloaded search results and turned them over to the client, who then analyzed the data personally.

The database search did not turn up any new procedures. Rather, researchers in the nuclear chemistry group learned that they were already employing some of the most advanced low-level waste techniques available. Nevertheless, they compiled a database that catalogued nearly 100 technologies and new procedures, all of which were uncovered during the database search. By implementing these sophisticated techniques, scientists will be able to perform more thorough and sensitive measurements of metal byproducts, in turn helping to reduce the introduction of potentially dangerous materials into the environment.

EVALUATING THE SEARCH EXPERIENCE

The information specialist found the most challenging aspect of the search to be identifying the exact nature of the technologies the client needed. The task was difficult because the original search parameters were very broad: in the initial stages, not even the client was certain of the types of technologies he wished to identify. Finally, as the specialist came to understand the field better and as she met with the client on various occasions, she was able to pinpoint specific technological applications which helped narrow the search.

One of the most important elements in defining the search, the specialist concluded, was having some background regarding the overall nature of the client's program and his long-term technological needs. This context was extremely useful both in retrieving information to meet immediate objectives and in identifying data that might be useful to the client farther down the road.

The study described here was initiated in 1993. Were the information specialist to conduct a similar search today, she would also use the Internet, since many organizations now increasingly discuss their research results through this burgeoning electronic medium.

SUMMARY

The foregoing case study illustrates how use of databases can help an organization maintain or verify technical information in its field. To maximize the effectiveness of this electronic resource, the specialist undertook the classic steps of defining the question, limiting the search, interfacing with the client, and revising the search based on updated specifications. Finally, the specialist provided the client with the search results for final analysis.

Not only can databases provide timely information on new developments in a given field, but their use can also help companies identify new strategies for maintaining the competitive edge. Databases will play an increasingly important role for businesses in the years to come. The successful manager will not underestimate the utility of this vital tool.

REFERENCES

Basch, Reva. 1993. *Secrets of the Super Searchers*. Eight Bit Books, Wilton, Connecticut.

Combs, Richard E., and John D. Moorhead. 1992. *The Competitive Intelligence Handbook*. The Scarecrow Press, Inc., Netuchen, New Jersey

Fuld, Leonard M. 1985. *Competitor Intelligence: How to Get It; How to Use It*. John Wiley & Sons, New York.

Patents and Technology Intelligence

MARY ELLEN MOGEE

"In spite of all the difficulties, patents statistics remain a unique resource for the analysis of technical change. Nothing else even comes close in the quantity of available data, accessibility, and the potential industrial, organizational, and technological detail. . . . We should not be cursing the darkness, but rather we should keep on lighting candles."

—Zvi Griliches

Patents are an important source of technological intelligence that companies can use to gain strategic advantage. This chapter explains the strengths and weaknesses of patent data, the types and sources of patent data, and how they can be analyzed for competitive intelligence purposes.

PATENTS AND THE PATENT SYSTEM

A patent is a property right granted by a national government for an invention. Most national governments grant patents which have effect only in the territory or the country that grants them. Firms apply for patents to protect inventions which may have commercial payoff. Patents award the firm a temporary period during which the firm may prevent others from using its invention. In return for this protection, firms disclose the specifications of the invention so that the knowledge enters the public domain. Patent laws generally require that the invention be new, not obvious to one skilled in the art, and useful.

Different countries have different patent systems which, while they differ, have been harmonized to a large extent to facilitate international trade through a variety of international conventions and treaties, the most important of which are the Paris Convention of 1883 and now the General Agreement on Tariffs and Trade (GATT).

As a general rule, it is necessary to obtain protection in each country in which one wishes to make, use, or sell an invention, or to prevent others from doing so.[1] When inventors believe they have made a complete invention, they file an initial (priority) patent application, usually in their home country. Under international law, inventors must file all foreign applications within one year in order to preserve the so-called "priority date" of the original filing. Each filing is independent of the others and is subject to the respective laws of the target countries.

In almost all countries, a patentee must pay fees to the patent office when the application is submitted, amended, examined, and published; the patentee also pays attorney's fees. Foreign applications typically cost more than domestic applications because of the need for translations and specialized legal counsel or patent agents in the patenting country. Once a patent right is granted, most countries require its owner to pay annual maintenance fees to keep the right in force. These fees rise with time, running in some cases to the thousands of dollars annually. Although it is difficult to get hard data on these costs, it has been estimated that the cost to patent an invention in the United States, Japan, and 10 European countries may be $140,000, not including the renewal fees.[2]

INFORMATION IN PATENTS

The patent process gives rise to a variety of public documents containing detailed information on inventions and inventing companies. These public documents can be used for competitive intelligence. Patent documents, that is, issued patents and, in many countries, published patent applications, contain a description of the invention and the official claims, information on the inventor and his or her organization, as well as other information. In the United States, only *issued patents* are published; if a patent application is not granted, it remains proprietary information. In many other countries, however, patent applications are automatically published 18 months after the priority application (that is, the first application in any country) is filed.

Companies use patent information for competitive intelligence in basically two ways. The more common way is as a current awareness tool. Many firms circulate patent abstracts to researchers and other technical people to ensure that they keep up to date on developments in their field.

The second way in which patents are used involves statistical analysis of large numbers of patents to discover broad patterns or trends that may be significant to the firm's technology management or strategy. Such patent analyses produce quantitative results that can be used in conjunction with technology intelligence methods based on expert opinion, which are prone to problems of bias and information inadequacy. This chapter focuses on patent analysis.

PATENTS AS TECHNOLOGY INDICATORS

An indicator is a statistic used to measure something intangible. The most familiar indicators are those used to measure national economic activity. Technology is often thought of as machines, devices, and hardware. In its most important aspects, however, technology is knowledge, which is intangible; the machines are merely the embodiment of the knowledge of how to build the machines. Technology indicators are statistics that measure technology indirectly. Patents can serve to quantify and measure, albeit indirectly, aspects of technology that are important to the firm and are called technology indicators in this context.

Technology indicators include research and development (R&D) expenditures, number of scientists and engineers, and number of scientific and technical publications, in addition to patents. Most are based on a simple "pipeline" model of the technological innovation process, such as shown in Figure 1.

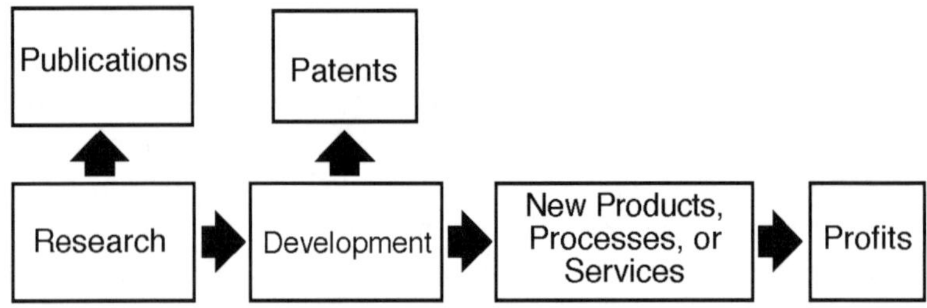

Figure 1. The pipeline model of innovation

The model seeks to convey the idea that investments in R&D lead to improved profits for companies, through the development and commercialization of new products, processes, or services. The innovation process so modeled needs to be understood as a probabilistic process—that is, one in which there is some probability that each stage will follow the preceding stage. Thus, while many studies have shown R&D to be positively associated with measures of economic value such as profit or productivity (Griliches 1984), for any given innovation project, there is a high failure rate between initiation of R&D and economic benefit. Moreover, economic benefits clearly depend on many factors besides R&D and innovation.

The model is an over-simplification in other respects as well. It does not reflect the cyclic and continuous aspects of innovation, that is, market-driven improvements in products and processes. Nor does it reflect the need for R&D to work in tandem with marketing, manufacturing, finance, and other corporate functional areas from the very start of the innovation process.

Despite the model's shortcomings, studies have confirmed one of its central premises: by examining data on patents, in addition to data on R&D investments, one can significantly improve one's ability to explain economic benefits statistically (Griliches 1990).

STRENGTHS AND WEAKNESSES OF PATENT DATA

A patent application is generally submitted shortly after the invention has been made and represents an invention that is judged by the inventor (or his or her organization) to be of sufficient novelty and potential economic value to warrant the expense of filing a patent application in one or more countries. Thus, patents are distinguished from R&D expenditures or from scientific and engineering personnel, both of which represent R&D investments that may or may not bear fruit. Patents are also distinguished from scientific publications in that patents signify perceived economic potential. Patents also have the advantage of generally appearing before a new product is introduced, making possible an early warning of a competitor's new product plans.

Patent data have several other characteristics that make them attractive for technology intelligence purposes. Patents are public information. Patents cover most technologies.[3] Electronic patent databases go back to the mid-1960s in some fields, particularly chemicals, and cover patents issued by an increasing number of countries. Patent data provide a much greater level of detail than other indicators, supplying information on individual inventions by individual inventors and organizations, broken down into very detailed technology classifications.

Further, studies have shown that the information disclosed in patents cannot be found in other places. Studies conducted by the U.S. Patent and Trademark Office (USPTO) and the American Chemical Society found that about 8 out of 10 U.S. patents contain technology not disclosed in the nonpatent literature (USPTO 1977). Another study found that technical experts in particular fields were unaware of half or more of the inventions and assignees revealed in patents in those fields (Mogee 1990).

Patent data also have shortcomings that have hindered their use as technology indicators. First of all, not all inventions are patented. Some inventions are not patentable subject matter; for example, some aspects of software, and pharmaceuticals in many countries. Moreover, a company may choose not to seek patent protection even if an invention is patentable. Companies generally screen their inventions for patenting, based on a rough cost-benefit analysis that trades off the cost of filing and maintaining a patent against the perceived risk of losing control of the technology in the absence of protection. Patents are sometimes obtained with no intention of commercializing the invention, but of preventing anybody else from commercializing it. The propensity to patent inventions varies across technologies, industries, firms, and over time and is generally related to variation in the efficacy of patents as a means of protecting intellectual property (Pavitt 1985). Despite these problems, studies have shown that when large numbers of patents are analyzed, the number of patents is positively associated with the level of technological activity. (Tests of validity will be discussed later.)

It is often pointed out that patent counts do not account for differences in the importance of inventions. This problem is not unique to patents, but is also endemic to other data that are widely used in technological analysis, including R&D expenditures and scientific and technical personnel (Comanor and Scherer 1969). Nonetheless, some patents are for "basic" inventions that provide the basis for many improvement inventions. Thus it is desirable to distinguish between "basic" and "improvement" patents and to identify clusters consisting of a basic patent and its associated improvement patents. Approaches used to overcome this problem include using data on patent renewal rates, on citation by subsequent patents, and on members of the international patent family to measure the value or significance of the patent.

Another often-noted problem with using patent data for analytical purposes is the lack of correspondence between patent classifications (for example, the U.S. Patent Classification System or the International Patent Classification) and other analytical categories. This disconnect has most often been noted with respect to using patent data in economic research (Trajtenberg 1987), but it is also a factor in doing corporate technological analysis (Mogee 1990). Approaches to overcoming this problem have included using firms as the unit of analysis (Griliches and associates at the National Bureau of Economic Research [Griliches 1984]) and using a search strategy that combines various techniques in computerized databases (Trajtenberg 1987, Mogee 1990, Schmoch 1990).

There are delays between the time the invention is made and the application is filed and then until the patent or application is published and appears in databases. These delays have caused patents to be criticized as not timely enough for competitive intelligence. Although there are delays in the publication of patents, these delays can be reduced by using international patent databases that cover published patent applications, which often appear before the corresponding U.S. patent. Moreover, as noted earlier, the technical information in many patents is never published elsewhere.

International comparisons using patent data have been hindered because of differing national patent systems. Patents issued by the USPTO have been used for most patent analysis to date, not only to study domestic U.S. technological activity, but also that of other nations patenting in the United States. The rationale for using U.S. patents to study international patenting has been the size and importance of the U.S. market and the accessibility and long time-series of U.S. patent data (Collins and Wyatt 1988). Moreover, studies of national-level patenting have found that the number of U.S. patents awarded to nationals of a country is closely related to the level of that nation's R&D expenditures (Soete and Wyatt 1983).

Analyses based on the patents of any single country are inherently limited in their ability to give an accurate picture of global technological activity. Indicators based on U.S. patents are biased toward the United States as the home country; hence, the United States cannot be included in comparative international studies based on U.S. patent statistics. Moreover, as technological capability spreads around the world, more and more new technology of interest to U.S. firms will be developed and commercialized outside the United States. Figure 2 shows that 40 percent to 50 percent of international patent families (that is, those inventions for which patent applications have been filed in more than one country) are not patented in the United States. Mogee Research & Analysis Associates have developed several ways of dealing with the issue of international comparability; these will be discussed later.

Other limitations stem from the fact that most patent databases are not designed to facilitate large-scale analysis. Although some computer hosts permit frequency distributions of key variables online, these may be quite misleading because without the raw data, it is difficult to know what is going into the analysis. Thus, it is generally preferable, although much more costly, to download the records in electronic form and convert them into a statistical data set. This task requires considerable programming skill and knowledge of international patenting and patent data. Derwent has published a software package (InfoView™) to conduct elementary statistical analysis of its Derwent World Patent Index (WPI) records. Companies may also write their own analytical programs or retain a patent analysis consulting firm that has already developed software.

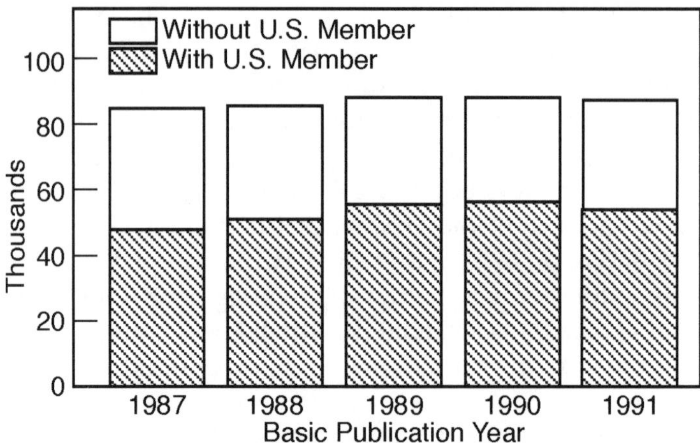

FIGURE 2. Worldwide international families and portion with U.S. members, WPI Database.

There is also the problem of cost. To obtain on-line patent data, one must pay a per-record fee plus a fee for the on-line time. For large projects, data costs alone may run into the thousands of dollars. CD-ROM databases may be more economical for large-volume users because the company pays an annual fee for a subscription to a year's worth of data (plus a one-time fee for the back-file), then uses the data as often as desired.

Finally, to conduct patent analysis and interpret results correctly requires a thorough understanding of the patent system and patent databases to avoid misleading results.[4] The use of patent analysis in competitive intelligence requires considerable skill and expertise. Conducting such an analysis may require participation of the patent, R&D, technical information, and planning departments within a company. Many patent analysis exercises may involve the use of outside consultants who have the necessary capabilities.

To summarize, patents are very attractive as a data source for technology intelligence. Although there are problems associated with the use of patent data, they are surmountable. Companies must invest in data, training, and, perhaps, consultants to take full advantage of patent analysis; but the value of patent data for technology intelligence warrants such investments.

TYPES AND SOURCES OF PATENT DATA

All patent data have their ultimate source in national (or regional, for example, European) patent offices. Patents are generally in the language of the country granting the patent.[5]

A typical patent will include a front page of "bibliographic" information, one or more drawings, a detailed description of the invention, and the legal claims. The bibliographic information may include the following:

- Title and abstract of the invention
- Name of the inventor and the assignee (owner) of the invention (typically the inventor's employer)
- Address of the inventor and/or assignee
- Date of application and date of issue
- Application number and patent number.

Countries with two- or three-step patent application systems may show the dates of interim steps. If the patent was first applied for in another country, the country, date, and number of this "priority" application are generally shown. References to "prior art," (earlier, related patents or literature) may be included, as well as whether patent renewal fees have been paid. Patent technology classifications, such as the U.S. Patent Office Classification or the International Patent Classification, are often included. The name of the patent examiner and patent agent may also be included.

Recognizing the value of patent data as technological information, national patent offices have sought to make the data easily and economically available. The USPTO led in making patent data available in electronic form, beginning in 1973. Today, patent data are published by many countries, as well as by commercial vendors.

Commercial vendors may purchase from the patent offices hard copies of the patents or computer tapes that contain the full text and drawings of the patents or the bibliographic information. These data are in turn made available in a variety of forms including on-line information services, CD-ROMs, and captive databases used as the basis for consulting services. The data available range from full text and drawings to bibliographic information to pre-analyzed patent indicators. Paper copies and full-text databases, such as Mead Data Central's LEXPAT and the European Patent Office's ESPACE, are generally used for legal patent searches or for current technical awareness. Patent analysis as defined here refers to the analysis of large numbers of patents (hundreds to thousands) and generally uses electronic bibliographic data.

Some databases that are not patent databases per se, such as CA SEARCH published by Chemical Abstracts Service and Biotechnology Abstracts published by Derwent Ltd., include patents among the scientific and technical literature they cover. Such databases often specialize in specific fields of technology and may have specialized search aids. Use of these databases can be helpful in identifying relevant patents for a patent analysis.

Many patent databases exist; only a few can be mentioned here.[6] Most of these cover the patents issued by a single country. U.S. Patents (published by Derwent Publications Ltd.) and CLAIMS (published by IFI-Plenum Data Corporation), for example, cover patents issued by the United States. FPAT (published by the French Patent Office, INPI) and JAPIO (published by the Japanese Patent Information Office) are other examples of single-country patent databases. Some of these are in the native language, for example, FPAT is in French and PATOLIS is in Japanese; others, for example, JAPIO, are in English.

Databases that cover patents issued by multiple countries include the Derwent World Patents Index (WPI), published by Derwent Publications Ltd.; INPADOC, published by the International Patent Documentation Centre in Vienna; and EPAT and EDOC, based on patents at the European Patent Office (EPO) and published by the French Patent Office. Patent family data, which link equivalent patents for the same invention that have been filed in different countries, are available on WPI and INPADOC, although there is a surcharge for family data on INPADOC.

On-line patent databases are carried by several different computer hosts or vendors, including Knight-Ridder Information Inc., Questel•Orbit, Mead Data Central, and STN International. Each of these varies in search procedures and capabilities; some offer elementary statistical analysis capability on-line. On ORBIT, the GET command allows one to obtain frequency distributions of key variables such as patent assignee code for a set of patent records. Corresponding capabilities exist in DIALOG and QUESTEL.

CD-ROM databases of patents include U.S. PATENT SEARCH (U.S. patent bibliographic data) and ESPACE (EPO patents), both available from MicroPatent.

To search patent databases, one generally uses patent classifications or words that appear in titles and abstracts. Searches may be done for particular technologies, organizations, inventors, and so forth. Patent database searching is notoriously difficult and requires specialized knowledge. A thorough knowledge of techniques for effective searching of the different patent databases and on different hosts is necessary.

Patent databases must be carefully evaluated to determine the best one for the purpose. Foreign patent documents and databases may not be in English. Patent databases differ in their coverage of technologies, years, and the types of patent documents included. For example, some databases include published patent applications, as well as other forms of protection such as utility models or petty patents. In countries where patent applications go through a series of steps with publication, some databases allow one to distinguish those patent applications that have progressed to the patent grant stage, and others do not.

PATENT ANALYSIS

Most patent analysis to date has used patents from a single country, most often the United States. The most common method of analysis has been simply to count patents. The number of patents or patent applications has been used as an indicator of the level of technological activity or output. As noted earlier, the issuance of a patent, or even a patent application, signals the existence of an invention that the applicant believes has potential economic value.

As also noted earlier, however, simple patent counts can be misleading for a variety of reasons. Not all inventions are patented, and the propensity to patent inventions varies across time, firms, industries, technologies, and countries (Pavitt 1985). Moreover, patents vary widely in their importance, implying that, for any given sample of patents, the correlation between the number of patents and the significance of the technology they represent may be quite low. Further, the distribution of patent values is highly skewed, implying that a small fraction of the patents in the sample will account for a large fraction of the sample's value.

Recently analysts have attempted to make use of other observable characteristics of patents in order to draw inferences about their underlying importance or economic value. These characteristics include the size and composition of a patent family (the collection of all patents, worldwide, covering a single invention);[7] the number and timing of subsequent patent citations (given by patent examiners when they establish the novelty of a new invention) (Trajtenberg 1987); and the timing of the decision to allow a patent to lapse (by failing to pay the annual maintenance fee most countries require to keep the patent right in force) (Pakes and Simpson 1989).

The following sections will describe ways of analyzing patent counts, patent families, and patent citations to provide competitive intelligence. Patent renewal analysis cannot currently provide useful information on individual companies.

PATENT COUNTS

Counts of patents have been used as a proxy for the level of technological activity—activity, such as R&D or engineering, that is aimed at developing or improving a technology—or the output of technological activity in companies. Studies have been done of fields of technology, industries, and nations (Pavitt 1985). Studies of patenting in companies are of primary interest for competitive intelligence, although studies at the other levels can provide important contextual information.

LEVEL OF TECHNOLOGICAL ACTIVITY

Patent counts can be broken down in many ways to reveal interesting aspects of technological activity. For example, companies may be compared according to the number of patents they hold in a particular field.[8] (One should take care not to compare across technologies, because the propensity to patent is known to vary across technologies). If one company has more patents than another, it indicates that the first firm has undertaken more technological activity in the field and has made more inventions. Other things being equal, one would expect this firm to be in a better position to develop new products, processes, or services based on this technology. Such comparisons can be made as part of a competitive technology assessment that determines the technological position of one firm relative to its competitors.

CORE TECHNOLOGICAL COMPETENCE

Using this same basic technique, it is also possible to compare companies with respect to the patent classifications on their patents. This comparison may be done in a couple of different ways. One way is to look at all patents assigned to each of a group of companies and to see how each company's patents break down by patent classification. Thus, if automobile companies are being compared, one might calculate each company's technological profile in terms of the number or proportion of its patents that fall into various patent classes such as engines, metal working, electrical systems, etc. Another indicator that may be calculated is the company's proportion of patents in one of these classes divided by the company's proportion of all patents. This is a measure of a company's relative strengths and weaknesses (compared within the firm) and has been interpreted as a measure of the firm's core technological competence (Patel and Pavitt 1994).

In this manner, it is possible to discern the particular technological directions or approaches a firm is pursuing. This investigation may reveal that the firm is pursuing technology that directly competes with another firm or, on the other hand, one that complements—for example, a needed material, a component, a process, or something that facilitates use.

INVENTORS

Particular inventors within the assignee firm may also be monitored to determine which inventors are especially prolific. Over time, changes in the names of inventors on the firm's patents may reveal that more researchers are being assigned to a particular field of technology or that they are being reassigned elsewhere. This finding would reflect increasing or decreasing priority and effort given to that field by the company.

TRENDS

Changes in a firm's patenting level over time may also be observed. A large increase in the number of patents may indicate a new emphasis on technology as the basis for competition or some other change in competitive strategy. An increase in particular fields of technology may indicate a major effort to develop an innovative new product. Such trend analyses, however, should not focus on the very short-term (for example, 2 to 3 years), because the high level of "noise" in patent data (that is, the year-to-year variation) makes it impossible to draw confident conclusions from year-to-year changes in the number of patents (Griliches 1990).

VALIDITY

Recent studies using patent statistics to illuminate the innovation process have found "a strong relationship between patent numbers and R&D expenditures in the cross-sectional dimension, implying that patents are a good indicator of differences in inventive activity across different firms" (Griliches 1990, p. 1702). This indicator exists despite the fact that the propensity to patent differs significantly across industries.

A statistically significant, but weaker, relationship exists between R&D and patents within firms over time. Economist Griliches has concluded that because of the high variance and skewness of patent values, patent counts probably are not good indicators of short-run changes in the output of R&D.

PATENT FAMILY DATA

In this kind of analysis, counts of patent families—that is, the collection of patent applications filed in different countries for the same invention—are used as an indicator of the level of technological activity. Use of international patent data, that is, data on patenting in more than one country, allows the analyst to see what competitors are inventing and patenting in other countries, as well as in the home country.

As noted earlier, there are several sources of international patent data. Thus, one may combine patents from different countries. This has been done by Schmoch and Grupp and others affiliated with the Fraunhofer-ISI in Germany, who use a combination of U.S., EPO, and, sometimes, German data (Schmoch and Grupp 1989). Archibugi has used a combination of U.S., EPO, and Japanese patent data (Archibugi 1992). A problem with simply aggregating national patent statistics, however, is that it results in multiple counting of a single invention across countries (if multiple applications have been filed).

An approach that eliminates this problem is to use the patent family as the unit of analysis. Databases that organize patents into families include the WPI and INPADOC.[9] Although it is a more time-consuming and expensive activity, patent families can be constructed based on the priority application number from different national patent statistics. Of these approaches, the one that has been used most extensively for competitive intelligence at the company level is the Derwent WPI.

WPI contains records from 33 major patenting countries and patent authorities (for example, the European Patent Office) organized into "patent families." A patent family consists of all the patent documents (that is, published patent applications and issued patents) pertaining to a single invention that have been published in various countries. The first patent document in the family to be published is the "basic" patent. The first application filed in any country is called the priority application because it establishes priority under the Paris Convention.

Patent families exist because it is generally necessary to file separate patent applications in each country in which protection is desired. There are some exceptions to this generalization. EPO patents and World Patent Cooperation Treaty (PCT) patents allow applicants to seek protection in more than one country using one application. In the analyses described here, EPO patents are not counted per se, but are instead broken down into their "designated states" and counted as patent documents published by those nations. For example, an EPO patent that designates France and Germany is counted as a French patent publication and a German patent publication. PCT patent applications are not counted until they appear as a patent publication in one of the designated countries because PCT applications must subsequently be prosecuted at the individual national patent offices, and many are not pursued to that point.

WPI records include information on the specific countries in which protection has been sought for each patented invention. This information can be used in two ways. First, it can provide insight into a company's strategy for exploiting its technology internationally. If a firm has applied for a patent in a country, one may infer that the firm sees potential economic value to be derived from making, using, or selling the invention in that country or in preventing a competitor from doing so. Second, this information can be used to make judgments about the economic potential of individual firms' inventions. Since seeking patent protection in multiple countries is expensive, one assumes that the more countries in which protection for an invention is sought, the greater the perceived economic value of that invention.

It is only fair to note that the WPI database has certain limitations. Like patent data in general, patent databases are subject to data-censoring in the most recent years—that is, patent applications may have been filed but not yet published in any country. The lag before publication is generally 18 months after the priority filing because most countries, other than the United States, automatically publish applications at that time. For this reason, records from the two most recent calendar years are incomplete.[10]

Another limitation of the WPI database is that, although it covers a wide range of countries, its historical coverage of Japanese patenting is selective. It covers chemical technologies thoroughly, but only a portion of electrical technologies, and no mechanical technologies at all. This selectivity may affect some, but not all, international comparisons. Some indicators are based only on those families with patent documents in multiple countries, and in these cases, Japanese-origin families with multiple members are included.

COMPANY-LEVEL ANALYSES

Indicators have been developed using WPI data that are useful in competitive intelligence in two ways: 1) to compare the technological positions of companies and 2) to describe the broader technological environment in which firms operate. The simplest of these indicators, number of patent families, is the international analog of patent counts and is used as an indicator of technological activity or output. Other indicators, however, make use of the patent family information that is not available in single country statistics.

Level of Technological Activity

To measure the level of technological activity, the number of patent families is counted. Each family, which corresponds to a WPI record, corresponds to a single invention. For most purposes, families are ordered by priority application year. The priority application date is used because it is the closest to the time the development work underlying the patented invention was actually done.[11] The level of technological activity in a firm is indicated by the number of patent families on which it appears as an assignee (that is, owner). It is further assumed that firms apply for protection first in their home country and that is the country in which the R&D was done.[12]

Another indicator of technology activity is the number of assignees active in the technology. An increasing number of organizations filing patent applications in a field of technology may indicate that companies see increased technological or economic potential in the technology, making it attractive to more participants. For this indicator, the number of unique assignees on patent families is counted for each year.

Technological Activity Intended for International Exploitation

The number of patent families is not adjusted for differences in national patent systems. Different national patent systems give rise to higher or lower levels of domestic patenting. These differences are particularly a problem in the case of Japanese patenting, where the domestic patent system and culture give rise to extraordinarily high levels of domestic patenting.[13]

This problem may be overcome by analyzing international families only, that is, families that represent inventions for which patent protection has been sought in more than one country.[14] Counting only international families removes domestic-only patenting, which may be affected by national patent systems, and is a better measure of the level of technological activity intended for international exploitation.

Technology Profile

The technology classifications appearing on WPI records can be used to develop technology profiles for companies, similar to those described earlier under analysis of patent counts. Table 1 shows that the technology profiles of Seiko-Epson, Corning Incorporated, and AT&T in the field of sol-gel processing of glass and ceramics are strikingly different. Such profiles can be used to examine the breadth of a company's technological efforts (that is, broad or narrow) and the particular areas in which it concentrates

TABLE 1
Technology profiles of three selected firms—sol-gel technology

SEIKO-EPSON
- Glass manufacture by sol-gel process (71%)
- Production and modification of silicon dioxide or hydrate (35%)

CORNING INCORPORATED
- Compounds of beryllium, magnesium, aluminum, calcium, strontium, barium, radium, thorium, and rare earths (25%)
- Compounds of zirconium, hafnium (25%)
- Forming glass hollow-ware (25%)
- "Other" glass-forming processes (25%)
- Electrical and electronic applications of glass (25%)
- Melting and casting of ceramics (25%)
- Oxide ceramics, including "technical" ceramics (25%)
- Electronic oxide ceramics (25%)
- "Other" oxide ceramic preparation (25%)
- Antiperspirants (25%)

AT&T
- Manufacture of guiding structures for fiber optics (83%)
- Manufacture of glass by sol-gel process (33%)
- Glass fiber manufacture (33%)
- Optical applications of glass fibers (33%)

its efforts, as well as to compare one company's technological directions to those of another. These profiles can be based on total families or international families.

Commercial Potential

A number of researchers have hypothesized that "external" patenting—that is, patenting by nationals of one country in countries other than their own—indicates a greater level of commercial value than domestic-only patenting (Basberg 1987; Schmoch and Grupp 1989; Soete and Wyatt 1982). A patent generally offers protection only in the country in which it is issued, and it is expensive to file multiple patent applications abroad in order to gain wider protection for an invention. One may assume that a company, or an individual, will seek protection for an invention in multiple countries only if the perceived potential commercial benefits from doing so exceed the costs of filing patent applications abroad. Following this logic, the more countries in which protection is sought for an invention, the greater that invention's perceived economic value.

While there is little evidence from formal validation studies to support this hypothesis empirically, Mogee (1990) found a statistically significant relationship between family size (the number of countries in which protection had been sought for an invention) and the number of subsequent citations received. Putnam[7] has also found correlations between family size and renewal rates.

Relative Technological Position

Faust and others have suggested that indicators of relative national technological position can be developed based on a country's share of foreign patent applications (Faust and Schedl 1983). Use of WPI allows one to identify those patent applications that are "foreign," that is, filed in countries other than the country where the priority application was filed.

Comparing foreign patenting eliminates the bias of domestic patenting and thus puts the countries on a more even footing. A similar indicator can be calculated for companies by calculating the number and proportion of foreign patents each company files in a technology. Duplicates within any single country should be eliminated, and countries designated through EPO should be counted.

Scope of International Technology Exploitation

The average size of a company's patent families, that is, the average number of countries in which it has filed for patent protection, is an indicator of the extent to which the company intends to exploit its inventions internationally. If a competitor firm has a large average family size, it may mean that it is pursuing international exploitation of its technology very aggressively; conversely, a small average family size may indicate that the competitor does not have much presence in the international arena.

Average family size may also be viewed as a rough indicator of the potential commercial value of the work a company is conducting. Note, however, that this indicator is affected by the foreign patenting policies of companies. Average family size tends to be larger for companies that are headquartered in countries with small domestic markets, but with strong trade ties to other industrialized countries.

Profile of Patent Countries

Patent family information can also be used as a rough indicator of a company's profile of patent countries—that is, the countries in which the company tends to seek patent protection. Table 2 reveals that selected companies patenting in the field of optoelectronic couplers differ in the number of countries in which they patent and in the countries in which they patent heavily or not at all. Knowing in which countries its rivals have filed patent applications and in which they have not may be of considerable interest to a company. The countries in which a company seeks protection may be indicative of its plans for marketing, manufacturing, or otherwise commercially exploiting its inventions. A company may also file patent applications in a country to block competitors from manufacturing or selling in that country.

The WPI database cannot be used alone to determine the status of actual patent protection a firm has in each country. For one thing, WPI covers only the major industrialized countries and a few newly industrialized countries. In addition, for many countries, including Japan, it is impossible to tell from WPI if a patent *application* has progressed to an *issued patent*. To obtain information for additional countries, one must use the INPADOC database, which

TABLE 2
Number and share of families having patent protection in selected countries—optoelectronic couplers data—selected companies

	Assignee[a]										
	SIEI	**AMTT**	**SUME**	**CSFC**	**INTT**	**PHIG**	**COGE**	**AMPI**	**MESR**	**BRTE**	**IBMC**
Families	110	47	47	40	39	26	24	23	22	17	15
Patents	527	274	122	178	189	151	200	105	128	176	77
Country											
U.S. Number	48	41	7	16	17	20	13	20	7	7	14
Share	44	87	15	40	44	77	54	87	32	41	93
Japan	26	19	36	7	5	8	4	3	1	7	5
	24	40	77	18	13	31	17	13	5	41	33
Germany	109	34	16	23	28	23	16	10	22	12	15
	99	72	34	58	72	88	67	43	100	71	100
France	57	34	15	40	16	24	21	10	12	12	15
	52	72	32	100	41	92	88	43	55	71	100
G. Britain	59	32	16	22	19	22	16	9	12	14	15
	54	68	34	55	46	85	67	39	55	82	100
Canada	3	12	7	6	3	8	5	5	—	5	2
	3	26	15	15	8	31	21	22	—	29	13
Australia	—	1	2	—	18	4	12	—	—	5	—
	—	2	4	—	46	15	50	—	—	29	—
Italy	37	16	6	18	11	12	14	8	11	12	4
	34	34	13	45	28	46	58	35	50	71	27
Netherlands	32	19	7	21	10	15	13	11	8	12	1
	29	40	15	53	26	58	54	48	36	71	7
Switzerland	30	9	1	2	10	1	13	4	7	12	1
	27	19	2	5	26	4	54	17	32	71	7

(continued)

TABLE 2 (continued)
Number and share of families having patent protection in selected countries—optoelectronic couplers data—selected companies

	Assignee[a]										
	SIEI	AMTT	SUME	CSFC	INTT	PHIG	COGE	AMPI	MESR	BRTE	IBMC
Belgium	22	11	—	2	10	—	14	6	7	12	1
	20	23	—	5	26	—	58	26	32	71	7
Austria	24	8	—	—	10	—	13	3	7	12	1
	22	17	—	—	26	—	54	13	32	71	7
Liechtenstein	27	2	1	2	9	1	13	2	6	12	1
	25	4	2	5	23	4	54	9	27	71	7
Luxembourg	7	7	—	—	—	—	—	2	7	12	—
	6	15	—	—	—	—	—	9	32	71	—
Spain	6	10	—	—	9	—	13	1	7	9	—
	5	21	—	—	23	—	54	4	32	53	—
Greece	6	—	—	—	—	—	1	—	4	8	—
	5	—	—	—	—	—	4	—	18	47	—
Portugal	1	—	—	—	—	—	—	—	—	—	—
	1	—	—	—	—	—	—	—	—	—	—
Sweden	27	18	8	18	11	13	14	6	9	12	1
	25	38	17	45	28	50	58	26	41	71	7

(a) SIEI - Siemens International
AMTT - American Telephone & Telegraph
SUME - Sumitomo Electric Co.
CSFC - Thomson CSF
INTT - International Telephone & Telegraph
PHIG - Philips Corp.
COGE - Alcatel Alsthom
AMPI - AMP Inc.
MESR - Messerschmitt AG
BRTE - British Telecom
IBMC - International Business Machines Corp.

covers about 50 countries. To obtain data on which applications have been granted, it is necessary to consult INPADOC or, in the case of Japanese patents, EDOC (the documentation file of the EPO, which is carried on Questel).

ANALYSIS OF TECHNOLOGICAL CONTEXT

Indicators of various aspects of the broad technological context have also been developed based on international patent records.

Global Technological Activity

Trends in the number of patent families per priority application year indicate trends in the level of global technological activity over time. This information can provide a company with a general picture of whether activity in a technology is increasing or decreasing. It is one of the indicators that goes into the life-cycle analysis (discussed below). Similarly, changes in the number of international patent families over time indicate trends in the level of inventions being generated for international exploitation.

National Technological Activity

The number of families broken down by priority country indicates the distribution of the technological activity across countries. This number can be further broken down by priority year to reveal trends in activity within each country. This information can help companies decide where to locate overseas R&D facilities or science and technology monitoring activities.

Patent Countries

The number of families that have members in each patent country is an indicator of the importance companies place on having protection in that market. Applying for patent protection in a country may signal an intention to market or manufacture in that country or to prevent national companies from manufacturing. The same indicator based on international families removes some of the effects of domestic patent systems, as discussed earlier. This kind of information may be useful in alerting a company to the countries in which there is much patented technology and those in which there is not. In those countries with many patent applications, technology-based competition is likely to be high, but so may be the rewards.

Technology Trade Patterns

International patent families can be broken down by priority country and patent country. Such a breakdown reveals the proportion of international families originating in a particular priority country that has a patent or application in a particular patent country. This breakdown reveals 1) the extent to which any source country is making a targeted "patent attack" on another country and 2) the extent to which the "patent market" of a country has been "penetrated" by another country. This information can be valuable in helping a company understand whether its home country technology market has been targeted by foreign competitors and what direction competition may come from.

Technology Life-Cycle Stage

Two analyses together serve to diagnose the life-cycle stage of a technology. One is the frequency distribution of company entry/exit categories. If a large proportion of the companies active in a particular period have stopped filing patent applications, a technology may be mature or obsolete. Table 3 shows, for example, that all of the major companies patenting in nitric acid production technology had dropped out of patenting activity by the end of the period studied. If a large proportion of the companies have just begun filing recently, the technology may be emerging or growing. Analyses of technologies that are clearly emerging or clearly mature/obsolete support this interpretation (Mogee 1990).

The other part of the life-cycle stage analysis is based on a model of technology development postulated by Richard Campbell (1982) who hypothesized that technologies go through life-cycle stages that can be characterized with patent data (see Figure 3). Three patent indicators are used: number of families, number of active firms, and concentration of patenting among the top four firms. The average indicator per year is calculated for multiple time periods and the patterns (for example, level and direction) are

TABLE 3
Number of firms with more than one patent family tabulated by year of first and last priority application nitric acid production

First Year of Activity	Last Year of Activity Pre-1975	1975-78	1979-82	1983-86	1987-90	TOTAL
Pre-1975	10	12	5	3	0	30
1975-78	0	1	1	2	0	4
1979-82	0	0	0	1	0	1
1983-86	0	0	0	0	0	0
1987-90	0	0	0	0	0	0
TOTAL	10	13	6	6	0	35

Life-Cycle Stage	Activity	Concentration
Emerging	Low, Increasing	High
Growing	High	Decreasing
Maturing	Stable	Stable
Obsolete	Low, Decreasing	High, Increasing

FIGURE 3. Modified Campbell life-cycle stage analysis framework

compared with the model to diagnose where the technology is with respect to its life cycle.

The life-cycle stage may be viewed diagrammatically as shown in Figure 4. The X axis represents the number of technologically active firms. The Y axis represents the number of patent families. The lines that divide the graph into four quadrants represent mean values. The lower left-hand quadrant represents relatively low numbers of families and low numbers of firms. This quadrant is characteristic of technologies that are emerging and those that are

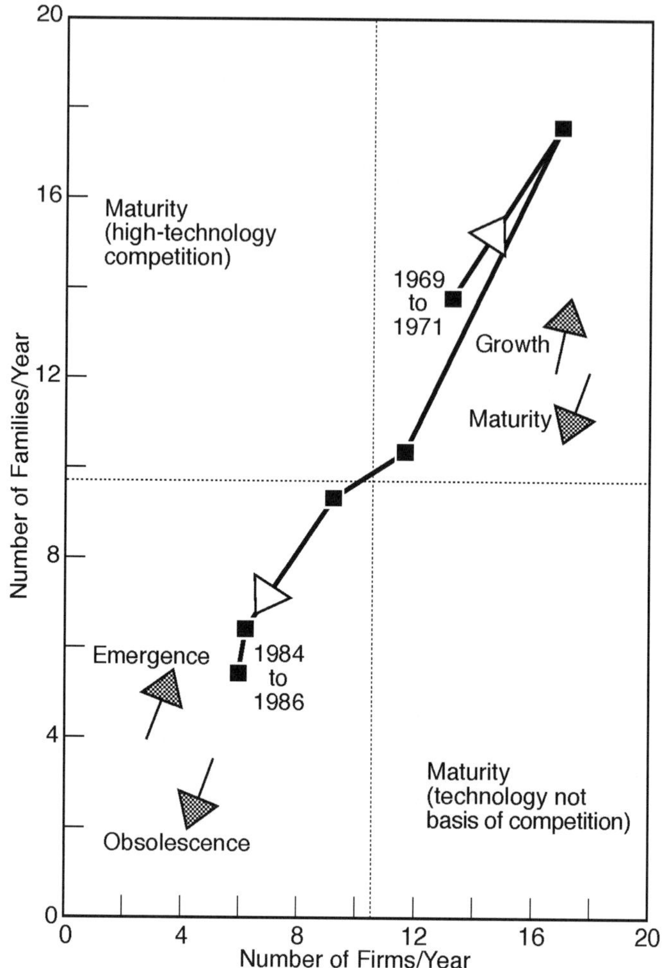

FIGURE 4. Life-cycle stage model—nitric acid production technology

obsolete. The difference is that emerging technologies are characterized by growth in both number of families and number of firms, while obsolete technologies are characterized by decline in both families and firms.

The upper right-hand quadrant represents relatively high numbers of families and high numbers of firms. This quadrant is characteristic of technologies that are in the growth stage of their life-cycle, as well as those that are in the mature stage. The difference is that for growth technologies, both the number of families and the number of firms are growing, while for mature technologies, both families and firms are relatively stable.

The upper left-hand quadrant represents high numbers of families, but low numbers of firms. The lower right-hand quadrant represents low numbers of families, but high numbers of firms. Both quadrants are interpreted as representing mature technologies, but different kinds of maturity. The upper left-hand quadrant represents a mature technology in which many firms have dropped out of activity, but in which there is still a high degree of technology competition among the remaining firms. The lower right-hand quadrant represents a mature technology in which many firms remain active, but in which the technology is no longer the primary basis for competition among them.

Figure 4 shows the interesting case of nitric acid production technology. This technology was already mature in 1969, the first year covered in the analysis. It experienced a small surge of growth in the early 1970s as a result of pollution control regulations. Since then, activity and the number of technologically active companies have declined, moving the technology into the obsolescence stage by the end of the period.

This kind of information can help firms decide whether, given the stage of the technology, it is in their best interest to make the investment necessary to enter a technology. Firms already active in a technology can use this information to assess the types of management issues they will need to address.[15] It can also help them decide when to get out of a technology.

Active Areas

The technology codes on the patent families a technology comprises can be analyzed to show the areas that are most active. A frequency distribution of the codes on each family is calculated, resulting in a list with the most frequently occurring codes at the top. This list can sometimes yield very interesting information, such as in the case of sol-gel processing, which clearly showed that most sol-gel activity was aimed at making glass and very little at making ceramics or glass-ceramics. This type of information can be useful in showing a firm whether its particular approach to a technology is already being heavily exploited. A code that does not occur frequently may represent a new approach or specialized niche.

Validity Test

A study of monoclonal-antibody based diagnostics (MAbs) found that the annual number of families, international families, families weighted by family size, and assignees was highly correlated (.94–.96) with the annual number of scientific and technical publications in that field. They were also fairly highly correlated with the number of new products in that field (.85–.87) (Mogee and Kolar 1994). For the field of optoelectronic couplers, these same patent variables were highly correlated with annual R&D expenditures on optoelectronics (.91–.96), not so highly correlated with the annual number of new product introductions (.72–.80), and still less highly correlated with the annual number of scientific and technical articles (.61-.68). Thus it appears that the patent variables are correlated with a variety of other indicators of the innovation process and are more highly correlated with different aspects of the innovation process in different technologies. This is consistent with the findings of Chakrabarti, who found different patterns of correlations, at the firm level, among the number of U.S. patents, publications, and new products in four industries (Chakrabarti 1990).

The study of MAbs and optoelectronic couplers also examined several simple regression models of the innovation process (Mogee and Kolar 1994). The equations represented the pipeline (linear) model of innovation using annual numbers of patent families, R&D expenditures, and publications as the independent variables and new products as the dependent variable. They incorporated various lag times to reflect assumptions about the sequence and length of innovation stages. All the models were highly statistically significant and explained a large part of the variance in the annual number of new product introductions (R^2=.71–.94). The unique contribution of the patent variable was often negligible in the presence of the R&D and publication variables. This result should not be interpreted as meaning patent data are of little value, however, because data on the other variables may not be available. R&D expenditure data in particular are generally not available at the industry or more detailed level.

Another study of sol-gel processing and nitric acid production compared patent family indicators to expert opinion (Mogee 1990). In both cases, experts were asked the degree to which the results of patent family analyses of the technology conformed with their knowledge of the field. Some analyses were assessed with a "conformance score" based on the following scale:

1 - Not at all
2 - Somewhat well
3 - Moderately well
4 - Quite well
5 - Almost completely
0 - Don't know.

Technology-level analyses of technological activity and life-cycle stage performed quite well for both sol-gel processing and nitric acid production, with average conformance scores ranging from 3.8 to 4.5.

Analyses at the national and firm level were assessed by asking for expert rankings on variables such as most active countries or firms. The expert rankings were averaged and correlated with the patent rankings, using Spearman's rho. These analyses did not perform as well, displaying moderate-to-negligible correlations. It should be noted, however, that similarity of rankings is a more stringent test of validity than the conformance score, which may account for the lower scores.

In many of the analyses, somewhat higher scores were obtained for sol-gel processing (an emerging technology) than for nitric acid production (a mature technology). The reason seems to be that many improvements in the mature technology are so minor they are not patentable, and many developments are held as trade secrets. In light of this, it is significant that the patent analysis of nitric acid production technology scored as well as it did.

PATENT CITATION DATA

Patents contain references to earlier patents and other technical or scientific publications. These references are the result of a patent examiner's "prior art" searches, which are required to establish the novelty of an invention claimed by a patent. The cited documents are judged by the examiner to be relevant to the invention, but do not bar the patent from being granted.

The motivation to reference is embedded in patent law, and because patents are subject to litigation, references are not made lightly. The applicant must bring to the examiner's attention any relevant prior art of which he or she is aware; failure to do so is considered committing fraud on the USPTO. The examiner must include references that were used to further limit the claims and specification in the patent application. In the United States, all materially relevant references are supposed to be placed on the patent. The references printed on the patent are those "officially of record," that is, the most relevant prior art. The patent examiner can be called into court to defend the references placed on a patent, and there are also internal PTO procedures for maintaining quality control over the references.

Thus, there is a strong rationale for interpreting references on patents as an objective and tightly drawn indication of the state of the art at the time the patent was filed. References are analogous to the legal boundaries of the technological area protected by the patent. (The patent claims are analogous to the "territory" that is protected).

Patent references are of particular interest for technology analyses because they offer a measure of importance or value that can be useful in evaluating the quality of patents and the work of companies or labs. They also offer a method of identifying links among patents and between patents and scientific and technical literature, which can be helpful in identifying competition and complementarities among companies and strategic areas of research and emerging technologies. They can also be used to measure the speed with which a technology is developing.

MEASURES OF IMPORTANCE OR VALUE

Several studies have found that the number of times a patent is cited by subsequent patents correlates with various measures of importance. Economist Trajtenberg (1987) found that the number of patents weighted by the number of subsequent citations was highly correlated with an independent measure of economic value of inventions. Technology analysts Carpenter, Narin, and Woolf (1981) found that inventions represented among the IR100 (an annual list of noteworthy innovations) were more highly cited than a random sample of patents. Narin, Rosen and Olivastro (1988) found that U.S. patents which are renewed are much more highly cited than patents which have been allowed to lapse. Mogee (1990) found the number of subsequent citations and number of international patent family members (another possible indicator of value) were correlated. Albert et al. (1991) found a high correlation between the number of times a patent was cited and expert ranking of its technological importance, but only for highly cited patents, that is, those with about ten or more citations. Putnam[7] has found a correlation between the number of subsequent citations and patent renewal rates.

Economists tend to use patent citations to measure economic value, while technology analysts use them to measure technological significance. It seems clear from the above studies that the number of times a patent is cited by subsequent patents is a function of its importance to the development of the field of technology. Although high technological quality may be a factor in commercial success, it is not the only such factor. Inventions may represent tremendous technological advances, but not have great economic value for a variety of reasons. Therefore, the number of subsequent citations of a patent is probably a better indicator of its technological significance than its economic value.

Patent references present some difficulties for analysis. The distribution of references is highly skewed so that only a few patents get many citations, while most patents get few or none. Therefore, standard statistical techniques such as averages can be misleading. A technique used to accommodate this is to limit the analysis to only the most highly cited top one percent of patents (Frame and Narin 1990, Mogee and Kolar 1993).

Citations also take time to accumulate, which means that the most recent patents will not have many citations to analyze. Thus, it may not be possible to derive much information from the citations of very recent patents. Older patents will tend to have more citations simply by virtue of being older. To deal with this, patents being compared should be drawn from the same time period.

The number of references given and citations received is a function of the field of technology. One way of dealing with this is to hold technology constant—for example, by making comparisons within a technology rather than between technologies. Another technique is to develop normalizing factors for each technology, as has been done by CHI Research, Inc.

Most studies have used the references on U.S. patents, which are placed there by examiners in the USPTO. Some recent studies, however, have suggested that U.S. patent examiners have a bias toward English language documents in their referencing practices and tend to reference a narrower range of technologies than examiners at the EPO (Claus and Higham 1982, Grupp et al. 1990). An unpublished study by Mogee that compared rankings of groups of patents by number of subsequent citations from the USPTO and the EPO found substantial differences between the rankings.

Analyses of the number of subsequent patent citations may also be conducted on the WPI database, which includes the references (to patents only—that is, not to literature) given on EPO and PCT applications. This analysis is done by searching for the patent numbers in the citation field. In this way, equivalent analyses can be conducted using patent families. For each patent family, the number of times any member of the family is cited is counted.

Using patent references, one can rank companies by the technological significance of their work in a field, that is, the contribution of their work to the development of the technology. Patent references have also been used to weight the number of patents or patent families. Trajtenberg (1987) found that patent counts weighted by the number of subsequent citations were more closely related to the economic value of the inventions than were unweighted patent counts.

RELATIONSHIPS

The references on a patent reflect the relationship of the patent claims to the prior state of the art. Therefore, they may be used to study relationships between the assignee firm and the firms that are assignees on the patents it references. Campbell and Nieves (1979) hypothesized, for example, that a firm whose patents give few references to patents held by other firms but receive many citations from those firms is in a position of technology dominance. As a result, it is likely to have the superior position in any licensing arrangement.

The references on a company's patents may tend to go to other patents owned by the same company or by other companies. The interpretation of these "self" and "other" references differs. "Self" references presumably indicate that a company has seen enough value in an invention to follow up on it with more technological activity. The existence of a cluster of patents owned by a single company connected by a high level of inter-citations, signals an attempt by the company to develop a tightly protected niche in technological space—probably a sign that it has what it thinks is an important core invention, which it has surrounded with multiple improvement inventions (Campbell and Nieves 1979).

The distinction between "self" and "other" references reveals an important aspect of a company's technology strategy—that is, whether it is building on its own work or the work of others. "Other" references may indicate that a company is building on the work of other companies. (Because references are placed on the patents by examiners, this building may not be done purposefully.) "Other" references may mean that the work of the referencing and cited companies is closely related.

Conversely, if a company's patents tend to be cited by its own later patents, it means that the company is building on its own work and has successfully protected its technology from being used by others. If its patents tend to be cited by other firms' patents, it means that the company's technology is flowing to others; the firm is in effect teaching other companies—probably not a desirable strategy in most cases.

This means of analyzing technology strategy can be represented graphically as in Figure 5 for optoelectronic couplers (Mogee et. al. 1992). The upper left quadrant represents firms that rely heavily on other firm's technology, while, in turn, preventing their rivals from imitating the technology they themselves develop. Two firms—Mitsubishi and Hitachi—are in this quadrant. They are apparently pursuing imitator strategies, but holding their own technologies more tightly than the median.

The upper right quadrant represents firms that build primarily on their own technology base and prevent others from building on that technology. Firms that fall in this quadrant include Kodak, Fuji, and ITT. Kodak and ITT are in an interesting position with respect to each other. Both are building on their own technology to the same extent, but ITT is receiving a larger share of references

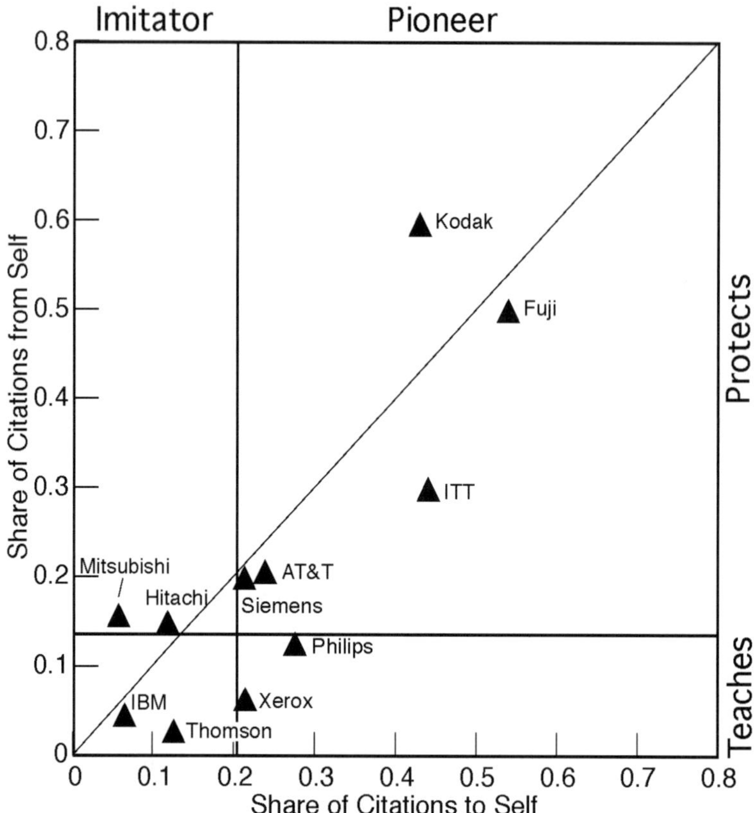

FIGURE 5. Patent citation map—optoelectronic couplers

from others, indicating that it is having a harder time keeping the new technology at home.

Firms like AT&T and Siemens appear to exhibit what could be called a balanced strategy. They are building on their own technology about the same as everybody else and are above median in their ability to keep others from building on their technology. In contrast, other firms such as IBM, Thomson, and Xerox are producing inventions that are relatively highly cited by others, which makes it harder to appropriate the returns on their investments in new technology—that is, they are relatively unsuccessful in keeping others from using their technology. The accuracy of technology strategy assessments made in this way is being explored in ongoing research.

TECHNOLOGY CYCLE TIME

The age of patent references has been used to assess the rate of progress in a technology. Studies of the scientific literature have found that in rapidly changing fields, the references tend to go to more recent articles. Recently an indicator of technology "cycle-time" has been developed, based on the median age in years of the references on a company's recent patents.[16] A shorter cycle time for a company is interpreted to mean that the company is developing new technology faster. It should be recognized, however, that occasionally a patent that references old patents may represent an important breakthrough.

RELATIONSHIP TO SCIENCE BASE

Occasionally patents refer to scientific articles. Such references indicate that the most relevant prior art was generated by scientific research and are more common in some fields, such as biomedicine, than others. The share of patent references that goes to the scientific literature tends to be higher in fields that are closely linked to science.

The study of the references a patent makes to science is of interest because it offers the possibility of identifying emerging technologies (which are often heavily based on scientific research), strategic areas of research (that is, areas of research that are moving into applications), and companies that are working close to the scientific frontier. Research has shown that fields of patented technology that heavily reference science are rated more closely linked to science by experts (Carpenter and Narin 1983). One problem associated with the analysis of patent references to science is that they are not in a standard format and are very difficult to process electronically.

Firms whose patents reference the scientific literature heavily are presumably working at the leading edge of technology. A study by Mogee (1996) of the field of implantable prostheses found that the top patenting U.S. firms drew on scientific research to a greater extent and more rapidly than did the top patenting foreign firms.

Companies that had won a Phase II award from the Small Business Innovation Research Program drew on scientific research even more extensively than the top U.S. companies and drew on it more quickly than the average for all firms.

Patent citation analyses that make use of data on the application date or assignee cannot be carried out on the WPI database economically because of the expense involved in retrieving the cited or citing records to record the data. Analyses using patent references to the scientific literature cannot be conducted on WPI because it does not include nonpatent references. For this reason, most patent citation analysis has been conducted with U.S. patents. Derwent Publications recently released a new international patent citation on-line database (PCI). However, it remains to be seen whether the structure and cost of PCI will make it amenable for analytical purposes.

SUMMARY

As markets and industries become more and more global and technology-based, increasing numbers of companies are looking for good sources of technology intelligence. Patent data, particularly international patent data, represent a source of data that has been relatively little explored by companies for this purpose. As this chapter has pointed out, however, academic researchers and consultants have been analyzing these data for more than a decade. They have developed technology indicators and methods of analysis that can be used to provide valuable information on companies' technological capabilities and strategies, as well as on broad trends in the technological environment. Some of the most forward-looking companies have begun to experiment with these methods.

The message, in short, is that patent data have much to offer companies in terms of competitive technology intelligence. As a source of technological data, as Griliches said, "nothing else even comes close." Companies that are serious about obtaining comprehensive, quantitative, objective technology intelligence should be using patent data.

REFERENCES

Albert, M. B., D. Avery, F. Narin, and P. McAllister. 1991. Direct Validation of Citation Counts as Indicators of Industrially Important Patents. *Research Policy* 20:251-259.

Archibugi, D. October 1992. Patenting as an Indicator of Technological Innovation: A Review. *Science and Public Policy*, pp. 1-13.

Basberg, B. 1987. Patents and the Measurement of Technological Change: A Survey of the Literature. *Research Policy* 16:131-141.

Bertin, G., and S. Wyatt. 1988. *Multinational and Industrial Property: The Control of the World's Technology*. Humanities Press, Atlantic Highlands, New Jersey.

Campbell, R. S. 1982. Patent Trends as a Technological Forecasting Tool. *World Patent Information* 5:137-143.

Campbell, R. S., and A. L. Nieves. 1979. *Technology Indicators Based on Patent Data: The Case of Catalytic Converters*. Battelle, Pacific Northwest Laboratories, Richland, Washington.

Carpenter, M., and F. Narin. 1983. Validation Study: Patent Citations as Indicators of Science and Foreign Dependence. *World Patent Information* 5:180-185.

Carpenter, M., F. Narin, and P. Woolf. 1981. Citation Rates to Technologically Important Patents. *World Patent Information*, pp. 160-163.

Chakrabarti, A. February 1990. Scientific Output of Small and Medium Size Firms in High Tech Industries. *IEEE Transactions on Engineering Management* 27:48-52.

Claus, P., and P. Higham. 1982. Study of Citations Given in Search Reports of International Patent Applications Published Under the Patent Cooperation Treaty. *World Patent Information* 4:105-109.

Collins, P., and S. Wyatt. 1988. Citations in Patents to the Basic Research Literature. *Research Policy* 17:65-74.

Comanor, W., and F. M. Scherer. May/June 1969. Patent Statistics as a Measure of Technical Change. *Journal of Political Economy* 77(3):329-398.

Faust, K., and H. Schedl. 1983. International Patent Data: Their Utilization for the Analysis of Technological Developments. *World Patent Information* 5:144-157.

Frame, J. D., and F. Narin. 1990. The United States, Japan, and the Changing Technological Balance. *Research Policy* 19:447-455.

Griliches, Z. 1990. Patent Statistics as Economic Indicators: A Survey. *Journal of Economic Literature* 28:1661-1707.

Griliches, Z., ed. 1984. *R&D, Patents, and Productivity*. University of Chicago Press, Chicago.

Grupp, H., T. Reiss, and U. Schmoch. 1990. *Knowledge Interface of Technology and of Science: Developing Tools for Strategic R&D Management*. Fraunhofer-Gesellschaft-ISI, Karlsruhe, Germany.

Howard, W. G., Jr., and B. R. Guile, eds. 1992. *Profiting from Innovation: The Report of the Three-Year Study from the National Academy of Engineering*. Free Press, New York.

Mogee, M. E. 1990. *International Patent Data for Technology Analysis and Planning*. Final Report to the Center for Innovation Management Studies, Lehigh University, Bethlehem, Pennsylvania.

Mogee, M. E. 1996. Benchmarking U.S. Competitive Technological Position in Implantable Prostheses with Data on New Products, Patent Families, and Patent Citations. *Management of Technology, Vol. V: Technology Management in a Changing World*, R. M. Mason, L. A. Lefebvre, and T. M. Khalil (ed.). Elsevier Advanced Technology, Oxford.

Mogee, M. E., and R. Kolar. December 1993. *International Patent Indicators of U.S. Position in Critical Technologies*. Report prepared for the Science and Engineering Indicators Program, Division of Science Resources Studies, of the National Science Foundation. Mogee Research and Analysis Associates, 11701 Bowman Green Drive, Reston Virginia 20190.

Mogee, M.E., and R. Kolar. 1994. International Patent Analysis as a Tool for Corporate Technology Analysis and Planning. *Technology Analysis and Strategic Management* 6:485-503.

Mogee, M. E., R. Kolar, and J. Putnam. 1992. *Extracting Useful Information for Technology Management from International Patent Records.* Final Report to the National Science Foundation, Washington, D.C.

Narin, F., M. Rosen, and D. Olivastro. 1988. Patent Citation Analysis: New Validation Studies and Linkage Statistics. *Handbook of Quantitative Studies of Science and Technology*, A.F.J. van Raan (ed.). North-Holland, Elsevier Science Publishers.

Pakes, A., and M. Simpson. 1989. Patent Renewal Data. *Brookings Papers on Economic Activity: Microeconomics*, M. N. Baily and C. Winston (ed.). Brookings Institution, Washington, D.C.

Patel, P., and K. Pavitt. May 1994. *Technological Competencies in the World's Largest Firms: Characteristics, Constraints and Scope for Managerial Choice*. STEEP Discussion Paper No. 13, Economic and Social

Research Council Centre on Science, Technology, Energy, and Environment Policy at the University of Sussex, Brighton, United Kingdom.

Pavitt, K. 1985. Patent Statistics as Indicators of Innovative Activities: Possibilities and Problems. *Scientometrics* 7:77-99.

Schmoch, U. 1990. *Wettbewerbsvorsprung durch Patentinformation: Handbuch fur die Recherchen-Praxis*. Köln, TUV Rheinland.

Schmoch, U., and H. Grupp. 1989. Patents Between Corporate Strategy and Technology Output: An Approach to the Synoptic Evaluation of U.S., European, and German Patent Data. *Science Indicators: Their Use in Science Policy and Their Role in Science Studies*, van Raan, Nederhof, and Moed (ed.). D.S.W.O. Press, Leiden, The Netherlands.

Simmons, E., and F. Rosenthal. 1985. Patent Databases: A Survey. *World Patent Information* 7:33-67.

Soete, L., and S.M.E. Wyatt. 1983. The Use of Foreign Patenting as an Internationally Comparable Science and Technology Output Indicator. *Scientometrics* 5:31-54.

Soete, L., and S.M.E. Wyatt. June 1982. *Domestic and Foreign Patenting in the USA and the EEC: Towards the Development of an Internationally Comparable Science and Technology Output Indicator*. Paper presented to the Workshop on Patent and Innovation Statistics, Organization for Economic Co-Operation and Development, Paris, June 28-30, 1982. DSTI/SPR/82.89, Organization for Economic Co-Operation and Development, Paris.

Trajtenberg, M. 1987. *Patents, Citations, and Innovation: Tracing the Links*. Working Paper 2457, National Bureau of Economic Research, 1050 Massachusetts Avenue, Cambridge, Massachusetts 02138.

U.S. Patent and Trademark Office, Office of Technology Assessment and Forecast. December 1977. The Uniqueness of Patents as a Technological Resource. *Technology Assessment and Forecast: Eighth Report*. U.S. Government Printing Office, Washington, D.C.

ENDNOTES

1. An important exception to this rule is the European Patent Office (EPO), which permits companies to file a single application and designate the members of the European Patent Convention in which it wishes the patent to have effect.
2. Private conversation with the C.E.O. of Competitive Technologies, Inc.

3. Technology coverage by patents differs somewhat from country to country. In the United States, computer programs are patentable, as is biotechnology, although there are some limitations.
4. Patenting patterns are affected by national patent laws and international patent treaties, the patenting process, and patent classification systems, as well as the ins and outs of various patent databases.
5. European patents may be in English, French, or German.
6. On-line patent databases are surveyed and summarized in tabular form by Simmons and Rosenthal 1985.
7. J. Putnam. 1996. *Invention and Information Disclosures with International Patent Rights*. Unpublished Ph.D. dissertation, Yale University
8. The patent assignee recorded on the patent or in a patent database is the owner of the patent at the time of issue or publication. Patents may be reassigned and may no longer belong to the company recorded on the patent. Reassignment databases exist for U.S. and Japanese patents, if current ownership is important to an analysis. If the analysis is concerned with technological activity, however, the assignee listed on the patent is probably the one that conducted the activity. Another problem with company data is the constant change in companies resulting from merger and divestiture activities. To trace such changes, it is necessary to consult other databases of corporate information. Some patent databases, however, such as the Derwent World Patents Index and databases held and published by CHI Research Inc., have unified companies' names to a significant extent.
9. INPADOC charges extra for family information.
10. In some technologies, more than two years' data may be incomplete, particularly if activity in a technology is very heavily U.S.-based and the technology is experiencing very rapid growth. This lag occurs because U.S. processing of patent applications in some rapidly growing technologies is extremely slow, and U.S. patents are not published until they issue as granted patents.
11. For administrative reasons, some inventions can have more than one priority application. In these instances, the earliest priority date is used to order the invention in time.
12. Bertin and Wyatt (1988) found this to be true in 90% of the firms they studied.
13. Bruce Stokes. May 21, 1988. The Culture of Patents. *National Journal*, pp. 1350-1354.

14. The operational definition includes families with more than one member (i.e., country patent publication) or families with one member where that member (country) is different from the priority country.
15. Howard and Guile (1992) suggest that the challenges faced in managing a technology vary according to the life-cycle stage of the technology.
16. Robert Buderi, John Carey, Neil Gross, and Karen Lowry Miller. August 3, 1992. Global Innovation: Who's In the Lead? *Business Week*.

Identifying Strategic Sciences and Technologies Through Scientometrics

J.P. COURTIAL,
A. SIGOGNEAU, and M. CALLON

A new discipline called scientometrics aims at measuring scientific and technical development by analyzing computerized scientific and technical information. This information is generally public and available to anyone. Scientometrics is not intended to develop the methods used in competitive scientific or technological intelligence that is oriented toward fresh information research. On the contrary, scientometrics concerns the intelligent use of existing data.

THE THEORETICAL CONTEXT

Scientometry evolved from a reflection on scientific development on the one hand (Price 1963) and the availability of numerous databases on the other.

SCIENTIFIC PUBLICATIONS

Well before the Second World War, statistics indicating the total number of publications in a given field in relation to time were derived from scientific publications. When charted into graphs, these statistics revealed regularities, often forming what is termed a logistic or S-shaped curve. Such curves show a slow, linear beginning in the number of publications; then exponential growth followed by an inflection point and repeated linear growth; and, finally, slowdown and stagnation.

This growth pattern can also be seen in various sectors of human activity, such as the total extraction of coal from a certain seam or the total number of miles of railtrack laid in a particular country. It can also be observed frequently in biology.

These observations led to a view of science as a deposit, and scientific discovery or innovation as living processes, instead of punctuating phenomena. Far from being defined once and for all, they improve progressively, reach maturity, etc.

However, these processes are controlled quantitatively by simple laws concerning the growth rate of publications or products sold. These laws can be used as basic elements in competitive scientific or technological intelligence. In fact, if the publications graph of a product or process shows a growth period, there is every reason to think that the product or process is new and promising. A number of indicators (for example the "signal" of the National Institute of Industrial Property in France) function in this way, based on the automatic detection of growth patterns in certain categories of the International Patent Classification.

Kuhn and other science specialists have attempted to define a scientific revolution from the standpoint of a paradigm (Kuhn 1970). A paradigm is the organizational element that regulates the practices of a scientific community. It becomes evident, not through the increase of publications in a field, but through the rapid growth in simultaneous citations of a small number of fundamental scientific articles. The Institute of Scientific Information (ISI) in Philadelphia calculates these sets, which it terms core articles of a research front (Small and Greenlee 1985). The research front is thus made up of articles citing the core articles. In this way, one can identify developing scientific fields without have recourse to an initial classification of the sciences, as is the case for patents. Experience has shown, however, that method articles (that is, articles whose first purpose is to describe new research tools or method) gain a clear advantage in this type of calculation.

Research fields where the cited documents become more and more recent (what the ISI calls the immediacy effect) can be calculated from the original citation. This calculation is a more accurate indicator than the simple enumeration of the increase in publications over time.

PATENTS

To date, the statistical enumeration of registered patents by appropriate category classification has revealed the accelerated development of generic technologies, for example, the rapid development of photocopying techniques. These enumerations prove inadequate, however, to the extent that highly innovative fields can exist without showing a quantitative increase in the number of registered patents. Moreover, enumeration does not allow for far-reaching identification of the technologies a firm views as strategic.

Calculations based on citation of the patent subject also exist. A key-patent is the name given to a patent which draws a series of others in its wake. A patent, in fact, is cited when it helps to evaluate another patent registered subsequently, either because the latter is close to it (and the difference needs to be indicated) or because it implies the technological complementarity of the former (technological trend).

In other words, whether a patent reflects attempts to get around or attempts to continue, its citation is a sure indication of its importance. Citation measurement is a way of pinpointing such patents, among which are numerous key technologies insofar as they bring about important technical development. However, as previously noted, the question of the strategic aspect of these technologies for a given firm remains unanswered.

Patent databases generally provide patent citations which appear on the front page. These citations are drawn up by examiners and are not necessarily the citations suggested by the depositors. This information is compiled with the greatest care and is legally binding. An examiner, particularly in Europe (EPAT database) can spend over five hours per patent and can consult (by computer) more than a thousand related patents.

In spite of the innate inventiveness which all patents imply, they are all more or less relatively close in fact. This aspect provides the basis for an analysis of technical trends, as suggested in particular by CHI Research.[1] This analysis reveals the patents which are bridgeheads to whole lines of patents. But, contrary to scientific articles, which are frequently cited, the most cited patents are quoted only a few dozen times and, in any case, are not numerous. Patents which lend themselves to trend analysis are, consequently, few in number and are known.

Other analyses based on patent citations, such as those suggested by Battelle,[2] are possible. These consist of building up (in a given technological field) a double-entry table of citations received for the patents of a set of given firms and citations made by the same firms. The "dominant" firms whose patents are frequently referred to thus emerge, without their having to borrow from outside.

As CHI has shown, citation analysis can also reflect the complementarity of firms. The analysis of citations can therefore give information on strategic firms, both in relation to each other and in relation to specific technologies.

Beyond very general ideas of developing technological fields and leading firms, therefore, the usual analysis of information contained in patent databases does not allow for *dynamics of technology* or for any identification of the strategic value of a technology for the firm.

NEW DEVELOPMENT MODELS OF INVENTION AND INNOVATION

Over the past 15 years the Centre de Sociologie (CSI) de l'Ecole des Mines de Paris has developed a theory of scientific knowledge construction and innovation construction (Callon et al. 1986). This theory is based on the idea of a sociocognitive or sociotechnical network. It has led to new mathematical tools and to new models of knowledge, to inventions, and to innovation development. These tools and these models are based on information available in most databases, scientific articles, patents, commercial information, etc.

Innovation is generally thought to arise automatically. The success of good products seems obvious. Their own qualities give them a place on the market. This way of thinking does not take account of the fact that innovation first entails change, that is to say, the rejection of existing structures.

The CSI has demonstrated that innovations can be studied only through the networks of alliances and disconnections they introduce. A successful innovation is one which has succeeded in enrolling the maximum number of partners through a series of successive adaptations. There is, therefore, a logic which can be followed.

Innovations do not tumble from heaven. In other words, an innovation is not a linear process leading from research to the market. It is a circular process comprising successive cycles, each cycle employing its particular "spokesman" for research, production, consumers, financial bodies, etc. A tool has even been proposed for describing the different phases of innovation: an "x" axis for the transformations made to the initial project, and a "y" axis for the growth in number of potential users.

THE SOCIOLOGY OF SCIENCE OR THE ANALYSIS OF SCIENTIFIC NETWORKS

The sociology of sciences similarly proves that an invention is the result of networks closely linking the social and the cognitive. Such networks are often termed "sociocognitive" for this reason.

Kuhn (1970) introduced the idea of a paradigm. As mentioned, a paradigm is the element organizing the practices of a research group. It is an idea which can be compared to psychological "good form." The paradigm therefore emphasizes the social aspect of research practices as opposed to traditional epistemology, which concerns only the strictly logical aspects of scientific knowledge. The idea of a paradigm, however, did not include social features in its construction. The notion of a sociocognitive network responds to this need.

The Idea of the Actor-Network and Translation

Any approach to either the sociology of innovation, the sociology of sciences, or the sociology of technics inevitably leads to the use of mathematical network tools.

The scientific or technological networks theory advanced by CSI holds that all science and all technology are bound by a network dynamic. It consists of identifying the knowledge and know-how network of a laboratory or firm from their publications and patent registrations in order to gain insight on their future publications or patents, or at least to obtain an idea of what these may concern. In the same way, when publications or patents of a given field are put together, the networks making up the structure of the field can be identified and foresight gained into the forthcoming publications or patents concerning it.

Coword Analysis

A new dimension has to be given to the usual networks of mathematicians, however. These networks are generally without any hierarchy and are made up of nodes and links. The current sociology of science considers networks simply as being organized in decreasing association gradients from central points.

The interaction among several networks is behind the dynamics of knowledge and techniques. Translation relationships become established between these networks, similar to translations from one language to another: communication is established between centers. This communication gives rise to invention or innovation.

It is therefore necessary to work in two stages. First, the intermediary interacting networks, or *actor-networks,* have to be identified. Second, they must be led to play the role of a full actor, even if they are mostly incomplete and are only partially known. To achieve this end, a computerized mathematical program has been created: coword analysis.

The following article taken from academic publications relating to polymer science found in the PASCAL database for 1973-75 is an example:

> "Crystallinity and the Effect of Ionizing Radiation in Polyethylene Vi Decay of Vinyl Groups", G.N. PATEL, in *Journal of Polymer Science*", Phys. Ed., 1975, Vol 13, p 361-367.

The publication is described by the following keywords:

Polymer ethylene	monocrystal	irradiation
crystallinity	IR	spectrometry
ionizing radiation	amount	vinyl
modifications	structure	

Keywords alone will not describe the contents of an article or what it is trying to prove. Nothing is like reading the article itself. Keywords can, however, help accurately identify research problems or themes which researchers automatically associate at any given moment.

The scientific article—or the patent—is itself an actor or an *actor-network*, that is, a momentary association of problems following a research logic presented by the author. In the above example, the article associates research on monocrystals with research on crystallinity and ionizing radiation. In other words, solving problems raised by crystalline polymers (or their obtainment) implies that problems relating to monocrystals should be solved first. As can be seen, the list of keywords is not an approximation of the contents of the article, but something entirely different—a particular way of highlighting researchers' strategies.

With the help of keywords, scientific articles can be described by their relational features with respect to each other, that is, by their function in the system of science in the making. In addition, bibliographical references of scientific articles can be interpreted as keywords of scientific networks linked by the articles. Articles linking several research fronts can also be identified in this way. However, as some keywords are more frequent in a document file than citations in bibliographical references (most scientific articles are cited only a few times), they reveal more clearly the logic of interactions between networks of all kinds (not just those acknowledging intellectual debts).

Coword analysis applied to scientific articles (as well as to patents and any other document describing innovations) is based on the scientific publications contained in a selective international database and entails studying the interface logic between publications through the emergence of the actor-networks they build up. To be more precise, the coword method (words being descriptors of articles) aims at identifying the words which are most frequently associated, leading to research themes and, consequently, to a classification of contents. In addition, the method aims to highlight potential or completed themes and the general dynamic behind the transformation of research.

In this way, words which will be in the center of strong associations and thus represent networks linked through research can be identified.

Figure 1, which was drawn up using the associated keyword network for articles appearing between 1973 and 1975 (approximately 2500), shows how the aggregate on the upper right associates a network built around crystallinity (crystallinity, RX diffraction, crystalline structure, etc.) and a network concerning radiation (ionizing radiation, radiochemical reticulation, and so on).

The method does not assign associations between "satellite" words linked to the central word. These words and their satellites do not necessarily lead to homogenous clusters in the sense of conventional classification techniques, for example. The homogenous networks will correspond to well-identified themes in a research field; the heterogeneous networks will correspond to potential or poorly identified themes.

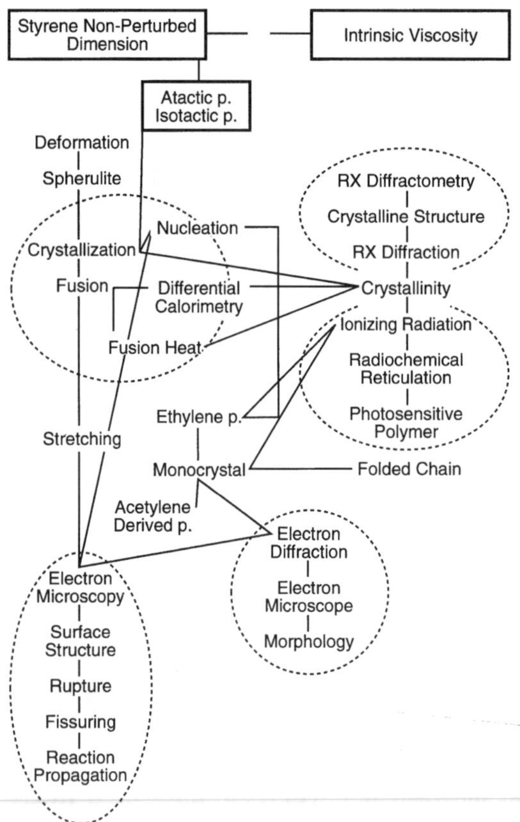

FIGURE 1. Partial keyword network for polymer academic science (1973–1975); clusters or subnetworks are indicated within general network.

On the one hand, therefore, it is necessary to determine from the available information in line with the database what relates to a scientific or technological network and, on the other hand, to give a simple, definite shape to the network obtained—its morphology—so as to have foresight regarding its dynamic.

SCIENTIFIC ARTICLE DATABASES

There are numerous general and specialized databases for scientific articles. Broadly speaking, databases correspond to the main scientific branches: CHEMICAL ABSTRACTS (chemistry), INSPEC (physics), BIOSIS (biology), MEDLINE (medicine), etc. The CHEMICAL ABSTRACTS base is the only one to enter both patents and publications relating to the same scientific field. It also supplies the codes of chemical compositions (Registry Number) and detailed summaries of publications.

General bases are not so widespread. They are interesting inasmuch as they facilitate the passage from one discipline to another and, consequently, cover fields which relate simultaneously to several disciplines. They are compiled through subscriptions to the best reviews concerning all disciplines; for example, the PASCAL database run by the Centre National de Recherche Scientifique in France (7000 reviews). In some cases, only the most important articles are retained; in others, all are retained.

The Institute of Scientific Information's SCISEARC (Science Citation Index) database (and SSCISEARC for human [social] sciences) is different in that it comprises 3500 reviews which cite each other reciprocally, with about a 15 percent limit of infrequent citations made from sources outside the reviews of the base. In other words, 85 percent of article citations contained in this base are articles of the base itself. It is therefore a coherent base from the standpoint of what is termed academic science, which has recourse systematically to citation as a means of giving an article legitimacy.

At the same time, the base computerizes the bibliographic references at the end of each article (citations). Consequently, the calculation of citations pertaining to each article, each author (Science Citation Index), each review (impact factor), etc., is automatically available.

THE PATENT BASES

The starting point is the analysis of patents registered by firms. It is generally admitted that patent bases contain information which is 80 percent original. No one knows how to use the information, however, principally because innovation goes beyond all analysis categories, particularly statistics. Patent bases are either commercial, and therefore international, or jurisdictional (corresponding to country base, European base).

WORLD PATENT INFORMATION BASE

The WPI(L) (World Patent Information–Latest) is a private database managed by Derwent, a British company which computerizes legal documents called "patent-documents" (requests for a patent, patents granted, modifications, issues, etc.) relating to patents in about thirty countries. In particular, Derwent enters registered patent requests in Japan. There are a great many of these (one request per single claim of the Western type), and the number should be taken into account for statistics. On the other hand, the requests thus make available a good deal of information even before the patent is granted.

The documents entered date back to 1963 (pharmaceutical products and agriculture), 1966 (polymers and plastics), 1970 (other chemical products), 1974 (other fields). They are organized by family around a priority patent, that is, generally around the first registered patent mentioning the invention (often a patent registered in the inventor's country of origin). Overall, there is thus an entry per invention which leads to statistics per number of inventions (and not by patent-document). The WPI(L) entry mentions the number of family members, in this way giving an evaluation of its importance. Companies owning the patents appear under a standard format, which facilitates accurate interrogations and statistical sorting by company.

Fortunately, the WPI(L) patent database (Derwent) provides a normalized title for each patent family of the base (a patent family is made up of all patents corresponding to the same invention as contained in a single priority patent: a family normally includes all foreign applications related to a domestic prior application). The normalized title is a normalized version of a family title given by

WPI(L) editors. Generally the applicant gives only a short, meaningless title recorded in the standard databases. The WPI(L) provides improved titles based on the whole text of the priority document. Furthermore, WPI(L) tries to use thesaurus terms. The normalized version is obtained by suppressing tool-words, normalizing words, and so on, through computer processing tools.

For instance, the title, "Appts. for high intensity treatment of solid particles—comprises means of adding fuel, particles and oxidizing gas to combustion chamber" is made of the priority patent original title "Apparatus for high intensity treatment of solid particles" to which new words are added in order to know more about the complete technology involved. The normalized title (IT field) consequently is "Apparatus high intensity treat solid particle comprise add fuel particle oxidation gas combust chamber." In some cases, WPI(L) adds in a specific field (called "AW") other words which are useful for understanding the context.

Apart from these "in-house" products, all the usual details concerning patents, that is, the important front page headings, citations of other patents, or the number of citations of scientific articles, plus a summary (frequently very extensive) in English of the entire patent-document, are given. However, if the examiner's citations of other patents (citations appearing on the front page) are mentioned, only the *number* of other documents (scientific articles) the examiner has cited is indicated.

The base contained about 5 million references to patent families in 1992. Its yearly growth rate is on the order of 300,000 new families of patents, representing 600,000 new patent-documents.

EUROPEAN PATENT DATABASE (EPAT)

The EPAT is the European patent database. In Europe, patent requests are published, hence registered, with the final approval being subsequently attached to the patent. At a preliminary stage, scientometricians do not distinguish between the patent request and the registered patent, knowing that most patents requested are registered.

The EPAT base presents the same interest for European scientometry as USPAT does for scientometry in the United States. It enumerates patents registered within the same legal framework—which does away with differences relating to national jurisprudence, particularly the artificial multiplication of Japanese patents in Japan—in liaison with a coherent economic framework which the market in European countries represents. It is therefore an ideal base from which to make statistical calculations from the viewpoint of European interests, the WPI(L) base tending more to competitive technological intelligence. (According to the field reviewed, there are 5 to 10 more patent documents in the WPI(L) base).

The EPAT base has the additional advantage of having patent titles and summaries in English, German, and French. Finally, except for certain references from the CHEMICAL ABSTRACTS base, for example, which are obtainable from this base only through a computerized access code, the same base generally clearly indicates all the examiner's references to other documents: number of patents cited, scientific articles (often review articles, taken sometimes from a set of documents partly specific to the examiner, as well as articles on applied science or even fundamental research).

Patent classification codes obviously cannot be used to identify the networks from which they arise: the information is too unsophisticated. It would be desirable to have a system of keywords such as the descriptors used for scientific articles in certain databases. The patents could be recoded through keywords derived from summaries. For ease of method, normalized uniterms of WPI(L) titles (also called interpreted titles) were used. These, in fact, supply information on the main points of a patent which link it to technological families and types of use, in short, to fabrication or process technological networks and to product technological networks.

It is thus interesting to try to use the normalized title as a list of keywords, a keyword being defined as a string between two space characters. (Using word processing techniques, this list of uniterms can be improved by joining a set of two succeeding words—for instance, joining "ice cream" to make "ice*cream"). The advantage of WPI(L) titles is that they account for uses, specific features, and a host of useful information for describing technology networks—information often absent from classification codes.

With these titles, we obtain both meaningful results and network properties as in the case of genuine keywords (scientific articles).

OTHER SCIENTIFIC AND TECHNICAL DATABASES

Apart from the large bases described above, a number of other specialized bases deal with specific scientific and technical fields. Among these is a database for conference proceedings ("grey literature"). Study reports requested by government agencies can prove particularly interesting, and more up-to-date information can emerge from scientific colloquia than from scientific articles. Civil engineering conferences can inform more on engineering know-how than can articles.

Conference databases present two types of problems, however. The publication of conference proceedings follows no set rules: they can be printed quickly or can take a long time to come out. Conferences which take place at regular intervals can be of interest for competitive intelligence; on the other hand, those with no obvious distinction can deflect its course.

COMMERCIAL EVENTS DATABASES

These bases are organized by commercial issues as indicated in publications aimed for the use of companies. An example of a commercial event would be the launching of a new product. PROMPT, INFOMAT, etc., are the principal bases covering industrial publications in all developed countries. These bases give competitive intelligence an insight into competitive commercial intelligence.

COWORD ANALYSIS: LEXIMAPPE SOFTWARE

The coword analysis method described here can be adapted to all types of data as long as the documents are described in terms of knowledge networks (scientific articles), know-how (technology, conferences) or applications (documents market) through the use of cowords.

Two words can be associated in many documents.[3] This connection is taken as an association index between words. (The usual index is the probability of obtaining the second word of the pair when the first one appears, multiplied by the same probability calculated in the other direction). After calculating links between words, coword analysis

- Orders links in decreasing order of their strength
- Selects from this list words having the most important links with about nine other words. This activity gives clusters of the most tightly linked words through a pathway (not the most tightly linked words all together); when a cluster of ten such words appears (when reading the word-pair list in decreasing order), the succeeding pairs made up of one of these words are deleted from the list (but the links are maintained between clusters for further calculation as external links)[4]
- Calculates centrality and density weights for each cluster. The density is the mean value of the internal links; the centrality is the sum of values of the external links.

Through connecting components, coword analysis indicates the themes that are aggregates of the keywords by which the documents are linked and behind which potential actors can be found. In the case of dense themes, these are sometimes organized around a model common to several documents or, in the case of central themes, sometimes organized simply around precise centers of interest shared by different documents. The cognitive strategies of researchers are represented by the keyword associations. As already indicated, these are sociocognitive categories and not stable cognitive categories or, even less, the cognitive categories themselves.

In conclusion, when LEXIMAPPE themes are not interpreted in a cognitive manner but are used as a means for identifying clusters of articles close to their strategic function in relation to the knowledge development network, coword analysis can point up the nature of these clusters. On the basis of a specific attribution rule—for example, the necessity to contain at least two keywords of the theme—any given document can be said to belong to a certain theme. When documents regarding a theme through laboratories, authors and countries are inspected, the most important actors, predominant laboratories, and countries, as well as their strong or weak points, can be identified.

After potential themes have been identified, the translation strength around these interests (density of the theme) and the strength of the links between themes (centrality of the theme) has to be evaluated in order to plot the morphology of the entire network.

Usually, using median values for centrality and density (values which divide cluster lists into two sets of equal size), we classify the clusters into four groups according to their degree of centrality and density. We also display the clusters on a "strategic diagram" (or graph) made by plotting centrality and density rank values along two axes.

The centrality will be interpreted as the degree to which the themes overlap (because the distinguishable themes of science-in-the-making do not generally have a definition which enables them to be strictly separated and are thus linked to each other). Density can be interpreted as the degree of theme development.

The origin of the axes is situated at the point of the median rank values of centrality and density. Under these terms, the centrality axis contrasts specific or isolated themes with overlapping themes, and the density axis contrasts context themes with the developed themes in the file studied. In other words, two divisions of an equal number are obtained of the theme, one relating to the vertical axis, the other relating to the horizontal axis, and four quadrants. This layout emphasizes the outstanding properties of translation networks.

Dense themes, that is, those with strong associations that correspond to articles whose lists of keywords are very close, are to be found in the upper right quadrant. In addition, these clusters are associated with several others. In other words, an article whose keywords belong to one of these clusters also contains the keywords belonging to other clusters. Related articles with multiple offshoots (that is, which affect multiple translations) are found in this quadrant because it represents the present strategic core of the network or its focal point. In principle, the major articles of the field corresponding to the file of selected articles are to be found here and, needing no further proof, will be those most often cited.

The lower right quadrant corresponds to articles which are widely different from each other (low density) but which are linked to a number of clusters (strong centrality). They represent centers of interest operating very general, major translations. This quadrant particularly holds promising research themes or, more generally, those representing loans from one preponderant network to other scientific networks, either relating to the future (promising themes), past (context themes) or situated outside the studied field (loans). This quadrant is therefore often called a transfer zone and is essential to the understanding of the field, although it plays a different role from the upper right quadrant.

The upper left quadrant corresponds to articles which are very close to each other, but which are specialized on a single theme. The specialized themes of a field can therefore be found here, whether signifying internal themes of the field which are sufficiently developed to represent autonomous sub-fields, or "imported" external themes, that is, those belonging to other fields and enjoying a new career in the field under study.

Finally, the lower left quadrant corresponds to themes which are neither central nor developed and which represent the boundary zones of the field under discussion. Clusters from this zone can work their way toward the right (through the development of their external links) or toward the top (through the development of their internal links) which will be the beginning of new development trends in the area.

To avoid any inconvenience arising from the threshold of the maximum number of words per aggregate, words which would have composed one theme only if the threshold were higher are related.

In this way, the strategic network of pathways leading from one cluster to another can be traced by using a selection rule. A pathway lies between two clusters, for example, from the moment there are at least three links among words belonging to the clusters studied and with a value superior to the lowest value of the internal link in one of the two clusters.

The term "crossroad cluster" is used for a theme which is associated with at least two other clusters obtained after it in the calculation algorithm. Hence, these links are between clusters defining the principal clusters which emerge first in the LEXIMAPPE algorithm and the secondary clusters which are an extension of the former are obtained. The analysis of trends, particularly for forecasts, only pertains to crossroad clusters, as has been shown in previous studies. Other clusters can, in fact, be linked to the momentary appearance of a cluster of articles which are associated, but which do not have true strategic value for the field.

In the case of keywords from scientific publications, we observed typical moves for crossroad clusters on the strategic diagram, for instance, from the lower right quadrant to the upper right quadrant. This move corresponds to an increase in density values for clusters (research themes) that were first central, and thus to a decrease in the centrality/density ratio.

Since normalized patent title words are a less controlled kind of information than keywords, we only studied changes over a period of time for clusters belonging to the upper right quadrant in the second period of time (clusters externally and internally linked over median values). For these clusters, we looked at earlier clusters (that is, those having in common most words or the most important as regards weight of links) in the first period of time. We compared the change in the centrality/density ratio (rank values) in time.

In this way, we obtain regular changes which show that the LEXIMAPPE clusters are a way of highlighting a regular dynamic in technological changes. In other words, technologies corresponding to the clusters are either consolidated or proliferate from a strategic position, or succeed in improving their strategic position from a consolidated state. The analytical coword diagrams are therefore a systematic way for pointing up the life cycles of technologies based on information provided by patents.

RESULTS OBTAINED

Coword analysis supplies an irreplaceable method for evaluating the true strategic aspect of a technology.

STRATEGIC TECHNOLOGIES IN THE FIELD OF THE CHEMICAL PURIFICATION OF RESIDUAL GASES

All the patents registered in the BO1D-053/34 sub-group in the International Patent Classification were selected. This sub-group is entitled "Chemical purification of residual gases"; for example, smoke, steam, oven efflux or exhaust fumes from combustion engines. Two hundred forty-two patents were obtained for the period 1985-87 and 291 references for 1988-90.

The coword analysis for the 1988-90 period brought to light 11 themes corresponding to a variable number of patents (Table 1). A single patent can correspond to two or more themes.

The association network between clusters reveals the specificity of a process with regard to a certain chemical compound (Figure 2). Treatment by water is frequently used as concerns carbon dioxide. It is, moreover, possible to relate the different processes either with the help of the techniques used or by those of the treated products. Denitrification methods are generally linked to the problem of treating exhaust fumes by catalytic processes.

The association network between clusters emphasizes a theme linked to all the others: the desulphurization of gases. In short, it is statistically impossible to register any type of patent without its containing a link with the problem of desulphurization.

The subject regarding the treatment of fumes containing heavy metals is also an example of a second central theme, together with the use of fluidized beds to eliminate sulphurized hydrogen.

The strategic diagram (Figure 3) shows another form of theme centrality consisting of retaining links with other clusters without itself being a technological crossroads-like theme. A case in point is the purification of gases containing carbon dioxide, a technology which appears in quadrant 1, along with the gas desulphurization theme in general. On the other hand, the elimination of sulphurized hydrogen through fluidified beds is too much of a heterogeneous theme to appear in quadrant 1.

Gas purification is not confined only to treating pollutants; patents are also registered for combustion techniques which reduce discharge. The strategic diagram shows that these processes are relatively well developed within the field.

It is possible to calculate the percentage of patents according to theme for any given country and to divide this percentage by the total percentage of patents registered by this country at the overall level of gas purification. In this way, what is termed the activity index of a country can be obtained on a theme (Figure 4).

Table 2 indicates the most important companies for strategic themes within the field. This helps to pinpoint more accurately certain aspects of specialization prevalent in different countries and to distinguish the activities of leading firms.

Experience has shown that the clusters obtained by coword analysis are generally far more numerous than the themes which

TABLE 1

List of word clusters, themes, and patent numbers obtained by applying the LEXIMAPPE method to a set of European patents published between 1988 and 1990 and related to the technological field "Chemical purification of residual gases."

CLUSTERS OF WORDS	THEME	NO. OF PATENTS
High centrality and density		
Gas[(a)]		
flue, waste, treat, sulphur, desulphurize	Treatment of effluent gases; desulphurization	220
Di-oxide		
carbon, scrub, aqueous, sulphuric	Treatment of gases containing carbon dioxide; scrubbing with aqueous solutions	34
Metal		
heavy, toxic, compound, alkali, solution	Removal of heavy metal compounds; treatment solutions: metallic compounds, alkali	37
High centrality and low density		
Dry		
lime, alkaline, cooling, hot	Gas treatment with dry sorbent; treatment with lime; cooling systems	24
Stream		
sulphur, hydrogen, zinc, fluid, bed, adsorb	Removal of hydrogen sulphide; absorbing compositions; fluidized beds, porous beds, . . .	24
Purification		
acid, washing, air, wet, temperature	Air purification; wet washing; acid solutions of treatment; acid production	42
High density and low centrality		
Ammonia		
denitrification, nitrogen, control, effluent	Denitration; treatment with ammonia	30
Reduce		
combust, emit, boiler, burner	Combustion devices (boiler, burner): technical process for reducing emissions	31
Heat		
halide	Heating devices; detoxication of halides	13
Low density and centrality		
Separate		
solid, particle, dust, reactor, process	Separation process: particles filtering, dust separator	20
Exhaust		
clean, catalyst, injection	Exhaust gases: catalytic treatment; injection	13

(a) Word in bold corresponds to the central word of each cluster.

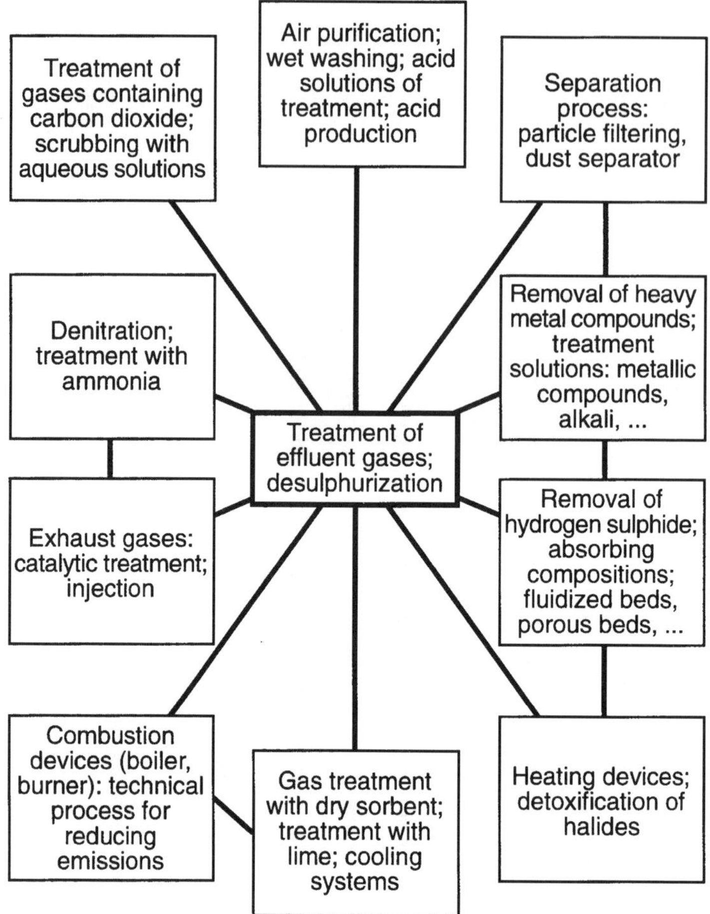

FIGURE 2. Association network obtained through coword analysis (LEXIMAPPE method) of the technological field of "Chemical purification of residual gases" (set of European patents published between 1988 and 1990).

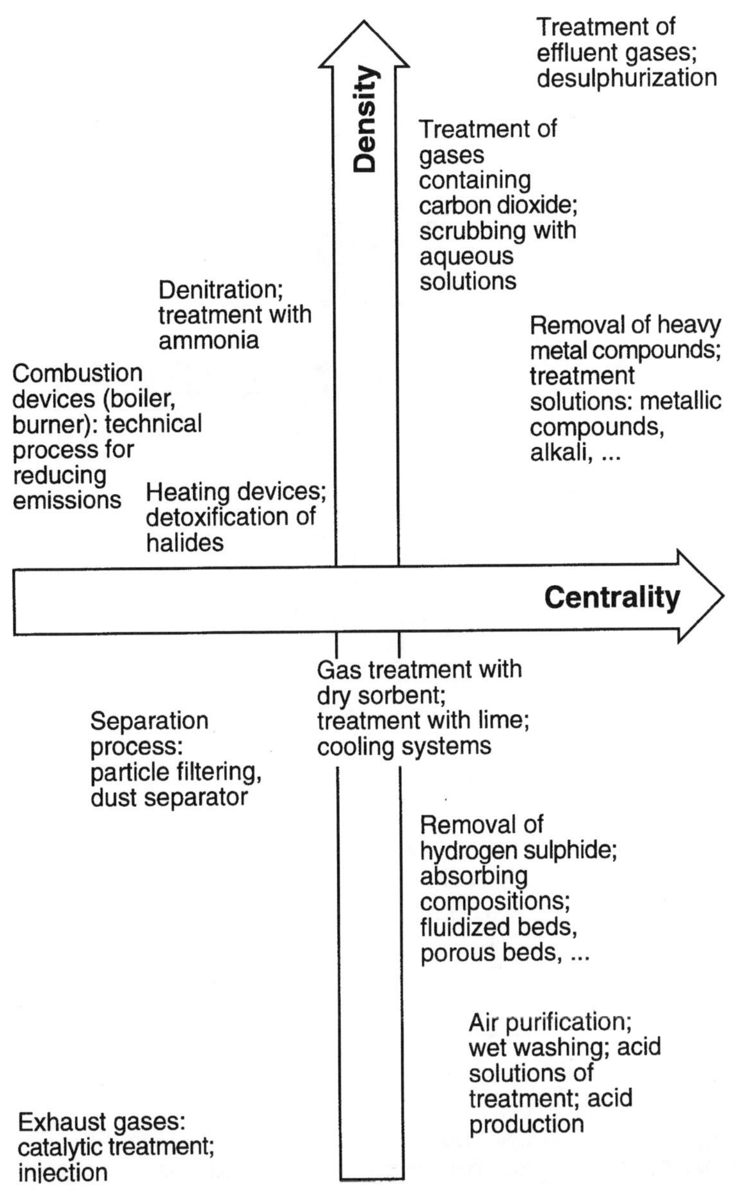

FIGURE 3. Strategic diagram obtained through coword analysis (LEXIMAPPE method) of the technological field of "Chemical purification of residual gases" (set of European patents published between 1988 and 1990).

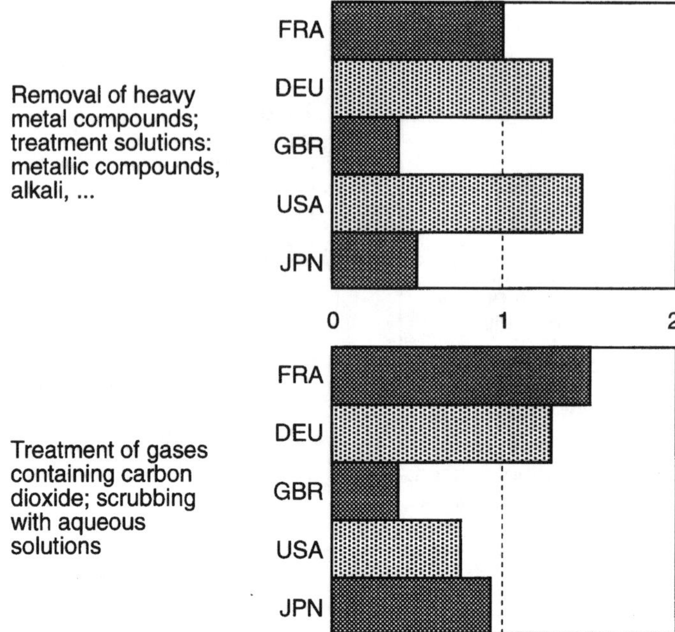

FIGURE 4. Activity indexes of main countries for strategic themes.

TABLE 2

Main firms filing patents on strategic themes of the technological field of "Chemical purification of residual gases" (extracted from a set of European patents published between 1988 and 1990)

Theme	French Firms	Main Firms (No. of Patents)
Treatment of gases containing carbon dioxide; scrubbing with aqueous solutions	Bertin & Cie L'Air Liquide Soc. Nat. Elf Aquitane	Bayer AG (3) Dow Chem Corp. (2) Chiyoda Chem. Eng. Co. (2) Shell Int. Res. Mij. BV (2)
Removal of heavy metal compounds; treatment solutions: metallic compounds, alkali, . . .	Inst. Fr. du Petrole Lab. SA Bertin & Cie L'Air Liquide	Brown Boveri Cie (4) Dow Chem. Corp. (3) Basf Ag (2) Japan Pionics Ltd. (2) Mobil Oil Corp. (2)

spring to the mind of experts (Courtial and Sigogneau 1994). They can also comprise a different structure: two technological themes which an expert would consider as different (for example, membranes and electrolytic processes for waste water) can make up a single cluster of patents if the technologies cannot be dissociated. Finally, the method is able to measure new technologies in terms of their strategic aspects: some new technologies entail the complete reorganization of a factory, and others are substitutes for a limited aspect of older technologies.

LINKS BETWEEN OTHER TECHNOLOGIES AND RESEARCH

To locate the leading technological fields involved in the development of techniques for gas purification, other associated codes of the CIB's sub-group BO1D-053/54 were identified (Table 3). The largest category is "chemical way to fight noxious chemical compounds."

To determine the links between technology and fundamental science, two research fronts with cowords relating to the problem of gas desulphurization were identified in the ISI database (Figure 5). As Figure 5 shows, work on the treatment of sulphur dioxide by

TABLE 3
Main International Patent Classification (IPC) codes linked to the technological field "Chemical purification of residual gases" (extracted from a set of European patents published between 1988 and 1990)

IPC Code	Title of Code	Number of Patents
A62D - 003/00	Chemical way to fight noxious chemical compounds; process to make them inoffensive	46
F23 - 015/00	Device planning of fume or vapor treatments	46
B01D - 000/00	Separation (B01: process or device, physical or chemical, in general)	31
C01B - 017/00	Sulphur; its compounds (C01: inorganic chemistry)	22

RF 89-1739:	"Coal char; reacting in surfactant-modified sorbents; SO2 removal; gasification kinetics; gaz carbon reactions"	USA .... 50% JPN .... 8% FRA .... 6% Total N = 48
RF 88-5544:	"Perovskite-type oxides; catalytic removal of sulfur-dioxide; sulfided la 1-XSRXCOO3; flue gas desulfurization; cobalt (III) complexes"	USA .... 26% JPN .... 39% Total N = 23

FIGURE 5. Research fronts (SCISEARC database/ISI) linked to the theme of "gas desulphurization."

catalytic processes is mainly carried out in Japan. France is not indicated on any of the identified research fronts.

The following example shows the observable regularities in the clusters obtained through coword analysis of 11 technological fields in a given area, rather than just one.

TECHNOLOGY DYNAMICS IN THE CASE OF FOOD PRODUCTS

The data used are patents from 11 subfields of the WPI(L) database in the food products section of the International Patent Classification (IPC). Each subfield corresponds to a specific IPC code. This code has been defined so as to have between 300 and 700 patents for a period of one or two years. For each subfield, two periods of time have been used in order to make comparisons over time. Table 4 lists subfields and the number of patents.

By applying coword analysis to patent family titles, we easily obtained understandable technological themes through clusters.

An example of a coword theme is given in pasta and oven cooking, Field A21 in the second period of time, by the following word list: fat, sugar, egg, wheat, add, water, preparation, rye, mixture. All words are linked to flour. The most important links are, in decreasing order, with the following words: fat, sugar, egg, wheat. This means that a lot of patents refer to pasta composition. All these patents contain the words flour, fat, sugar, egg and wheat. In

TABLE 4
Food product subfields

Subject Area	IPC Code	First Period Year	First Period Inventions	Second Period Year	Second Period Inventions
Alcoholic beverage	C12+, except C12M,N,P,Q	1985	437	1989	315
Oven cooking; pasta	A21+	1985	714	1989	603
Meat and fish	A22+	1985	555	1989	389
Food	A23B+	1985	524	1989	505
Dairy products	A23C+	1985	329	1989	337
Fat	A23D+	1983-85	352	1988-89	356
Pet food	A23K+	1985	498	1989	475
Nonalcoholic beverage	A23L-002/00	1982-85	212	1987-89	253
Canned food	A23L-003/00	1982-85	306	1987-89	277
Sugar and starch	C13+	1984-85	44	1988-89	276
Leather and skin	C14+	1984-85	531	1988-89	522
TOTAL			4942		6457

addition some of them contain such words as "add" (that is, specific features to add to pasta) or "rye" and so forth.

The theme flour was already present in the first time period. However, new words appeared in the second time period: fat and sugar. The appearance of these words means that the novelty concerning pasta flour patents lies in fat- and sugar-related problems. Referring to patents containing these words, we can see that dietary problems related to fat and sugar are a new general purpose for patents.

The location of themes on the strategic diagram is also another indicator for the general importance of corresponding patents. Themes on the upper right quadrant are of strategic importance. In the case of the theme "dough," which belongs to this quadrant for both time periods and corresponds to most patents, patents corresponding to the theme in the first period of time are cited 0.9 times (median value). In general, patents of the field are cited 0.6 times. This number indicates that citation criteria are related to strategic positions of themes. In other words, looking at the location of themes within the strategic diagram is a way of identifying patents that will be the most cited, without resorting to citations.

Furthermore, Figure 6 indicates changes in the centrality/density ratio over time for a list of 25 themes. These themes are present in both time periods and, in the second period, are in the upper right quadrant of the strategic diagram. Clearly, if this ratio is below 1, it will increase and vice versa. This property is well established (for 100 percent of themes below 1 [10 themes] and 80 percent [12/15] of themes above 1).

If we want to use this general property—checked with 11,399 patents for 11 different subfields—as a predictive one, we must follow themes that will appear in the next period of time in the upper right quadrant of the strategic diagram. This tracking is not easy to do, as the content of themes changes over time. If we define a theme by the list of words it contains, some themes have two or more successors. As described in earlier studies on polymers, a theme often splits into two or more themes or merges with another, another way of expressing the fact that technologies are constantly evolving. Thus, in the first period of time, we must consider a large list of themes not necessarily belonging initially to the upper right quadrant.

The main purpose of this account is to point out some properties of the dynamics of technology. Results suggest that technology

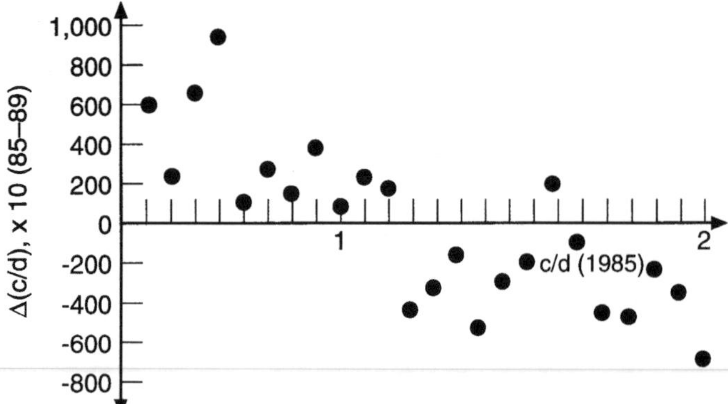

FIGURE 6. Changes in centrality/density ratio (Y axis) from year 1985 to year 1989, according to year 1985 value (X axis).

located well within a technological network will increase in development (density), whereas, a well-developed technology in a less strategic position will improve its links. Patents on a new flour composition—a strategic position for a lot of doughs—will develop improvements. On the other hand, patents on a high-frequency bread oven will, for instance, develop baking-control software programs in order to obtain bread whose particular quality corresponds to customer tastes.

LINKS WITH COMMERCIAL EVENTS

In the second analysis period, the patents theme regarding doughs-ovencooking led to new words: flour, sugar and fat (Figure 7). This result principally concerned the Japanese firm

4/8 (C) DERWENT
AN 89-148723 (20)
XA Bread-like cake prodn. -by kneading **flour** mixed with **sugar**, protein cracking enzyme, etc. ... and adding **fats** (J5 172.82)
DC D11
PA (ASAE) **ASAHI** DENKA KOGYO
NP 2
PN J89021940 B 890424 DW 8920
J57029243 A 820217 DW 8920
PR 80JP-103240 800728
AP 80JP-103240 800728
IC A21D-008/04 A21D-013/00
AB Process comprises kneading a flour mixed with sugar (10-30 wt. %), additives and protein cracking enzyme to make a dough, and inserting roll-in fats, in an amt. of 10-50 wt. % based on the dough.
Used for food prodn. plants. (J57029243-A) (5pp Dwg. no. 0/0)

PATENT: WPI(L)

0686284
JAPAN-**ASAHI** DENKA LAUNCHES BAKERY FATS
JapanScan (JS) November, 1989 (page 5)

Asahi Denka has a range of **fats** for **flour** confectionery and bread, including a fat with added **sugar** to improve yeast fermentation and a fat for Western flour confectionery.

PRODUCT: Bakeries (FOBR); margarine and cooking fats
EVENT: New products and technology
COUNTRY: Japan (JP), Far East (FEA)

EVENT: INFOMAT INTERNATIONAL BUSINESS

FIGURE 7. Market-patent link—finding a market event corresponding to a particularly innovative patent.

ASAHI DENKA. It was possible to find a commercial event related to the launching of a new product by this same firm in the INFOMAT commercial operations database and therefore to correlate a technological invention with a commercial innovation.

SCIENTIFIC DYNAMIC

Because LEXIMAPPE clusters are not cognitive themes, but provisionally translated overlapping problems, their content generally changes when the file or reference period is changed. If we go from an academic science file (that is, fundamental science), for example, to an applied science file, the same technological stake will not be translated in the same way.

Such a change applies to any given type of file viewed over time. Generally speaking, the problems or keywords of a given LEXIMAPPE cluster are associated differently as time goes by. Certain words disappear. Words of a cluster can be found later in two or even three different clusters. It would, for example, be possible to give preference to a cluster containing the highest number of words common to the initial theme or to a cluster whose words in common with the initial theme played the determinant role from the point of its strategic positioning (words contributing most to the cluster as regards its centrality or density). In fact, all successive developments observed in a field over time are interesting: they indicate how the different aspects of a given theme have different trajectories.

The strategic diagram regarding environmental research efforts published in *Science* and *Nature* from 1986 to 1989 (top of Figure 8) reveals the actors that can be used to describe the construction of the field. Four strategic clusters are particularly emphasized: hydrology of surface water; pollution (linked in particular to waste disposal); paleoecology (climatic action on ecosystems); and, with recent events in mind, volcanic eruptions (eruption of Lake Nyos in Cameroon) concerning sudden gas discharges. The contextual themes relate to marine ecology and human action. Specialized themes deal with studies in polar regions and on the paleoenvironment, as well as acid rain. Marginal themes, though still ones that are considered significant science and that are published in the most reputable scientific reviews, are air pollution, the greenhouse effect, and the ecosystems of freshwater or tropical forests. It

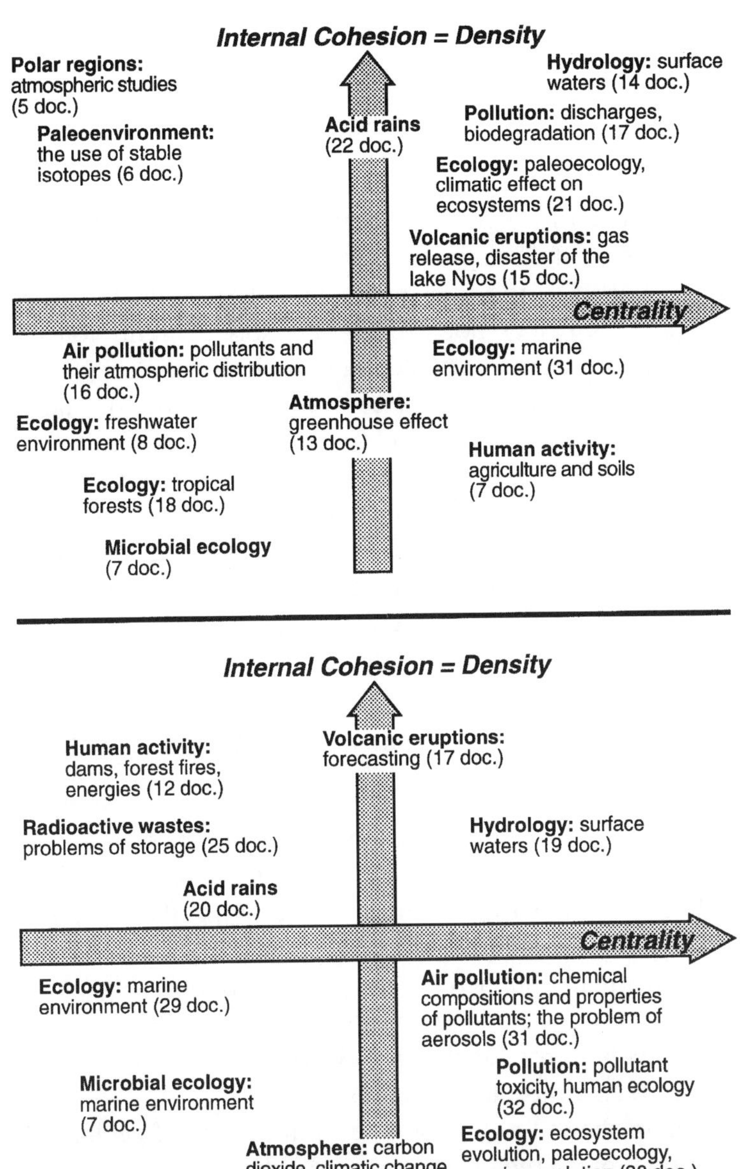

FIGURE 8. Strategic diagrams obtained through coword analysis of *Nature* and *Science* articles linked to the field of environment (PASCAL/CNRS database). Publication years for top diagram are 1986–1989, for the bottom 1982–1985.

can thus be seen that "significant science" does not reflect the weight of these different themes in public opinion, the most strategic (surface-water hydrology, for example) being the least spectacular.

Although these themes are like scientific sub-disciplines, they should be taken for what they really are—actors involved in the advancement of knowledge and whose description, through key-words, is linked to the role they genuinely play in this progress. This description does not express any sort of definition of the themes and even less the reflection of logical links.

From the preceding period (see bottom of Figure 8), paleoecology and studies in pollution and human action on nature became strategic, and marine ecology moved from being a marginal element to a context level. The specialized character of research on acid rain was stepped up, with a slight growth in its centrality. Research into the greenhouse effect appeared and problems related to the study of radioactive waste disappeared (doubtless because they can be found in a different context).

THE NETWORK OF STRATEGIC PATHWAYS BETWEEN CLUSTERS

In the case of environmental research, the links between clusters and the paths leading from one cluster to another are shown in Figure 9 (top). For example, a pathway from ecology (scientific) to hydrology, passes through microbial ecology, then to pollution linked to public or industrial waste disposal.

The same map obtained for the previous period (Figure 9, bottom) showed other crossroad clusters and other pathways such as the ones leading from acid rain to hydrology, passing through air pollution, then atmospheric studies.

This map shows the link between three types of ecological science in relation to the environment, dividing the research area to a certain extent in the manner in which they translate the research problems: study of ecosystems, microbial ecology, and marine ecology. In the following time period, this dynamic propelled marine ecology—as well as fresh-water milieu ecology—away from being negotiated as a mere item in a set of roles to clear autonomy in relation to environmental problems.

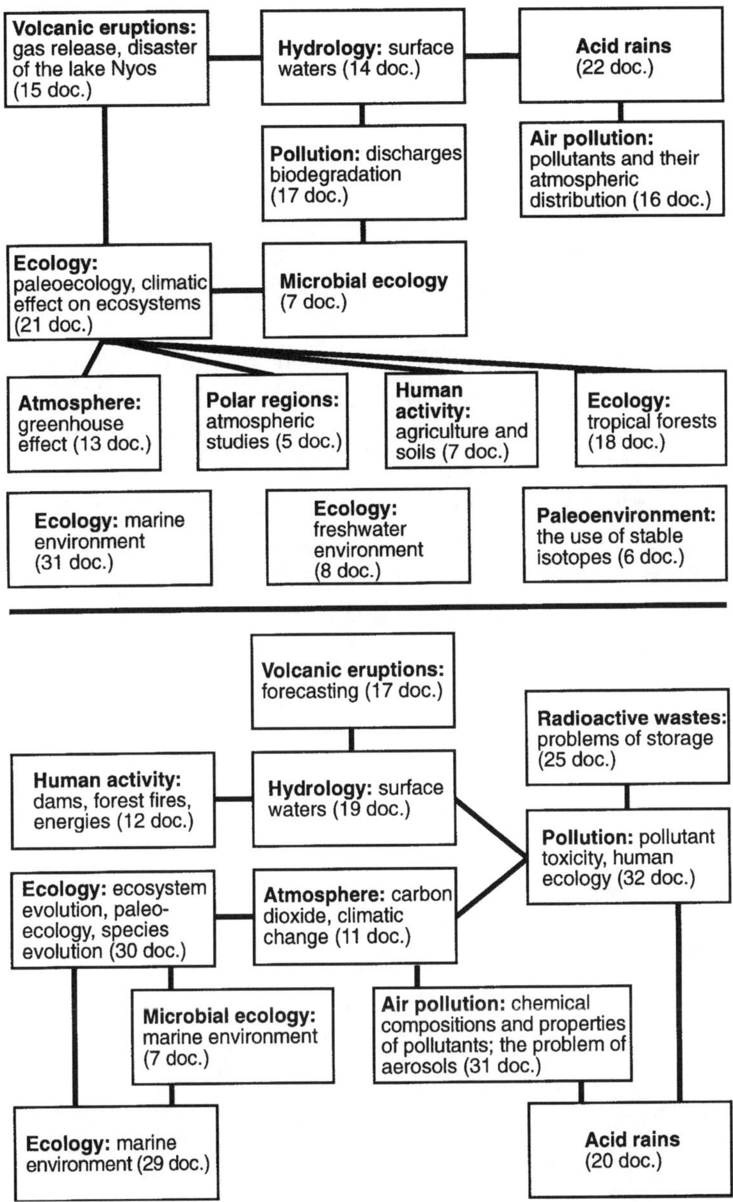

FIGURE 9. Association networks obtained through coword analysis of *Nature* and *Science* articles linked to the field of environment (PASCAL/CNRS database). Publication years for top diagram are 1986–1989, for the bottom 1982–1985.

TECHNOLOGY CYCLES

If four or five time periods are considered instead of only one or two, it would no doubt be possible to follow continuously the variations in density and centrality values of LEXIMAPPE clusters. In certain cases, typical centrality graphs would be found, for example. This type of calculation has, in fact, been made for articles concerning polymer science and technology (Callon et al. 1991). Clusters in which centrality increased continuously have been obtained.

The tracing of centrality diagrams in relation to time is therefore an additional method for analyzing the life-cycle of a technology. Centrality (c) and density (d) values, as well as the number of articles published over a given time period (n) or articles accumulated (na) in relation to time from both academic science publications and from all types of publication are indicated in Figures 10 and 11, respectively, for the theme of liquid crystals.

For the given time period, it can be seen that the centrality of the theme passes a peak in the case of strictly academic polymer

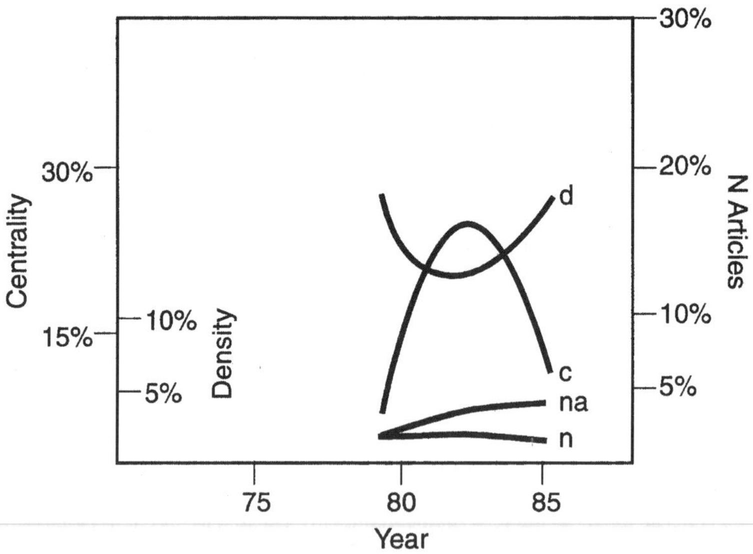

FIGURE 10. Polymer academic science: "Liquid Crystal" theme life cycle.

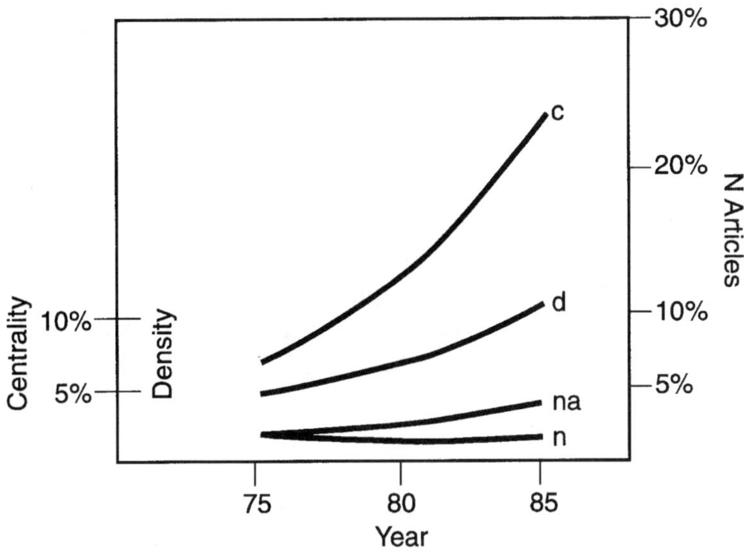

FIGURE 11. All polymer publications: "Liquid Crystal" theme life cycle.

science, although it is a continually growing subject for all scientific and technical publications on polymers (applied science publications being predominant). In other words, the strategic aspect of the theme is completely different according to the fundamental or applied reference network.

CONCLUSION

Scientometrics offers a method through which the strategic aspect of a technology can be identified through the simple analysis of complementary patents, without having to resort to unusual, rather uncertain, or complex methods.

The methodology used shows how it is possible to reveal a dynamic specific to technology in both its conceptual phase and its industrial application. Computer simulations can be undertaken (Courtial et al. 1994) which allow technologies to be considered at different strategic stages according to the viewpoint of the partners involved: research laboratories, the market, rival companies or complementary firms. A technology can be strategic at different moments—from the position of academic research (it is promising and within the scope of laboratories), industrial applications (company workplaces are prepared to use it), or consumer use (consumers are ready for it). The analysis of technological solidarity networks can, in each case, give the required information.

Coword analysis can very quickly identify the predominant technological or scientific themes implicit in a considerable number of documents; it is not necessary to read the documents themselves. Some calculations have been based on a body of 7,000 to 20,000 documents (Kostoff 1994).

Contrary to usual statistical methods, this method can reveal inconspicuous research areas which, in fact, have the peculiarity of linking several technological or scientific fields together and are thus highly innovative ("needle-in-the-haystack" capability). Promising research fronts to be found at the intersection of several technological or scientific fields can be highlighted.

Having a possible resort to the complete text implies that, in principle, all types of documents can be handled. The method can thus provide links between different classifications of documents; for example, the geographical and scientific organization of documents (scientific articles, patents, reports, press cuttings, etc.). It is possible in this way to pinpoint regional scientific solidarities which are useful for managing scientific or technological establishments.

The interest in working with technological networks by the analysis of cowords for sets of patents is to be able to demonstrate various strategic aspects according to the reference network. A technology can be strategic for a company, or group of companies, without being strategic from the viewpoint of the considered field, and vice versa. Coword analysis based on a variety of files is therefore the only method for testing a technology's strategic aspect.

REFERENCES

Callon, M., J. Law, and A. Rip. 1986. *Mapping the Dynamics of Science and Technology*. MacMillan, London.

Callon, M., J. P. Courtial, and F. Laville. 1991. Coword analysis as a tool for describing the network of interaction between basic and technology research: The case of polymer chemistry. *Scientometrics* 22(1):255-205.

Courtial, J. P., T. Cahlik, and M. Callon. 1994. A Model for Social Interaction Between Cognition and Action Through a Key-word Simulation of Knowledge Growth. *Scientometrics* 31(2):173-192.

Courtial, J. P., and A. Sigogneau. 1994. How to Use Scientific and Technological Information to Reveal Strategic Technologies. *International Journal of Technology Management, Management of Technology Flow Across Industrial Boundaries* (Special Issue) 10(1):31-44.

Kostoff, R. N. 1994. Database Tomography Origins and Applications. *Competitive Intelligence Review* 5(1):48-55.

Kuhn, T. 1970. *The Structure of Scientific Revolutions.* The University of Chicago Press, Chicago.

Price, D. J. De Solla. 1963. *Little Science, Big Science*. Columbia University Press, New York.

Small, H., and E. Greenlee. 1985. Clustering the Science Citation Index Using Co-citations. *Scientometrics* 7:391-409 (Part I), *Scientometrics* 8:331-340 (Part II)

ENDNOTES

1. R. Narin, CHI Research, Inc., 10 White Horse Pike, Haddon Heights, NJ 08035
2. G. Stacey, Battelle Europe, Centre de Recherche de Genève, 7 route de Drize, CH 1227 Carouge, Genève, Switzerland
3. Word association analysis can be derived from signification linguistic models based on the idea of co-occurrence or collocation. This subject has been dealt with by R.N. Kostoff or F. Smadja, see F. Smadja, "Extracting Collocations from Text. An Application: Language Generation," Ph.D. thesis, Columbia University, 1991.
4. Another possibility could be to keep words from the association list as far as clusters are built. We may obtain many more clusters which are slightly different from each other and thus may gain a more precise picture of the field.

Practical Use of Competitive Technical Intelligence:
Superconductor Business Applications and Opportunities

CHRISTINE LEBOULANGER and
FRANÇOISE PERDRIEU-MAUDIÈRE

Developing and exploiting advanced materials will be one of the main challenges for companies and laboratories around the world in the next decade. The vast product potential and the strategic business role of materials technology and manufactured articles will require traditional materials industries and high-tech firms to make important investments in these materials. High-temperature superconductors are one of these advanced materials. Although still not in widespread use because more research and development (R&D) is needed, high-temperature superconductors offer the prospect of radical change in many fields.

This chapter provides a picture of the companies and countries that dominate emerging markets and applications for superconducting technology, emphasizing the nature of relationships between participating firms and their impact on market structure and competition. Indicators based on patent data are used to describe the active companies, the characteristics of their positions, and the evolving nature of the industry in major countries of the world (Campbell 1983). This research illustrates the kind of patent analysis that can provide a useful background of basic, industry-wide, global information for companies entering markets growing out of this exciting new field.

SUPERCONDUCTING TECHNOLOGY

Traditional low-temperature superconducting technology has been in use for many years, primarily for electric power generation and transmission. However, its potential has been limited owing to the need for very elaborate and expensive cryogenic support equipment to maintain extremely low temperatures. Finding materials that are superconductors at higher temperatures has been a long-sought goal. The current set of room-temperature/high-temperature superconductors that generated so much excitement was precipitated by IBM's discovery of the first high-temperature superconductor in April 1986.

The growth of entrepreneurial activity by many research teams; the investments of large private sector firms; the research programs funded by the government in the United States, Japan, and in a few European countries all show the importance of the stake in this high-tech industry.

The stakes are high because superconductors seem to offer the potential for entirely new and promising industrial fields, as well as to contribute to the growth of closely related industrial activity (e.g., other electrically important materials and cryogenics). It is not the immediate importance of superconductivity for industry—considerable as it may seem—which seems to dictate R&D choices, but rather its potential importance for the future. As suggested by the applications in Table 1, the growth potential of this technology appears enormous. New applications of high-temperature superconductors in fields such as electric power generation and transmission, electronic magnets, strong magnets, and transportation now seem achievable in the foreseeable future.

SUPERCONDUCTIVITY R&D AND COMPETITIVE TECHNICAL INTELLIGENCE BASED ON PATENTS

An important characteristic of superconductivity is that, probably more than any other present-day technology, it was discovered and is being developed as an international technology based on multiple contacts, projects, and joint operations that extend beyond any single country's borders. This active involvement by many government, R&D, and commercial organizations suggests

TABLE 1
Technological changes resulting from the discovery of high-temperature superconductors

Electric power	Power zero resistance High-efficiency power storage High-efficiency generation, transmission & distribution
Electronic magnets	Fast-switching communications Medical diagnostics and research—nuclear magnetic resonance Communication capacity increases Infrared sensors
Strong magnets	Effective high-energy physics equipment (colliders, fusion machines)
Transportation	High-speed trains (magnetic levitation) Efficient ship drive systems (magnetohydrodynamics)

an important need for careful intellectual property protection for superconductor developments on a global scale. This need is very likely part of the reason for the huge number of patents (21,243 patents) during the eight years from September 1986 to mid-1994 (Leboulanger 1993).

The patent data used here come from the multidisciplinary patent data bank WPI (World Patents Index of Derwent Publications Ltd.); the set specifically studied includes 14,094 patents covering the period from mid-1986 to mid-1993. Owing to the delay in issuing patents in some countries (including the United States), the lastest data set lacks representativeness; thus, the analyzed set has been restricted to the end of 1991 (13,128 patents). All the countries dealing with superconductivity have been studied, but only those holding more than 50 patents have been extensively analyzed. The statistical part of the results (but not the bibliometric one) has been updated to mid-1994.

The importance of superconductivity and the large number of patents raises several competitive technical intelligence issues. The widely accepted domain of intelligence is to recognize important events and trends and to understand their significance for the user (Bucki and Pesqueux 1993). Patents have been shown to be a valuable intelligence information resource to help identify and understand both technology- and company-related events and trends. Already, patent databases are considered to be a unique and valuable bibliometrics tool for recognizing and understanding superconductor-related scientific activity around the globe.

The creation of networks of a variety of organizational participants in the field constitutes one of the basic mechanisms that has allowed the rapid emergence of the broad area of superconductivity. The increased number of sophisticated analysis tools coming from the information and decision sciences has made it possible to obtain precise descriptions of the state of these technical networks. For instance, numerical indexes established from technical connections between patents have made it possible to identify a variety of non-obvious significant publications, linked in technical and business relationships. Some of the most important publications in the field can be readily identified because they are referred to frequently in later patents. With knowledge of these publications and with strategic information about the geographical and industrial origin of these major patents, analysts are now able to confirm or question ideas about the most important countries or firms in this field.

CHARACTERIZING POTENTIAL COMPETITORS AND NATIONAL POSITIONS

The leading companies and dominant countries can be identified from the patent activity. Likewise, the major emerging markets can be seen from the distribution of those patents by country or region.

CONCENTRATED AND OLIGOPOLISTIC MARKETS

Because of the lack of understanding about the basic science and mechanisms of high-temperature superconductivity (HTS), discoveries essentially come from small incremental advances or iterations, i.e., from the accumulation of experience. Consequently, virtually all existing patents are "technician" patents without any particular commercial value because, at this early stage, the lack of scientific knowledge makes each patent difficult to use. Nevertheless, patenting continues at a rapid pace, and a study of the geographical locations of patents by originating nations reveals that much of the effort seems to be concentrated in a few countries, predominantly Japan, the United States, France, Germany, and Great Britain.

Relative Analysis of the National Potentials

Clearly, superconductivity is limited to the organizations located in the major industrial countries (Figure 1). This geographical picture suggests the presence of a hierarchical market system dominated by the Japan/USA/Europe triad, with minor countries or under-systems weakly linked. Europe is limited to three countries—Germany, France, and Great Britain—a roughly homogeneous group (similar levels of development, similar legal systems, etc.). Their involvement is not fully homogeneous, however, because of disparities such as the level of R&D spending and

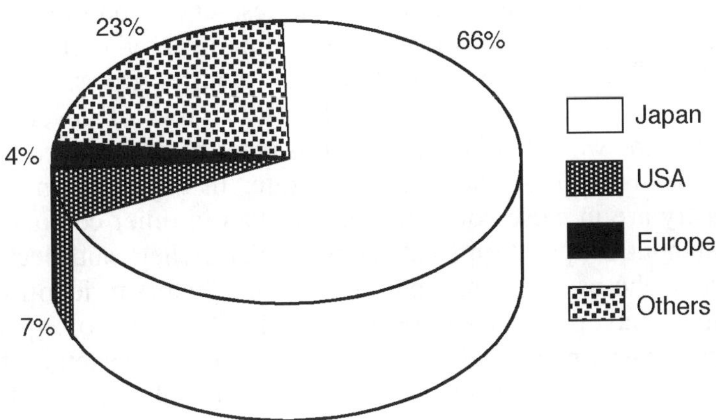

FIGURE 1. Number of superconducting patents, by country.

the scientific and technical directions of their research efforts (Leboulanger 1993).

Part of the explanation for this national concentration is that superconductivity is one of a series of technologies in which technology transfer processes play a crucial role. Transfer sciences refer to the process of rapidly bridging the gap between basic science in the laboratory and technology development in industry (OECD 1992). Successful transfer of superconductivity technology to commercial applications is limited to countries that have appropriate scientific and commercial technology infrastructure. Hence, in spite of the technical ease and low level of funding needed to participate in some of the superconductivity scientific research programs, the variety of materials science disciplines needed to actually develop commercial technology becomes a significant barrier to entry for the countries that lack a strong technological basis.

In this industry, the Japanese supremacy seems indisputable, with the United States as the closest follower (Leboulanger 1993). However, Japan and the United States already appear to show an important disparity that cannot be justified by traditional explanations of differences between the countries; for example, Japan's historical pattern of systematically imitating other countries' developments or the use of patent strategy distinctions such as differences between large or short patent, dominant or servient patent, or major or minor patent.

A valid explanation of this phenomenon may lie in the different national environments that support innovation. According to social, economic, and political realities, each country has to develop appropriate technological solutions adapted to its own situation. Thus, as the complexity of this industry grows, scientific policy in the United States that limits the role of government restricts the ways in which the various types of existing producers and the users of science can cooperate. In Japan, science and industry are in close contact, more so than in other countries. A permanent cooperation exists between researchers and decision-makers who use some social and economic factors to identify the business and operational opportunities. The high level of Japanese patent activity may result from the variety of existing actors (business, government, academia) who are closely linked in collaborative relationships and can therefore pursue some related, although not necessarily identical, R&D objectives.

Comparison of Small and Large Firm Positions

Because the market is uncertain and the task of keeping a direct watch on the potential implications of the latest developments by competitors is difficult, indirect measurement tools such as scientometric methods are essential for identifying and tracking the innovative firms. Scientometric methods can reveal emerging industrial partners and small technology development companies. Studies of patent activity over the last years show the nature and rate of participation by firms in a given field. The information contained in patent literature is an excellent source for identifying both potential follow-on inventions and probable emerging competitors.

The superconductor industry is a trans-national industry insofar as a few large firms control the international networks and are at the origin of almost all research in the world (Table 2) (Leboulanger 1993). This concentration is continuing and seems to be driven by the formation of oligopolies based on the depth and extent of technical and commercial knowledge.

The formation of these oligopolies tends to restrict the potential for small start-up firms to participate. This trend is accentuated

TABLE 2
Leading companies in superconductor technology

Company	No. of Patents
Sumitomo	1649
Mitsubishi	1539
Toshiba	1314
Hitachi	1215
DKB	1202
Matsushita	811
Fuyo	365
Siemens	156
General Electric	121
Westinghouse	52
IBM	50

because integration into such networks requires some form of acceptance or acknowledgment from existing network members, typically large entrenched firms. Thus, smaller entrepreneurial firms, sometimes viewed as a primary stimulus to innovation, are not yet able to play a very important commercial role in this industry.

Their wide commercial network gives the largest companies a decisive advantage over the smaller innovative firms. For instance, if the financial, technical, and commercial "staying power" of small firms to remain independent is limited, larger firms have acquired and exploited the smaller companies' technological results. Under these conditions, large firms, which are often less dynamic technologically, are able to absorb the smaller innovative companies just as their innovations, know-how, scientific, and technical potential become commercially attractive.

According to the list of the biggest assignees, a few technology specialist firms can patent the results of the totality of research, while a great many other assignees patent only occasionally. In addition, among firms that patent once, only some patent several times and only a minority can patent regularly. It appears that a "technological momentum" is established in these firms in that they can focus on the latest technology advancements and exploit related technical barriers to gain incremental patent positions. This corresponds to a model of "cumulative advantage" in the marketplace, often used in economics to explain the concentration of firms.

The long-term survival of these smaller firms appears uncertain because this industrial activity is mainly closed to science and strongly linked to research, which is more likely to be concentrated among a few large companies. Thus, the competition appears to be driven more and more by technological advances among the oligopolistic competitors. This suggests that the large multinationals who work inside some strongly concentrated market structures play a major role.

In the superconductor industry, the strong industrial concentration can easily lead to a global oligopolistic supply structure. The dominance of large firms in this industry seems to be imperative (Nègre 1987). Research is easily accessible to the large companies, even though the value of the results is not always determined by firms of a particular size. In this industry, a flood of patents has been issued by large firms that also appear to be the most innovative. Thus, in this high-technology field, being large appears to be an important condition to being able to ultimately exploit the technology with commercial products.

In addition, the concentration in the superconductor industry appears to be driven by the relation between the size of the firms and their ability to sustain the costs of further innovation. In early stages of development, information on an invention is reasonably accessible to everybody. The follow-up pursuit of commercial innovation is accessible only to the firms that are able to generate enormous resources to develop the research (Le Duff and Maïsseu 1988). Consequently, these firms usually have to capture some early market share if they want to begin to recover the cost of the risk they assume. For instance, with regard to the three European countries (Germany, France, Great Britain) active in this area, only a few companies or public laboratories pursue the development of superconductive material technologies. These national pioneers are committed to heavy R&D efforts and, most of the time, monopolize government R&D spending (Perdrieu-Maudière 1993).

International Distribution of the Market Share

An understanding of the geographical distribution of patents is necessary to assess the nature of the potential market. While many companies will patent only in their parent nation, a large number of firms will also patent in countries where they intend to do business in the future. The foreign countries in which a company files patents are its strategic markets; otherwise, the company would not incur costs to patent in these locations. Companies that anticipate participating in a specific country's market are also likely to patent in foreign countries.

The geographical distribution of patents shows a preponderance of developed countries. A sort of "mutual invasion" of other countries by the United States and Japan is evident by looking at active patenting states (Table 3) (Leboulanger 1993). The more prominent countries belong to a number of oligopolistic competitors, i.e., those that can sustain a worldwide competition. The oligopolistic effect can be identified through a "reciprocal dependence" of these countries in two ways: first, in terms of patent citations (countries whose patents cite each other) and joint agreements and, second, through the reciprocal recognition apparent in cross-

TABLE 3
Countries where American, French, Japanese, German, and British patents have been filed

	Great Britain	France	Germany	United States	Japan
Austria	—	—	—	1	—
Australia	18	9	9	102	41
Belgium	1	—	—	4	—
Brazil	3	9	—	26	2
Canada	6	13	7	129	68
China	2	8	4	18	59
Denmark	4	7	—	24	4
European Patent Office	50	83	188	317	579
E. Germany	4	—	—	—	1
W. Germany	13	22	353	71	140
Finland	7	9	1	10	8
France	3	146	9	24	33
Great Britain	73	3	10	36	70
Hungary	—	—	—	5	—
Israel	1	—	—	18	—
Italy	—	—	—	6	—
J0*	23	29	58	211	—
J5*	3	5	12	26	—
J6*	13	17	49	58	—
J8*	—	—	2	3	—
J9*	—	—	—	1	—
Korea	—	—	—	—	2
Luxembourg	—	—	—	1	—
Netherlands	1	—	—	6	3
Norway	6	10	3	19	3
Portugal	—	8	1	1	—
Spain	1	2	—	4	—
Sweden	2	—	1	7	—
Switzerland	1	—	3	2	1
U.S.	26	39	103	653	319
USSR	—	—	—	—	3
World Patents	30	15	40	136	54

*All Japan—reflects WPI's method of dealing with Japanese system of dating its patents based on the Imperial year.

country patenting, which suggests a choice of potential superconductivity markets (e.g., the pattern of links between Japanese firms patenting in the United States and, correspondingly, similar U.S. firms patenting in Japan).

While most of the Japanese patents are concentrated in Japan, many of the American titles are issued all over the world. This could suggest a qualitative weakness of the Japanese patents in the sense that new Japanese patents may be minor extensions of existing ones. A country's patent law may encourage a flood of incremental patents in the originating country to protect domestic markets (Savignon 1971) from more fundamental advances from external countries. This kind of effect could occur worldwide in other large invention-exporting industrial countries, although the data on this are not clear.

While national patent law is designed to promote the diffusion of innovation, its global purpose is to serve as a basis for business negotiations. So Japan, where patenting is aimed at protecting intellectual property, could attack the international marketplace with a few strong publications and close its domestic market with a plethora of incremental patents. Such a dichotomy does not appear in the American system because the law does not affect domestic and foreign patents differently. In addition, patent coverage is so expensive that potential patentees have to plan their international filing strategy accordingly and patent only in the most important foreign markets. These conclusions are supported by the absolute numbers of patent distribution. Indeed, in absolute value, the number of Japanese foreign patents is far greater than that of America (Leboulanger 1993).

The number of countries in which both Japanese and U.S. patents are filed (foreign patent location [FPL] countries) indicates the degree to which the technology has been internationalized. This indicator of foreign penetration shows the geographical concentration of patents: the variation in the number of FPLs up to this period is low. This distribution may result in a sort of stabilization of markets and, since companies patent in the countries where they wish to market, the pattern may signify that patenting countries know the major areas of expected competition. Patenting in potential overseas markets allows a firm to establish a patent position against the existing or potential domestic competitors in their own market, i.e., to prevent them from taking developments in superconductivity to the marketplace or from acquiring or increasing their competitive advantage from their domestic location. Indeed, establishing a strong presence in non-existing but potential future markets affords the firms an *ex ante* comparative advantage.

The patent filings by Japan, the United States, and Europe show that this triad monopolizes the pattern of foreign patenting. Such a global dimension seems to be in the center of the nationwide patent strategy, even though it is a phenomenon quite independent of the spatial expansion. This suggests the notion of preference for culturally closer markets, although this geographical preference tends to decline as awareness and certainty about the market's potential increases. In the superconductor industry, the uncertainty about the structure and nature of future markets and the desire to avoid high risks and cultural problems could partly justify the geographical preference.

Increasing interest in European markets (since the 1960s in the United States and the 1980s in Japan) may eventually lead to emergence of a strong European superconductor target market (Perdrieu-Maudière 1993). The European presence in this case, however, is limited to three countries: Germany, France and Great Britain. The Japanese presence in these states is not neutral, especially in the United Kingdom (Michalet 1989). Germany appears to be the most serious contender or the most important potential market. The presence of other countries can be justified by the existence of a few nationwide firms that are potentially dangerous in some areas (Philips of Netherlands, for example) or by certain market opportunities (Italy, for example).

The early markets for this industry may be limited to Japan, the United States, Germany, France, and the United Kingdom—the biggest patentees in superconductivity. In addition, the choice of some countries can be linked to a preference for discreet protection (Denmark or Australia) or for a patent tax haven (Liechtenstein). A company will sometimes wish to patent without any publicity. This firm will then choose a less inspected country in order to buy time to develop its technology before obtaining another patent-pending, during the priority year, in a country with strong property right protection. Switzerland is suggested as an example here because of the substantial presence of foreign industrial laboratories working in the superconductor field—Asea Brown Boveri, IBM-Zurich, for example, or Spectrospin, a worldwide leader in magnetic resonance imaging and spectroscopy.

RELATIVE POSITION OF COMPETITORS

Competition in the development of practical HTS applications is already strong among the leading companies of "high patenting" nations. Analyzing the characteristics of the various strategies pursued by these countries and firms—and especially their chance of success—is instructive.

Competition for Dominance

If a nation or an organization manages to identify some emerging opportunities beyond the constraints inherent in a foreign innovation, the cumulative effect could be quite significant and the innovation set on despite a technological dependence. Technological dependence is defined as the situation in which a nation's lack of domestic technology and know-how obliges it to import most of the technology it uses. This can be examined by *patent citation analysis*. A patent citation (that is, when a patent is referred to a later patent document) is an indication of the technical value of the earlier patent. *Citation analysis* indicates the interdependence between patents and the basic technologies they cover.

According to this definition, neither Japan nor the United States is technologically dependent. Using several foreign technologies involves a concentrated source of foreign supply and thus a strong dependence. Even though it appears that the United States depends more on Japan in terms of patent citations than Japan does on the United States, the United States cannot be characterized as a technologically dependent country. Japan has mostly adapted many foreign patents to its needs. It seems difficult to assert that this country is more dependent than another.

Rather, technological dependence should be an increasing function of the level of economic and industrial development, of the organizational capabilities, and of the existing technical or scientific potential. So, the key question does not directly concern the interdependence, but rather deals with its underlying dynamics and the use of its emerging opportunities.

If the global economy is viewed as a system (Dufourt 1979), it appears that each country is more or less dependent on the inherent interacting process. In Japan, which has succeeded in appropriating American technological discoveries, the *dominance effects* have been favorably converted in *multiplier effects.*

In theory, a priority patent might use the domestic science. In other words, a national scientific publication might have a greater chance of being cited in a national patent than in a foreign patent: the so-called *territory effect.* This effect is partly linked to the center of patent examination. Indeed, the patent examiners try to know what has been done before through their own national stock of patents before they search somewhere else. Additionally, some stocks—the American stock for example—are viewed in priority.

In the case of Japan, if the aim is to promote technological diffusion, the territory effect should be important. In the case of America, if the idea that it is the biggest science producer is pursued, the territory effect would be equally manifest.

The study of patent citations shows that if the international production and circulation of technology suggests an international technological hierarchy of different economies as centers of technological production, the international circulation provides for and breeds this hierarchy with Japan as a leader.

Dominance and Uniqueness Measures

These key factors come from a bibliometric analysis of the patent situation vis-a-vis the patentor and patentee countries. If we use an indicator of *"dominance,"* I = R/D, where

R = number of citations a country or a company has received
D = number of citations a country or a company gives

it appears that Japan controls technology better than the United States does (Leboulanger 1993). This result corresponds to the lead Japan holds in production of technology. However, the indicator result for the United States is surprising if we consider the fact that the United States is the origin of the first developments in high-temperature superconductivity.

To investigate this, the *"uniqueness,"* U, is determined (U = S/T) where

S = the number of self-citations
T = the total number of citations for a country.

A self-citation occurs when, for instance, a Japanese patent cites an earlier Japanese patent. The total number of citations is simply the number of times Japanese patents are cited by any other country's patents.

The high Japanese uniqueness result, 1.32 (see Table 4), shows that this country tries to protect its market on a large scale and to maintain its technological advantages through some "technological borders." This means that many new Japanese patents are in the same areas as older patents and describes technology that builds on older Japanese technology. This strategy supports efforts to contain the territorial expansion of off-shore competitors by obtaining some *barrier* patents close to the activity domains of the country. This strategy essentially consists of building some strong walls to serve as market barriers to other countries in a domestic market. Interestingly, as is the case with U.S. or European patents, Japanese patents overall receive more citations than they give references. This result suggests that the term "imitator" cannot be used for Japan.

The United States has a self-citation rate of 0.74, suggesting that its strategy is to exploit and improve on strong off-shore patents. Both Japan and the United States are trying to win a leadership position. Even their cooperative, multilateral agreements do not cover up the underlying struggle. For generic technologies, these pioneers must choose between dependency and competition.

Germany would appear to be an *aggressive follower* country with the undeniable domination of Siemens, which competes with major American firms in some research areas (Perdrieu-Maudière 1993). France undoubtedly takes advantage of its basic research. These laboratories made many discoveries, for instance, Chevrel

TABLE 4

National level superconductivity citation matrix

Countries	Received (R)	Citations Given (G)	Reference Ratio R/G
Japan	557	421	1.32
United States	211	264	0.80
Germany	112	151	0.74
Great Britain	30	30	1.00
France	27	40	0.67

phases and the first organic superconducting material. Its industrial experience in low temperature will be important for further progress in that area. Finally, the British contribution may seem to be less significant based on these data, but it plays an interesting part in instrumentation with the know-how of Oxford Instrument.

The European patents make few references to others, indicating an absence of strong technological dependence between those countries.

Key Success Factors in Competitive Positions

In superconductivity, most of the big Japanese patentees use an *offensive strategy* associated with *technological pioneers*. The *defensive strategy* seems to be the strategy of smaller patentees. Such a result suggests a kind of sharing of roles between the large and the smaller patentees. The large firms that can support expensive new R&D tend to make direct frontal attacks to target new superconducting breakthrough developments, while the smaller firms tend to follow the leaders and carve out niche technology applications.

In the United States, three large companies emerge: IBM, AT&T-Bell, and Westinghouse. Their indicators of dominance are very strong, while the territory indicators are low, suggesting that these firms are following offensive strategies. This may well be because their high levels of R&D funding allow them to pursue their own wide-ranging internal programs for HTS development. Generally, the large American firms, like similar Japanese companies, hardly ever use self-citation, so they may have adopted some technology specialization based on inventions by others.

Start-ups should not serve as the catalyst for innovation in American industry because it clearly adopts (i.e, references other patents) more technology than it provides to others (i.e., receives citations to its patents). These firms must be able to exploit technology with little funding because most small firms probably do not have large financial support (Leboulanger 1993).

In Europe, the most cited company is Siemens. Siemens also uses self-citations quite often. This suggests a defensive patent position through both patent coverage on the avalanche of potential applications and self-citations. Nevertheless, Siemens appears to be the European company most capable of being a serious competitor to Japan and the United States (Perdrieu-Maudière 1993).

IDENTIFYING EMERGING TRENDS IN THE NATURE OF COMPETITION

A study of the technical characteristics of patents allows us to identify the research emphasis of the leading patentees. It is possible to show the evolution of activities that indicate the strategies of the subject firms. A bibliometrics analysis of patents also helps to characterize the impact of technological evolution on participating firms and to understand the sources and stages of the technology innovation process.

This technological evolution affects the growth and maturity of a sector of activities; on one hand, technological change can open new opportunities for growth, and, on the other, these changes make old skills obsolete, opening up the need for growth (Strategor 1992). Technological change can also affect strategic industrial segmentation because firms working in different sectors or lines of business can nevertheless be in competition; moreover, it can create additional distinct segments of activities because of special market niches created by use of new technologies. Consequently, technological evolution can have significant effects on existing company positions because it creates or alters their relative business strengths and weaknesses.

POSSIBLE SHIFTS IN CORE TECHNOLOGY COMPETENCIES

Often, using a high-performance technology allows a firm to improve certain components of its cost structure, thereby providing itself a competitive advantage. Then, competitors may have no choice other than acquiring this technology themselves in order to remove the cost advantage. Sometimes, a technological innovation can serve to offset the advantage of long-standing experience in an area or of the market share a firm enjoys, possibly forcing a redistribution of the relative positions among firms.

The Experience Effect: Amplification or Destruction

By its characteristics, the history of superconductivity can enforce new rules in the global competitive game. Two main periods appear to be important: the first one, 1911-1986, concerns low-temperature superconductivity, and the second one, since mid-1987, covers the emergence of high-temperature superconductivity.

High-temperature discoveries opened the possibility of technology applications which were inconceivable until then. Thus, this new technology calls into question the value of expertise in low-temperature superconductivity. Firms with skills in low temperature are faced with deciding whether old experience can be successfully refocused on the new technology without significant risk or whether these old skills must be abandoned.

A scientometrics analysis of patents indicates that the discovery of high-temperature superconductors has energized the superconductor field in terms of patent publications. The process of exploring the new technology varies between countries. Some countries are characterized by research efforts in both low- and high-temperature technology that are, for the most part, quite different (e.g., United States, Great Britain). In other countries, the same researchers work in both fields (e.g., in Japan for many R&D programs). Finally, other country's research indicates that low-temperature patents are still a priority (e.g., high-temperature in France). Many patents about low temperature have been issued since 1987, indicating that interest in the technology is still present.

Also, using the *"immediacy"* measure of patents (immediacy is defined as the average age of issue date for a set of patents), the speed at which knowledge is being assimilated can be measured and the maturity of the field evaluated. In theory, if patents in a technical area most often tend to reference only very recent patents (i.e., those with low average age or high immediacy), an area of rapidly changing technology is suggested. On the other hand, patents that refer only to old material (i.e., patents with a medium or high average age) suggest an area characterized by only minor variations on old technological themes. This kind of information allows the flow of knowledge between the different actors to be evaluated and provides an early indication of a possible shift in the technology paradigm in a field.

From Scientific Advantage to Commercial Advantage

Analyzing the average age of cited patents allows us to analyze the shifts in technological emphasis for various countries (Leboulanger 1993). For example, if the average age of Japanese self-citations is compared with the average age of the Japanese patents cited in American patents, Japanese self-citations fall into three periods. The first period (1986-1988) would square with the use of low-tempeature experience to build capability in the high-temperature area. The second period (1988-1989), where the average age of patents decreases, shows the emergence of high-temperature as a prominent new field of investigation. The break is not clear, however, because the older technology is not completely abandoned; that is, research is continuing even if declining. The third period (1989-1990) shows increasing use of older references.

The United States seems to use old Japanese technology. On the one hand, this suggests that some researchers are using outdated Japanese research; on the other hand, it suggests that the old technology still has some intrinsic value.

Europe's role in this competition comes from its older knowledge that can sometimes be used for current applications (Perdrieu-Maudière 1993). However, Europe's contributions could undoubtedly be strengthened even if official European joint programs are opened to other nations. It is a risk to see European firms as isolated from attractive sectors. This danger is not hypothetical for the electronics sector: most patents in this field are issued to Japanese patentees (85 percent). The reason is not merely the enormous resource requirements; the inequality between partner contributions also plays a role. For instance, it is possible that Germany is not as interested as Great Britain in such cooperative agreements. This suggests that the impact of foreign competitors is significant in the quest for alliances, as illustrated by agreements in electronics such as those concluded between Siemens, Toshiba, and IBM.

The patent data indicate that many researchers have assumed that the mastery of certain low-temperature technologies would provide an advantage for high-temperature technologies. Initially, patents emphasized the most recent high-temperature results. Then, owing to the inherent difficulties of this new technology, patenting tended to shift back to older technologies, suggesting a resurgence of interest in low temperature. For instance, the discovery of the HTS oxides has breathed new life into the low-temperature industry. Indeed, even if diverse new and old technological skills (such as those of the ceramists for the new materials and those linked to metallurgy for the older ones) are required for success, low-temperature experience would constitute a real advantage for the firms that use it. The low-temperature market alone is estimated at $300 million/year.

Establishment of Barriers to Entry

Innovation most often involves modification of a business' key success factors; however, it can also create entry barriers that restrict some firms from shifting to adopt the new technology. Owing to a lack of will or means, some firms that do not have enough control in this technology area may consider exiting the market altogether. Other organizations having some competence in the field of the innovation may choose to enter the market.

It is possible to explain the limited presence of smaller firms or, at least, their concentration on small or more mature applications. Smaller organizations are most predominant in low-temperature applications because their skills in the new technology enable them to invest even when the returns on investment are uncertain. Moreover, superconductivity patents issued after 1987 are like guarantees to protect the possibility of participating in a future market. The patentees or patent acquirers use them to create barriers to entry and to exploit some dominating positions in promising sectors. Other firms have either left the business altogether or have taken over in some of the niches left by the pioneers.

SUPERCONDUCTIVITY AND MARKETS

According to various studies, the economic potential of the high-temperature sector is enormous. Famouth Associates have forecast a market of $375 million before 2000. This market could be increased by a factor 10 if some room-temperature superconductor components were used (ADITECH 1987). According to the Nikkei Research Institute, the potential markets of all superconductors would be more important ($12.4 billion in 2000 and eventually $85 billion) if all potential applications of room-temperature superconductor materials were used. Such potential is too great to ignore, and certain firms will try to capture these opportunities. To identify these firms, it is necessary to look at the new superconductor industry as having four principal areas of emphasis:

- Basic materials in fields similar to those of today
- Basic materials in fields other than those known today
- Existing manufacturing and bonding industries
- Cooperation between basic materials industries and manufacturing and bonding industries.

How will a company approach its role in high-temperature superconductivity, and how will it pursue its research and development? Firms appear to be interested in the new material field for three reasons:

- Experience and activity in the existing materials field with interest in a similar emerging field (e.g., development of superconductive ceramics by the suppliers of ceramics, for example)
- Interest in development corresponding to particular needs of users (e.g., computers, electronics)
- Interest in a field of products that substitute for the current products of the firm (e.g., entry in the superconductor market by the suppliers of power cables).

Patents can indicate where each firm fits in these groups. Patents also suggest areas of a firm's strength in the emerging superconductivity industry. If research and development in the new materials industry continues to evolve, it appears that

- Basic materials firms that have accumulated some technologies and some experienced staff for long-term research and development would hold a good position if they are interested in this market.
- Businesses other that those involved in basic materials, such as venture capital firms, may also be interested. For instance, materials industries in different but related fields are beginning to be interested, as indicated by their increasing investigations of superconductivity. Materials with good electrical, magnetic, chemical, optical, and thermal properties need much more creative research and these "related materials firms" seem to be good candidates.
- Suppliers of superconducting materials are not limited to the production of new materials (composition), but can innovate by

trying to improve production processes (processing). New processes are constrained on the one hand by the envisioned applications and on the other by the properties of the superconductor materials. Although the superconductive phases of materials were discovered at different periods, the mastery of the techniques and processes for producing and molding the materials has not had the same experience. A significant example is the thin films that are useful both for the study of high-temperature components in a good crystalline state and for all the low- or high-temperature electronics applications. The potentially enormous progress in materials processing depends on the mastery of several emerging technologies for ceramics (e.g., oxygen atmosphere control during processing, cathode pulverization for metals, sputtering, lithography, and sputtering of particles by a stream of plasma).

While potential applications depend on inherent technologies, their rapid development is also linked to future commercial promise and to other development efforts going on throughout the industry.

TECHNOLOGICAL EVOLUTION AND STRUCTURE OF COMPETITION

In the superconductor industry, evolution of the structure of competition is subject to the emergence of new applications, which depend on overcoming technical difficulties and on the level and timing of investment in potentially attractive opportunities. These new applications can be investigated by patents.

To obtain a good understanding of the probable evolution of a field, it seems useful to understand the dynamics at the beginning of the innovation process. For electrical power generation, the economic criteria should be determinant. If the total number of patents in this field is important, it is because the mastery of high-temperature superconductors allows new applications that can potentially revolutionize the industry.

In electronics, other superconductors (arsenium or gallium) compete with the classical or low-temperature superconductors. Only some significant, cost-effective technical performance breakthrough with high-temperature superconductors could prompt firms to opt for a change of technology.

Two fundamental innovation processes are possible for superconductors:

- Incremental improvement of existing technology—evolutionary gains in low-temperature superconductivity, which occur by *market pull* (demand in markets for better low-temperature technology)
- Dramatic addition and substitution of fundamentally new technologies—revolutionary gains in high-temperature superconductivity, which occur through *technology push* (a new capability available for market applications).

Most applications are essentially concentrated in a restricted group of fields, which suggests a specialization. The participating companies are strongly internationalized (the large organizations through their network of foreign subsidiaries and the smaller firms through their international contacts). In addition, the active firms are clearly committed to international trade and research.

On the other hand, the existing firms in these fields are also cooperative organizations. But the diversity of specialization among these firms permits collaborations to develop new technologies or applications. Development of new technologies provides new opportunities for product differentiation among firms, thereby fostering competition.

It seems necessary to identify a country's or a firm's contribution to a technical field to see if organizations emphasize defense of their patent positions in some preferential fields or applications, a strategy that may drive the international competition to patent elsewhere.

Research Strategies and Business Strategies

Using the International Classification of Patents or the technical classification of the patent (i.e., World Patent Index [WPI]) and the patent numbers of major firms allows us to evaluate the concentration of the assignee's research efforts. In addition, it is possible to know the different sectors where firms have research emphasis because classifying patent activity by technical field tends to reflect the areas where technological progress is most important to the assignee companies (Pavitt 1985). Even if such a patent classification is not the best starting point to determine the content of the innovative activity (e.g., when counting patents does not provide much information on the state of the technological art of a given field), it nevertheless enables identification of the strategic research fields of interest and trends in the R&D investments of certain countries or organizations.

Two main application fields appear in this industry: electronics and electrotechnics (Figure 2) (Leboulanger 1993). To characterize firms in these industries, it is valuable to identify the authors of publications covering these fields and to identify similarities or differences in company characteristics of existing and potential competitors. If the publication results differ from the company characteristics coming from patent groups for the same application fields, the difference may provide useful information.

Discrepancies between general literature and patents could indicate that the potential applications of issued patents are not directly connected to the core business of the firms as described in other publications. The discrepancy could indicate either a diversification or a specialization strategy. Specialization can be checked by assessing the importance of existing productive capacities in

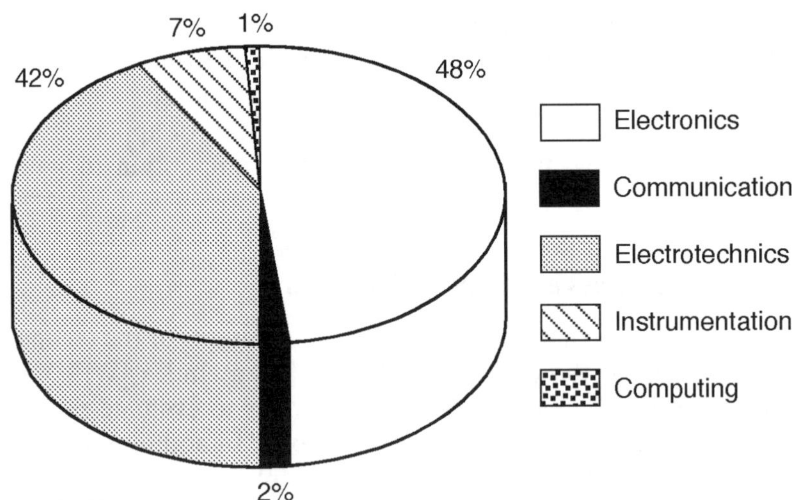

FIGURE 2. Main application fields in superconductors according to the World Patent Index.

terms of cost and experience; current investment levels may not permit companies to easily diversify through reinvesting elsewhere. However, in this case, diversification is possible in the sense of a *concentric diversification* (Bienaymé 1971), i.e., production of new goods that are still closely tied to existing product lines, but are targeted at incrementally different markets or customers.

Among Japanese *keiretsu* groups and vertically connected groups, three pioneers in superconductivity exist (Leboulanger 1993). For the *keiretsu*, Sumitomo, Mitsubishi, and DKB dominate, with 74.83 percent of patents with applications in electronics and electrotechnics. Among the vertically connected groups, Toshiba, Hitachi, and Matsushita lead, with 85.29 percent of the relevant patents.

If each of these six industrial groups is broken down by activity sector, it appears that, for the *keiretsu*, Sumitomo is not the strongest in electronics/electrotechnics applications, although it is a leader from a global standpoint. This could mean that Sumitomo protects itself intensively in many fields so as not to overlook any potential market, while establishing a leading position through an aggressive patenting initiative. For the vertically connected groups, Toshiba's lead position is confirmed.

An attempt at potential electronics/electrotechnics market-sharing between the six biggest Japanese groups is suggested by patents, which is not surprising, since these industrial leaders tend to be the more cooperative groups.

In the United States, General Electric (GE) dominates with 19.54 percent of patents having electronics/electrotechnics applications. IBM and universities (considered here as an entity) follow with 12.34 percent, and Westinghouse with 11.05 percent. GE's strong position is essentially the result of its electrotechnics activity (80 percent of its superconductivity patent portfolio). It would seem that GE pursues a strategy similar to that of Sumitomo: it strives for an unshakable position. GE is both the first American patentee and the firm that would seem to have the greatest financial resources. IBM ranks second because of its electronics activity, particularly that related to memories and hybrid circuits (70 percent of its portfolio). These two firms concentrate on their core business (Perdrieu-Maudière 1993). The strength of the university patent activity is quite surprising. However, their patenting could be linked to the cooperative research contracts between universities and industry.

The same is true for Europe (Perdrieu-Maudière 1993). The major research organizations focus their new patents within the framework of their existing core activities. The German firm Siemens is a good example; it ranks just behind GE in the area of electric power generation. The major French patentee in this area is CGE Alsthom. The Centre National de Recherche Scientifique (CNRS) and Thomson confine themselves to electronics (their patents claiming such an application represents 70 percent of their portfolio). The British presence is essentially characterized by its contribution to electrical instruments (measuring magnetic and electric variables). Oxford Instruments is the principal player in this area.

This focus on core business, with some patenting related to downstream product integration, suggests a broadened interpretation of the group strategy, particularly with reference to the concept of the "technological tree" (CPE 1988). The tree concept shows branches of incremental improvements derived from the basic "truck and roots" of main line production.

The use of superconductors in the electrotechnics field is subordinated to real progress made in the area of low- or high-temperature superconductor materials. Their use varies according to the importance of the advantages or drawbacks of competing systems. In addition, many potentially attractive superconductor projects are not yet possible as long as certain technical barriers remain unaddressed by relevant breakthroughs in superconductor technology.

The lack of sufficient basic theory makes the ultimate economic and commercial value of a patent very hard to evaluate. Each new bit of technological progress can destroy promising current lines of research or can re-open closed investigations that were abandoned as unpromising. The *a fortiori* patent value of a patent family can thus vary from one extreme to another, depending on follow-up developments.

A New Technological Global Order—Strategic Alliances

Competition is limited neither by national nor industrial sector borders. Basic competitive forces seem to be driving the industry toward continued internationalization of the main resources such as knowledge and financing, as well as the production and marketing of new applications. However, this study demonstrates that, although huge multinational firms organized around the principle of vertical integration dominate the industry, a new form of entrepreneurial cooperation called the "strategic alliance" has emerged.

The motivations for traditional forms of economic cooperation such as joint ventures and licensing agreements have usually stemmed from the desire to control property and distribute research costs. Motivations for strategic alliances, on the other hand, have additional dimensions such as gaining access to uniquely qualified technical specialists and exploiting the ingenuity of others. Through such arrangements, both firms will have access to technology that neither could have developed individually. Nowadays, firms are quicker to recognize that they cannot always be world leaders in all technology areas relevant to their business. Another motive for strategic alliance is the desire of both partners to create demand and gain access to a potentially lucrative market. Finally, natural economic forces acting to consolidate existing oligopolies undoubtedly constitute still another motivation for the wave of strategic associations.

COOPERATIVE RELATIONSHIPS AMONG GLOBAL COMPETITORS

The struggle between a few large Japanese and American firms characterizes the superconductor industry's paradox, which involves both competition and cooperation. Large Japanese and American companies compete with each other. They do not cooperate in this area very much despite the rising worldwide cooperation and *global interdependency* among many firms.

REPRESENTATION OF BILATERAL RELATIONSHIPS

The relationship between Japanese and American superconductor firms can be characterized as "ago-antagonism" (Bernard-Weil 1992, 1993), an idea found in mainstream Judeo-Christian philosophy. Ago-antagonism is a systemic concept in keeping with an ancient tradition of modeling both the universe and ourselves in antagonist binomes. Such modeling forms the basis of bilateral strategies whose objective is to avoid the perverse effects of unilateral strategies. Indeed, ago-antagonist systems characterize the practices and principles of many present-day bilateral strategies. This model (see Figure 3) can be represented with a horizontal line, each end corresponding to one of the ago-antagonist forces, intersected by a vertical axis. The top of the vertical axis represents the international market, while the receiver or receptor (the entity or nation that wins international supremacy) is at the lower end of the axis.

The U.S./Japanese race toward worldwide supremacy in the superconductor industry can be regarded as antagonist and agonist, regulated by the international market, which is necessarily neutral and serves to balance the two opposing forces. The model requires complete polarity of the protagonists, and exchanges are strictly regulated. Finally, each pair in the ago-antagonist network oscillates between the affirmation of autonomy and hierarchical dependence. These relationships help create the links which constitute systems. Recent developments in the superconductivity industry can be traced to systems such as these.

One characteristic of the ago-antagonist systemic is the *constituting division,* which precludes all direct contact between elements of the pair under threat of penalties that will split up the elements of the system. Likewise, under the ago-antagonist system, duality

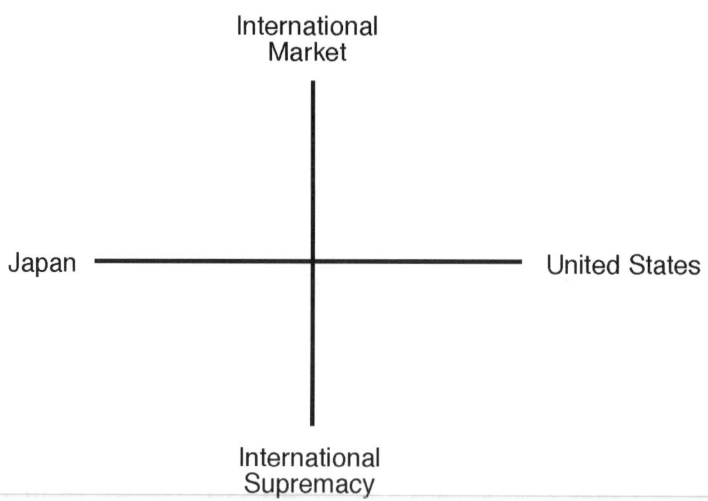

FIGURE 3. The ago-antagonist model.

must be maintained; pairs may not unite to create synthesis. Under this approach, moreover, competitors employ “partnering” behavior in conjunction with adversarial behavior.

Collaboration enables parties to gain advantage over traditional competitors, form networks, and evaluate new product options before choosing a market penetration strategy. In addition, collaboration allows partners to benefit from learning about each other, thus obtaining a more global business knowledge and capability. Indeed, combining divergent abilities is becoming increasingly necessary for successful competition in global markets. Finally, joint programs in pre-competitive research enable participants to reduce the costs and risks inherent in such activities.

On the other hand, the ago-antagonist approach allows all partners to resist or to launch an attack on those who are not members. It is a means of testing the relations of influence or dominance between the partners. There is competition, though it manifests itself in other ways. The global effect of all of this is a kind of global network.

CONCENTRATION AND SPECIALIZATION

Patent-based competitive technical intelligence to date shows patent-related activities concentrated on a few potential applications. This concentration is apparent throughout the global market in the relationship of existing and potential competitors. Globalization comes from two processes—the willingness by firms to seek out the required technological skills from anywhere in the world and the internationalization of the competition. This globalization can be seen through the expansion of superconductivity participants throughout the world, especially through signing of cooperation agreements. Because of these general characteristics, superconductivity is both affected by and a contributor to globalization.

The concentration-specialization strategy found in this industry is not necessarily accompanied by a geographical expansion of the network of international collaboration suggested by related patents. This strategy can be considered global because it takes place at the supra-national level, e.g., similar to relationships of members in the European Patent Treaty and the Patent Cooperation Treaty. Superconductivity is a worldwide industry in which the strategic positions of the competitors are completely determined by their international positions (Porter 1982). The firms entering the market must compete in a global market right away.

Finally, patent-based competitive technical intelligence shows a redistribution of the leading positions between the large international companies and countries, e.g., a relative American weakness and a Japanese thrust are indicated in recent trends. Moreover, analysis of this competitive technical intelligence suggests that the characteristics of this key technology are not the real determinants of the future structure of the industry. The wide variety of company participants around the world and their linked relationships, rather than the nature of the technology or the size of the individual firms, is likely to dictate the future directions of this important industry. The pattern of participants around the world and their relationships must be constantly examined.

CONCLUSION

The patent analysis in this chapter has provided a unique picture of the emerging markets, the companies, and the national competitors that are developing applications for superconducting technology. Patent indicators were used to describe the active companies, their competitive positions, and the nature of the industry in the major active countries of the world.

The analysis has identified important trends in the international market structure and potential competitive environment as superconducting technology applications approach commercial use. A key finding is the pattern of relationships between firms, especially the appearance of cooperative relationships in technology development. This analysis demonstrates the use of patent data as a valuable means to characterize and explore the structure and future directions of the attractive international high-technology market for superconducting materials.

REFERENCES

ADITECH (Mission d'information scientifique et technique). 1987. Développements recents des matériaux supraconducteurs au Japan. *Ministére des relations extérieures* (3):2-40.

Bernard-Weil, E. 1992. La systémique ago-antagoniste. *Techniques & Documentation*. Lavoisier, Paris.

Bernard-Weil, E. 1993. Étude systémique du rituel hébraïqie des sacrifices. Contribution au problème des stratégies bilatérales. *Revue Internationale de Systémique* 7(3):233-262.

Bienaymé, A. 1971. *La croissance de l'entreprise.* Bordas, Paris.

Bucki, J., and Y. Pesqueux. 1993. Intelligence d'un système—L'analyse décisionnelle des systèmes. *Revue Internationale de Systémique* 7(1):71-102.

Campbell, R. S. Campbell. 1983. Patent Trends as a Forecasting Tool. *World Patent Information* 5(3):137-143. Pergamon International, London.

Centre de Prospective Economique (CPE). 1988. *Stratégie et compétitive dans l'industry mondiale*. Economica Publishers, Paris.

Dufourt, D. 1979. L'économie mondiale comme système. *Sciences des Systèmes*. PUL, Lyon.

Leboulanger, C. 1993. Analyse technométrique des relations ago-antagonistes entre le Japan et les Etats-Unis: cas de l'industrie des matériaux supraconducteurs. Unpublished doctoral dissertation. University of Caen, France.

Le Duff, R., and Maïsseu, A. (ed.). 1988. *L'anti-déclin ou les mutations technologiques maîtrisées*. Entreprises modernes d'Édition, Paris.

Michalet, C. A. 1989. L'échiquier industriel mondial. *Les Cahiers Français* (243):11-14.

Nègre, C. 1987. Impératif de la masse critique. *Les Cahiers Français* (234):1-48.

Organization for Economic Co-Operation and Development (OECD). 1992. *La technologie et l'économie: les relations déterminantes*. Paris.

Pavitt, K. 1985 Patent statistics as indicators of innovative activities: possibilities and problems. *Scientometrics* (7):6-17.

Perdrieu-Maudière, F. 1993. *Analyse technométrique d'une industrie en émergence: les supraconducteurs*. Unpublished doctoral dissertation. University of Caen, France.

Porter, M.E. 1982. *Choix stratégique et concurrence*. Economica Publishers, Paris.

Savignon, F. 1971. *Brevets d'invention et développement industriel.* Cahiers de l'ISEA (Institut de Science Economique Appliquée, Laboratoire du Collège de France Associé au CNRS) 5(2):353-359.

Strategor. 1992. Collective volume, InterEdition, Paris.

PART IV

Using Competitive Technical Intelligence: Applying Results to Obtain Value

PART IV
Editorial Introduction

Intelligence is valuable only if it is used by the organization's decision-makers and if it directly contributes to successful company business performance in its applications. This is a tall order, and attempts to sort out the contributions of intelligence have proved difficult. Clearly, however, careful attention to how intelligence may be used is an important component of actionable intelligence products. The three chapters in this section focus on how intelligence information can be applied in a company. The authors point out that competitive technology intelligence has provided valuable inputs to a variety of decisions and actions in a number of companies. They also point out that simply producing good intelligence is not enough. Intelligence professionals must follow the message through to implementation, often enlisting help in the form of a champion or advocate to carefully manage intelligence "ideas" to achieve their potential impact.

In the first chapter, Tom Krol, Jim Coleman, and Pat Bryant describe the wide variety of services their competitive technology intelligence (CTI) unit provided at Marion Merrell Dow (now Hoescht Marion Roussel). While the authors address CTI benefits as applied to a pharmaceutical company, the ideas and concepts they illuminate are readily transferable to most other industries, particularly those with a high-tech focus. A CTI unit can benefit a company by helping to improve planning assumptions; eliminating negative surprises; improving portfolio management; enhancing decision-making ability; improving the process of selecting research projects and allocating resources to them; and increasing awareness of threats from unscrupulous competitors. Many different branches of the company will benefit from a CTI unit—senior management, research and development, sales and marketing, product development, and legal, to name a few.

Hervé Penan describes an unusual application of intelligence principles in his chapter. He shows how firms can enhance their competitiveness through the use of standards in negotiating contracts with clients. Standards are a way to implement intelligence findings about clients to maximize a firm's contracting advantage. Standards can help minimize risk and enable firms to position themselves advantageously when negotiating with potential clients. Standards are an important component of the innovation process. Because, contrary to popular belief, innovation is primarily a collective, non-linear process consisting of a series of individual efforts contributing to a final product, standardization indicates the parties' interest in a project. In other words, it promotes the circulation of a firm's know-how within its network and reveals the link between know-how and market requirements, which makes the project visible. For these reasons, Penan argues that standards should be included in all innovation contracts and should be carefully and iteratively negotiated among parties.

In the final chapter, Gary Stacey introduces the important concept of expressing intelligence findings as "ideas." He discusses the critical role of ideas in making technical intelligence systems effective. The author argues that because the purpose of business intelligence activity is to produce ideas on how company performance can be developed or enhanced, it is essential that a company be receptive to new ideas and provide an environment which supports idea generation. Conventional business management procedures generally do not provide an atmosphere that allows creativity and, hence, ideas to develop and flourish. In this chapter, Dr. Stacey emphasizes the importance of nurturing the intellectual capital that is ultimately the backbone of corporate success. According to Stacey, transforming ideas into strategic business activities consists of generating ideas, then communicating, nurturing, screening, implementing, and harvesting them.

Range of Services Provided by Competitive Technical Intelligence

THOMAS F. KROL,
JAMES C. COLEMAN, and PATRICK J. BRYANT

The competitive technical intelligence (CTI) unit is expected to provide a wide range of services for a wide range of clients. In the context of this chapter "range of services" is used to denote *what is provided to whom*. Competitive technical intelligence is competitive intelligence within the research and development (R&D) arena.

Competitive intelligence involves three steps. First, publicly available competitive technical and R&D data that could affect the company's business are *collected*. Second, these data are *organized* and thus, transformed into competitive technical information. Third, the information is *analyzed* to a point at which strategic and tactical decisions can be made. The final step—analyses—is the key characteristic of a CTI unit, and it is the competitive intelligence resulting from analysis that adds value to the corporation.

The basic tools used to provide traditional competitive business intelligence are also used for competitive technical intelligence. The differences lie in the type of data being analyzed and the training and experience of the analysts.

An important congruency between business and technical intelligence units is that both gather competitive data and information from a wide variety of valuable sources, including associates within the company.

Figure 1 illustrates the information flow between CTI and its clients. Note that CTI clients are also potential sources of competitive information. As the saying "chance favors the prepared mind" suggests, increased awareness of one's primary competitors should be accompanied by increased efforts to monitor these competitor companies and/or products companywide

Material for this chapter was obtained through many years of experience in the pharmaceutical industry, but the concepts and ideas are readily transferable to most industries, especially those with a high-technology focus.

In this chapter, we will review the clients upon whom CTI may have significant impact. This list may not be all-inclusive, and it may not entirely reflect the reader's client base. Nevertheless, readers are encouraged to take notice because the concepts and ideas presented may provide insight as to how a CTI unit can provide even greater value to similar units within their own organization.

To be successful, services provided by the CTI unit must have impact on the decision-making processes of individuals, departments, or teams identified as clients. The underlying assumption is that CTI will benefit both R&D and the company as a whole. If

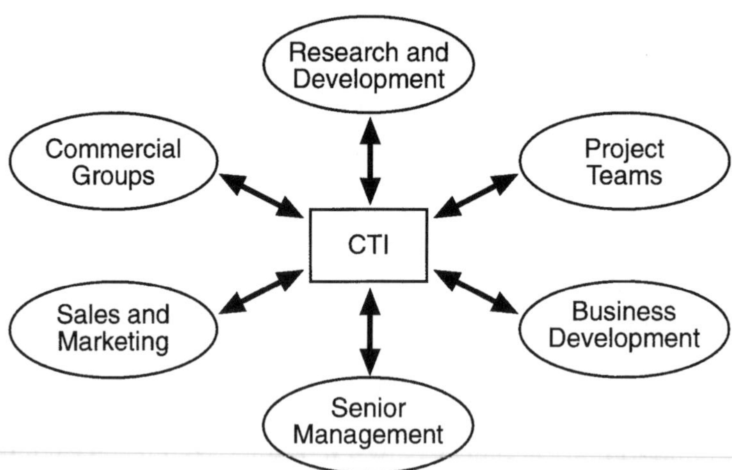

FIGURE 1. Clients for competitive technical intelligence

implemented correctly, the CTI unit should provide the following benefits to any company:

- Improve planning assumptions
- Eliminate surprises from the science and technology aspects of the business, surprises that could eventually result in lost revenues
- Improve R&D portfolio management and prioritization of projects and products
- Provide the basis for better tactical and strategic decisions
- Improve decisions regarding the best way to acquire new technology (for example, should the new technology be developed internally, an alliance be formed, or an acquisition made)
- Improve selection and evaluation of research projects (for example, should the project be approved, continued as is, or terminated)
- Improve resource allocation (for example, are appropriate resources such as staffing, facilities, equipment, and budget being invested based on competitor timing)
- Gain better insight on internal strengths and weaknesses
- Increase awareness of threats to proprietary technology from unscrupulous competitors.

Clients who use services provided by a CTI unit vary among industries and within industries; however, some basic business functions are found within almost all high-technology industries. These common functions are outlined below:

- Research and development
  –research
  –development
  –regulatory
  –product portfolio prioritization
- Commercial groups
  –strategic development
  –commercial development
  –market research
  –business intelligence
  –licensing and business development

- Senior management
- Other
  –equity investment review committee
  –project and product teams
  –sales and marketing
  –legal.

This chapter will focus on the interactions between the clients listed above and the CTI unit.

RESEARCH AND DEVELOPMENT

Research and development is the life blood of any company that develops high-technology products, such as pharmaceuticals. It is the source of all new products, whether they result from internal or external R&D. However, in addition to innovation, creativity and efficiency are needed to bring new products to market ahead of the competition. One recent article noted that

> *Most pharmaceutical companies get the greatest leverage from intelligence efforts in the area of R&D, because this is the basis of competition. . . .* (Esposito and Gilmont 1991)

This statement holds true for many other high-technology industries that depend on innovation and creative exploitation of these innovations to achieve success.

In the pharmaceutical and biotechnology industries, CTI is becoming more important as the level of competition increases. Cost containment efforts in health care are challenging and changing the way companies perform their R&D. Senior managers are rethinking R&D investments. Some of these changes are reflected in trends such as reducing product pipelines by concentrating on those future products with a high-value potential, streamlining processes, increasing use of consultant groups, and establishing more licensing agreements.

If a CTI unit is to be successful, it must have good relationships with R&D associates. Development of these good relationships is fraught with multiple hurdles, which include turf battles, perceptions that the CTI unit will kill projects, "information is power" attitudes, and introversion (Matteo and Dykman 1994).

Good communication, establishment of rapport, and fostering of a team approach over time will improve these relationships. Good communication with technically trained associates requires excellent listening skills. Rapport is established as the technical competence of the CTI analyst is exhibited. It is built gradually over time and is nurtured by open communication and a genuine interest in individuals and their work. Fostering the team feeling is a continuous challenge and is achieved by working together on projects and solving problems together. R&D scientists may develop the wrong opinion about CTI if the benefits are not promoted in the appropriate ways, and this could be catastrophic to the success of the CTI unit.

Another way to improve R&D relationships and enhance the CTI process is to perform needs analyses. A needs analysis can often be combined with an educational component about CTI and its value. The technique(s) used for needs analyses should be appropriate to the culture of the organization. They will be effective as long as needs are identified and monitored and clients are kept informed of progress in meeting their needs. Needs analyses for CTI clients should be a continuous process.

RESEARCH

Research represents the scientists, engineers or other technical experts, and their managers. These are the people who discover potential new products or identify leads which may result in future products.

In the pharmaceutical and biotechnology industries, the research unit represents biologists, biochemists, molecular biologists, molecular geneticists, chemists, toxicologists, and other highly trained professionals. In these industries, an important function associated with the research unit is to provide enough scientific data that clinicians within the development arm of the company are comfortable in administering the potential drug product to humans and, therefore, can file an investigational new drug (IND) application.

Research groups can benefit from CTI in multiple ways. CTI techniques can be used to identify similar research projects, therapeutic targets, and/or compounds being developed by other companies, institutions or individuals. In the development state of a research project, that is, before product discovery or selection of a lead, scientists are typically aware of two to three similar competing technologies and/or research units, but often are not aware of others that should be considered potential competitors. The CTI unit helps identify other technologies which may be threats or, at this stage, may be viewed as potential opportunities.

The CTI unit can also benefit research scientists and managers by identifying stage of development and results of competitor research projects, products, or targeted areas of intervention. Examples of a target area in the pharmaceutical industry are a new enzyme, receptor, or transcription factor which may be modified in hopes that therapeutic benefit will be derived. Information about the stage of development is important because it gives an idea of the status of an internal project relative to the competition. Awareness of results on competing projects or products may help confirm that the target is a viable approach, or it may allow better strategic decisions in terms of directions for the discovery effort.

The CTI unit can increase awareness of current and future technologies that lead to potential collaborations. The collaborations may be formal, for example, a research agreement or alliance, or informal, for example, establishment of relationships with other researchers or institutions.

A further benefit is that provided by continuous monitoring of evolving science and technologies and communication of appropriate advances to the scientists. In the pharmaceutical and biotechnology industries, such communications help scientists identify new targets or proposed new targets for drug development. This process is especially important for evolving technologies such as gene therapy, gene transcription factors and their modification, and amplification or blockage of genes related to diseases.

Discovery research managers who must decide which lead compounds or products to select for future development or which ones to discontinue can make better decisions with CTI. It may help give research management the rationale for requesting a better product candidate based on currently available and/or competing technologies. Even at very early stages of development, clear decision points can be identified if products being developed can be compared with external research activity. For example, if most competing technologies for a given disease state are administered orally and product X does not have the potential to be dosed orally, it should be discontinued and another lead compound which can be dosed orally should be identified.

DEVELOPMENT

CTI plays a pivotal role in various stages of the development of new products. A very important function of the CTI unit is to identify and continuously monitor the progress of critical competitors. Critical competitors are defined as those competitors that have a high likelihood of taking away significant market share of a company's product by the time it gets to market.

Simply identifying critical competitors raises red flags in the minds of development associates so that when they hear or read something about one of these competitors, they report it to the CTI unit. This process makes the competitive information identified by development associates available to other decision-makers throughout the company. Analysis of the competitive information gathered by the CTI unit provides valuable insight into future trends and helps in numerous tactical and strategic decisions made by development scientists and management.

Product development is unique to each industry; thus, the time to develop a product and the expertises involved vary among industries. In the pharmaceutical industry, development scientists and managers are the associates who devise and execute plans to move a drug from preclinical stages, that is, studies prior to human testing, through registration and approval to market. For a drug, this process takes approximately 6 to 8 years. Developmental functions for pharmaceuticals include formulation preparation (tablet, capsule, syrup, patch, sustained release, etc.), clinical studies (studies in humans to show safety and efficacy), long-term toxicological studies, and many other support studies. Development culminates its efforts with the filing of a new drug application in the United States or equivalent filing outside the United States.

To reduce cycle time, CTI techniques can be used to identify unique developmental approaches which are targeted to decrease development time. This type of analysis may involve benchmarking studies or modified benchmarking studies (Bookhart 1993). When the competitive information collected is combined with developmental approaches used across industries, unique and innovative strategies and plans may be developed.

CTI can also be used to identify developmental findings and difficulties encountered by competitors. This information can then be integrated with internal plans and used for tactical decision-making and planning as it relates to a company's product. In the pharmaceutical industry, tactics are perhaps most important as they relate to the clinical program plan, which is developed to coordinate all clinical studies. Well-executed studies must be done so that when the drug receives approval for marketing, it is approved for the desired indication, and sales, marketing and advertising efforts are being coordinated. Timeliness is the key to success for this process since a developmental plan is not easily changed once clinical studies have begun.

Competitive information can be very beneficial in differentiating a company's product from those of the competition. Simply identifying critical competitors and their stage of development is not enough. Often the critical competitors' key attributes, potential/actual advantages and disadvantages, and their future potential require comparisons to a company's internal product. For instance, designs of pivotal trials, the most important clinical trials that demonstrate a drug is efficacious and safe, can be modified in an attempt to obtain slightly different labeling from regulatory agencies.

CTI can also play an important role in linking the efforts of functional units within an organization. In the pharmaceutical industry, development scientists often work closely with clinician researchers in the field. Up-to-date knowledge of and experience with treating and tracking patients is an incredible asset in determining needs and identifying other uses or indications for a drug. It is important for the CTI unit to communicate with development scientists and the investigators involved with the study of the drug. The latter can help assess new potential indications and determine if it will be advantageous to obtain regulatory approval to use the drug to treat a new indication. Additional benefit comes from investigators' thoughts on the hurdles and changes in the health care arena for the institution and practice specialty.

The CTI unit can provide valuable economic information. In the pharmaceutical industry showing that a drug is cost-effective or that it saves money when used long-term is becoming an important aspect for product success. Responsibility for this task falls to the pharmacoeconomic unit, which is usually composed of clinicians who have some epidemiological and health care experience. The CTI unit works with this group to identify when competitors are instituting pharmacoeconomic studies and what they are measuring. Although such studies are not currently required for drug approval, regulatory agencies are paying close attention to the financial aspect of new drugs and their ultimate benefit to society. CTI helps to identify if a competitor is doing pharmacoeconomic studies and to analyze the extent of the studies, the tools used to measure economic benefit, and the degree to which the tools have been validated. The future acceptance of these studies by health care providers, as well as an evaluation of whether a similar approach should be considered for an internal product, is crucial. These analyses have layers of detail, and, if these details are known, a sound strategy can be put into place.

REGULATORY

Regulatory groups within a company can benefit from CTI. For pharmaceutical companies, the regulatory unit represents those individuals who interact most directly with regulatory agencies—the government bodies that must approve a product before it can be marketed. In the United States, the regulatory agency for pharmaceuticals is the Food and Drug Administration (FDA). In addition to their function of communicating with regulatory agencies, the regulatory group is consulted whenever drug development regulations come into question and to assure that governmental guidelines are followed throughout the development of a product.

The CTI unit helps the regulatory department by identifying critical competitors and their key attributes. Regulatory associates can track more closely what is happening with these competitors and their regulatory status. Once identified, competitor products and companies can be followed more closely.

CTI helps in identifying when regulatory applications are submitted to agencies. For pharmaceuticals in the United States, an investigational new drug application must be filed 30 days before a drug can be studied in humans, and a new drug application must be filed and approved by the FDA before the drug is marketed.

Analogous processes occur internationally. CTI techniques are used to calculate the time a competitor's product has taken to proceed through regulatory hurdles. Perhaps these hurdles can be avoided by planning appropriate scientific studies or finding creative ways to satisfy regulatory agencies. At a minimum, the time it takes regulatory agencies to act on similar products can be used in estimating market timing.

The CTI unit helps compare the R&D capabilities of competing companies to those of its own company and estimate how long a product may be bogged down in a regulatory agency. Capabilities may include anything from the competitor's history with a given section or subsection of an agency to its ability to file a new drug application or equivalent in a computerized format which may be acceptable to the regulatory agency.

The CTI unit can help analyze and predict the potential success or failure of competitors' formal regulatory filings. In the pharmaceutical industry, the CTI unit can help regulatory units identify and evaluate competitors' pivotal trials, which are eventually scrutinized by regulatory agencies to determine the safety and efficacy of a drug prior to its approval for use. Based on these studies, one can make educated assumptions about regulatory allowances for labeling of competing or similar products and how this may affect a product.

The CTI unit can help in terms of planning international submissions. CTI techniques can be used to identify how other competitors have filed or plan to file. This knowledge may affect how and in what order a company makes its regulatory submissions. It may also provide insight to alternative submission strategies which may allow a company to beat the competition to market in certain countries.

Interactions with the regulatory group provide a good example of how information should flow back to the CTI unit. In the United States, the FDA usually hires experts to critically evaluate a new drug application and, subsequently, to recommend whether the FDA should approve or not approve a drug for marketing based on scientific proof of efficacy and safety. This group of experts is called an Advisory Panel. In most instances the FDA follows this panel's recommendations. Regulatory associates frequently attend FDA Advisory Panel meetings in the United States. These meetings may now be purchased on videotape; however, much more can be learned by attending the meetings personally. In addition, important relationships and side conversations that occur before, after, and during breaks can provide additional insight.

PRODUCT PORTFOLIO EVALUATION AND PRIORITIZATION

CTI can play a pivotal role in prioritizing the product pipeline. Pharmaceutical and biotechnology companies have research pipelines and product pipelines (see Figure 2). Research pipelines are composed of projects which do not yet have a lead compound, that is, a single best potential product from a series or unit of potential products. Product pipelines are composed of lead compounds and different products at various stages of development.

Each pharmaceutical company and/or biotechnology company has a unique combination of research projects and products in the pipeline. The pipeline changes over time as more is learned about given projects. Some projects may be discontinued or put on hold because resources are allocated according to a prioritization process. Every company has some type of prioritization process. It may be as simple as one individual's decision or as complicated as numerous people rating projects and products based on numerous factors. Regardless of the process used for prioritization, CTI can help by analyzing the competitive environment.

Analysis of the competitive environment typically includes one or all of the following:

- Identify critical competitor products
- Analyze the key characteristics, attributes, strengths, and weaknesses of a critical competitor's products and the future impact

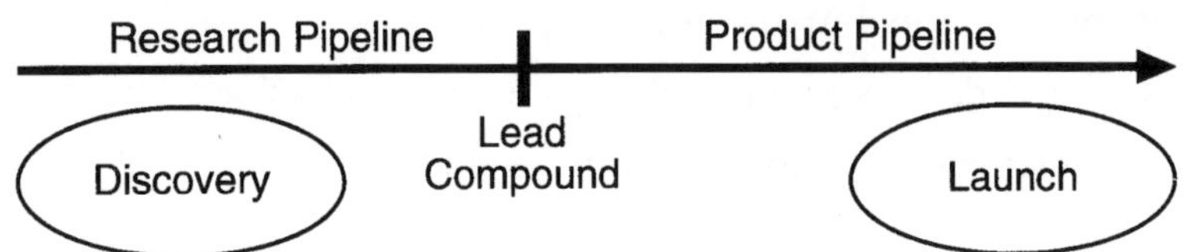

Figure 2. Research/product pipeline

these products will have on a company's product and market. A good analysis helps address issues such as

–product differentiation and its significance
–appropriate patient groups or market niches
–means for capitalizing on competitors' weaknesses.

- Analyze nontraditional products that may affect your market. For example, in the pharmaceutical industry, it is important to analyze nondrug therapies and the potential impact they may have on a company's product
- Analyze major technologies which could affect the future of the product
- Analyze the future environment and how this will affect the product.

These analyses provide the basis for rating products in terms of differentiation from competition (both marketed and under development) and market timing in relation to competing products and/or technologies. This information then becomes part of the prioritization process along with many other key points of evaluation such as cost and difficulty of development, market size, probability of success, etc.

COMMERCIAL GROUPS

Commercial units within a company have significant need for CTI. Commercial units are groups that assess and determine the commercial viability of new products. They also evaluate and attempt to maintain the commercial viability of existing products. Although most companies are structured differently, several basic commercial functions are needed to operate successfully. These functions include, but are not limited to

- Strategic development—develops long-term business strategy
- Commercial development—directs and coordinates all efforts committed to a product worldwide
- Market research—assesses size and desirability of marketplace internationally

- Business intelligence—acquires and communicates information related to competitors' current products
- Licensing and business development—constructs and negotiates the best business agreements to make the company viable and competitive in the future.

STRATEGIC DEVELOPMENT

Strategic thinking is something all associates of a company should do. However, in large technology-based companies, it is often important for one individual or group to specialize in this area to continually evaluate and plan strategies for existing and future product lines, markets, and the entire company. By interacting with strategic thinkers, the CTI unit has the potential for great impact on the corporation since recommendations at this level are often thoroughly evaluated by the senior decision-makers within the company.

The CTI unit can help strategists by filling their needs for competitive information and intelligence as it is required for strategy-based decisions. To develop a strategy, it is important to understand what the current environment is, who the major players and principal competitors are, and how the current game is played.

When the strategist ventures out of current state analysis and into future state analysis, CTI becomes even more important. CTI can be helpful in identifying existing state-of-the-art technology, but it is essential in determining future state-of-the-art technology as it relates to internal products and companies.

The CTI unit may work with strategists to supply best guess scenarios for the future. CTI helps to identify technologies that are likely to be available for identifying and/or evaluating various product targets in 5, 10, and 15 years and how these technologies will affect the company's current strategy.

This information is important because, while these technological changes are not necessarily direct competitors, they may have a significant impact on the future viability of a company's products. A good example in the pharmaceutical industry is estimating what changes would occur if a diagnostic test for Alzheimer's disease became readily available and widely accepted.

The CTI unit works with strategists to come up with unique ways to evaluate areas or companies in a "big picture" kind of way. For example, CTI techniques can be used to identify which companies are current leaders in the area of neurological disorders and how this may change in 5 or 10 years.

One of the biggest challenges to any company involved in health care concerns health care reform in the United States. Many changes are already under way. With this degree of change, CTI becomes more important than ever in evaluating how health care reform will affect R&D. For example, Harris and Associates (1993) estimate that by the year 2000, more than 90 percent of the U.S. population will have health care coverage through managed care organizations. This arrangement will have considerable impact on the availability of patients for certain types of clinical studies because a majority of certain patient populations may be accessible only through managed care organizations. Managed care has focused on cost reductions and not on conducting research. These issues may significantly impact clinical studies in the near future.

COMMERCIAL DEVELOPMENT

Commercial development refers to those units charged with developing business and marketing strategy across the globe and maintaining some consistencies between countries. In addition, they are responsible for the overall coordination of each facet of product development, including some of those being performed by R&D. The commercial development unit tries to roll up all the pieces and create a strategic and tactical plan for executing product launches in various countries.

Perhaps the largest benefit CTI provides to the commercial development unit comes from working on competitors' status and strategies throughout the world. It is often necessary to break competitor products up by their status in each targeted country. This perspective is extremely helpful to commercial development associates who plan individual strategies and an overall strategy.

By knowing which competitors are at which stage of development throughout the world, CTI helps the commercial development unit compare its product to those of the competition. This information also helps the commercial development unit develop plans to promote similar product attributes throughout the world, while maintaining individuality by country.

The commercial development unit also needs to be aware of the critical developmental issues which may be specific to the competitor's company. The CTI unit can help identify hurdles that may be unique to different parts of the world.

The CTI unit can also help by making the commercial development unit aware of any potential breakthroughs that may be expected and when. Alternative technologies that are not necessarily breakthroughs can be identified and monitored for their potential impact.

MARKET RESEARCH

Market research either performs primary market research or hires others to do it, if needed, and uses existing information that may be relevant. The services provided by the CTI unit may be important to market research analysts because they often do not have a technical background, but are asked to find answers to questions such as how physicians and pharmacists view the technical merits of a drug product.

The CTI unit can help identify critical issues related to currently marketed products or those being developed today. It can help market researchers identify key questions to ask interviewees, for example, especially with regard to future therapeutic interventions.

Also, CTI can help market research analysts get up to speed technically and can identify the appropriate assumptions used in sales forecasting models.

The CTI unit can help market researchers put together a competitive picture of the future so they can identify or verify the appropriate position for a product for which they are conducting market research.

The CTI unit can also help market research associates by creatively modifying an existing product's technical features to provide a more accurate new product profile and image to the potential customer. For example, an analogy would be combining an existing product with a new technology to enhance therapeutic activity or safety profile.

CTI can also help to identify breakthrough technologies that could affect market size. For example, a breakthrough technology in the pharmaceutical industry is one that has the potential to permanently change the way a disease is treated.

BUSINESS INTELLIGENCE

Competitive intelligence can be categorized as either technical or business. The distinction is primarily based on differences in expertise required for analysis and type of data being analyzed (Bryant et al. 1994). These differences can set the stage for natural division between the two groups. Many corporations need both types to maximize competitive advantage.

Technical intelligence and business intelligence (BI) groups can reside in the same department, but often exist in different divisions of the company. For this reason, the groups must have a good working relationship to ensure open communication and collaboration on related, often complementary, competitive intelligence projects.

Because both units track different competitive information, a synergistic relationship occurs as products are analyzed and competitive intelligence projects are under way. The CTI unit acts as a consultant to the BI unit and vice versa, as needed.

The CTI unit helps BI evaluate the technical merits, attributes, and limitations of the competition, whether the product is marketed or soon to be marketed. Such evaluations may be very important because business data often reflect underlying assumptions about scientific attributes, merits, limitations, etc., which may or may not be accurate.

LICENSING AND BUSINESS DEVELOPMENT

Licensing and business development (L&BD) associates are responsible for identifying, negotiating, and signing contracts for new business opportunities—new products, technologies, or research agreements.

The CTI unit identifies and evaluates new business opportunities that affect R&D and, potentially, other parts of the organization. If the CTI unit is truly an interfunctional and international operation, it can work very closely with L&BD to identify new business opportunities when certain constraints are identified up front.

A key to this process is establishing clear constraints up front and working closely with L&BD as the effort progresses. The business opportunity may range from finding a late-stage product for a co-promotion or a co-marketing arrangement to expanding the company into a new area of R&D.

New business opportunities may also come from a different direction, such as a business opportunity that results from an R&D technology need. For example, the R&D organization may perceive a need to expand rapid screening assays for quick evaluation of chemical or peptide libraries. In pursuit of this technology, the L&BD unit may decide that it is better to purchase an entire company or portion of a company because the need is estimated to increase over time.

The CTI unit can help identify potential licensing candidates, projects, or products. The CTI unit can help identify and initially review new products (in much the same way as business opportunities are identified and evaluated) which may fit criteria the strategists have identified.

Because of their technical background, analysts in the CTI unit have an added-value function with regard to emerging products. In many instances, it is necessary to cut through rhetoric or "hype" about an emerging product and get to the facts. In this way, the CTI unit can help eliminate less desirable licensing opportunities and prioritize the remaining, desirable ones.

CTI techniques can be used to identify and evaluate competitive activity relative to a licensing opportunity, whether it be a business venture or licensing candidate. One of the most important aspects of any business opportunity is a critical evaluation of its potential success when integrated with a company's strategy. CTI can help in this process by providing a competitive assessment of the capabilities or products of other companies or institutions and their capacity for taking a product to market. Although the competitive assessment should not be the only basis for the decision, it may be important enough to make or break a potential business opportunity or licensing arrangement.

The CTI unit can identify and help evaluate potential acquisition targets. The environment in many industries is one of increasing competitiveness as the total market grows at a slower pace. In this environment, it is becoming more commonplace for companies to merge, make partial or full acquisition of smaller companies, or expand dimensions of business by purchasing a distribution channel or generic company.

The strategy for a merger or acquisition will determine the impact CTI may have on the opportunity. If the strategy is of purely a business nature, CTI will have minimal impact; however, if technology is part of the focus, CTI has the potential to have significant impact. The CTI unit can help by evaluating the competitive situation for an entire company's pipeline of products and determining each product's future role.

The CTI unit can identify licensees for company products which have potential, but do not fit the company's strategy. In the pharmaceutical industry, only 1 in 5000 new compounds ever gets to market (Halliday et al. 1992). As a product progresses from discovery to market approval, it must pass certain milestones. With each stage of development, the cost of doing the necessary research increases. Therefore, companies are wise to cut losses as early as possible by determining whether a product is unsuitable for further development. In some cases the product may not fit the company's future strategy, and, therefore, may be considered an out-licensing opportunity.

Products can be deemed out-licensing opportunities at any stage of development. CTI can help identify potential licensees, based on current R&D activity in a given field across the globe. If constructed properly, arrangements such as these can be a win-win proposition for all companies involved.

SENIOR MANAGEMENT

Any competitive intelligence function, whether business- or technology-focused, must work closely with senior management to show benefits and gain continued commitment and support. Top management needs to be a staunch supporter of CTI so that the entire organization can contribute (Gilad 1994). Top-down support of CTI will provide leadership and incentive for the entire organization to accept competitive intelligence activities at all levels.

The most significant impact on the corporation is made at the senior management level. Senior management is most commonly interested in the current and future competitive environment for a project, product, opportunity, or business arrangement and often has very insightful and detail-oriented questions. In working with senior managers, CTI analysts are stretched to make recommendations, outline scenarios, and answer hard questions.

CTI can help senior managers in all of the previous ways mentioned if or when a project, product, or business opportunity progresses to that level of decision-making. CTI can also help senior managers identify trends, threats, and opportunities on a large scale. Many CTI projects for senior management are termed mega-projects because they can take hundreds to thousands of analysis hours and significant resources to complete. These projects may involve analyses of selected companies, specific processes, management styles, or competitive strengths and weaknesses. They may get as detailed as developing executive profiles and anticipated scenarios based on previous decisions and the experience of a competing senior manager.

OTHER AREAS

Companies design corporate structures many different ways with numerous functions and areas of expertise, any of which may have use for CTI. These other areas often discover the potential of CTI through word of mouth by key clients. The impact CTI may have on these areas is often hidden but is, nonetheless, significant and positive.

EQUITY INVESTMENT REVIEW COMMITTEE

The current business climate has created consolidation in several industries. The methods may include buy-outs, mergers, shared owners, joint ventures, and other creative ways to attempt to create future value. It is becoming more and more commonplace for large companies to purchase equity in smaller companies as a measure of good faith when the two companies enter into a joint agreement, whether it be with R&D, marketing, or both.

Because equity ownership represents significant investments (in the pharmaceutical and biotechnology industries, generally $5 million to $50 million) these investments must be reviewed periodically. The CTI unit can help review these investments by evaluating how the equity company is performing relative to the competition, both now and in the future. This analysis can be as superficial or as detailed as is needed. For example, one could perform competitive analyses on each project and product an equity partner has in its pipeline and on the market.

PROJECT AND PRODUCT TEAMS

Although the accountability, leadership philosophy, and exact composition of project and product teams differ among companies, most new projects and products will be implemented through a team composed of cross-functional units to reconcile problems and share plans. Typically, project and product teams are charged with design and review of overall development plans, integration of tasks, and strategic and tactical decisions. The CTI unit can help these teams in their strategic and tactical decision-making.

CTI can affect project teams in a significant way by identifying critical competitors and analyzing what they mean to the company's product. CTI can identify the competitor's difficulties and help design alternative strategies, recognize the competitor's advantages and disadvantages, and identify differentiating characteristics for a company's product. CTI techniques can also be used to identify niche markets, for example, patient groups competitors have targeted. In addition, CTI presentations often create awareness of upcoming hurdles and help team members realize the repercussions of missed deadlines.

Critical competitor strategies can be approximated, and wargaming or modified wargaming can be performed (Kurtz 1992). Wargaming is the process of identifying a company's most critical competitor, gaining all competitive information available about the competitor, and then bringing the company's decision-makers together to act as if they were their own counterpart at the competing company. Many questions and scenarios can be addressed. The result is a better understanding of what the competition may be doing.

SALES AND MARKETING

By their nature and basic function, sales associates are focused on selling the most products possible. Marketing is charged with doing whatever it takes to enhance sales of existing products. Both sales and marketing need to focus on existing competitors with whom they interact on a daily basis. Although most of the competitive information and intelligence needs of sales and marketing are related to traditional business competitive intelligence (that is, competitor promotional plans, sales tactics, marketing plans, pricing), the CTI unit can interact with sales and marketing functions to the mutual benefit of both units. Competitive intelligence units can act as a catalyst between these often non-integrated divisions of corporations.

The CTI unit can also identify future competitors. This information helps sales and marketing understand the importance of using certain selling tactics today because of the competitors who are expected to come to market tomorrow. It also gives them an appreciation for how the environment will be changing in the future, and another topic to discuss with potential customers.

Competitive information and intelligence on future competitors may be very useful to sales and marketing as they prepare to interact with potential customers. The CTI unit can help sales understand the technical differences between existing and future competitors and the significance of the differences. The CTI unit can also help sales and marketing construct appropriate assumptions for sales forecasting estimates.

One of the main missions of marketing is to differentiate products in the marketplace. The CTI unit can be a valuable asset to marketers as they strive to exploit the benefits of products.

The CTI unit can help sales and marketing efforts to preserve market share of existing products. For instance, in the pharmaceutical industry, CTI can assist in several ways:

- Identify new indications being studied by competitors and interpret the potential impact these changes may have on its own products
- Identify generic activity in clinical trials
- Identify new and improved formulations in clinical trials.

In much the same way as the regulatory group can be a source of competitive information, sales and marketing associates can also be good sources because they interact with customers. In some cases, these customers are consultants or clinical investigators for R&D—for another company! Sales associates are very helpful in terms of determining what the competitor's sales force is doing. This information can help determine when a competing product may be licensed for marketing.

LEGAL

In high-technology companies, legal activities are traditionally divided into several units, including litigation, business contracts, copy approval, intellectual property. By far, the intellectual property group interacts most with the CTI unit.

The CTI unit interacts with intellectual property attorneys in several ways. CTI techniques can be used to identify competitors who can then be monitored in terms of patent activity. As Mogee notes in her chapter in this volume, much can be learned about a company's R&D unit based on its patent activity over time.

The intellectual property attorneys can help the CTI unit in determining the extent and length of patent protection certain companies have. In the pharmaceutical industry, this information is important because it takes 10 to 12 years to develop a drug, and a patent may have 5 or fewer years of exclusivity left. In addition, under the Waxman-Hatch amendment, new chemical entities are allowed additional years of exclusivity.

Although in most instances the CTI unit and the legal department do not interact directly, each may use the other as consultants for various projects.

INTELLIGENCE COUNTERTACTICS

An additional companywide service the CTI unit can provide is education about competitor tactics. This service is especially pertinent to those associates in a company with access and knowledge of proprietary technology and trade secrets. The need to protect these important assets cannot be overstated because, as the competition increases, so does the need for competitive information and intelligence. The temptation for some companies to use unscrupulous, unethical and/or illegal tactics is a reality, and some foreign governments help local companies in these endeavors (Nugent 1992). An awareness and protection program can be put in place with the help of an internal security unit.

While it is not our intent to extensively review these illegal and unethical tactics or how to avoid them, the following are some of the more common methods employed by some companies:

- Breech of a nondisclosure agreement
- Theft and unauthorized copying of documents or computer diskettes
- Trespassing
- Bribery, extortion or blackmail
- Aerial photographs of internal areas of plants under construction
- Obtaining employment for the sole purpose of learning and disclosing proprietary information, processes, or trade secrets
- False representation or disguised interviews (for example, phone calls from graduate students working on a research paper)
- Coercion
- Remote surveillance, for example, devices that will monitor a room through a telephone, even though the phone is not off the hook (in 1991, non-U.S. firms spent over $200 million on "bugs")
- Garbology, that is, searching through garbage/trash (practiced by foreign governments, has been raised to a science)
- Facsimile interception devices
- Cellular and portable phone interception devices
- Devices that allow a competitor's computer to be read through emissions
- Use of foreign hotel employees to obtain copies of businessmen's facsimiles, to learn of guests' arrivals, and to obtain guests' office or hotel room keys.

For additional information on tactics and protective maneuvers to avoid being hurt, the reader should review Carlton (1992) and Nugent (1992).

PRIORITIZING THE WORKLOAD

With so many clients, the obvious question is how does one prioritize the CTI tasks and requests? The answer is simple: Prioritize based on those CTI activities that will have the greatest impact on the success of the corporation. This guideline is true in almost every instance.

Positive impact on the success of the corporation should be CTI's primary mission (see Bryant, Coleman and Krol, this volume). The priority given and resources allocated to each client unit is directly related to the impact CTI has on the future success of the company.

Figure 3 illustrates this concept as it relates to range of services provided. The method of communicating competitive information and intelligence is tailored to the needs of the client and balanced with relative impact on the corporation.

A useful exercise for established CTI units is to determine which clients have the greatest impact on the success of the company and

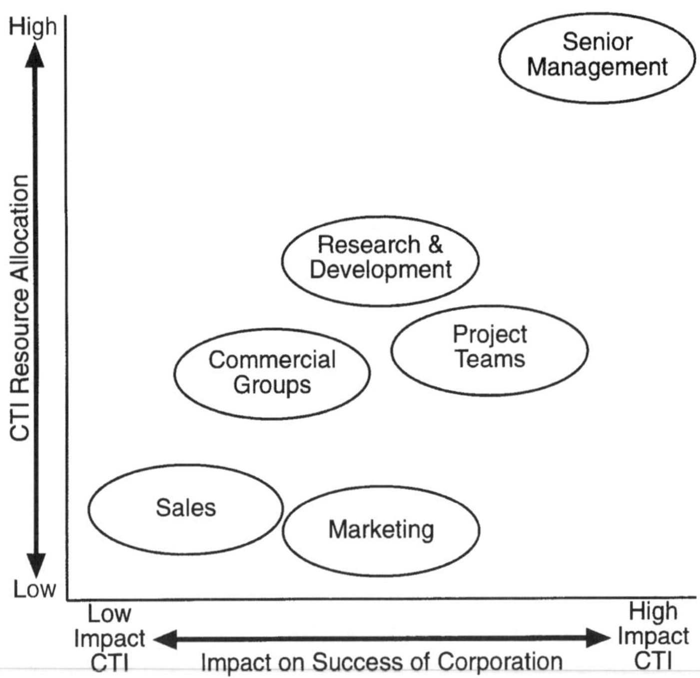

Figure 3. Impact of competitive technical intelligence on the success of a corporation

calculate where current CTI resources are allocated to determine what changes, if any, should be instituted. Recently formed CTI units may not have such a large and diverse client base, and they should not.

Beginning CTI units are doomed to failure if they try to satisfy everybody at one time. The need to build slowly should not, however, preclude finding out what competitive intelligence is needed by whom.

Designing a CTI unit is much the same as starting a small business (see Bryant, Coleman and Krol, this volume). The CTI unit needs a strategic plan and should concentrate on a focused client unit. This unit should include at least one heavy-weight champion, as well as those clients who will have the greatest impact on the success of the corporation. The initial client group can then be expanded based on need and potential benefit and as resources to the CTI unit expand.

Two other methods of operation can help to distribute workload. First, the best interest of the CTI unit is served not only by educating associates about the competitive intelligence process, but also by teaching them to perform analyses themselves and consult the CTI unit if they come across an insurmountable hurdle. A key component is to incorporate the findings of these analyses into the CTI unit's filing system, database, etc., so that the information is accessible to the entire corporation for strategic and tactical decisions.

The second way to distribute workload is to maintain and update competitor profiles on internal pipeline projects and products. Such maintenance saves time for the CTI unit because competitor reports are available very quickly. The price paid is up-front time in getting all competitor analyses automated and implementing a process for evaluating the changing environment routinely.

FACTORS AFFECTING RANGE OF SERVICES

Several other factors relate to the range of services a unit provides:

- Budget for the CTI unit
- Reporting structure and political environment

- Number of analysts and expertise
- Age/experience of CTI unit.

To some extent, the factors above may limit the range of services a CTI unit can provide. The most important word of advice is to work with the clients who have the greatest impact on the success of the corporation and convince them of the value of CTI.

REFERENCES

Bryant, P. J., T. F. Krol, and J. C. Coleman. Summer 1994. Scientific competitive intelligence: a tool for R&D decision making. *Competitive Intelligence Review* 5(2):48-50.

Bookhart, S. M. Spring 1993. Benchmarking: A natural progression beyond competitive analysis. *Competitive Intelligence Review* 4(1):44-49.

Carlton, S. A. 1992. Industrial espionage: reality of the information age. *Technology Management* 35(6):18-24.

Esposito, M. A., and E. R. Gilmont. December 1991. Competitive intelligence: doing corporate homework. *Pharmaceutical Executive*, pp 68-71.

Gilad, B. 1994. The New Old Paradigm of Competitive Intelligence. *Business Blindspots*. Probus Publishing Company, Chicago, Illinois.

Halliday, R. G., S. R. Walker, and C. E. Lumley. 1992. R&D philosophy and management in the world's leading pharmaceutical companies. *Journal of Pharmaceutical Medicine* 2:139-154.

Harris L. & Associates, Inc., Harvard School of Public Health, Department of Health Policy and Management, and Institute for the Future. 1993. Special Report SR-534. Menlo Park, California

Kurtz, C. J. March 27, 1992. Competitive wargaming. *Proceedings of the 7th Annual Society of Competitive Intelligence Meeting.* Society of Competitive Intelligence Professionals, Alexandria, Virginia 22314.

Matteo, M. A., and E. H. Dykman. Summer 1994. Building credibility, champions and a mandate for competitive assessment. *Competitive Intelligence Review* 5(2):26-30.

Nugent, J. H. March 6, 1992. Foreign competitive intelligence: a personal view. *Proceedings of the Seventh Annual Society of Competitive Intelligence Meeting*, pp. 277-287. Society of Competitive Intelligence Professionals, Alexandria, Virginia 22314.

Technological Intelligence Through Standards Analysis: The Standards Baseline

HERVÉ PENAN

In informal polls of the most intractable problems of management science, our colleagues in the field have repeatedly cited competitive intelligence. This topic is intractable because it is sometimes ill-defined, complex, and not amenable to study through simple discipline-bound frameworks of analysis. One major purpose of this book is to present specific technological competitive intelligence concepts, describe various technological competitive intelligence practices, and demonstrate their relevance in strategic decision making.

The standards baseline is one of the specific concepts for technological competitive intelligence. One of the main characteristics of industrial companies is that they convey scientific and technological information: each company generates, uses, and communicates scientific papers, patents, standards, and regulations. The effective strategy of the firm depends on the way in which it coordinates, filters, and pools these types of information in a standards baseline. In this chapter, we emphasize both the problem of evaluating standards information and the technical difficulty of an in-depth analysis of standards for strategic decision-making.

Two contrasting aspects of competitive intelligence through standards are addressed: one strategic, on the role of standards in the dynamics of innovation, and the other, more operational, on the optimal use of standards in contractual relationships. We intend to demonstrate that technological competitive intelligence is based on the design and the implementation of a standards baseline.

THE INDUSTRIAL USE OF STANDARDS

Standards issues in the competitive technological intelligence of industrial firms are growing in complexity because of the opening of markets, the explosive growth in international standards literature, the horizontal nature of standardization, and the need for inter-operability of products and processes.

Each industrial project, if it is to have a successful outcome, needs a system of reference supplied by standards. A firm must also ensure that its research and development fall within the scope of existing standards. If not, its products may be rejected in favor of those of its competitors who conform better to standards in force. This is especially true if products are exported where a tried and tested approach in line with known standards is often more easily accepted than an innovation that is outside the scope of the usual standards framework.[1]

STANDARDS AND THE INNOVATIVE PROCESS

Innovation and standards have often been argued to be opposed insofar as it is difficult to associate creation, on the one hand, with the prevailing order on the other. A standard defines a product in terms of its manufacturing process, materials, performance, etc.—all of which, on the face of it, are contrary to innovation because they fix the techniques and characteristics of a product. Conformity to a standard and innovation are mutually exclusive. This position is based on a reductionist interpretation of the contents of all standards. The simple answer is to recall that standards are principally concerned with the potential performance of a product or service, rather than the means of attaining the required level of performance.[2] Modern standards set targets, leaving firms to innovate and develop appropriate technical solutions.

A more profound critique is developed around the nature of standards and the process of innovation. The collective nature of standards and broadcasting of their contents into the public domain is incompatible with the original and confidential nature of the classic idea of innovation.

This argument is based on a mythical view of the innovation process (Callon 1994) as a linear procession of relatively discrete phases, beginning with the solitary and mysterious conception of an inventor, followed by the development of a prototype, the production of a good, and its launch into the market where a user will (or will not) leap upon it! An innovation must necessarily break with its scientific and technical environment and will only appear in its finished form before its clients. In this view, a standard is "... a document established by a recognized body, that provides, for common and repeated use, rules, guidelines of characteristics for activities or their results, aimed at the achievement of the optimum degree of order in a given context"[3] and cannot therefore play a role in the innovation process. At best, it authenticates the know-how embodied in an innovation.

This view of the innovation process has little ground in reality and leads firms to make a sub-optimal use of standards. No myth is more dangerous than that of ". . . innovation spotlighting a genial and solitary inventor. . . seeming to spring unpredictably into view. . .opposing vested interests." (Callon 1994). This myth sanctions the separation between the scientific and technical content of innovation and the context of its conception and use.

While it is unnecessary here to go into the numerous developments in the critique of the linear view of technological innovation,[4] it is useful to recall that the dynamic of innovation is that of a network (Callon 1991). An industrial firm develops a network to exploit competencies; actors of varying status (universities, laboratories, firms, public research institutes, clients) participate in this network. Innovation is primarily a collective process, which can be understood in terms of an accumulation of competencies and the convergence of interests and various alliances within a network rather than in terms of improvisation, breakthrough, and competition in a hostile environment. In this model, rather than appearing as a by-product of the innovation dynamic, standardization is a critical success factor in an industrial firm's innovation process.

STANDARDS AS AN INTEREST MECHANISM

To innovate, the interests of a group of actors must be translated into the innovation project (Akrich et al. 1988). An innovation project is usually only partly concerned with existing standards. The technical and economic feasibility of a project often requires that certain standards be modified or new ones proposed. A draft standard, linked to an innovation project, divides the actors of a techno-economic network into three distinct camps:

- Those who ally themselves with and support the draft standard because they are interested in its technical characteristics
- Those who oppose the draft because they support other technical options closer to the characteristics of their know-how
- Those who are indifferent to the draft standard, neither allies or adversaries.

In attempting to propose a standard, a firm draws a demarcation line between the detractors and allies of its innovation project; this line reveals the structure of its network. When a firm has collected the scientific and technical information to develop the first draft of a text, it seeks a consensus for its draft among various partners.

The first draft of a standard is prepared by a standards commission made up of representatives of the various actors in the techno-economic network: producers, distributors, users, government, laboratories, etc. This commission examines the first draft and formulates technical and commercial observations necessary for the development of an agreed-upon draft.

The content of the standard is thus the outcome of successive arbitration between technical possibilities, the choice of users represented on the commission, and costs and deadlines related to its elaboration. The draft standard is revised over time to take account of the expectations and requirements of the actors in the firm's network or, in other words, to interest them. It reflects the final links and interactions that are established, made, and unmade among potential clients, institutional actors, the firm, and its competitors. From this collective experience, a common strategy is born to support one or several draft standards in the framework of national, European, or international standardization.

The search for alliances should be carefully timed in the innovation process to avoid any misunderstandings among partners, to consolidate the position of allies within the network, and to marginalize adversaries to the project. A late launch of the standardization phase can result in considerable added costs for the firm and a risk of having to radically transform an initial draft which has already required significant network investment. Undertaken too soon, standardization can give dangerous publicity which compromises the success of an innovation, particularly if the delivery of the product is delayed, for example, as a result of organizational strategy.

National standards commissions and international and European technical committees serve also as fora for industrialists in the same sector. It is possible to learn—in some cases, a great deal—not only about the draft standards under consideration, but also about the way in which know-how is distributed within a techno-economic network (Penan 1992). Studying standards under development means following the promoters of an innovation project in the alliances they make and in the force of the case they make to win standards over to their side.[5] Standardization promotes the circulation of a firm's know-how within its network; reveals the link between know-how and market requirements; and, by extension, makes its innovation projects visible. For this reason, the management of draft standards should be integrated into innovation projects.

After the role of standardization in technological innovation has been reviewed, a second critical issue in the use of standards—that of their optimal use in contractual relationships in the industrial domain—can be developed.

CONTRACT SPECIFICATION ISSUES

During contract negotiations, firms are faced with ever-more complex standardization requirements from both national and multinational standards organizations.[6] Leaving aside the situation in which client needs are not covered by a contractual relationship (often the result of an insufficient dialogue between the client and supplier), the contract specification issues are of three types:

under-specification; over-specification; and correct standards specification, i.e., properly negotiated.

UNDER- AND OVER-SPECIFICATION

A contract can be described as *under-specified* when the client's technical requirements are either completely or inadequately translated. Standardization contributes to contractual under-specification when technical needs are specified without reference to any standard. This situation can relate to an implicit client need and, as such, constitutes one of the riskier ones for a supplier. In fact, Article 1160 of the "Code Civil" states that customary clauses may be read into a contract, irrespective of whether they are spelled out. A judge may use standards to interpret a contract where they form part of the customary usage of a profession and where their non-observation would constitute a breach of professional conduct.

Standards play the role of annexes to contracts, i.e., they have contractual value insofar as the contractor knows that they are a part of the contract and that they can be taken into account. For this to be valid, the annex has to be made public, which is always the case with a standard even if it has not been given to the other party. Jurisprudence will refer to standards in force at the time of the contract's signing. A basic precaution any supplier should take is to contractualize through negotiation the standards that apply, limiting them to those which are familiar.

A contract can be described as *over-specified* when it includes tasks which do not correspond to any implicit or explicit client need. Imprecise, erroneous, redundant, incompatible, obsolete, or defunct standards can often be found in calls for tender of large procurement agencies concerning one, or sometimes more, supply areas. The ISO definition is often not specified and, consequently, the status of secondary standards (i.e., standards which depend on another standard) is not defined.

A typical case is where general reference is made to a generic series of norms defined by the acronym of the standards agency responsible for their development.[7] For example the U.S. military standard MIL-STD-454[8] cites some 400 individually applicable standards which, in turn, cite several hundred standards. In consequence, the documentation applicable to the contract has no bounds.

The contract is, thus, over-specified; standards serve to cloud the issue and are reduced to the role of a regulatory umbrella. Each party uses a double language in contractually accepting these standards references, fully aware that they cannot meaningfully be used or associated with the supply. Over-specification can also result in the delivery of a higher quality than necessary to meet client requirements and can penalize the supplier in terms of cost of the service.

Disregarding the caricature in which a supplier meets none of the client's needs and where no standards specifications are used leaves what might seem to be an almost miraculous convergence of existing needs, standards specifications, and supply. On completion of a contract, if delivery does not meet requirements which have been correctly specified, the supplier is placed in a situation of breach of contract with all the ensuing financial and legal consequences. On the other hand, if delivery meets the existing needs, correctly specified using a body of standards clearly identified by the two parties, quality has been attained through standards specification. Unfortunately, this situation is not the most common, notably because of legal interference in the use of standards in contracts and the absence, given the lack of analytical tools, of a precise evaluation of the standardization risks.

LEGAL INTERFERENCE

Standards and related documentation were initially devised to be used in an optional and consensual fashion (leaving aside regulatory requirements). Their increasing use in contracts has given them a legal role in contract law ("loi des parties").[9] This trend is not, in itself, contentious and is the basic link between standardization and quality.

What is regrettable is that the use of standards in contracts too often lends itself to being used as an insurance policy for any potential claim against the supplier. In these circumstances, those who draft contracts do not hesitate to cite sets of standards (with which they are not necessarily familiar) in the relevant (or irrelevant) technical areas for the supply of a good or service. The vast array of standards is multiplied by their pointless, incoherent, duplicative, and incompatible use corresponding to over-specification as described here.

International usage, however, as formalized by ISO, does conceive of standards being used as a reference in "place of detailed provisions within a regulation."[10] It goes without saying that a standards-maker expects these requirements to be defined before a standard is selected, whereas, in practice, their citation in contracts represents a misuse of standardization. Indeed, the obvious impossibility of meeting blindly accepted, contradictory standards requirements reduces standardization to a costly constraint. In numerous cases, the client seeks to be covered against potentially bad workmanship, whereas the supplier tends to accept standards without negotiation in order to keep the competition out. The perseverance of this type of contractual situation can distort the image of standardization within a firm.

In this doubly distorted context of a superfluity of incorrectly cited standards, standardization can still supply some relevant guidelines in drawing up a contract. These guidelines are based on a legal concept defined by ISO as "strength of reference."[10] Three types of reference are defined which, if systematically used, allow the identification of a coherent set of documents to be applied in line with specified practices:

- Indicative reference: a reference to standards which states that one way to meet the relevant requirements of technical regulation is to comply with the standards referred to.
- Exclusive reference: a reference to standards which states that the only way to meet the relevant requirements of technical regulation is to comply with the standards referred to.
- Mandatory reference: a reference to standards the application of which is made compulsory by virtue of general law or exclusive reference in a regulation. For example, in France, standards approved by the Association Francaise du NORmalization can only be deviated from in certain public procurement contracts with prior approval.[11]

The negotiation of the strength of reference to standards documentation in contracts establishes the list of standards references that are applicable to the supply. It is then necessary, in contractual terms, to specify the procedure by which each document (particularly those cited as exclusive references) will be applied in practice.

Here again, a relevant standardization concept exists, that of "tailoring" a standard defined as a ". . . process by which individual requirements (sections, paragraphs, sentences) of specifications, standards and related documents, are evaluated to determine the extent to which they are most suitable for a specific system or equipment acquisition and the modification of these requirements to ensure that each achieves an optimal balance between operational needs and costs. . .."[12] The purpose of contract negotiation is, thus, to establish the list of relevant standards with a strength of reference, and, in agreement with the client, to adjust the set of standards which are exclusive references where there is an explicit requirement concerning their application.

THE STANDARDS BASELINE

The use of the concept of tailoring standards cited in a contract is necessarily linked to a prior definition of a finished set of standards embracing the know-how of a firm. This set is termed the standards baseline of the firm. National and international standards commonly applied by the firm are assembled in a "coherent set of standardisation documentation to be used in the client/supplier relationship, except for specific requirements."[13]

Thus, the standards baseline is a structured set of documents whose use is the result of a consensus not only within the firm and all its units, but also between the firm and its clients. Two essential criteria determine the standards to be included in the standards baseline of the firm:

- A high usage frequency by clients, measurable through the statistical study of emerging standards, for example, in the calls for tender to which the firm responds. Statistics collected on the basis of a sample of business transactions reveal two types of standards: multi-project (cited twice or more by clients) and mono-project (cited only once by the same sample). A multi-project standard is an obvious candidate for inclusion in the firm's standards baseline.

- An appropriate degree of proximity of the content of standards to the prevailing know-how in a firm at a given date.

This second point necessitates an audit of the scientific and technical competencies of a firm.

AN AUDIT OF COMPETENCIES

The principal obstacle to establishing a standards baseline is related to the need to link the standardization climate of the firm with its internal know-how: the standards baseline is a competence register. In classic terms, the concept of competence refers to knowledge and know-how, standard processes, and procedures, in brief, all that has been acquired through training and practice necessary for a given operator to accomplish a given task (Parlier 1994). The task, narrowly defined, is the objective assigned to an operator; in a wider sense, it includes instructions, guidelines, the mechanisms used to accomplish the objective, and also the conditions under which the task is performed.[14]

It is, in consequence, necessary to distinguish the defined task (what is expected of the operator and described in a set of procedures) from the effective task (what is done in reality). To state that the standards baseline is based on the technical know-how of the firm, presupposes that the tasks are rigorously defined and performed and that only through following instructions can a result be guaranteed. This is often far from being the case. Operators often need to define instructions in their absence, to redefine them when they are ill-adapted to the context, or to complete them when they include an implicit dimension.

The construction of a standards baseline thus becomes an essential prerequisite for controlling the quality of the service by decoding what is implicit in its accomplishment. This step is an opportunity for a firm to clarify its conception of the task, to examine the agreed-upon definition, and to incorporate in a contract the relevant technical detail which would not have been taken into consideration without the juxtaposition of described tasks to the standards baseline.

From this juxtaposition of the similar and the different, the firm develops a capacity to formalize and explain through the comparison of selected technical aspects of its know-how. In this way, the purpose of the development of the standards baseline is the translation of competencies into standards to be kept and applied to accomplish a given task.

The collective nature of the standards baseline must be emphasized. From the moment when several operators are necessary to complete a contract, the purpose of the standards baseline is, on the one hand, to identify, bring together, and share the necessary competencies so that each operator can participate in a co-operative endeavor and, on the other, to allow each operator to acquire new competencies necessary for the attainment of the task. The standards baseline is an opportunity to exploit each individual's competencies and to make them accessible and usable to other members of the team. It can serve as a space for the construction of a firm's know-how, where each member acquires, through sharing, the complementary competencies needed to act.

POTENTIAL ADVANTAGES

Setting up a standards baseline reinforces the position of a firm during negotiations and allows greater control of the risk linked to contract performance. In the negotiation phase, before standards are contractualized, the firm has the possibility of convincing its counterpart of the advantages, in terms of costs and deadlines, of giving preference to the standards in its baseline. Indeed, if it is accepted that the standards baseline is a translation of the know-how of the firm, its application to a particular output requires no additional investment in modifying existing procedures with the resultant impact on costs on anticipated deadlines. The contractual requirements are not, in consequence, subject a priori, to any random effects.

Standards documentation, linked to internal application procedures which determine the application and adjustment rules, ensures that performance meets the client's expectations.

On the other hand, it is understandable why clients often do not use strictly specific internal baselines which are not linked to standards documentation: a priori, they obviously cannot be known to the client and are thus the subject of extreme caution. On the contrary, a pre-established and demonstrated path between a known standard and internal procedures enhances the credibility of the supplier.

The existence of a standards baseline avoids the need for the firm to reveal restricted or confidential internal procedures and also allows the firm to optimize the level of information supplied to the client. Simply publicizing the technical contents of standards documentation, which are of necessity understandable to the client and not easily challenged because they are drafted by recognized (and sometimes competing) industrialists, suffices to oil the negotiations.

Finally, in having a standards baseline, a firm can require a similar document from its main sub-contractors and co-contractors. This can serve as a control and dialogue mechanism, which can be brought to the fore in negotiations with a client as appropriate. The standards baselines of a firm and its regular sub-contractors should obviously be coherent and complementary.[15]

TOWARD AN ASSESSMENT OF THE CONTRACTUAL RISK

The concept of risk can be generically defined as the possibility that something will happen which could negatively affect a firm's ability to successfully complete its project. The standards risk can be considered to be the specific contractual risk related to the negotiation of standards that are to be referred to in the contract.[16]

In the case of contractual over-specification, a firm blindly accepts a set of standards suggested by the client. In addition to the fact that ignorance of the standards is a potential source of error in the contract (considered by the courts to be inexcusable between professionals), the non-negotiation of standards exposes the firm to the risk of error in estimating the costs of the service. This estimated risk can, for a given task, correspond to the difference between the forecast cost of the service delivered according to the standard proposed by the client and the forecast production cost of the same service according to the internal usage of the firm as reflected in the estimate. The assessment of the standards risk is thus linked to the precise calculation of the direct and indirect costs of adjusting a task to a standard.

Theoretically two typical cases are possible:

- The risk of exceeding the estimate—For a given task, whatever the level of application of a standards document, the forecast cost of production according to the client's standard is higher than the forecast cost of the production linked to the standards baseline of the firm. The estimate runs a high probability of overrunning and exceeding a price the client will find acceptable for the service under consideration.

- The risk of under-estimating the margin—For a given task, whatever the level of application of the standards document, the forecast cost of production according to the client's standard is less than the forecast cost of production linked to the standards baseline. There is little likelihood, if any, of exceeding the estimate. However, the buyer is deprived of exploiting the evident room for manoeuvre to obtain a lower overall price for the service.

In practice, according to the level of application of standard retained in the contract, the estimate will either be exceeded or not. For example, contrary to the more customary international practice, the American Society of Mechanical Engineers' Y14.3M standard[17] obliges users to provide plans drawn in the North American style, i.e., inverting the trihedral projection. Clearly, a firm cannot invest in computer-assisted design and modify its know-how to satisfy this standard for one project only. In this situation, the firm can decide on one of three courses:

- Limit the impact of the standard to an aspect which is not central to delivery (where technically possible)
- Sub-contract the element subject to the standard to a provider who has the required know-how
- Make the necessary investments (material, internal training, and the setting up of internal procedures) if it is important for strategic reasons that the firm's know-how be compatible with the standard. This decision corresponds to integrating the new standard into the firm's standards baseline.

To be competitive, a firm must identify those standards which can be of most benefit in contracts and which its sector makes most use of. It can gain advantage in positioning itself with reference to these standards in order to negotiate with its clients more effectively.

The standards risk in the client-supplier relationship can thus best be minimized by selecting standards as close as possible to the firm's standards baseline and by specifying in contracts the strength of reference of the standards cited, accompanied by the annexing of negotiated adjustments.

CONCLUSION

Technological competitive intelligence remains one of the most controversial areas of management science because it involves, quite literally, the most basic question of exactly which technological targets the company strategy should aim at and exactly how progress toward achievement of these targets should be measured.

This chapter argues that standards play a critical role in the technological competitive intelligence process of industrial firms. Design and implementation of a standards baseline seem to be relevant in both innovative processes and contractual risk management.

It must be emphasized, however, that effective use of standards analysis can be construed as the extent to which decision-makers actually employ technological information in evaluating business alternatives. The problem of fostering the use of standards information in strategic decision-making appears to be acute. Technological competitive intelligence emphasizes the interweaving of both technical and scientific activities into business.

REFERENCES

Akrich, M., M. Callon, and B. Latour. November/December 1988. A quoi tient le succès des innovations? 1. L'art de l'intéressement 2. Le choix des bons porte-paroles. *Annales des Mines, Gérer et Comprendre* 11/12:10-16.

Callon, M. 1991. *Réseaux technico-economiques et irréversibilités. Les figures de l'irréversibilité en économie*. EHESS Editions, Paris.

Callon, M. March 1994. L'innovation technologique et ses mythes. *Annales des Mines, Gérer et Comprendre* 3:15-19.

Parlier, M. 1994. La compétence au service d'objectifs de gestion. Chapter V of *La compétence, mythe, construction ou réalité ?* F. Minet, M. Parlier, S. de Witte. (ed.). L'Harmattan, Paris.

Penan, H. 1992. Gestion du capital immatériel en milieu industriel: de l'environnement aux compétences technologiques. *Actes des XIemes Journees Nationales des IAE, Edition Economica* II:757-777.

ENDNOTES

1. This is also true for products of interest to the public sector where reference to standards is compulsory.
2. P. B. Jensen (*Guide d'interprétation des normes ISO9000*, Association Francaise de NORmalization, 1990) reviews the interpretation rules for standards systems.
3. International Standards Organization (ISO) definition of a standard appearing before the number of each standard that it publishes.
4. For a systematic review of the classic model of innovation, see P. Mustar, *La création d'enterprise par les chercheurs. Dynamique d'intégration de la science et du marché*. Doctoral thesis in Socio-Economy and Innovation, Ecole des Mines de Paris. 1993.
5. For a detailed discussion of the critical role of standardization in the development of a technological innovation in the field of road direction, see the September 1989 attempt the partners in the CARMINAT (PHILIPS-SAGEM) project and the representatives of the ALISCOUT (SIEMENS) project made to standardize the road/vehicle liaison (Mangematin, V. 1992. Entre Marketing et innovation: la gestion du début du processus de compétition technologique. *Recherche et Applications en Marketing*, Vol. 4); in television, the elaboration of the D2Mac-Paquet standard. (Meadel, C. March 1994. Les belles images de la télévision. Une histoire du D2Mac. *Annales des Mines, Gérer et Comprendre*)
6. There are currently some 9000 standards agencies located all over the world whose output is estimated at more than 600,000 documents. This figure increases by approximately 10% per annum. The number of standards applicable to the strategic operations of any given industrial firm is usually significant.
7. Some reference procedures and/or the obligatory application of standards in public contracts (e.g., those specified in Decret No93-1235 of November 15, 1993, modifying Decret No84-74 of January 26, 1984, determining the statute of standards) can have the same effect if they are not applied consistently in contracts.

8. *Standard General Requirement for Electronic Equipment*, Rev. M, 1989.
9. F. Ghestin. 1993. Traité de droit Civil—La formation du contrat. *LGDJ*, 3 edition. Paris.
10. International Standards Organization-CEI, Guide n2, 1991.
11. Compare Decret 93-1235 of November 15, 1993, modifying Decret 84-77 of January 26, 1984, establishing the statute of standardization and the Circular of July 5, 1994, relative to standards references in public procurement and contracts subject to European Community procedures.
12. MIL-STD-962B, 3.3, 1988.
13. NFX50-711. 1994. "La démarche normalisation dans l'entreprise, inventaire et description des outils."
14. For a detailed discussion of the concepts of task and activity see J. Leplat, G. de Terssac, 1990, *Les facteurs humains de la fiabilité dans les systemes complexes,* Editions Octarès; V. de Keyser, 1991, Work analysis in French language ergonomics: Origins and current research trends, *Ergonomics* 34, 6.
15. Such working practices are facilitated by the current developments in Electronic Data Interchange (EDI).
16. G. Lamand, 1993, La maîtrise des risques dans les contrats de vente, Association Francaise de NORmalization.
17. American Society of Mechanical Engineers. 1994. Y14.3M. "Multi-view and sectional view drawings."

The Rationale for Competitive Technical Intelligence Systems: Producing Ideas That Create Intellectual Capital

G. S. STACEY

This chapter is about ideas. Without ideas, business cannot derive value from all the information created and the data processed. It follows, therefore, that the effective and efficient organization of a competitive technical intelligence system depends on a clear understanding of why such a system needs to be set up. Most systems have evolved from corporate information systems, patent offices, libraries, or technology-watching units. These units engage in the relatively passive acts of assembling, processing, recording, and distributing information aimed at minimizing risk and uncertainty.

The thesis of this chapter is that the objective of a competitive technical intelligence system is to extend beyond these passive acts. A competitive technical unit should promote creative intellectual effort and risky thinking in uncertain fields. **The main purpose of a technical intelligence system should be to get ideas about actions that will lead to opportunities to defend, grow, or improve one's business and that will create business assets**

Seeing the competitive technical intelligence system this way encourages a business or other organization to deploy its resources so as to support both the creative act that generates the idea and the subsequent personal actions that develop the concept. Knowing the end objective helps focus the system and assure that it adds value to the business enterprise or organization.

Ideas and intellectual effort are difficult or impossible to manage using conventional business management procedures. Accounting principles cannot effectively be applied when the investment and returns cannot be monetized. However, creativity, ideas, and intellectual effort are critical to the future success of enterprises (Quinn 1992).

From the recent literature, for example, the Tom Peters Seminar, "Crazy Times Call for Crazy Organizations" (1994, Chapter 2), we see that revolutionary organizational forms are needed because less and less of companies' capital is in the form of physical capital and more and more is in the form of intellectual capital. Herein is also a quote from James F. Moore: "For most companies today, the only sustainable competitive advantage comes from out-innovating the competition."

Writing in *Fortune* magazine, Thomas A. Stewart reviews the importance of ideas as assets and the difficulty of dealing with such assets with traditional parameters for evaluation of investments and return. Companies are struggling with how to define and measure human capital, know-how, and patent portfolios. One company (Skandia in Sweden) makes a distinction between human and structural intellectual capital. Human intellectual capital is embodied in employees' knowledge and skill, while structural intellectual capital is represented by the internal processes that link, develop, enhance, and deliver the human capital—company communication systems, market knowledge, the customer base. When only 20 percent of a company's intellectual capital is actually employed and this capital represents three or four times the value of the company's physical capital, there is immense opportunity to improve by using more, developing it more effectively, and valuing it properly in the allocation of resources (investment) for growth (Stewart 1994).

The competitive technical intelligence system is one way to enhance the value of a company's intellectual capital by fully using or exploiting ideas. The intelligence system discussed below is oriented toward technical intelligence; thus, the ideas generated are likely to be in the form of a technical innovation. The system needs to support the identification, definition, and evaluation of these ideas. The system also needs to provide information to help identify which ideas and related actions have the greatest potential to successfully generate return for the business. Clearly, the competitive technical intelligence system needs to do more than assemble, process, and record information.

If the system needs to support the innovation process, it is important to be clear about what innovation is for the business enterprise. In the American Heritage Dictionary of the English Language, innovation is "To begin or introduce something new, be creative."

For a business, this definition of innovation is too restrictive. The innovation process must embody more than this; it must also have an end that is consistent with the objectives of the business. Innovation can be technology-based to improve a product or process. It can be "non-technical" in terms of organization, service, or other nonmaterial aspects of the business.

Innovations, however, must eventually bring a return. They must become business assets. Thus innovation implies getting an idea, developing it, applying it, and benefiting from it, most often in terms of improved business. The benefit is usually in the form of increased sales of products or in reduced cost of production or product delivery. It can also be in the form of improved quality, greater range of services by the product, and improved image. More imaginative or risky innovation may take the form of creating products and services for a wider range of customers or delivering to latent or unimagined customer needs.

THINKING

An important corollary of the concept of getting ideas is that, because it involves creative intellectual effort, someone must think. For this reason, formally assembling, processing, evaluating, screening, selecting, distributing, and communicating information and intelligence must be aimed at stimulating the intellectual effort that is absolutely essential to getting ideas. If all of the formal processes do not stimulate or perhaps otherwise directly support intellectual effort, they are truly a waste of resources. In fact, some systems create such a vast array of undigestible information that using them dissipates and consumes intellectual effort.

Thus, we see that the initial act in creating assets for a business through the innovation process is to get an idea. The word "get" is used because ideas can be one's own; they can come from others in the company; from the outside; or from all sorts of lateral thinking about customers, possible needs of non-customers, future customers, alternative technologies, competitors, suppliers. They can come from inside, from outside, from people in completely different fields, from children.

Note that all ideas come from people. Someone must think, imagine, dream, create, solve, or otherwise "get" the idea. This is a personal and relatively intimate effort and act. Offering ideas is like offering a part of oneself. This is why the process of treating ideas must be managed carefully, sometimes differently from the way other, more well-developed assets might be managed. For example, if ideas are roughly or discourteously rejected, people stop offering them, turning off the stream that feeds the company's survival and growth process.

FAILING

Ideas emanate from a creative process that is nonlinear and generally contrary to traditional logic. Furthermore, many, if not most, ideas will eventually fail (see Norman 1989). Thus, the process must be stimulated and often renewed by the competitive intelligence system. The system must ensure that the flow of ideas continues even though the ideas predominantly fail.

The competitive intelligence system can support the creative process which involves definition of the problem, estrangement from (that is, escaping, taking distance from, or even forgetting) the problem, and stimulation to seek solutions. The creative process does not involve evaluation. Formal tools such as brainstorming, storyboarding, nominal group technique, and word and picture analysis all defer evaluation to another phase. The evaluation process blocks creative thinking. For this reason, evaluation must be done separately and with extreme care.

To mitigate the problem of predominant failure, the culture in which the ideas are generated must strongly support nontraditional ideas and must not penalize failure. Often, this culture is contrary to the ongoing operation of traditional business, where following the rules is rewarded and failure is punished. This conventional model is under strong attack today (see Peters 1994, Chapter 2), but most companies still operate by these conventions, especially as the push to be "lean and mean" continues.

It is probably too much to expect that entering into a competitive technical intelligence system will be effectively preceded by a cultural revolution (encouraging ideas and recognizing the importance of failure) in a company. Therefore, companies that recognize the value of the stream of unconventional ideas are resorting to creating compartments or units of people who obey the new rules: innovation cells, skunkworks, greenfield plants, etc.

The method for paying for these compartments is highly variable. Some companies set funds aside on "faith"; others allow the compartments to charge a fee for the ideas; and others encourage the compartments to market ideas externally, if they are not adopted internally.

Ideas, creativity, and innovation arise from a highly irregular process that may be discontinuous and nonreplicable. Conventional thinking about business depends upon the interchangeablity of people with similar skills. The production line model also depends on the similarity of a product at different stages of development and the detachment of the producer from the actual product at any point. One half-assembled automobile is just like another half-assembled automobile. While many businesses are reconsidering this concept of production, it is absolutely clear that one half-assembled idea or innovation is nothing like another half-assembled idea or innovation. For this reason, ideas and innovations are successes when pursued by a champion, not when passed down a production line of idea manufacturing and given to someone else to finish.

CHAMPIONING

The promotion, care, and nurturing of ideas comes from a champion. One should not expect that ideas can be given to an "incubator" unit for growth. Generally, ideas cannot be given to anyone. They can draw people to them, and they can be pursued doggedly by a champion; but if given to someone else, they are almost sure to fail. The person or unit to whom the idea is given will often spend more time proving that the idea will not work than showing how to overcome all possible objections. Alternatively, the response of a champion to objections or barriers takes the form

This way will work . . .

An alternative that will work is . . .

This can be overcome with . . .

Here are the ways around this . . .

It will work because we could also . . .

Instead, we will do it this way . . . .

Recognizing the strong difference between managing ideas and managing a company's physical assets leads to the conclusion that a competitive intelligence system that supports the evolution (that is, the generation, innovation, and harvesting) of ideas will differ from a conventional corporate information system.

Next, we review a model technical intelligence system and the entire idea-evolution process (creation of intellectual capital) to examine how they relate and integrate.

A MODEL TECHNICAL INTELLIGENCE SYSTEM

The model of the technical intelligence system used for the following discussion involves six specific steps:

1. Plan—Understand user needs and establish actions to meet them.
2. Collect—Seek out and gather data and information.
3. Analyze—Convert data and information to intelligence.
4. Deliver—Transmit selected information to individuals who can benefit from it.
5. Apply—Realize value from technical intelligence in decision-making and actions.
6. Evaluate—Review the effectiveness of the technical intelligence in meeting needs and identifying corrective actions.

While it is essential to organize a system for technical intelligence, putting this system in place does not guarantee success until the system is associated (overlaid or underlain) with the philosophy that the objective is to create assets from ideas and not to distribute information or enhance knowledge. Many companies have been successful in creating intellectual capital without a formal technical intelligence system. Nevertheless, the exigencies of the technical business environment of today will result in a high payoff for the company that is organized to gather, organize, and distribute such intelligence.

The objective, though, must always remain the creation of intellectual capital. Information and knowledge are the raw materials for creating and enhancing intellectual capital.

THE CREATION OF INTELLECTUAL CAPITAL

Intellectual capital is not amenable to a standardized process for its creation. However, to improve the way it is created, there must be an attempt to identify the principal actions that lead to its creation. Following are actions that contribute to the successful innovation of ideas. These steps are not meant to be rigidly defined, and there is probably overlap among the means of accomplishing them. Nevertheless, a business that becomes effective at these steps will become effective at creating and benefiting from intellectual capital.

Ideas must be

- Generated—Producing ideas requires creativity and intellectual effort.
- Communicated—Ideas must be transmitted from one person to others; they must be shared.
- Nurtured—Fresh ideas are usually very fragile so they must be strengthened.
- Screened—Not all ideas can be developed, so some must be put aside.
- Developed—To create intellectual property, ideas need to be proved, improved, tested, demonstrated, and converted into "property" that can be used.
- Implemented—The intellectual property must be used in products, services, or processes. This implementation requires

significant investment in, for example, process changes or new product development.

- Harvested—Return from the intellectual capital comes from reduced costs, improved performance, improved quality, enhanced image, etc. Normally, at this stage, the value of the property is monetized and can be reflected on the bottom line in a conventional accounting system.

Clearly, there are strong relationships and even outright parallels between these steps and the six tasks of operating a unit aimed at competitive technical intelligence described earlier. This section concentrates on the importance of ideas to ensure that the true objective of a competitive technical intelligence system is to create intellectual capital rather than just to introduce a process for assembling, recording, processing, and distributing data and information.

GENERATING

Ideas are the fundamental building block of intellectual capital for a company. Therefore, ideas need to be encouraged, celebrated, and rewarded. For example, in one Japanese company, everyone in the company was expected to be sensitive to the needs of the company and to continually seek ideas for the application of new technologies to solve customer (internal and external) needs.

With a relatively small effort, a burst of ideas (hundreds) for a business can be generated at any point in time. The consulting business is based on this fundamental point and creates its value this way. This burst of ideas can be generated through workshops, brainstorming sessions, idea generation exercises, etc. Therefore, if a company does not have enough good ideas at any point in time, it can get them quickly and easily. However, the greater question in generating ideas is how to sustain a flow of ideas over time.

There is a question of quality also. Generally, quality of ideas will improve over time if there is an accommodating acceptance of different or unusual ideas. The accommodating acceptance consists of treating ideas and the people who offer them with respect and acknowledging the value even for ideas that are not developed further.

The "unloading" process for the backlog of ideas is important to sustaining the flow. Once these ideas have been proffered, the mind is free to deal with new alternatives and is less apt to rehash ideas of the past. Experience from formal idea-generating exercises (normally of several days duration) shows that after the first wave has been unloaded, the next wave of ideas is very rich in content and value.

Generating ideas is a highly creative process. The principal steps are understanding the problem, estrangement, and viewing the problem from a new perspective. Creating these conditions is very important if new ideas are to be generated. As stated above, workshops of various types can produce a flood of ideas quickly.

A technical intelligence system can support this process by providing the opportunity for people to be exposed to problems (some companies link people by computer for communicating and discussing potential company problems); by providing estrangement (one company publishes a newsletter on interesting and provocative subjects seemingly unrelated to the principal business lines); and by viewing the problem from a new perspective (encouraging staff to devote a certain amount of time and providing related information and materials to pursue subjects that are of high personal interest but are outside the traditional business domain).

Of course, the technical intelligence system must assemble and distribute traditional sources of background information about the business and the future, if this function is not already done elsewhere in the business. This information may be in the form of customer surveys, business scenarios, technology forecasts, competitors actions, etc. Presenting this type of intelligence to people in the company must be done in a way that provokes ideas (and perhaps also documents the ideas that occur as the intelligence so presented is assimilated).

Beyond this, there is a need to unfocus the view. People need to be encouraged to look beyond the current products, production processes, customers, and customer needs. They need to exit from their "box" of traditional thoughts and the relative tranquility of the associated environment.

People who work in a company experience the same general background and view of the business and future. As a result, the ideas that emanate from this milieu will be similar. Therefore, it is important to cultivate diversity among staff, backgrounds, cultures, information sources, and means of communication. Independence of sources and methods is essential to having a varied range of possibilities. In sum, the great importance of tolerating divergent views gives an added dimension to the mission of a technical intelligence system that is aimed at creating intellectual capital.

The result of effectively generating ideas will be not only a burst of ideas to deal with special subjects as appropriate, but also a steady stream of ideas that invigorate thinking and stretch the business views about opportunities that create success. In fact, there will certainly be more ideas than can be pursued—a topic that is discussed in more detail later in the section on screening.

COMMUNICATING

In the creation of intellectual capital, communication has several important aspects. Three are discussed here. First, aside from the infrequent solitary genius, most people get ideas when they engage in an exchange with other people. Ideas originate and develop as people communicate with each other. The back and forth repartee is a very creative process for many people. Concepts can be expressed, challenged, modified, extended, strengthened, and improved very easily and quickly. The after-work sessions of teams in Japanese companies are said to be a principal source of ideas because the formal hierarchy and associated stigma of an unacceptable idea have been abandoned. The face-to-face exchange is highly creative.

Second, before ideas can pass to subsequent levels of development and become intellectual capital, they must eventually be communicated to others. Ideas that reside only in someone's head (or are written on a memo in a file) will not serve to advance the idea to higher levels of development. To advance, the ideas must be documented so they can be communicated.

Third, publicity can be a means of recognition and reward for individuals in the system, a way to elevate in importance the fact that ideas are fundamental to the success of the company. Also, positive representation of people with fresh ideas encourages the flow of ideas for the future.

Several approaches for communications are relevant to the technical intelligence system. The actions and mechanisms differ depending upon the alternatives: face-to-face exchanges, documentation of ideas, and visibility for recognition and reward as explained above.

Face-to-Face Exchanges

The technical intelligence system for a company or organization can, of course, encourage face-to-face meetings. Such meetings, generally, are more of a cultural aspect of the business organization, and the technical intelligence system probably cannot be expected to modify company culture. It is possible, and appropriate, to recognize the rules that lead to successful communication about ideas. These rules can be distributed, and people can be informed and trained on them.

Also, clearly operating the system to recognize the difference between creation and evaluation can show the difference and importance of the distinction. Ideas arrive from a process of creation in which "killer phrases" are banned (in discussion or other communication). In the creative phase, participants are not allowed to object to an idea; rather, their responsibility is to add or build so the idea can work, not to explain why it will not (in someone's opinion) work. The operating phrases and thoughts must be

Furthermore, if we do . . . it will work (work better).
By adding a . . . it will succeed.
To make it more attractive to a larger group of users, we can . . .
I can extend that even further by . . .
It would be even less costly if . . . .

Another role for the technical intelligence system can be to provide the actual forum for face-to-face exchanges of ideas. In particular, since many systems are now being oriented toward linking by computers, local area networks, and telecommunications, the forum for face-to-face (in a matter of speaking) meetings can be created on-line. This type of communication is already popularized by Internet.

For a company to create intellectual capital, of course, the distinction between internal and external communications and exchanges needs to be evaluated carefully. Exchanging ideas freely on the Internet might compromise the possibility of defining the idea as property, a delicate point as yet unresolved (except to say that what is on the Internet is public) and of concern to companies wishing to maintain the security of their own property.

Internal, secure systems can still provide the mechanism for face-to-face exchanges for the creation and discussion of ideas. In fact, the anonymity of the computer system and screen may encourage participation by people who normally might be reluctant contributors. It also appears that certain rules of comportment on the computer system are required to avoid abusing participants (an interesting and evolving episode in today's computer communications).

Documentation

Until an idea is written down or otherwise transcribed into a form that can be conveyed to another person, it has no chance of being effectively converted into intellectual capital and managed as an intellectual capital asset. Once it has been documented, it can be explained to others; it can be evaluated; it can be developed. More specifically, it can also be protected by patenting or other formal legal means. At this point, it becomes intellectual property and advances significantly beyond being an idea.

Know-how is often cited as the counter example to documentation because it is not written down, but rather, resides in the knowledge base and capability of people who have experience with processes and methods. The current business environment of reengineering and becoming lean and mean has been accompanied by an associated scramble to document this know-how (using artificial intelligence systems, for example) so that the experience is not lost. In fact, after documenting, know-how can often be improved, extended, and taught.

Visibility

Overall visibility for the technical intelligence system and the results of the work by people in the company is important to create the environment that emphasizes the importance of ideas and their development. In this regard, a certain amount of publicity is appropriate. This publicity usually appears in an internal newsletter that is brief and stimulating and recognizes successful (and unsuccessful) ideas.

External publicity can also achieve the same objectives. The results of a competition for ideas among people at car companies in Japan were the subject of a television report. One of the winners was a young man who designed a commuter car that folded into a briefcase. It looked a bit like a go-kart. He was televised driving it on the road to show that it worked. Although the car company is not likely to be produce this car, the recognition this young man received, with the attendant publicity, practically assures that he will continue with a stream of ideas for the future. Of course, he may set up his own business to produce and sell the commuter briefcase car himself. Even in this case, the recognition and resulting opportunity will inevitably encourage ideas from others.

The overall result of efforts in these areas is to steady the flow of ideas, to convert ideas into documentable intellectual property assets, and to reward people and recognize the fundamental importance of ideas to the success of the company.

NURTURING

Investments in new ideas for products, services, and processes tend to be weak when compared with investments in existing business elements (products, processes, internal and external services). As a result, companies have found it important to permit these ideas to grow and develop before they compete for funds with investments in existing products and processes.

Ideas can be thought of as seeds that need careful nurturing and access to some resources so they can gain strength. This process has sometimes been called incubation. At the Singapore Institute for Standards and Industrial Research (SISIR), a special incubation program provides inventive people with access to equipment, laboratory space, some limited resources, and contact with technical and business expertise. In this way, ideas can be developed so they can withstand more rigorous evaluation and analysis essential to demonstrating the potential for investment. Nurturing of some type is essential to encourage the creative expression of new ideas.

At the Battelle Memorial Institute, funds were allocated to a unit called Corporate Technical Development. This unit had the responsibility for calling for ideas and allocating central funds to encourage the development of ideas to the point that they could potentially be converted into an intellectual property asset. The normal business channels would view the ideas as too risky or too uncertain to justify funding from resources that would otherwise go to the bottom line. Battelle recognized that investments in new ideas could not compete for resources aimed directly at the bottom line, especially when the bottom line was being squeezed by current business conditions.

Paradoxically, the need for new ideas and concepts is often most urgently felt when the bottom line is squeezed hardest. This fact argues strongly for a relatively steady commitment of resources to the nurturing of ideas, a commitment that, by nature, would have to be small so it could suffer the cycles of good and bad business years.

A commitment to nurture ideas strengthens them, signals the importance of ideas to the future of the company (or a country like Singapore), and encourages people to look for ideas and offer them. In addition, it is important to recognize clearly that most of the resources committed to nurture ideas will not pay off directly. Many, if not most, ideas will, sooner or later, fall by the wayside. A steady hand is needed and must be supported by the technical intelligence system so the flow is encouraged.

Once its results are being used, the technical intelligence system can support and nurture ideas. In some cases, the technical intelligence system is contained within a unit that is responsible for development and growth of intellectual capital. In this case, some resources are devoted to nurturing ideas. These resources might variously be called incubation, technical development, seed money, or predevelopment funding.

The amount of resources devoted to nurturing is often less than one percent of a total R&D budget. Most company officers would like to push the envelope out to the point that funds for nurturing ideas represent up to 10 or 20 percent of the R&D budget.

Creativity is still needed in incubation because there are not enough resources to incubate all ideas. For this reason, it is important to leverage in as many ways as possible to allow ideas to grow.

SCREENING

Screening is where 80 or 90 percent of the ideas must be rejected. Screening is also where people could be potentially discouraged and demotivated. For this reason, screening must be done in the most positive manner possible. At this point, the value of a competitive technical intelligence program will grow or will be reduced to zero. In one chemical company, the ideas gleaned from competitive technical scanning were handed to a blue-ribbon committee of well-respected people to screen and pass on to other parts of the organization for action. Naturally, most of the ideas were rejected, and only a few were passed on to others. Those people whose ideas were rejected became highly demotivated and subsequently stopped offering ideas. The stream of ideas dried up.

To create a positive screening process that will encourage a continuing flow of ideas

- Set a context. Sometimes the context is based on the company vision (if there is one).
- Screen effectively. Do not throw the baby out with the bath water.
- Decide if the company wants evolution or revolution, or both.
- Define the methods of screening that will be used at a later stage so incubation is aimed at answering the relevant questions.
- Involve people in the process of creating a "humane" and effective screening process for seeking and creating ideas. In one company, this process involves people in the creation of scenarios about the future business, technical, and customer environment.

The system may be simple, using clearly stated and defined criteria and weights, or complex, involving weighting, pairwise comparison, criteria setting, and evaluation such as, for example, the analytical hierarchy process of Saaty (1988).

In the end, the company must be able to sustain ideas that fail, without demotivating the idea generators. Most (90 to 95 percent) ideas will not be successful. A high rate would be one in ten or one in twenty ideas that are successfully implemented and become an asset to the company.

How can a company sustain such a level of failure and still have people freely exercise their creativity? By celebrating all ideas, including those that are not accepted. Value them because they clarify focus or define non-directions; use them as ideas for sale elsewhere or to another company; patent them and get royalties from licensing them, but celebrate! An "un-useful" idea is infinitely better than no idea at all.

DEVELOPING

The next step in the business innovation process is to develop the idea. Even after incubation, young ideas will remain weak in the face of other investment alternatives. The technical concept might not be proven, the manufacturability might be questionable, the quality or performance potential unknown, the acceptability to potential customers not evident. These unknowns make new ideas highly vulnerable. For this reason, ideas need to be developed before being placed in competition with other possible investment alternatives. They need development until they become strong enough to compete.

The resources devoted to developing ideas are much greater than those needed for incubation. For this reason, not as many ideas can be developed (or one might say pre-developed). Nevertheless, critical questions about the ideas and their application must be answered before the more significant resource commitments and implementation are undertaken. These activities often take place in somewhat isolated centers which might be called, for example, the predevelopment department, the skunkworks, the innovation cells.

For the competitive technical intelligence system to function effectively, these centers either must be involved in the system definition of scope or must be free to assemble their own information based on their own knowledge and needs. The scope of interests of such centers is usually not "mainstream" for the business, and the information that these centers use and need might be viewed as stimulating or a distraction to the core businesses. For this reason, the intelligence needs of these groups must be handled with understanding and perspicacity.

The sources of resources for the development of ideas are actually vast. Not all development must be done with "high power" bottom-line-consuming R&D funds. It can be extremely effective for a competitive intelligence system to develop knowledge, data, and associated relationships (for example, with industry associations and external centers of excellence) to ensure that all possible resources can be brought to bear. Some examples of sources include the following:

- Use company R&D money.

- Look for others in other company business units who are interested in cooperating.
- Support idea development through purchasing policy. Many purchasing departments are not organized in this way (in fact, many are organized to the contrary), but they can be an important unexploited resource for practically any company.
- Get unions to help.
- Look for business associations (industry, consumer, product, etc.) linkages.
- Look for public support.
- Form alliances with suppliers to ensure their commitment of resources and effort.
- Give people freedom with some of their time and some small resources.
- Combine with public resources.
- Network with people in centers of excellence such as universities where work on the subject is already under way.

There is no single place where all of these resources are assembled and rationalized in most companies. No one really has interest in all of them. In fact, usually no one has interest in much more than one of them. For this reason, an important element in developing a competitive technical intelligence system can be to survey, develop, and maintain contacts with such sources to make them available to the rest of the company during the development process.

IMPLEMENTING

Implementing involves taking an idea to production or changing a company process or method. Usually, an existing process or method is to be changed. Most ideas also can find a logical place (group, unit, level, organizational function) where they could be implemented. And, of course, most companies have production plants that are amenable to being modified to produce new or different products.

The biggest difficulty in implementing new ideas, however, is the resistance of the "old line" cadre, who will fight tooth and nail to prove that the old way (technology, method, product) will do everything any new way might claim. Witness the fact that NCR nearly died of this inflexibility.

In another case, the manufacturer of large electrical home appliances (white goods) wanted a washing machine with electronic controls. Whatever the "electronics" group could think of to do, the "mechanics" group would prove they could do it better. To halt the contest and make progress toward electronics-based machines, the company started a completely new plant of "electronics" people at a completely different site. Over time, production at this plant replaced the "mechanics" production. A true greenfield plant was needed to break out of the old box. To effect this type of break, companies today are developing approaches that encourage continuous learning in their staff, clearly offering a role and responsibility to the competitive technical intelligence function (Senge 1990).

Most companies are not completely out of their historical patterns and boxes. For this reason, it may remain necessary to establish new units in forms like greenfield plants, innovation cells and teams, and spin-off companies.

HARVESTING

Not all innovations will become assets, but every one must be aimed at becoming an asset in some way. Ideas come from many sources and thus can be generated both by a special source or unit, such as a skunkworks, and/or by any or all other people in the company. The former should be set off so that it has the freedom to produce the ideas. In the latter case, the entire business perceives itself as the incubator for ideas. How can ideas that come from differing sources be finally harvested?

The principal view of harvesting consists of thinking of converting the value of the asset into money. This method should be coupled with other ways of achieving gain for the business or organization from the asset. Nevertheless, the principal way of harvesting is to incorporate the idea into the business. Incorporating ideas or harvesting involves people with the willingness and freedom to differ.

In a company primarily oriented toward development, production, and distribution, significant freedom and creativity might be viewed as detrimental to an overall focused effort in the main lines of the business. This view is especially true for highly structured environments.

Changing to looser arrangements in which each individual is expected to be more creative and active in developing and using new ideas should be approached with caution lest the historical basis for success be undermined. In this case, a skunkworks approach in which the source of ideas is separate from the source of new developments may be best. The problem of transferring the ideas to use in production and products needs special attention in this case.

In one particular case, for a consumer appliance company whose product life cycle was very long, internally generated new innovative ideas created uncertainty for people involved in the product development cycle. In this case, an external (or well-separated) idea-generation system was judged more reasonable and potentially effective. This decision led to consideration of a variety of alternative, externally based arrangements leading up to harvesting and the act of harvesting itself.

Each company, business, or organization has important characteristics that result in an arrangement that is appropriate for their circumstances. These characteristics relate, for example, to cost, degree of integration needed, degree of development needed for the idea, time involved to put in place, number of company people who must be involved, company culture (idea-accepting or idea-adverse), urgency of need for new ideas, and existing organization elements and relationships. Therefore, a company might harvest through any of the following mechanisms: innovation cell follow-through, skunkworks, idea broker or manager, intellectual property office, technology transfer (in and out) office, networking internal/external, royalties, patents, recognition, financial rewards, and advertising and publicity.

In most of these examples, the competitive technical intelligence system can serve the company or organization by identifying and, in some cases, promoting the harvesting activity. For example, at a large international chemical company, one person was assigned responsibility for finding incoming, useful technology and for transferring company-owned technology and ideas out. In fact, such a "unit" could be viewed as a cost and revenue center and could engage in activities that are central to the competitive technical intelligence function.

In another case, all of the intellectual property of an R&D group of a large British defense company was given to one "intellectual property office" that was required to deliver a certain amount of profit to the bottom line from managing income and expenses (including internal exchanges).

CONCLUSIONS

The value a competitive technical intelligence system adds is demonstrated by a system that stimulates creativity, encourages ideas, and pushes them to the point that they produce a return for the business. The system can be viewed as the motor for the ideas or the nonphysical assets of the company. These are the inventive, innovative, creative, intellectual, know-how-based, traditionally nonquantifiable, or intangible assets.

To deliver the value-added of a competitive technical intelligence system, it is important to integrate it into the process of creating, innovating, and harvesting ideas. The principal factor for success is transforming the concept of an intelligence system from one that assembles, processes, and records information to minimize risk and uncertainty to one that supports creativity, facilitates risky thinking and effort, and explains uncertainty about the future so advantage and opportunity can be sought. This transformation needs to occur either across the business for those with a creative culture or, for businesses with a limited creative culture, in support of special compartments that have the responsibility and authority to generate new ideas and business.

REFERENCES

Ashton, W. B., and G. S. Stacey. 1995. Technical Intelligence in Business: Understanding Technology Threats and Opportunities. *International Journal of Technology Management* 10(1):79-104.

Moore, James F. May-June 1993. Predators and Prey: A New Ecology of Competition. *Harvard Business Review*, p.75.

Norman, Donald A. 1989. *Design of Everyday Things*, p. 105 ff. Currency Doubleday, New York (ISBN 0-385-26774-6).

Peters, Tom. 1994. *The Tom Peters Seminar: Crazy Times Call for Crazy Organizations.* Macmillan London Ltd.

Quinn, J. B. 1992. *Intelligent Enterprise*. The Free Press, Maxwell Macmillan International, New York.

Saaty, Thomas. 1988. *The Analytical Hierarchy Process.* Beccles, Suffolk.

Senge, Peter. 1990. *The Fifth Discipline: The Art and Practice of the Learning Organization.* Currency Doubleday, New York.

Stewart, Thomas A. October 3, 1994. Your Company's Most Valuable Asset: Intellectual Property. *Fortune*, pp. 28-33.

PART V

Contemporary Business Intelligence Issues

PART V
Editorial Introduction

This final section contains a single chapter addressing the outlook for competitive technical intelligence in firms and laboratories and an appendix containing an inventory of some of the most important information resources on science and technology.

Brad Ashton discusses the future of technical intelligence in business. He includes a range of ideas on topics such as increasing demand in companies for competitive technical intelligence services; the consequences of advances in computer, information, and communication technology; and improvements in analysis methods.

Future Directions in Competitive Technical Intelligence

W. BRADFORD ASHTON

The formal practice of developing technical intelligence in American business is only in its infancy. Although many firms carry out various intelligence functions, they are not usually called "technical intelligence," and only a small number of U.S. companies have organized competitive technical intelligence (CTI) programs. Most firms simply do not make a focused CTI effort a high business priority.

There are, however, signs that this situation is changing. A larger and rapidly increasing number of U.S. firms gather general business or competitive intelligence, and some science and technology (S&T) matters are handled in these activities. Competition based on new technology is on the rise around the world. As having the technology advantage become a more prominent component of overall company strategy, the importance and practice of gathering CTI will undoubtedly increase. More CTI organizations will form, and many existing CTI activities and units will grow. In short, CTI will begin to mature as a business and technical discipline, and the signs of this evolution will become increasingly apparent in the near future.

This chapter highlights several broad areas where significant changes in the practice of CTI are likely in the future, including trends in CTI business practices and in the production and use of intelligence in business. The production of intelligence involves collecting, storing, and analyzing input data, while the use of intelligence involves disseminating the intelligence findings and applying them to strategy, decisions, or actions.

THE GENERAL OUTLOOK FOR COMPETITIVE TECHNICAL INTELLIGENCE IN U.S. BUSINESS

According to many intelligence professionals the outlook for continuing CTI growth throughout U.S. business is very good, especially where advanced technology is a core element of business strategy. Increased interest in CTI is already apparent in the largest professional organization dealing with competitive business intelligence, the Society of Competitive Intelligence Professionals (SCIP). Recently, research and development (R&D) has been a SCIP membership subgroup with high annual growth in new applications.

Moreover, in an on-going investigation into the practice of technology intelligence, the Industrial Research Institute (IRI) has uncovered strong interest in CTI by member companies. A recent survey in which recipients could self-assess their company's CTI practices against norms of intelligence excellence and could express a need for educational and training materials to improve their intelligence operations had a response rate of over fifty percent. IRI's counterpart in Europe, the European Industrial Research and Management Association, has identified similar levels of interest there, where strong interest in technology monitoring has been evident.

Trends in the use of CTI in industry depend on a variety of factors, but the future of CTI is tied most directly to future directions for both public and private R&D. As indicated in other chapters in this book, CTI is important when changes in any particular area of technology are imminent, rapid, and driven by advances and players from outside the main technical fields of focus (see, for instance, Kodama 1992 and Bower and Christensen 1995). Many companies scan, scout, or monitor technology activities to track

R&D advances and construct profiles of the technology strengths and weaknesses of competitors, other firms, or laboratories. But the continued success and growth of CTI depends on continued demand for its services and continued investment of resources to produce and deliver intelligence products.

The basic driving forces behind demand for CTI are the pressures on business to develop technology-based competitive advantages and the nature of the R&D to produce them. New technology needs are motivated by factors such as the current and expected nature of competition in a market, the costs of the product and the process, and the prospects for acceptable payoffs from R&D investments. And if recent history is a guide, the outlook for continued high levels of global competition and growing public and private R&D is very good.

Although most companies that rely heavily on technology for competitive advantage could benefit from some form of technical intelligence activity, certain types of companies have a strong need for a formal and continuing CTI program and would gain substantially from establishing one. These companies typically

- Operate in a technologically dynamic industry environment where
  - –the pace of technological change in the industry is rapid, or
  - –entirely new or different technologies are likely to surface or to be needed within five years.
- Emphasize technology-intensive products and processes where
  - –technology is an important differentiating factor in product features, pricing, or service strategy
  - –the rate of new product introduction is high
  - –market entry timing is important to the success of the business, or
  - –regulatory approval of new products is complex, time-consuming, and costly.
- Manage a significant R&D portfolio investment in an environment where
  - –the business is R&D-intensive, with a high ratio of R&D to sales dollars, or
  - –early decisions to kill unpromising R&D projects are important.

- Expect a high share of near-term business revenue growth from new products.

Firms in high-technology industries such as chemicals, telecommunications, computers, pharmaceuticals, medical equipment, aerospace, transportation, petroleum refining, electronics, scientific instruments, image processing equipment, energy, and transportation fit these criteria and seem to be the industrial groups where the present level of CTI activities is most likely to expand. These industries typically invest heavily in R&D to develop new products and processes. Also, some service industries, such as banking, publishing and data processing, that rely heavily on information technologies are potential beneficiaries of CTI and could also represent areas of high growth potential.

TRENDS IN ORGANIZATIONAL STRUCTURE AND ROLES

As use of CTI becomes more widespread in industry, existing CTI organizations will undergo a variety of changes through a natural maturing processes and adaptation to new demands for their services. Three of the areas for this change are discussed here: organizational structures, staff roles, and organizational roles.

ORGANIZATIONAL STRUCTURES

The successful CTI unit can be organized in a number of different structures. In fact, success appears to be influenced more by the unit's leadership, staff, and culture than by the organizational structure.

The fact that no single, best organization form has appeared, however, suggests that companies will continue to experiment with a variety of structures and reporting arrangements. The CTI staff are often part of a larger, centralized corporate competitive intelligence, technology acquisition, R&D management, or corporate/strategic planning unit. As the CTI function within these corporate units grows in size, complexity, or influence, a more independent CTI will often evolve. Some common organizational structures are summarized below (based on descriptions in Quinn 1985):

- Central Unit—Responsibility is assigned to a specially created core CTI unit with dedicated staff and a specific charter for technology intelligence functions.
- Decentralized Groups—CTI is conducted throughout the operating units of the company, such as in product divisions or business units, with each unit group gathering and processing its own intelligence.
- Combined Operations—CTI functions are given to a centralized group, but key intelligence staff are located in or "loaned" from operating units (for example, as collectors or information sources).
- Diffused—No formal structure for CTI is established; staff throughout the company are expected to perform the CTI function as part of their other job responsibilities and to pass information and results up through the management chain.

Regardless of organizational form, CTI activities depend heavily on a firm's library or information center resources and systems. With the proliferation of on-line information sources and customized databases, many traditional company libraries have evolved into multi-dimensional business/technical information centers with a variety of information sources, tools, and staff skills.

New organizational concepts for libraries that reflect growing company commitments to total information management are emerging and future CTI functions for some companies may fit better in this framework. One such concept with potential for CTI is the information analysis center (IAC), which combines traditional library or information center functions with decision-oriented analytical services. The centers are designed to provide senior technical staff, lab managers, and chief executive officers with more confidence in their decisions about technology. A number of companies and the U.S. Department of Defense have used the IAC approach (Lesko and Steve 1995).

Information analysis centers are analogous to military "war rooms" or industrial "crisis management centers" and have several features that make them attractive as technical intelligence organizations. They provide a readily accessible knowledge base of information, data, technical skills, analytical tools, and facilities to meet the needs of its users. Although similar to high-quality traditional libraries, IACs are unique in several respects:

- They acquire and process information from any pertinent source and in all media, which gives their information variety and quality.
- They maintain up-to-date inventories of current information in designated S&T areas as it becomes available from around the world.
- Their processing, storage, and retrieval mechanisms are tailored to the organization and its needs.
- Subject matter experts analyze information both in the selection and in the output stages.
- Synthesized information in selected subject areas is packaged and disseminated according to expressed or anticipated user needs.

The technical staff and information specialists in IACs work in partnership with clients to determine technical priorities; interpret research, development, test, and evaluation data; assess product performance and support process requirements; and recommend steps that will lead to the desired results. In day-to-day problem-solving, IACs have demonstrated that no matter which tool, technique or machine is used, it is ultimately ideas that count. The beginning of the scientific and engineering process is the idea, and generating ideas is a very human thing.

An emerging informal organizational concept with important potential for CTI applications is the “knowledge cell.” A knowledge cell is a topic or theme-fixed group of company staff dispersed throughout an organization, but in regular contact through meetings, e-mail, phone, or other information exchanges. The cell is organized to explore and learn about a business or intelligence issue or topic. Its mission is to develop a common understanding, future vision, or point of view on a priority question or issue (such as a key intelligence topic) and to identify action items to capitalize on the collective knowledge of the cell. Knowledge cells have been used to generate multiple points of view about a topic or to develop and execute a technology or market strategy for an emerging technology application or product concept. However, they have excellent potential for developing and interpreting technical intelligence (Battelle 1996).

STAFF RESOURCES

As CTI becomes a more accepted input to technology acquisition, R&D, and business strategy decisions and as companies increase their use of CTI, a community of expertise among CTI practitioners will begin to form. A pool of experts with a formalized knowledge base will develop and the collective professionalism of CTI work will increase. As this transition occurs, three aspects of CTI staff resources will require more attention: specialized staff roles, training and development, and use of experts.

Specialized Staff Roles

Successful intelligence functions typically have a number of formal specialized roles, ranging from collectors and analysts to information specialists and managers. In addition, informal specialized roles—such as gatekeepers and champions—are also likely to develop. As a CTI activity matures, these roles have proved valuable in keeping CTI visible and supported in companies. One of the best ways to create effective CTI organizations is to promote the efforts of these individuals.

Gatekeepers are individuals who are naturally effective at collecting diverse bits of information, screening them for usefulness, and passing them on to appropriate recipients. They often are good intelligence collectors because they are sensitive to company needs, recognize the significance of certain pieces of external information, and see how to apply it in useful ways. Champions know how to develop useful S&T intelligence from external information and push it through organizational bureaucracies to effective application. They constantly draw attention to the contributions intelligence staff make to the organization's success. As a result, customers looking at their suite of important resources tend to see the CTI unit in the forefront.

Training and Professional Development

At the moment, there are very few educational or training opportunities for CTI in business or engineering schools. Professional organizations such as the Society of Competitive Intelligence Professionals offer periodic CTI information or training programs, but these efforts are only in the early stages. Entry-level training in CI is available through a variety of CI consulting firms, but advanced training for practitioners is virtually non-existent. Clearly, as the need for and use of CTI grows, professional education and training activities must also increase.

Use of Experts and Consultants

Most companies cannot afford to maintain all needed S&T skills in-house and therefore will outsource to external experts such as university professors, consultants, or vendors (see Krol et al. 1993). Partial reliance on sources outside the firm offers important advantages. External experts can introduce some "disinterested objectivity" into decision-making and can inject new data and fresh thinking into the firm's traditional cultures. In addition, using some external staff disguises the fact that a company is using CTI methods. Finally, outside expertise is often needed to cope with the array of new databases; specialized intelligence collection, analysis, or dissemination tools; and new security technologies.

Many companies already have established expert networks to link them with key individuals inside and outside their laboratories and have selectively convened expert panels or focus groups of relevant technologists to help diagnose technology changes or research directions. On-line services with relatively quick access to a wide variety of experts are also now available and are likely to improve as companies demand quicker access to the right expert. Use of outside experts will undoubtedly continue and probably increase in the future, especially given the rapid pace of change in technology and business.

THE ROLE OF COMPETITIVE TECHNICAL INTELLIGENCE IN THE ORGANIZATION

Many professionals expect the role of CTI to increase from narrowly focused R&D or technology acquisition problem-solving to encompass a broader range of company functions. Various forms of CTI are used in many technology-oriented companies, although the two most common activities appear to be scouting for technology and tracking competitors. A good example of technology scouting is the Air Products Technology Clearinghouse

(APTECH) at Air Products and Chemicals, Inc. APTECH staff search out new pre-commercial opportunities such as product extensions, research that is ready for development, and technology improvements and peripheral know-how that business developers or researchers can pursue. APTECH staff use more that 140 regular sources and thousands of network contacts to scout for over 10,000 specific interests of Air Products staff worldwide. Since the inception of the clearinghouse in 1988, over 500 unique technologies and over 1000 unique and valuable information items reach customers every year, sometimes finding their way into product or process advances (Brenner 1992, 1996).

The competitor tracking program at BOC Group, an industrial and specialty gas company, is another informative example (Kydd 1996). The objectives of BOC's competitor tracking program are twofold: 1) through a monthly information digest, keep R&D staff regularly informed on all important technical news, publications, and patents from key competitors, and 2) from a computerized profile of all technical information collected during the year, develop an annual strategic profile for each major competitor. Company profiles are based on a variety of literature, patent, and other data, and each is computerized so it can be tracked over time for inputs into appropriate decisions.

Besides functions such as monitoring, technology scouting, and competitor tracking, CTI can, in principle, serve a variety of other company needs. Examples include decisions about technology strategy and acquisition, R&D program planning, technology commercialization, and production operations. After several years of service, one competitive technical intelligence group in the pharmaceutical industry moved from filling simple, direct information requests for R&D management to providing some form of intelligence information service to the following company organizations (Krol et al. 1996):

- Research and Development—laboratory research and development, regulatory groups, product portfolio evaluation, and prioritization
- Commercial groups—strategic product line development, commercial development, market research, business intelligence, licensing, and business development
- Senior management—corporate managers and their staffs

- Others—equity investment review, project and product teams, sales and marketing, and legal.

This wide variety of intelligence users grew gradually as a result of careful management of company intelligence activities and care in delivering high-quality intelligence products.

TRENDS IN DATA STORAGE, RETRIEVAL AND COMMUNICATION

An array of technical and human information sources for business intelligence use has become widely available. The busy schedule of technical meetings and high-performance, low-cost computer and communication technology, exemplified by large databases and the Internet, have made information overload a serious problem for most intelligence analysts. These trends show no signs of abating. The increasing availability of verbal, written, and electronic source data, as well as continuing improvements in information storage, retrieval, and communications technology, point to enormous changes in the way intelligence is collected and stored. Information overload will continue to be a significant problem for all information professionals, not just for intelligence providers and users. But, the growth in information can be managed as users become more knowledgeable, user information needs become clearer, and data retrieval and analysis tools improve.

Several aspects of information technology will impact the collection, storage, retrieval, and communication of intelligence data. Five aspects discussed here are multimedia data sources and data fusion, data storage and warehousing, rapid data screening, automated communications, and groupware.

MULTIMEDIA DATA SOURCES AND DATA FUSION

The explosion in digital computer, electronics, and telecommunication technology suggests that static and dynamic multimedia data sources will find applications in business and technical intelligence. Real-world media images, audio, and video integrated with artificial computer-world text, graphics, and animation hold enormous potential for combining literature, video, taped voice, and even real-time system performance data for intelligence purposes. Recent technological advances have made it economically feasible to digitize and compress real-world media for use in digital computer or network environments; multimedia data fusion has already been demonstrated and is in use. The basic value is to improve the speed, accuracy and completeness of communicating information or transferring knowledge within an organization (Fetterman and Gupta 1993).

In the future, computer operating systems, networks, and database management systems will incorporate multimedia technology so other product developers can exploit the advantages of each media source. The personal computer is already a "personal communicator" capable of handling audio, high-capacity removable storage (CD-ROM), and motion video. The personal computer is now moving toward full multimedia networking of client server configurations. Multimedia is likely to change the way some intelligence functions are carried out because it delivers information in intuitive, multi-sensory ways that allow people to experience information rather than simply to acquire it. It is possible to foresee intelligence collected from audio and video sources merged with text and graphics to deliver recommendations to users. These advances would improve an analyst's or user's ability to experience ideas and concepts interactively for better understanding.

Multimedia opens up a whole new method of delivering information that can provide multiple connected pathways through a body of information, allowing users to jump easily from one topic to related or supplementary information. This capability will make complex ideas much easier to find and understand and communicate.

DATA STORAGE AND WAREHOUSING

Data in many forms that are relevant to intelligence work continue to proliferate from a variety of internal and external sources. To store the vast electronic files of data collected in routine and special business operations, many companies are now developing "data warehouses" that can hold as much as four terabytes (roughly equivalent to 160,000 four-drawer filing cabinets of text). Computer storage costs are declining and are expected to continue downward, suggesting that storage capacity will not be a limiting factor.

Since the notion was first described in 1991, data warehousing has emerged as a premier enabling technology for corporations seeking to unlock the contents of huge stores of internal and external data, especially the Internet. Data warehouses are specially designed electronic databases optimized for retrieval and analysis. They are accompanied by a series of powerful data access and transfer software to extract data from a variety of original sources. The information can then be cleansed, compiled, and integrated into the warehouse where it can be easily queried for business and intelligence analysis. Data warehousing is designed to ease the creation of useful knowledge from the large amounts of information that most companies have accumulated.

Future data warehouses will be flexible environments made up of technologies that store massive amounts of external intelligence data, consolidate it into separately designed relational databases, manage it, and organize it into subject-oriented formats that are optimized for end users to access and analyze.

RAPID DATA SCANNING, RETRIEVAL AND SCREENING

Advanced tools—both on-line services and sophisticated statistical data analysis software—for quickly searching and screening large data sets are also becoming available. These tools rapidly detect and identify those parts of large or linked databases that meet the user's criteria for relevance and usefulness, thereby reducing the time intelligence analysts spend reviewing source materials that may ultimately prove useless. Some tools also provide the capability to browse documents, extract information, mine databases, and construct queries to multiple data sources. Future progress should make services such as automatic document zoning/paragraph retrieval, automatic summarization, document link analysis, cross-language retrieval, and seamless access to multiple databases routine.

Concepts such as structured user information profiles, co-word analysis, co-citation analysis, and numerically weighted source selection criteria are being used in data scanning, search, and retrieval algorithms. Co-word analysis and related techniques use computer algorithms, based on the occurrence pattern and physical proximity of words, to extract and order data from large text files and to show the connectivity among identified technical themes and sub-areas supporting the themes. Document citations to other literature sources are also important quantifiable information sources for intelligence analysis because they provide a means of tracing scientific and technological developments in time or to other developments (see, for instance, Kostoff 1993).

Given the vast amounts of data available, continued progress on advanced screening tools is likely to occur, further helping analysts avoid information overload. One such tool already on the horizon is automated indexing or referencing mechanisms by which the document reviewer identifies how and where the recipient can use and apply the information in the document. Emerging computerized intelligent agent technology, which permits capabilities such as search algorithms that learn and create personalized communities of related information sites on-line, provides an exciting window to the future of rapid, customized, and comprehensive database search and screening tools.

Eventually, natural language processing (NLP), with high potential value for intelligence analysis, will become a routinely used tool. NLP is a range of computational techniques for analyzing and representing naturally occurring text. It functions at more than one level of linguistic analysis and its purpose is to achieve human-like language processing and understanding. An NLP system will allow information seekers to express themselves naturally with all requisite detail and will understand the underlying meaning, complexity, and subtlety of a query or documents being searched. The basic approach is to break natural language text into semantic representations that reveal concepts and relations between words and the co-occurrence of these items; other features of the text which cannot be determined by co-occurrence are also analyzed (Liddy 1994).

AUTOMATED COMMUNICATIONS AND DATA TRANSFER

Telecommunications systems and related functions are one of the most rapidly changing areas of intelligence-related technology. Improvements in the speed, capacity, reach, and cost of communications links are likely to have profound effects on everyday life, as well as on business activities.

Movement of high-quality documents between sites began with the simple fax and the computer modem. When integrated services digital network (ISDN) lines become widely available, digital faxing and database transfers will allow users to receive letter-quality documents via the telecommunications network. Remote imaging systems will be used to transmit these documents between organizations, bypassing the post office, private deliverers, and current fax technology, and revolutionizing document delivery.

Data exchange is beginning to appear analogous to the transportation of physical materials. In fact, in many cases, "information transportation" can substitute for the physical movement of people and goods, saving significant amounts of time and money and providing greater convenience for the consumer or the worker. Examples include what is sometimes called the advanced telecommunications market, that is, video-conferencing, home shopping, tele-working, distance education, tele-radiology, interorganizational document transfer, and automatic meter monitoring.

Each data transfer application relies on specific software and hardware products that permit users to conduct personal and professional business remotely. Analysis of advanced telecommunications focuses on the businesses that produce these products; namely, video codecs (coders/decoders), voice/call processing equipment, integrated services digital network customer premises equipment (ISDN CPE), remote imaging systems, multimedia software, and automatic meter monitoring equipment. The continued growth of advanced telecommunication applications provides significant opportunities for collecting, analyzing, and disseminating intelligence.

COMMUNICATIONS AND GROUPWARE

Using common data and software, groupware systems link a network of computer users to permit them to work jointly on documents, schedule meetings, route electronic forms, access shared public folders, and send e-mail. The intranet capabilities of Internet-based group systems to simultaneously connect employees, customers, and suppliers to vital information are now important. When linked to the Internet, integrated groupware platforms will provide added capabilities for information sharing, Web browsing, software distribution, client-server messaging, field-level replication, as well as better capabilities for developing programmable data-processing applications.

Since its introduction in 1989, Microsoft's Lotus Notes has been synonymous with groupware, but now several competitors with new capabilities have appeared. Novell, Netscape Communications, and Hewlett-Packard have taken steps to enter this market. Recent groupware releases include further advances such as more intuitive user interfaces and integrated cc:mail.

Rapid growth in groupware is expected to continue unabated and, with linkage to Internet, there is no telling what groupware markets will look like in the future. The payoff in ease of communication and information sharing and distribution is significant. With these potential advantages, groupware is already spreading into intelligence applications, especially where many data input or user sites need to link often and rapidly to each other and to common data.

TRENDS IN INTELLIGENCE ANALYSIS

Analysis is the process by which information and data are interpreted to produce intelligence findings and recommendations for actions. Understanding user needs is the key to selecting and using effective analysis tools (Ashton 1996). In the future, advances in a variety of tools and techniques from several different fields will permit new ways for analyzing intelligence data and presenting the results. Advanced modeling, computational, display, and interactive tools will increase the speed, capacity, and comprehensiveness of intelligence analysis. Speed will be improved by administrative gains such as wider acceptance of CTI in companies and better training of analysts and by new computer-based analytical tools, databases, and communication methods. Analysis capacity will increase as the number of participants from dispersed locations and the number of analysts, tools, or data sources that can be linked in the analysis process also increases. Finally, analysis will become more comprehensive through the integration of the range of possible perspectives or viewpoints on the input data. This integration will be achieved through analysis approaches that rapidly generate, link, and evaluate a variety of interpretations.

Four developments in intelligence analysis are highlighted in this section: integrated modeling and display approaches, group analysis methods, information visualization technology, and knowledge-based analysis systems.

INTEGRATED MODELING AND DISPLAY TECHNIQUES

Future CTI strategy and management methods will increasingly rely on advanced conceptual and computer tools for data analysis. One of the main emerging trends is the "integrated or multi-source" analysis approach, which permits several types of input data to be combined efficiently for simultaneous analysis (combinations of patent data, technical literature, and expert judgment, for instance). Three of the most important candidates for integrated analysis of CTI that are likely to be improved and see increased use are technical literature analysis, scenario analysis, and technology forecasting.

Technical Literature Analysis

Scientometrics and other bibliometric analysis tools are common approaches to developing S&T intelligence. Technical publications and patents are analyzed to characterize technology change, competitors, key scientific personnel, and S&T issues. The increased availability of electronic databases; improvements in computing capabilities, bibliometric techniques, and the multimedia potential of databases themselves; and the availability of bibliometric software are likely to further demonstrate the value of these methods. In the future, literature analysis will be aided by new tools that can efficiently search very large data sets for key words or topical patterns, use natural language processing technology to extract semantic meanings, link the results with other data, create visual displays, and incorporate expert judgment in support of the analysis. Some of these applications are already available in certain text processing software.

Continued progress in co-occurrence and statistical diagnostic tools such as co-word and co-citation analysis for analyzing text, coupled with human judgments about topic relatedness, is making analysis of massive data sets of literature easier and less expensive. The document content information obtained from these methods allows the user to relate technical R&D thrusts to institutions, journals, people, geographical locations, and other R&D categories. The methods can be applied to any text database, consisting, for instance, of mixtures of published papers, reports, news items, and internal documents such as memos. Further technical progress in these areas, such as work to increase the speed and usefulness of extracted and summarized information content, will make it likely that they will be used extensively in the future.

Aside from other bibliometric techniques using keywords, abstracts or complete text, citation analysis and co-citation analysis also provide insights into activities within specific scientific and technological areas. One important approach to evaluate scientific literature is the Science Model described earlier in this volume by Klavans (Klavans 1996). A database of scientific literature published up through 1994, the Science Model can be manipulated using co-citation analysis to identify the research communities that produce a body of publications. As Klavans notes, a research community is a group of researchers who follow a similar route to the solution to a scientific/technical problem. Identifying these researchers and their research themes is important to industries that are interested in rapidly capitalizing on scientific progress.

The future also holds promise for combining scientometric analysis with other intelligence analysis tools such as expert judgment and market, personal, or corporate data. Patent data can already be integrated with scientific literature data for simultaneous analysis from a single data source. The data on each patent or literature source document includes references to earlier literature, citations received from later literature, filing and/or publication dates, names of inventors or authors, and the originating company. Analysis of these sources is focused on summarizing the technology content of individual documents and identifying the links between a document and the literature it references, as well as the literature that references it. These relationships are useful for identifying characteristics such as the set of companies and authors working in common technology areas, differences in the nature of work by various parties, and the timing of various advances or breakthroughs. Special tools are being developed and applied to permit analysis of the patent and literature data to answer questions regarding technological "position," possible future rates of technology diffusion, and markets for technological concepts and areas (Mogee 1996).

Scenario Analysis

Scenario analysis is a formal process for trying to picture the future by developing structured description(s) of hypothetical characteristics or events. Scenarios are constructed to understand the role of causal factors and outcomes in possible future situations. Business scenario planning examines possible futures of a business operation under a variety of operating strategies and external environments. By surfacing, challenging, and adjusting the assumptions about key variables, executives can evaluate the performance of a company under alternative scenarios. The process allows management to "pressure test" plans and forecasts and to develop contingency actions for potentially hazardous developments (Ellis 1993).

Scenarios have become very popular over the past decade. They are now a basic tool for many corporate planning and company intelligence organizations, and their use is expected to increase. Computer-based analysis methods, such as those developed by Battelle and Shell Oil, are an important aspect of scenario use and new tools are emerging (Millett 1992; Ramsey 1992). Scenarios have been used to create future competitor profiles, describing characteristics such as markets, products, distribution strategy, distinctive skills, competitor advantage and ability to defend it, and vulnerabilities. In the future, scenarios will also be applied more extensively for forecasting technological progress and expected market performance, probably using computer tools with advanced features such as interactive interfaces, visualization, and real-time hypothetical decision-making. The energy industry is one in which technological change and its link to possible industry futures has been studied extensively with scenarios (Stokke et al. 1990). The RICOH Corporation has used scenarios to anticipate future product needs and plan its R&D agenda (Okimoto 1991).

Like many other group-based analysis techniques, the real value of the effort is not the scenario itself. Scenarios are only hypothetical guesses about the future; the chance of any one set of proposed events actually occurring is very small. Rather, scenarios provide managers and other busy staff with a structured format within which to think about the future, and this thought process may influence their behavior more than the scenarios produced.

Technology Forecasting

Technology forecasting is an important analysis method for technical intelligence or other planning purposes. The technical approaches for producing forecasts range from simple judgmental forecasts to formal quantitative models and scenario methods that predict future characteristics of new technologies (Martino 1994). Technology forecasts will often use multiple tools or approaches to integrate the results with expert judgment and probability estimates more explicitly than is done today.

All forecasting is a process of exercising judgment; new or improved tools and techniques are being designed to facilitate that judgment, particularly group analysis approaches such as scenarios now being applied by many companies. Quantitative predictive techniques can be used in conjunction with workshops where attendees contribute their insights. Automated methods that elicit judgments from a person and input them to an analytical program are being developed and used now (see, for example, Benson et al. 1995). New software is expected to support decision-making more time- and cost-effectively than traditional analytical models and methods.

One important example of using experts in technology forecasting is the Delphi Method, which is a technique for systematically creating a convergent forecast of future technology characteristics based on the judgments of a panel of experts in the technology area (see, for instance, Robeson 1988 and Martino 1994,). The method operates on the idea that experts may change their forecast of a technology's future characteristics in the face of feedback on the range of judgments supplied by the panel as a whole. Each Delphi estimation round consists of collecting expert estimates and then calculating group statistics on the panel's overall estimates, feeding the group numbers back to the panel members, and permitting members to revise their view in the face of feedback. Consensus on the forecast is usually reached.

New interactive tools that permit analysts to combine expert judgment (for example, modified Delphi procedures are already used) and quantitative results, as well as improved methods for addressing typical senior management questions, should become available. At present, most forecasting tools require quantitative data and methods and technical experts to derive results, often without methods to integrate the components. The development of better interactive computer tools should change this. Also in the future, the need for specialized analysis support should decrease in some applications as the tools become more directly usable by senior decision-makers.

Emerging Tools

Many techniques from other fields are just emerging from fundamental development to the point where practical applications will be possible soon. For example, concepts and techniques that hold promise for intelligence analysis include computational linguistics, pattern recognition, fuzzy logic, group decision techniques, complexity/chaos theory, weak signal processing, and war gaming.

GROUP ANALYSIS METHODS

A number of analysis tasks are best performed by a group rather than by a single person. For example, groups can quickly generate a wide range of ideas on a topic because members of the group can react to each other's thoughts. As a result, groups are excellent mechanisms for certain intelligence activities such as generating ideas about how to interpret a set of information, collecting several different views on an intelligence issue, or getting several parties to agree on a recommended course of action. In the past 20 years, a number of tools, sometimes called decision support systems, have been developed to help groups perform analysis functions more efficiently and comprehensively (see, for instance, Higgins 1994)

Given these advantages, systematic use of groups for intelligence analysis seems likely to increase in the future. Two of the most popular group methods are *brainstorming* and *consensus formation*, which are efficient and effective methods for generating useful ideas and reaching agreement on a choice. Brainstorming is a group process for rapidly generating and characterizing a set of creative ideas on a topic. The initial emphasis is on generating the ideas; the ideas are not evaluated until later. The power of the technique is the ability to build on and combine ideas. The method is structured, but the goal is to produce as wide a variety of creative thoughts as possible, recognizing that public sharing of ideas tends to stimulate other ideas. In consensus forming, the goal of the group is to process an idea to the point where all members of the group can agree to it or accept it—hence, the term consensus.

Electronic Brainstorming

One group method that also takes advantage of emerging computerized communication capabilities is electronic brainstorming (Gallupe and Cooper 1993). Electronic brainstorming (EBS) allows working groups to generate an abundance of ideas anonymously. Applied to intelligence analysis, EBS could be used to generate ideas for additional intelligence data sources or to create multiple interpretations of analysis results for further evaluation. Experience has shown EBS to be useful for large and small groups, for a variety of topics, for groups that meet face to face, and for those that are dispersed (globally, as well as locally).

Consensus Formation

One of the most popular consensus methods is the Nominal Group Technique or NGT (Delbecq et al. 1975; Thomas et al. 1989), which is a structure for efficiently generating, clarifying, and prioritizing ideas related to a problem statement from a group of individuals. In intelligence applications, NGT would be useful for developing collective interpretations of events, selecting follow-on actions, and identifying future topics or issues to monitor. Many group techniques are now supported with computer software to permit efficient processing, widespread application, and improved training.

INFORMATION VISUALIZATION TECHNOLOGY

One of the most important areas where advances in handling data will pay intelligence analysis dividends is in information visualization (IV) technology (see, for example, Gershon and Eick 1995; Wise et al. 1995). IV systems extend traditional scientific visualization of physical phenomena to include diverse types of information (for example, text, video, sound, or photos) from increasingly large heterogeneous data sources. IV systems improve the analysts' ability to identify, explore, discover, and understand complex situations from large numbers of documents that otherwise would be overwhelming to read.

The basic idea is that text from the sources is transformed to a two-dimensional spatial representation that preserves the informational characteristics of the original sources. The spatial view may then be visually browsed and analyzed in ways that avoid language processing and that reduce the analysts' mental workload. These visualizations result from a content abstraction and statistical projection of the original document. The text is transformed into a new visual representation that conveys information by image instead of prose.

Undergoing rapid development, IV technology is becoming faster, more user-friendly, and comprehensive. With further gains in computing power and capacity, desk-top personal computers will be able to handle highly complex information sources and permit highly flexible user interactions. In addition to helping analysts identify and screen important items in a data set, improved visualization technology holds promise for helping analysts process the information; that is, improve their interpretation of information and their ability to develop recommendations for action. Analysis aids such as Gantt charts, hierarchial or tree structures, influence diagrams and "knowledge maps" (see Howard 1989; Covaliu and Oliver 1995) could all provide useful graphic displays of complex intelligence situations.

KNOWLEDGE-BASED SYSTEMS

Knowledge-based systems, in the form of either decision science modeling or expert systems, represent a powerful new opportunity for analyzing technical intelligence. Decision science modeling attempts to represent well-defined business decision problems (such as evaluating a well-defined R&D portfolio) by quantitative models that can be manipulated to identify, study, and implement the most advantageous choices for users. Expert systems, on the other hand, are used when the rigorous conditions of formal decision science models are not present. In these cases, the basic approach is to capture an expert's individual decision rules or heuristics as the problem-solving mechanism. As discussed below, both of these knowledge-based methods can be tailored to certain analogous intelligence situations to provide experience-driven analysis insights.

Expert Systems

Expert systems are generally defined as computer-based systems that go beyond organizing and retrieving information to embody human reasoning and expertise. They consist of decision-making heuristics (or inference engines) contained in "knowledge bases" of information and hands-on human experience (Liberatore and Stylianou 1995). Operating on the basis of available information, expert systems either assist with or make decisions. Given a set of observed facts or conditions, expert systems access the experiential reasoning logic in the knowledge base by various inferencing schemes. They differ from traditional information systems in their knowledge content and, often, in the way they execute their functions and interact with users.

Expert systems technology can provide an effective approach for encoding the experience and knowledge of expert intelligence analysts. However, unlike other expert system applications in fields such as manufacturing, the goal in intelligence is not to replace the evaluation of expert(s) with a computer program. Rather, the goal is to draw out and capture the knowledge and experience of expert(s) and previous intelligence analysis situations and make it available for current analysis. The knowledge and experience for intelligence analysis would have to be captured in usable knowledge bases; this process is beginning to be explored for some intelligence applications and further exploitation of intelligence expertise is likely (Eom 1996).

DATA MINING AND FORMAL INFERENCE SYSTEMS

The term "data mining" (sometimes called "knowledge discovery" in databases) refers to a set of techniques used to extract useful decision information from databases—that is, to "turn data into knowledge" by discovering patterns in vast dispersed company databases. Data mining covers a variety of techniques such as statistical analysis, neural nets, machine learning, and pattern recognition, as well as sophisticated graphical tools.

Induction and case-based reasoning (CBR) are data-mining technologies that solve decision problems by storing, retrieving, and adapting past cases that are similar to the present situation (Althoff et al. 1995). A case is defined as the description of a problem and its solution. Induction extracts the knowledge of company specialists from their decision-making behavior as embodied in historical cases and builds decision trees for problem-solving. It identifies patterns among cases, rank orders the decision criteria according to their discriminatory power, and partitions the cases into families. The user can access cases at any node of the tree, "mine" data using graphical editors and knowledge browsers, and interactively modify the tree.

When a new problem is encountered, CBR recalls similar cases and adapts solutions that worked in the past for use with the current problem. Unlike induction, case-based reasoning does not require that a tree structure be generated before problem-solving. A new problem is solved by finding similar past cases and adapting their solutions. CBR offers flexible indexing and retrieval and fuzzy matching.

The number of applications in various domains is growing rapidly (Auriol et al. 1995). The most common systems focus on tangible problem-solving (for example, troubleshooting complex equipment) via "help-desk" areas. However, application to complex, time-sensitive intelligence situations (for example, assessing a newly identified but unforeseen competitor) is on the horizon.

TRENDS IN DELIVERY

Ineffective delivery and inadequate use of intelligence findings are the most troublesome problems facing virtually all business intelligence professionals today. Even the best intelligence is not worthwhile if someone in a position to act on recommendations does not recognize the intelligence as important and put it to use. And, unfortunately, unused intelligence is a basic problem for most otherwise highly effective intelligence operations.

Intelligence results and analysis findings have been distributed to users in many ways, ranging from formal reports or presentations to electronic mail and one-on-one conversations. Examples include custom reports, personal communication, on-line competitor files, memos, presentations, newsletters, regular meetings, CI seminars, bulletin boards, and special retreats. The best method depends on a number of factors, including the nature of the information to be distributed, the style and preferences of the target audience, cost, and urgency. However, regardless of the method chosen, some one-on-one discussion of key results is usually necessary. Personal conversation provides the opportunity for analysts to help inform and convince users directly, for particularly important points to be emphasized, and for users to ask questions and probe at issues.

Just as computer and communications technology will continue to improve intelligence collection and analysis techniques, new tools should also assist in making the delivery of intelligence more efficient and effective. Based on experience to date, two trends in intelligence delivery seem likely. First, given the improvements in computer and communication technologies discussed earlier (such as groupware), more rapid, widespread, and visual dissemination seems bound to happen. Even today's electronic communication systems are permitting speedy and extensive dissemination of text, graphics, and messages in nearly real time. However, the advances in visualization techniques mentioned earlier will continue to stimulate wider use of graphic displays of complex information. Visualization technologies, including multimedia mechanisms already entering the marketplace, will become even more prevalent in all intelligence systems. And as the complexity of the relationships in intelligence analysis and recommendations increases, visualization tools will become increasingly important for both analysts and users.

Second, given the importance of direct personal interaction in many company activities, including intelligence matters, we expect that dissemination via video conferencing (including 3-dimensional video) and face-to-face meetings will continue to increase. It is difficult for essential nuances in important intelligence findings to be conveyed solely through written material; there just is no real substitute for personal contact.

TRENDS IN APPLICATION

Technical intelligence produced today has had limited application. Companies have tended to recognize the importance of using

CTI to monitor changes in S&T areas of interest around the world and to understand a competitor's R&D pipeline. Yet, many additional areas of company operations are affected by technology and are potential customers for CTI products. In this volume, Krol, Coleman, and Bryant outline several business functions besides R&D—including commercial groups, senior management, and sales and marketing—where technical intelligence has proved useful in the pharmaceutical industry. It appears that these opportunities are likely to be pursued, if only because the need for intelligence is strong; it also appears that CTI applications will be scrutinized in company reviews to ensure that valuable intelligence impacts are being created.

MORE EFFECTIVE USE OF INTELLIGENCE IN COMMON COMPANY SITUATIONS

CTI results can be directed at current or potential use of technology in company products, processes, and management functions by focusing on activities to acquire, develop, exploit, and retire technology systems. In addition to the obvious R&D applications, a variety of other business functions such as strategic planning, external acquisitions, and production operations can benefit from CTI. Tables 1 and 2 summarize the main business areas where current information on external S&T activities and companies is directly relevant and which, therefore, can benefit from the more complete awareness provided by technical intelligence.

Table 1 covers the technology strategy and external acquisition functions; Table 2 covers the technology development and use functions. *Technology strategy* concerns (for example, the role of technology in business strategy, entry into new technology-driven markets, and protection of key technology property from exploitation by others) all depend on what competitors are doing in S&T and on the direction and pace of technological change in areas relevant to a firm. Information on a variety of S&T trends and on technology-oriented organizations will help in the selection of *technology acquisition* approaches and the use of technology partnerships.

Table 2 addresses three areas that support internal technology development and use. *R&D program development and management* also depends on S&T developments in organizations outside the

TABLE 1

Company S&T functions affected by competitive technical intelligence—technology strategy and acquisition

Business and Technology Strategy	
Strategic Technology Roles and Directions	• What role advanced technology will play in business, vision, goals, and strategy • Which technology-based business and market directions to pursue • Which core technical competencies to create and/or nurture
Technology Needs and Opportunity Evaluation	• What priority to assign current product, process, and operations technology needs • Which new technology applications (product, process, service, or operations developments) to pursue • Whether to enter a technology-based product line with strong competitors
Technical Information and Property Security	• How to protect intellectual property (for example, trade secrets, patents) • How to protect sensitive company information
Technology Acquisition	
Technology Acquisition Planning	• How best to acquire a new technology: internal R&D, external purchase, licensing-in, hiring or partnering • How much to invest in technology acquisition and R&D budgets
Technology Collaboration Choices	• Whether to enter into a joint technology development venture with another organization and what gains to expect from it • Which technology partners to consider and what terms of agreement to establish
Technology Acquisition Implementation	• What external technology sources to pursue • How to get the best bargain from external acquisitions

TABLE 2
Company S&T functions affected by competitive technical intelligence—technology development and use

R&D Program and Portfolio Management	
R&D Investment Portfolio Decisions	• Which new product development initiatives or improvements to make • What allocation of R&D funds to near- versus long-term projects • Whether to terminate or delay work on a project or in an S&T area
Technical Research, Product or Process Development Strategies	• Which technical approach to take in developing new product or process technologies • What technical objectives to set for R&D programs
Technology Deployment Investments or Divestiture Actions	
Product and Process Investment Decisions	• Which new product options to select for investment • Which capital expenditures to make for facility or process technology needs
Technology Transfer Mechanisms	• How to transition new know-how from R&D to manufacturing operations • Whether to permit external disposition of technology and how to transfer or limit distribution of rights or results (sale, license or cross-license out, trade partner)
Production and Delivery Operations	
Manufacturing and Distribution Operations	• How to qualify suppliers, customers or partners • What kind of technology training and operational procedures to establish
Technology Maintenance and Replacement	• What technology maintenance, repair, and replacement policies to use • How to trouble-shoot product or manufacturing technology problems

firm, especially those engaged in similar or competing R&D work. With regard to *technology deployment and use*, knowledge of competing technology developments in the market is essential for making capital investment and divestiture choices that will generate an attractive economic return. Finally, conducting *production activities* so as to get the most out of and maintain process technologies also depends on progress in supplier and resource technology outside the firm.

Current technical intelligence systems are rarely applied to all five of these areas. However, as the capabilities of emerging CTI systems and user confidence in them rises, this spectrum of applications will eventually be covered.

INCREASING EVALUATION OF CTI PROCESSES AND IMPACTS

The use of CTI in companies will increase as its potential benefits become more widely recognized—something that often occurs through formal evaluations designed to measure the impacts of intelligence services. CTI operations and results should be checked periodically to see how well they address user needs and how much ultimate value they provide to the organization. Typical evaluation processes are designed to improve future CTI programs by upgrading the efficiency and effectiveness of operations and by ensuring that CTI results have demonstrable benefits (Goodhue 1995). Reviewing intelligence programs involves comparing yardsticks of the program's performance against the resources used and management expectations for impact. Evaluations usually occur at least annually when decisions about future-year funding for CTI programs are made. Evaluations are likely to be more hard-hitting in times of tight company budgets.

Many companies already evaluate their intelligence operations; however, with the growth of CTI programs, more attention is likely to be paid to deliberate evaluation efforts. Recent discussions of this topic by Herring (1996) and Bryant et al. (1996) propose several measures of effectiveness for intelligence operations. In addition to linking intelligence to financial performance (revenues gained or not lost), one of the most important measures is "what the client did differently as a result of the intelligence process."

A FINAL COMMENT

Competitive technical intelligence is just beginning to emerge as a discipline and as a profession, but all indicators point to a rapid growth. The need to become competitive and stay that way is requiring technology-oriented organizations to operate in the rapid-response mode. Decisions-makers who must act under this pressure need real-time information upon which to base their decisions. Technical intelligence-gathering activities in many corporations have proved invaluable in providing such information. More and more corporations are beginning to see the benefits of CTI and are either establishing in-house CTI units or seeking CTI from outside consultants. Improvements in computers and communications technology will change the way intelligence is produced, increasing the ease and effectiveness with which CTI is collected, stored, and analyzed.

REFERENCES

Althoff, K. D., E. Auriol, R. Barletta, and M. Manago. 1995. A Review of Industrial Case-Based Reasoning Tools. *AI Intelligence*, A. Goodall (ed.). Oxford University Press, Oxford, UK.

Ashton, W. B. 1996. An Overview of Business Intelligence Analysis Methods for Science and Technology. *The Art and Science of Business Intelligence Analysis: Intelligence Analysis and Its Applications.* B. Gilad and J. Herring (ed.). JAI Press, Inc. Greenwich, Connecticut.

Auriol, E., S. Wess, K. D. Althoff, M. Manago, and R. Traphoner. 1995. INRECA: A Seamlessly Integrated System Based on Inductive Inference and Case-Based Reasoning. *ICCBR 95, First International Conference on Case-Based Reasoning*, M. Veloso and A. Aamodt (ed.). Springer Verlag, Heidelberg, Germany.

Battelle Memorial Institute. August 1996. Knowledge Cells: Exploring a Corporate Future Vision. *B- TIP Technology Spectrum*. No. 76. Columbus, Ohio.

Benson, P. G., S. P. Curley, and G. F. Smith. October 1995. Belief Assessment: An Underdeveloped Phase of Probability Elicitation. *Management Science* 41(10):1639-1653.

Bower, J. L., and C. M. Christensen. Jan.-Feb. 1995. Disruptive Technologies: Catching the Wave. *Harvard Business Review*, pp. 43-53.

Brenner, M. S. December 1992. Technology Scouting at Air Products. *les Nouvelles* 27(4):185-189.

Brenner, M. S. Fall 1996. Technology Scouting and Technology Intelligence. *Competitive Intelligence Review* 7(3):20-27.

Bryant, P .J., T. F. Krol, and J. C. Coleman. March 1996. Actionable Competitive Technical Intelligence with Measured Impact. *Conference Proceedings*. 10th Annual Conference—Washington, D.C. Society of Competitive Intelligence Professionals, Alexandria, Virginia.

Covaliu, Z., and R. M. Oliver. December 1995. Representation and Solution of Decision Problems Using Sequential Decision Diagrams. *Management Science* 41(12):1860-1873.

Delbecq, A., A. Van de Ven, and D. Gustofson. 1975. *Group Techniques: A Guide to Nominal and Delphi Processes*. Scott Foresman, Glenview, Illinois.

Ellis, J. Spring 1993. Proactive Competitive Intelligence: Using Competitor Scenarios to Exploit New Opportunities. *Competitive Intelligence Review* 4(1):13-24.

Eom, S. B. September-October 1996. A Survey of Operational Expert Systems in Business (1980-1993). *Interfaces* 26(5):50-70.

Fetterman, R. L., and S. K. Gupta. 1993. *Mainstream Multimedia: Applying Multimedia in Business*. Van Nostrand Reinhold, New York.

Gallupe, R. B., and W. H. Cooper. Fall 1993. Brainstorming Electronically. *Sloan Management Review* 34(1):27-36.

Gershon, N., and S. G. Eick. November 1995. Visualization's New Tack: Making Sense of Information. *IEEE Spectrum* (SPC) 32(11):38-56.

Goodhue, D. L. December 1995. Understanding User Evaluations of Information Systems. *Management Science* 41(12):1827-1840.

Herring, J. 1996. Measuring and Communicating Intelligence Effectiveness to Management. *Proceedings SCIP 1996 Annual Conference*. Society of Competitive Intelligence Professionals, Alexandria Virginia.

Higgins, J. M. 1994. *101 Creative Problem Solving Techniques*. The New Management Publishing Company. Winter Park, Florida.

Howard, R. A. August 1989. Knowledge Maps. *Management Science* 35(8):903-922.

Klavans. R.A. 1996. Identifying the Research Underlying Business Technical Intelligence. *Keeping Abreast of Science and Technology: Technical*

Intelligence for Business, W. B. Ashton and R. A. Klavans (ed.). Battelle Press, Columbus, Ohio.

Kodama, F. July-August 1992. Technology Fusion and the New R&D. *Harvard Business Review*, pp. 70-78.

Kostoff, R. N. Spring 1993. Database Tomography for Technical Intelligence. *Competitive Intelligence Review* 4(1):38-43.

Krol, T. F., J. C. Coleman, and P. J. Bryant. Fall 1993. Consultant Evaluation for Scientific CI in the Pharmaceutical Industry. *Competitive Intelligence Review* 4(4):43-46.

Krol, T. F., J. C. Coleman, and P. J Bryant. Spring 1996. Competitive Technical Intelligence and Commercial Decision Making. *Competitive Intelligence Review* 7(1):28-37.

Kydd, P. H. Jan-Feb 1996. Tracking Your Competitors. *Research Technology Management* 39(1):12- 14.

Lesko, J., and M. Steve. July 1995. Information Analysis Centers Speed the Search for Answers and Solutions. *Battelle Today*. Number 82. Battelle Memorial Institute, Columbus, Ohio.

Liberatore, M. J., and A. C. Stylianou. 1995. Expert Support Systems for New Product Development Decision Making: A Modeling Framework and Applications. *Management Science* 41(8):1296-1316.

Liddy, E. D. May 24, 1994. Information Retrieval via Natural Language Processing or an Intelligence Digital Librarian. Presentation at the ASIS Mid-Year Conference. School of Information Studies. Syracuse University Syracuse, New York.

Martino, J. 1994. *Technological Forecasting for Decision Making*. McGraw Hill, New York.

Metz, P. D. May-June 1996. Integrating Technology Planning with Business Planning. *Research Technology Managment* 39(3):19-22.

Millett, S. M. March/April 1992. Battelle's Scenario Analysis of a European High-Tech Market. *Planning Review* 20(2):20-23.

Mogee, M.E. 1996. Patents and Technology Intelligence. *Keeping Abreast of Science and Technology: Technical Intelligence for Business*, W. B. Ashton and R. A. Klavans (ed). Battelle Press, Columbus, Ohio.

Okimoto, A. October 1991. Creative and Innovative Research at RICOH. *Long Range Planning* 24(5):13-23.

Quinn, J. J. 1985. How Can Companies Keep Abreast of Technological Change? *Long Range Planning* 18(2):69-76.

Ramsey, G. March/April 1992. Recent and Classic Articles on Scenarios. *Planning Review* 20(2):32- 34.

Robeson, J. F. 1988. The Future of Business Logistics: A Delphi Study Predicting Future Trends in Business Logistics. *Journal of Business Logistics* 2:1-14.

Stokke, P. R. et al. 1990. Scenario Planning for Norwegian Oil and Gas. *Long Range Planning*. 23(2):18-24.

Thomas. J. B., R. R. McDaniel, and M. J. Dooris. 1989. Strategic Issue Analysis: NGT + Decision Analysis for Resolving Strategic Issues. *Journal of Applied Behavioral Science* 2:189-200.

Wise, J. A., J. J. Thomas, K. Pennock, D. Lantrip, M. Pottier, and A. Schur. 1995. Visualizing the Non-Visual: Spatial Analysis and Interaction with Information from Text Documents. *Proceedings of the IEEE Symposium on Information Visualization '95*. N. Gershon and S. Eick (ed). IEEE Computer Society Press, Los Alamitos, California.

APPENDIX
Science and Technology Information Resources

Compiled by
ANNE JOHNSON and JEAN TIBBETTS

This appendix contains a list of some of the most important sources of information on science and technology. The purpose of the list is to illustrate the wide range of available data sources and, therefore, is by no means comprehensive.[1]

The appendix is laid out as follows: Section I contains a description of some major information services that provide access to databases. Section II provides information on specific databases, including key databases devoted to business, patents, and science and technology. In the latter category are specialized databases focusing on aerospace; agriculture; biotechnology; chemistry; communications; computers; energy; environment; medicine; metals; pharmaceuticals; and international science and technology databases.

Section III describes electronic bulletin boards; Section IV lists some federal agencies supporting science and technology-related databases, and Section V contains a discussion of federal technology transfer organizations. Non-federal technology transfer organizations are found in Section VI. Section VII details some books and directories considered helpful in monitoring technological developments. Section VIII lists some of the more important technology-related newsletters, and Section IX lists some trade associations serving technology professionals. Where appropriate, telephone numbers and World Wide Web addresses are also shown.

Many data are now available on the World Wide Web, an increasingly popular network of networks used to access a variety of on-line media. Many organizations support a homepage—an electronic storefront—through which detailed technical information can be made available, along with general information about the organization itself. Firms provide data, products, and services, either free of charge or for a fee, on the Web. Some of the databases described in this report, for example, have recently become accessible via the World Wide Web.

In some cases, the Internet address given is that of the company that compiles the database. In other cases, the address is linked to a vendor. Most Internet sites listed here provide further information on the databases referenced; usually access to the database itself involves a fee. However, the section on energy databases lists some Internet homepages that are free.

I. INFORMATION SERVICES

These organizations, often referred to as vendors or hosts, maintain a number of different databases and sell access to them. Some of the individual databases developed by these companies are described in Section II.

Name: **Cambridge Scientific Abstracts**
Number of Databases: 6
Contact: Cambridge Scientific Abstracts
7200 Wisconsin Avenue, Suite 601
Bethesda, MD 20814
(301) 961-6750
Internet: http://www.csa.com

On-line databases specializing in water, mechanical engineering, pollution, and life sciences.

Name: **Dialog**
Number of Databases: over 500
Contact: Knight-Ridder Information, Inc.
2440 Camino Real
Mountain View, CA 94040
(415) 254-7000
Internet: http://www.tig.com/IBC/Dialog.html

Business and technical databases on both U.S. and international companies. Material is available in either full-text or abstract form, depending on the individual database being used. Main subject areas include business, news, science, medicine, technology, and law.

Name: **Dialog DATA-STAR**
Number of Databases: 300
Contact: Knight-Ridder
One Commerce Square, Suite 1010
Philadelphia, PA 19103
(800) 221-7754
Company headquarters is in Bern, Switzerland.
Internet: http://www.rs.ch/www/rs/press.html

Focuses mostly on European businesses, but has some information on U.S. companies.

Name: **Dow Jones News/Retrieval**
Number of Databases: 60
Contact: Dow Jones & Company, Inc.
World Financial Center
200 Liberty Street
New York, NY 10281
(212) 416-2000
Internet: http://bis.dowjones.com/djnr.html

Business and financial news from business and trade magazines and newspapers.

Name: **Information Retrieval Service**
Number of Databases: 60
Contact: European Space Agency National Center
c/o Department of Trade and Industry
Room 392 Ashdown House
123 Victoria Street, London SW1E 6RN
(44) 01 212 5638
or ESA-IRS
8-10 rue Mario Nikis
F-75738 Paris Cedex 15,
TLX 202746
(33) 1 5369 7203
Internet: http://www.esrin.esa.it/htdocs/esairs/esairs.html

Europe's largest concentration of scientific databases. Topics covered include aeronautics and space; agriculture and food; biology and botanics; biomedicine and pharmacology; business and economics; chemistry; computer science; engineering; environmental science; energy; metallurgy; news; physics and nuclear science; telecommunications; and transportation.

Name: **Knowledge Express**
Number of Databases: 20
Contact: Knowledge Express Data Systems
One Westlakes
1235 Westlakes Drive, Suite 210
Berwyn, PA 19312
(610) 251-0190
Internet: http://www.ceds.com

Largest commercial provider of technology transfer information in the United States. It provides information on recent research at over 75 major universities, 650 federal laboratories, the public health service (National Institutes of Health, Substance Abuse and Mental Health Services Administration, Centers for Disease Control, and the Food and Drug Administration), the Department of Energy, the Department of Agriculture, Small Business Innovation Research (SBIR) winners, as well as information on federal research grants and company information.

Name: **LEXIS-NEXIS**
Number of Databases: 5620
Contact: Reed Elsevier
Dayton, OH 45401
(800) 227-9597
Internet: http://www.lexis nexis.com/lncc/about/newsrelease/toc.html

Approximately 34 subjects are covered. Information comes from over 1,000 newspapers, magazines, wire services, broadcast transcripts, and other news sources, as well as hundreds of key trade publications.

Name: **MicroPatent**
Number of Databases: 15
Contact: MicroPatent
250 Dodge Avenue
East Haven, CT 06512-3358
(203) 466-5055
Internet: http://www.micropat.com

Specializes in U.S. and international patent data.

Name: **NewsNet**
Number of Databases: 812
Contact: NewsNet
945 Haverford Road
Bryn Mawr, PA 19010
(800) 952-0122 or (610) 527-8030
Internet: N/A

Sources include newsletters trade journals, industry magazines, and newswires. More than 40 subjects are covered, including aerospace, biotechnology, electronics, financial services, computers, defense, environment and more. NewsNet also operates **Newsflash**, an electronic clipping service, which scans over 17,000 articles each day.

Name: **Questel•Orbit**
Number of Databases: over 100
Contact: InfoPro Technologies
8000 Westpark Drive
MacLean, VA 22102
(703) 442-0900
Internet: http://www.questel.orbit.com/patent/pt-dbs.html

Specializes in the following areas: business; chemistry; energy and earth sciences; engineering; health, safety and the environment; materials science; and patents and trademarks.

Name: **Ovid Technologies** (formerly CDP Technologies)
Number of Databases: 80
Contact: Ovid Technologies
333 - 7th Avenue
New York, NY 10001
(212) 563-3006
Internet: http://www.ovid.com

Biomedical, academic, and general bibliographic and full-text databases.

Name: **STN International (Scientific Technical Network)**
Number of Databases: 180
Contact: Chemical Abstracts Service
2540 Olentangy Road
P.O. Box 3012
Columbus, OH 43210
(614) 4473729
Internet: http://www.fiz-karlsruhe.de/stn.html

A division of Chemical Abstracts Service, STN offers information on chemistry; engineering; health and safety; mathematics; physics; geology; biotechnology; medicine; energy; materials science; pharmacology; government regulations; and more. STN focuses on technologies originating in Japan and Germany.

II. DATABASES

There are nearly 8000 publicly available databases currently in existence. Methods of use vary. Some databases are available on-line, others can be found on CD-Rom. Increasingly, databases can be accessed via the Internet. In many cases, the user pays a one-time fee to access the database; in other cases, the user pays on a per-use basis. The type of information contained in the databases also varies. For example, some databases contain primarily bibliographic information, while others contain abstracts or full-text documents.

The following is a list of some of the most important databases in the areas of science, technology, and patent information.[2] They can be obtained either by contacting the companies themselves or by contacting the vendors listed in the previous section.

A. DATABASES: COMPANIES/BUSINESS/TECHNOLOGY

The databases described in this section specialize in information covering the business side of the technology development enterprise. Typically, they feature financial and market information on high-tech companies.

Name: **ABI/INFORM**
Number of Records: over half a million
Producer: UMI, Ann Arbor, MI
Internet: http://www-rlg.stanford.edu/cit-abi.html
Access: Available through Dialog

Information covering such areas as accounting, banking, computers, economics, energy, engineering, finance, health care, human resources, insurance, international trends, law, management, marketing, public administration, real estate, taxation, telecommunications, and transportation. ABI/INFORM is the oldest and largest business database.

Name: **Company Intelligence**
Number of Records: 171,000 plus
Producer: Information Access Company, Foster City, CA
Internet: http://www.rs.ch.www/rs/datastar.html
Access: Available through Dialog or Information Access Company

Information on over 200,000 public and private U.S. companies and 31,000 international firms. For each company, records provide name, address, telephone number, geographic area, business description, SIC codes, financial data, size of company, annual sales, and names of company executives. Each company record contains references to current news items and cross-references on each company from newspapers, business publications, and wire services.

Name: **Corporate Technology Database (CTD)**
Number of Records: 35,000
Producer: CorpTech, Woburn, MA
Internet: http://www.corptech.com:3600/
Access: Available via Data-Star, Knowledge Express, and Questel•Orbit

Profiles of over 40,000 public and private U.S. companies or corporate divisions that develop or manufacture more than 100,000 types of high-tech products. Names, addresses and phone numbers of executives, annual sales figures, export activities, rate of growth, ownership information, product lists. Covers manufacturers of advanced materials, artificial intelligence, aerospace technology, biotechnology, chemicals, computers, medical technologies, energy, environmental manufacturing, photonics, robotics, telecommunications, and others.

Name: **Disclosure Database**
Number or Records: nearly 12,500
Producer: Disclosure, Inc., Bethesda, MD
Internet: http://www.rs.ch.www/rs/ds/DSCL.html
Access: Available through Dialog

Summaries of companies' 10-K; 10-Q;10-3; 8-K, and 20-F corporate SEC filings.

Name: **Dun's Electronic Business Directory**
Number of Records: 8.6 million
Producer: Dun & Bradstreet Information Services, Parsippany, NJ
Internet: http://www.dnb.com
Access: Available through Dialog

Descriptions of the products and services of over half of U.S. businesses. Information is accessible by company name, location, and SIC code.

Name: **Freedonia Industry and Business Research Studies**
Number of Records: 600 plus
Producer: The Freedonia Group, Inc., Cleveland, OH
Internet: http://www.rs.ch/www/rs/ds/tbgi.html
Access: Available through Dialog, Data-Star, and other vendors not listed above

Full text of over 600 industry-specific studies and reports published by the Freedonia Group. For each industry, there is an overview of threats and opportunities, growth markets and products, competitive economics, industry outlook and structure, company profiles, acquisitions and divestitures, international competition, and market share. Includes industry forecasting and analysis by product and industry.

Name: **Moody's Corporate News - U.S.**
Number of Records: 13,000
Producer: Moody's Investors Services, New York, NY
Internet: N/A
Access: Available through Dialog

Current and past stock reports for over 13,000 publicly owned companies.

Name: **PROMT** (Predicasts Overview of Markets and Technologies)
Number of Records: N/A
Producer: Information Access Company, Foster City, CA
Internet: http://www.rs.ch/www/rs/ds/ptsp.html
Access: Available on Dialog

Information on trade and industry, company intelligence, business newsletters, aerospace and health. Sources are trade and business journals, newspapers, and research reports.

B. PATENT DATABASES

The following list contains information on those databases specializing in patents. Each one has a slightly different emphasis.

Name: **LEXPAT**
Number of Records: N/A
Producer: Mead Data Central, Dayton, OH
Internet: http://www-l.openmarket.com/lexis-nexis/db/lexis-nexiscopyright.html
Access: Available on LEXIS-NEXIS

Full texts of U.S. patents issued since 1975, the U.S. Patent and Trademark Office Manual of Classifications, and the Index to U.S. Patent Classification.

Name: **ESPACE**
Number of Records: N/A
Producer: Derwent Direct, Arlington, VA
Internet: http://www.derwent.co.uk
Access: Available on Data-Star, Dialog, and Ovid

Since the European Patent Office, unlike its American counterpart, publishes patent applications as well as actual patents, the ESPACE series of databases offer early awareness of patent activity in Europe. Each of the eight ESPACE databases has a slightly different focus to address different searcher needs.

Name: **PatentScan**
Number of Records: N/A
Producer: Derwent Direct, Arlington, VA
Internet: http://www.derwent.co.uk
Access: Available on Data-Star, Dialog, and Ovid

Information on U.S. patents granted between 1975 and the present. Allows user to search for patents in a given area of interest using key bibliographic data found on a patent's front page. This includes patent classification and assignee, application data, issue date, and inventor name.

Name: **Derwent World Patents Index and Derwent World Patents Index Latest**
Number of Records: over 6 million patent documents
Producer: Derwent Direct, Arlington, VA
Internet: http://www.derwent.co.uk
Access: Available through Dialog, STN and Questel•Orbit

Data from nearly 3 million inventions represented in patent documents from 30 patent-issuing authorities around the world. Records contain bibliographic information, full abstract for patents issued from 1981 to the present, International Patent Classification codes, and Derwent subject codes. Subjects include pharmaceutical patents (1963 to the present); agricultural chemical patents (1965 to the present); and polymer and plastics patents (1966 to the present).

Name: **U.S. Patents**
Number of Records: 1.4 million
Producer: Derwent Direct, Arlington, VA
Internet: http://www.derwent.co.uk
Access: Available through STN, Questel•Orbit, and Dialog

Complete patent information, including front-page and full claim information, with references, on U.S. patents issued since 1971. Covers all technologies.

Name: **U.S. Patents Full-text**
Number of Records: N/A
Producer: U.S. Patent and Trademark Office, Washington, D.C.
Internet: http://town.hall.org/patent/patent.html
Access: Available through Dialog and STN

Complete text of all patents issued from 1971-1979, 1980-1989, and 1990-present.

Name: **CLAIMS**
Number of Records: over 2.3 million
Producer: IFI/Plenum Data Corporation, Wilmington, DE
Internet: http://questel.orbit.com/patents/database/html
Access: Available through Dialog, STN, and Questel•Orbit

CLAIMS is a family of several patent databases that provides access to over 2.3 million patents issued by the U.S. Patent and Trademark Office. Citations cover nearly all fields of technology. Among the databases are CLAIMS, the base file; CLAIMS Uniterm with uniterm subject indexing for chemical and chemically-related patents; CLAIMS Biblio/Abstract files featuring bibliographic references; and CLAIMS Reassignment and Reexamination File.

Name: **JAPIO**
Number of Records: 4.5 million
Producer: Japanese Patent Information Organization
Internet: http://www.bedrock.com/cgi-bin/wwwwais
Access: Available on STN, Dialog, and Questel•Orbit

Comprehensive English-language access to Japanese unexamined patent applications in all areas of science and technology. Citations are bibliographic, but abstracts are available for all applications originating in Japan.

C. SPECIALIZED SCIENCE AND TECHNOLOGY DATABASES

The databases described in this subsection focus specifically on science and technology. The first group (general) offers information in a variety of scientific fields. The others, as the headings suggest, specialize in one particular field of science.

General

Name: **Applied Science and Technology Index**
Number of Records: over 600,000
Producer: H.W. Wilson Company, Bronx, NY.
Internet: http://www2.infoseek.com/titles?qt=%22applied+science+and+ technology+index%22
Access: Available through Silver Platter and Ovid

Citations from books, articles, interviews, new product reviews, and other publications focusing on applied science and technology. Includes coverage of aeronautics and space science, chemistry, computer science, electronics, energy resources and research, food industry, machinery, metallurgy, plastics, textiles, transportation, and various fields of engineering.

Name: **Conference Papers Index**
Number of Records: N/A
Producer: Cambridge Scientific Abstracts, Bethesda, MD
Internet: http://www.fiz-karlsruhe.de/confsci.html
Access: Available on Dialog

Index of significant scientific and technical papers that have been presented at scientific meetings. Seventeen disciplines and more than 150 meetings are covered.

Name: **Congressional Information Service**
Number of Records: nearly 300,000
Producer: Congressional Information Service, Bethesda, MD
Internet: http://www.cahners.com/reedelsv/cis.html
Access: Available on Dialog

Index of congressional documents, including hearings, committee reports, documents, and others. Also includes references to the *Federal Register.*

Name: **Current Contents**
Number of Records: N/A
Producer: Institute for Scientific Information, Philadelphia, PA
Internet: http://www.rs.ch/www/rs/ds/CCCC.html
Access: Available through Data-Star, Dialog, and Ovid

Bibliographic information on current research in a variety of fields, including life sciences; agriculture, biology and environmental sciences; physical, chemical, and earth sciences; clinical medicine; engineering, computing, and technology; as well as social and behavioral sciences.

Name: **Federal Technology Report**
Number of Records: Newsletter
Producer: McGraw-Hill, Inc., New York, NY
Internet: N/A
Access: Available on-line through Nexis, Dow Jones News/Retrieval, and Dialog

Full text of Federal Technology Report, a newsletter describing business opportunities at U.S. federal laboratories under the purview of the Departments of Energy, Defense, and Commerce.

Name: **Technology Access Report**
Number of Records: Newsletter
Producer: Technology Access, Novato, CA
Internet: N/A
Access: Available through NewsNet and Knowledge Express

Full text of Technology Access Report, which covers the transfer, management, and commercialization of technologies originating in universities, hospitals, federal and state laboratories, and other sources.

Aerospace

Name: **International Aerospace Abstracts Database**
Number of Records: over 1.9 million citations
Producer: American Institute of Aeronautics and Astronautics, Washington, D.C.
Internet: N/A
Access: Available through Dialog

Citations, including abstracts, to worldwide literature on research and development in 76 areas relating to aerospace. These include aeronautics; astronautics; chemistry; materials; engineering; geosciences; mathematics; computer sciences; physics, and space science. Also covered are the economic, managerial, and policy aspects of the aerospace industry. Sources are books, conference proceedings, journals, monographs, patents, and dissertations.

Name: **Aerospace/Defense Markets and Technology (A/DM&T)**
Number of Records: over 286,000
Producer: Information Access Company, Foster City, CA
Internet: N/A
Access: Available through Dialog and Data-Star

Abstracts and some full texts of the international literature on the defense and aerospace industries. Offers information on products; companies; technologies; and air, sea, and land defense systems. Among the subjects covered are new technologies and their applications; defense budgets and weapons systems appropriations; defense policy; military trends; new orders and sales trends; operations; contracts; companies; government regulations; market data; and information on launches of missiles, space stations, shuttles, probes, and satellites.

Agriculture

Name: **Technology Transfer and Agriculture**
Number of Records: N/A
Producer: University R&D Opportunities
Internet: N/A
Access: Available through Nexis

Reports on commercially valuable research and technology transfer methods in companies, universities, and government laboratories in the U.S. and around the world. Includes information on issues, priorities, new technologies, new applications of agricultural crops and techniques, technology transfer organizations, and processes.

Name: **CRIS** (Current Research Information Service, USDA)
Number of Records: around 30,000
Producer: USDA/Cooperative State Research Service, Beltsville, MD
Internet: gopher://nature.Berkeley.edu:70/11/other_information/CRIS
Access: Available on Dialog

Information on federal and state-supported research in agriculture, food and nutrition, forestry, veterinary medicine, and other fields. This database is compiled by the U.S. Department of Agriculture.

Name: **TEKTRAN** (Technology Transfer Automated Retrieval System)
Number of Records: over 20,000
Producer: USDA Agricultural Research Service, Beltsville, MD
Internet: http://www.nalusda.gov/ttic/tektran/tektran.html
Access: Available through Knowledge Express or directly through the host.

Results of USDA research on genetic engineering, human diseases, safeguarding crops and animals from diseases, and pest control.

Biotechnology

Name: **Bioscan**
Number of Records: over 1000
Producer: The ORYX Press, Phoenix, AZ
Internet: http://www.oryxpress.com/books/bscan.html
Access: Available through Knowledge Express

Business, financial, personnel, R&D, and product marketing information on over 1000 biotech companies located around the world.

Name: **Biotech Business News**
Number of Records: Newsletter
Producer: Worldwide Videotex, Boynton Beach, FL
Internet: N/A
Access: Available on NewsNet, Dow Jones News/Retrieval, Compuserve, Nexis, and Dialog

Complete text of Biotech Business, a monthly industry newsletter. Covers recent developments in the biotechnology industry and focuses on research, new products, regulatory issues, and company information.

Name: **Biotechnology Newswatch**
Number of Records: Newsletter
Producer: McGraw-Hill, Inc., New York, NY
Internet: http://www.bio.com/
Access: Available on Nexis and NewsNet

On-line version of Biotechnology Newswatch newsletter, which covers the field of biotechnology as well as the international biotechnology industry. Contains both technical and business information, including biomass conversion, enzyme and fermentation processes, recombinant DNA technology, genetic engineering, company earnings and products, new ventures, and patent disclosures.

Name: **Biotechnology Research Abstracts**
Number of Records: over 36,000 citations
Producer: Cambridge Scientific Abstracts, Bethesda, MD
Internet: http://www.CSA.com
Access: Available through Cambridge Scientific Abstracts

Information covers medical, agricultural, pharmaceutical, chemical, energy, and environmental applications. Subjects include genetic engineering, cloning vectors, gene manipulation, site-directed mutagenesis, biotechnology products, and patents.

Name: **Biosis Previews**
Number of Records: 9.3 million
Producer: BIOSIS
Internet: http://www.biosis.org/htmls/common/bde.html
Access: Available through Data-Star, STN, Dialog, and Ovid Technologies

Original research reports, reviews, and selected U.S. patents in biological and biomedical areas. Sources include periodicals, journals, conference proceedings, reviews, reports, patents

Chemistry

Name: **Chemical Abstracts**
Number of Records: over 16 million entries
Producer: Chemical Abstracts Service, Columbus, OH
Internet: http://www.questel.orbit.com/cgi-bin/wwwwais?%22cheical+abstract%22
Access: Available through STN

Bibliographic information on 68,000 publications held by over 350 libraries around the world. National Union Catalog codes are provided for each title, indicating which libraries carry the publication. Contains scientific and technical literature pertaining to the chemistry, chemical engineering, and chemical sciences fields. Sources include journal articles, patents, monographs, and conference proceedings.

Name: **Chemical & Engineering News**
Number of Records: Newsletter
Producer: Chemical Abstracts Service, Columbus, OH
Internet: http://www.pubs.acs.org/hotarcl/index.html
Access: Available through STN and Nexis

Full text of Chemical and Engineering News, the weekly publication of the American Chemical Society. Articles highlight news from the industry and feature technological and business information.

Name: **Chemical Industry Notes**
Number of Records: 990,000
Producer: Chemical Abstracts Service, Columbus, OH
Internet: http://www.rs.ch./www/rs/ds/cind.html
Access: Available through Dialog and Questel•Orbit

Information from chemical business magazines, newspapers, newsletters, and journals on such topics as facilities, pricing, production, sales, corporate activities, government involvement, and people.

Communications

Name: **Edittech's International High Tech Alert**
Number of Records: Newsletter
Producer: Edittech's International High Tech Alert, San Jose, CA
Internet: N/A
Access: Available through NewsNet

Full text of Edittech's International High Tech Alert, a weekly newsletter focusing on developments in the area of international high technology. Provides news, commentary, and product reviews on the communications industry.

Computer Technology

Name: **Computer Database**
Number of Records: over 500,000
Producer: Information Access Company, Foster City, CA
Internet: http://ww.rs.ch./www/rs/ds/cmpt.html
Access: Available through Data-Star and Dialog

Abstracts and indexing of journals focused on computers, telecommunications, and electronics. It includes information on hardware, software, peripherals, and computer services. It also provides information on computer, telecommunication, and electronics companies.

Energy

Name: **Coal and Synfuels Technology**
Number of Records: Newsletter
Producer: Pasha Publications, Inc., Arlington, VA
Internet: N/A
Access: Available through NewsNet and Nexis

Text of Coal and Synfuels Technology, a weekly newsletter focusing on coal combustion technology. Primary emphasis is on clean burning processes. Technologies covered include flue-gas desulpherization, fluidized-bed combustion, hot gas clean-up, coal liquefaction and gasification technologies, among others.

Name: **Energy and Environment**
Number of Records: N/A
Producer: Sandia National Laboratories, Albuquerque, NM
Internet: N/A
Access: Available through Nexis

Articles on waste minimization, management and remediation; renewable energy R&D; and fossil fuel R&D. It is designed to facilitate the transfer of technology between government and industry.

Name: **Energy Conservation News**
Number of Records: Newsletter
Producer: Business Communications Company, Inc.
Internet: http://www.vyne.com.bcc/bcc-newsletters.html#conservation
Access: Available through NewsNet

Full text of Energy Conservation News, a monthly newsletter focusing on technological and economic facets of energy conservation. It covers such subjects as natural gas, wind, photovoltaics, solar modules, cogeneration, conventional power, renewable energy, and power pooling. Also includes statistical, technical, and analytical data on public utility consumption costs, regulations, energy conservation programs, and methodologies for analyzing energy savings.

Name: **Energy Information Database**
Number of Records: 87,000
Producer: International Research and Evaluation, Bloomington, MN
Internet: N/A
Access: International Research and Evaluation (612) 888-9124

Citations to energy-related publications from such sources as annual reports, dissertations, conference papers, corporate filings, fact sheets, feasibility studies, journal articles, monographs, legislation, research reports, and technical reports. Topics covered include solar energy, bioconversion and biomass, wind energy, photoconversion, ocean energy, and more.

Name: **Energyline**
Number of Records: 167,000
Producer: Bowker A&I Publishing; Reed Publishing, New York, NY
Internet: http://www.questel.orbit.com/cgi-bin/wwwwais?energyline
Access: Available through Questel•Orbit and Dialog

Citations from journals, reports, monographs, surveys, and conference proceedings. Topics include economics, U.S. policy and planning, international issues, research and development, resources and reserves, environmental impacts, electric power transmission and storage, fuel production, and nuclear power.

Name: **Energy Design Update**
Number of Records: Newsletter
Producer: Cutter Information Corp., Arlington, MA
Internet: N/A
Access: Available through NewsNet

On-line version of the Energy Design Update, a monthly newsletter on energy-efficient building design and construction. Among the topics covered are regulatory trends, standards, legal decisions, as well as profiles of highly energy-efficient homes in North America. Also contains research news and new product information.

Name: **The Energy Report**
Number of Records: Newsletter
Producer: Pasha Publications, Inc., Arlington, VA
Internet: N/A
Access: Available through NewsNet

Complete text of The Energy Report, a weekly newsletter devoted to a discussion of U.S. energy policy as it relates to coal, natural gas, nuclear, and other energy sources. It also contains information on energy conservation, cogeneration, electric power, renewable energy, legislation, environmental issues, tax issues, activities of the U.S. Department of Energy, as well as data on fuel prices and trends.

Name: **Energy Science and Technology Database**
Number of Records: over 3 million citations
Producer: U.S. Department of Energy
Office of Science and Technology Information
Oak Ridge National Laboratory, Oak Ridge, TN
Internet: http://www.doe.gov/html/osti/estsc/essrch.html
Access: Available through Dialog and STN

Worldwide references to basic and applied scientific and technical research literature. Includes citations of articles on biology; biomedicine; chemistry; coal, gas, oil, and hydroelectricity; conservation technology; direct energy conversion; energy policy; engineering; environmental science; geosciences and geothermal energy; hazardous waste materials; human genome project methodology; isotope/radiation technology; materials handling; metals and ceramics; nuclear and thermonuclear power; renewable energy sources; and synthetic fuels.

Name: **Nuclear Science Abstracts**
Number of Records: nearly 950,000
Producer: U.S. Department of Energy
Office of Scientific and Technical Information (OSTI)
Oak Ridge National Laboratory, Oak Ridge, TN
Internet: hhttp://www.doe.gov/osti
Access: Available through Dialog

All unclassified nuclear information collected by the U.S. Department of Energy from mid-1948 through mid-1976. Covers scientific and technical reports, patents, conferences and other meetings, journal articles, theses, dissertations, and monographs. Subjects include reactor technology, particle accelerators, nuclear materials and waste management, radiation effects, isotope and radiation source technology, metals, ceramics and other materials, fusion energy, biomedical sciences, physics, engineering, and chemistry.

Name: **Oil & Gas Journal Energy Database**
Number of Records: over 150,000
Producer: Oil & Gas Journal, Tulsa, OK
Internet: http://www.pennwell.com/database.html
Access: Available through Nexis and General Electric Information Services (800) 345-4618

On-line databases of energy statistics from a variety of public sources, covering all facets of the domestic oil and gas industry. Includes data on drilling and exploration; production; reserves; refining; imports; stocks; exports; consumption and demand; natural gas; prices; financial; transportation; offshore; and other miscellaneous information.

Name: **UNESCO International Directory of New and Renewable Energy Information Sources and Research Centers**
Number of Records: nearly 4000
Producer: UNESCO
7 Place de Fontenoy
75352 Paris 07 SP, 1 rue Miollis,
75732 Paris, Cedex 15, France
(33) 1 45 68 1000
Internet: http://gopher.unesco.org.org:70/0/db/ch/unesd

Information on new and renewable energy technologies, as well as research under way at national governmental organizations and education and training institutions in 172 countries. Also references journal articles and other publications on the subject of renewable energy.

Name: **Worldwide Energy**
Number of Records: Newsletter
Producer: Worldwide Videotex, Boynton Beach, FL
Internet: N/A
Access: Available through NewsNet

Complete text of Worldwide Energy, a monthly newsletter carrying news and information on all types of energy sources and applications, including oil, gas, coal, nuclear, electric, solar, and other alternative energy sources. Also covers R&D, as well as energy conservation products and processes.

Other Energy Databases on the Internet

Name: **Alternative Fuels Data Center (AFDC)**
Producer: National Alternative Fuels Hotline, Arlington, VA
Internet: http://www.afdc.nrel.gov

Internet site operated by the U.S. Department of Energy's National Renewable Energy Laboratory. The AFDC collects information on vehicles running on alternative fuels and participating in programs sponsored by the Alternative Motor Fuels Act. The Center also maintains information on research reports conducted for both the Biofuels Systems Division and the Fuel Utilization Data and Analysis Division of DOE's Office of Alternative Fuels.

Name: **Energy Efficiency and Renewable Energy Clearinghouse (EREC)**
Producer: NCI Information Systems, Inc., Merrifield, VA
Internet: http://www.eren.doe.gov

EREC is a Department-of-Energy-supported clearinghouse that provides informational materials, technical assistance, and referrals on energy efficiency and renewable energy. Specialists provide information to callers immediately over the phone, or they may prepare a written response and a package of relevant information after receiving a request. EREC offers information on renewable energy, commercial, residential, and industrial technologies and can provide technical assistance on a wide range of energy-efficiency-related topics, including the design of systems and structures; comparison of systems, appliances, and components; system troubleshooting; and advice on financing and business development. All information is provided free of charge.

Name: **GTI Online**
Producer: IEA International Center for Gas Technology Information
Washington, D.C.
Internet: http://www.gasinfo.dk/gasinfo

The International Energy Agency Center for Gas Technology was established in 1995 to promote the commercialization of gas-related technologies throughout the global gas industry. The database provides detailed information focusing on five key areas: life extension and safety of gas transportation systems; technologies for commercial and residential markets; gas distribution technologies; natural gas storage portfolios; and technologies which reduce investments and/or operating costs for non-giant gas fields. In addition, the ICGTI offers a question-and-answer board; a service provider board; an electronic library containing, among other things, summaries of natural gas technologies; a listing of industry events; and references to state-of-the-art gas technologies. Access is free for citizens of IEA member countries. Hence, any company headquartered in the U.S. may use the database, since the U.S. Department of Energy has paid U.S. IEA membership. Nonetheless, users are asked to contact the Center to register.

Environment

Name: **Waste Treatment Technology News**
Number of Records: N/A
Producer: Business Communications Company, Inc.
Internet: http://www.vyne.com/bcc/bcc-newsletters.html#waste
Access: Available through NewsNet

Information on technologies, critical developments, and analysis of new concepts in waste clean-up, control, recycling, and disposal. Covers acid rain, water, nuclear, and toxic solid wastes.

Name: **WasteInfo**
Number of Records: N/A
Producer: Waste Management Information Bureau,
Harwell Laboratory, UK
Internet: http://sunsite.nus.sg/bibdb/pub/silverplatter/
silverplatter219.html
Access: Available through Questel•Orbit

Bibliographic references regarding all aspects of non-nuclear waste management, including coverage focusing on waste treatment and disposal, waste recycling, environmental hazards of waste, waste management policy, legislation and regulations, and economics.

Medicine

Name: **Cancerlit**
Number of Records: 1 million
Producer: National Institutes of Health, National Medical Library, Bethesda, MD
Internet: http://sunsite.nus.sg/bibdb/pub/silverplatter/silverplatter035.html
Access: Available through STN, Dialog, and Ovid Technologies

Bibliographic citations on nearly all cancer-related topics. Sources include journal articles; government reports; technical reports; meeting abstracts and papers; and monographs, letters and theses.

Name: **Medline**
Number of Records: over 7.8 million citations
Producer: National Institutes of Health, National Medical Library, Bethesda, MD
Internet: http://www.sils.umich.edu/~nscherer/Medline/MedlineGuide.html
Access: Available through STN, Ovid Technologies, Nexis, and Dialog

Nearly 8 million bibliographic references to medical literature throughout the world. Records date as far back as 1966. Medline is considered the most significant medical database. It can provide an up-to-date list of specialists around the world having expertise in very narrow disciplines.

Metals

Name: **Aluminum Industry Abstracts**
Number of Records: 160,000 citations
Producer: ASM International, Materials Park, OH
Internet: N/A
Access: Available through Dialog

Citations, with abstracts, to technical and business literature relating to the properties, production, processing, and applications of aluminum. Sources include scientific and business journals, patents, government reports, conference proceedings, translations, dissertations, press releases, and books.

Name: **Metadex**
Number of Records: 1 million
Producer: ASM International, Materials Park, OH
Internet: N/A
Access: Available through Dialog, Data-Star, Questel•Orbit and STN

Comprehensive international coverage of all aspects of metals and alloys, including specific alloy designations, intermetallic compounds, and metallurgical systems. Coverage includes materials, properties, processing, and products. Sources include journals, conference papers, reviews, technical reports, books, dissertations, and patent and government reports.

Pharmaceuticals

Name: **AIDSDRUGS**
Number of Records: over 300
Producer: National Institutes of Health, National Medical Library, Bethesda, MD
Internet: www.nlm.nih.gov/factsheets.dir/aidstrials_drugs.html
Access: Available through Ovid Technologies

A dictionary of chemical and biological substances being evaluated in AIDS clinical trials. Also describes agents which were tested in closed or completed trials.

Name: **Pharmaceutical News Index**
Number of Records: over 400,000
Producer: UMI, Ann Arbor, MI
Internet: N/A
Access: Available through Dialog

News and analysis of the U.S. and international pharmaceutical scene. Contains information on drugs, medical devices, cosmetics, pharmaceutical companies, new products, regulation, and market strategies. Sources include leading pharmaceutical newsletters and Investext reports

D. INTERNATIONAL S&T DATABASES

The databases described in this section are excellent sources of information regarding scientific developments in other countries, especially in Europe and Japan.

Name: **CHEM-INTELL Chemical Plant Database**
Number of Records: 23,000
Producer: CHEM-INTELL, London, England
Internet: N/A
Access: Available through Data-Star

Information on over 23,000 chemical plants around the world producing organic and inorganic chemicals, including petrochemicals, fertilizers, polymers, synthetic rubber, and fibers. For each plant, information is given on location, current and planned capacity, processes used, feedstocks, toxicity data, and more.

Name: **ITBOD (International Technology and Business Opportunities Database)**
Number of Records: 30,000
Producer: Klenner International, Ormond Beach, FL
Internet: N/A
Access: Klenner International (904) 673-4339

Contains over 30,000 technologies available for licensing in 56 technical categories. Use of this database can help firms promote their technologies, identify technologies needed for enhancing product lines, and learn about competitors.

III. ELECTRONIC BULLETIN BOARDS AND OTHER ON-LINE SERVICES

Among other things, these electronic mail services enable users to contact experts in their fields. Because bulletin boards involve the use of human sources rather than data files, however, success in obtaining specific technical information can be sporadic. However, it is just possible that a user will encounter someone having expertise in a given field or someone who can suggest such an appropriate expert.

CompuServe	(800) 848-8199
America On-line	(800) 827-6364
Delphi	(800) 544-4005
GEnie	(800) 638-9636
Prodigy	(800) 776-3449
Microsoft Network	(800) 426-9400
Amnet	(312) 553-1085

IV. FEDERAL AGENCIES HAVING SPECIALIZED DATABASES

The federal agencies listed below are among those having specialized science and technology databases. Most focus on federally funded research and development efforts. Many of these databases can also be accessed through Knowledge Express, described in Section I of this appendix.

U.S. Department of Agriculture

TEKTRAN database
See page 523 for more details.
(301) 504-5345

CRIS database
See page 523 for more details.
(301) 504-5345

Agricola database
(301) 504-5479

U.S. Department of Commerce

Patent and Trademark Office (703) 308-0322

National Trade Databank (202) 482-1986

National Institute of Standards and Technology (301) 975-6501

National Technical Information Service
U.S. Department of Commerce
5285 Port Royal Road
Springfield, VA 22161
Internet: http://www.fedworld.gov/ntis/ntishome.html

NTIS FedWorld database (703) 487-4778
NTIS Federal Laboratory Technology database (703) 487-4650
NTIS Federal Research in Progress database (703) 487-4650
Internet: http://www.fedworld.gov/ntis/fedrip.html
NTIS Federal Applied Technology database (703) 487-4929

NTIS offers a variety of databases containing information on the results of U.S. government-sponsored research, development, and engineering, as well as analyses provided by various federal agencies, contractors, and grantees. NTIS makes available information about activities at such agencies as the National Aeronautics and Space Administration, the Department of Energy, the Department of Housing and Urban Development, the Department of Commerce, and the Department of Transportation. NTIS also provides on-line information on Japanese technical and scientific literature.

U.S. Department of Defense

Technology Applications Information Service (TAIS)
(703) 693-1563

Ballistic Missile Defense Organization's Strategic Defense Initiative (SDI) database contains information on over 2000 cutting-edge technologies for re-use in commercial markets.

U.S. Department of Energy

Energy Science and Technology Database
Office of Science and Technology Information (OSTI)
Oak Ridge National Laboratory, Oak Ridge, TN
(615) 576-9362

OSTI is the clearinghouse for information on the Department of Energy.

U.S. Department of Health and Human Services

Food and Drug Administration Bulletin Board: "Electronic Docket"
(lists 510K approvals)

National Institutes of Health
National Library of Medicine
(301) 496-0822
(see page 532)

The National Science Foundation

Science and Technology Information System
(703) 306-0214
http://www.NSF.Gov or
STIS@NSF.Gov.

Among other things, this system provides information on the results of research funded by NSF.

The Securities and Exchange Commission

SEC's Electronic Data-Gathering and Retrieval Service (EDGAR) database provides free data on corporate finances. Information is based on companies' SEC filings.
Internet: http://www.sec.gov/edgarhp.htm

V. FEDERAL TECHNOLOGY TRANSFER ORGANIZATIONS

The federal government and some of the states offer assistance facilitating the transfer of technology from government laboratories to the private sector. The National Technology Transfer Center and the National Technology Transfer Network are two key organizations dedicated to this mission.

National Technology Transfer Center (NTTC)
Wheeling Jesuit College
316 Washington Avenue
Wheeling, WV 26003
(800) 678-6882 or (304) 243-2456
Internet: http://iron.nttc.edu

The NTTC helps facilitate the transfer of technologies developed at federal labs to the private sector. Data are available through NTTC's "Business Gold" electronic bulletin board and through other databases.

National Technology Transfer Network

Northeast Regional Technology Transfer Center	(508) 870-0042
Southeast Regional Technology Transfer Center	(904) 462-3913
Mid-Atlantic Regional Technology Transfer Center	(412) 648-7000
Mid-Continent Regional Technology Transfer Center	(409) 845-8762
Midwest Regional Technology Transfer Center	(216) 734-0094
Far West Regional Technology Transfer Center	(213) 743-6132

In 1991, the U.S. government and NASA established six regional technology transfer offices to provide business, engineering, scientific information, and education services to the public, private, and academic sectors to enable them to acquire and apply technologies developed by NASA and within federal laboratories. These six centers compose the National Technology Transfer Network.

VI. OTHER TECHNOLOGY TRANSFER ORGANIZATIONS

NERAC is a not-for-profit center offering technical assistance and technology transfer services. Staff also conduct on-line searches for clients, drawing on nearly 150 databases.

Contact: NERAC
One Technology Drive
Tolland, CT 06086
(203) 872-7000

VII. BOOKS AND DIRECTORIES

Literally hundreds of books and directories provide information on sources of high technology. Below are some of the most commonly used general purpose directories.

BioScan
The ORYX Press
4041 N. Central Avenue, #700
Phoenix, AZ 85012-3397 (602) 265-2651

Business Researchers Handbook
Washington Researchers, Ltd.
P.O. Box 19005 - 20th St. Station
Washington, DC 20036 (202) 333-3499

Company Profiles
Thomas Publishing Company
One Penn Plaza
New York, NY 10001 (202) 695-0500

Corporate Technology Directory (CorpTech)
CorpTech
P.O. Box 281
Wellsley Hills, MA 02181-0003 (617) 932-3939

Corporate Yellow Book
Monitor Leadership Directories, Inc.
104 Fifth Avenue, Second Floor
New York, NY 10011 (212) 627-4140

Directory of American Research and Technology
A&I Bowker/Reed Reference Publishing
New York, NY (212) 734-3855

Directory of Corporate Affiliations
National Register Publishing
121 Chanlon Road
New Providence, NJ 07974 (800) 521-8110

Directory of Directories
Gale Research Company
BookTower
Detroit, MI 48226 (313) 961-2242

Dun's Market Identifiers (on microfiche)
Dun and Bradstreet Information Services
3 Sylvan Way
Parsippany, NJ 07054-3896 (800) 526-0651

Dun's Million Dollar Directory
Dun and Bradstreet
3 Sylvan Way
Parsippany, NJ 07054-3896 (800) 526-0651

Encyclopedia of Associations
Gale Research Company
BookTower
Detroit, MI 48226 (313) 961-2242

Encyclopedia of Business Information
Gale Research Company
BookTower
Detroit, MI 48226 (313) 961-2242

Federal Laboratory and Technology Resources
U.S. Department of Commerce
National Technical Information Service
5285 Port Royal Road
Springfield, VA 22161 (703) 487-4650

Federal Regulatory Directory
Congressional Quarterly, Inc.
1414 - 22nd Street, N.W.
Washington, DC 20037 (202) 887-8500

Federal Yellow Book
Monitor Publishing Company
104 Fifth Avenue, Second Floor
New York, NY 10011 (212) 627-4140

Financial Yellow Book
Monitor Publishing Company
104 Fifth Avenue, Second Floor
New York, NY 10011 (212) 627-4140

Findex Directory of Market Research Reports, Studies, and Surveys
FIND/SVP
500 Fifth Avenue
New York, NY 10110 (212) 627-2347

Government Research Centers Directory
Gale Research Company
BookTower
Detroit, MI 48226 (313) 961-2242

Higher Education Directory
Higher Education Publications, Inc.
6400 Arlington Blvd., #648
Falls Church, VA 22042 (703) 898-0662

How to Find Information About Private Companies
Washington Researchers, Ltd.
P.O. Box 19005 - 20th St. Station
Washington, DC 20036 (202) 333-3459

International Corporate 1000 Yellow Book
Monitor Publishing Company
104 Fifth Avenue, Second Floor
New York, NY 10011 (212) 627-4140

Manufacturing Industry USA
Gale Research Company
BookTower
Detroit, MI 48226 (313) 961-2242

Market Share Reporter
Gale Research Company
BookTower
Detroit, MI 48226 (313) 961-2242

National Trade and Professional Associations of the United States
Columbia Books, Inc.
1212 New York Avenue, N.W., #330
Washington, DC 20005 (202) 898-0662

North American Research Directories
Synergistic Technologies
P.O. Box 14847
Research Triangle Park, NC 27709 (800) 972-8501

Research Centers Directory
Gale Research Co.
BookTower
Detroit, MI 48226 (313) 961-2242

Standard & Poors Registry of Corporations
McGraw Hill, Inc.
25 Broadway
New York, NY 10004 (212) 208-8702

State and Regional Associations of the United States
Columbia Books, Inc.
1212 New York Avenue, N.W., #300
Washington, DC 20005 (202) 898-0662

Technology Opportunities
Washington Researchers, Ltd.
P.O. Box 19005 - 20th Street Station
Washington, DC 20036 (202) 333-3499

The Medical and Healthcare Marketplace Guide
MLR Publishing Co.
229 South 18th Street, Rittenhouse Square
Philadelphia, PA 19103 (215) 790-7090

Ward's Business Directory of U.S. Private and Public Companies
Gale Research Co.
BookTower
Detroit, MI 48226 (313) 961-2242

VIII. NEWSLETTERS

The newsletters listed below are among those providing information on new developments in science and technology. They can be an excellent source of leads, and in many cases, they offer useful analysis of trends in their respective fields.

Genetic Technology News
Inside R&D
Technical Insights, Inc.
(201) 568-4744

New Technology Week
King Communications
(202) 638-4260

Technology Access Report
Technology Access
(800) 733-1556

The Wall Street Transcript
The Wall Street Transcript Corporation
(212) 747-9500

The Pink Sheet (pharmaceuticals)
The Gray Sheet (medical devices, diagnostics, and instrumentation)
The Blue Sheet (health policy and biomedical research)
F-D-C Reports, Inc.
(301) 657-9830

IX. ASSOCIATIONS

Licensing Executives Society (LES) On-line

LES is a trade association representing patent attorneys, technology scouts, technology managers, as well as other professionals. LES On-line Services, available to members only, includes a placement opportunities database, special presentations, a technology transfer calendar, Technology Express News, and an on-line membership directory.

Contact: LES
1800 Diagonal Road, Suite 280
Alexandria, VA 22314
(703) 836-3106

Society of Competitive Intelligence Professionals (SCIP)

SCIP is a trade association of approximately 2,800 professionals working in the area of business intelligence. The organization seeks to make the business community aware of the importance of staying abreast of new developments through use of legal methods of intelligence-gathering.

Contact: Society of Competitive Intelligence Professionals
1700 Diagonal Road, Suite 520
Alexandria, VA 22314
(703) 739-0696
Internet: http://www.scip.org

ENDNOTES

1. Because the world of information technology is changing rapidly, some of the information contained in this appendix, which was compiled in mid-1995, may be dated.
2. Some of this information was gathered from individual company sources and some was taken from *Gale's Directory of Databases 1994, Volume 1: Online Databases.* Detroit: Gale Research, Inc.

Author Biosketches

W. Bradford Ashton
Pacific Northwest National Laboratory
901 D Street, S.W., Suite 900
Washington DC 20024-2115
(202) 646-5240
(202) 646-7825 (Fax)
E-mail: wb_ashton@pnl.gov

Dr. Ashton is a Senior Program Manager at Pacific Northwest National Laboratory's Washington, D.C. office. He has more than 20 years' experience in management and analysis of advanced energy technology development programs. Currently, he develops and applies advanced tools for R&D program planning and information analysis methods to support government and industry clients. He has led development of computer information systems for R&D investment planning and patent trend analysis and has developed original analysis methods for evaluating technology investment and monitoring technological change. He has authored more than forty technical and planning publications.

Justin L. Bloom
President
Technology International, Inc.
11600 Georgetowne Court
Potomac MD 20854
(301) 983-8247
(301) 299-5322 (Fax)
E-mail: jlbloom@bellatlantic.net

As a Senior Foreign Service Officer, Justin Bloom served as Counselor for Scientific and Technological Affairs at U.S. Embassies in Tokyo and

London from 1975 to 1983. Today, he is President of Technology International, Inc., in Potomac, Maryland. Technology International is a small consulting firm that specializes in studies of foreign science and technology policies and in monitoring international technical developments. A graduate of the California Institute of Technology, Mr. Bloom spent his early career years as a research and senior project engineer. He was also an official of the U.S. Atomic Energy Commission. Mr. Bloom is author or co-author of more than 70 publications.

Patrick J. Bryant
Director
Drug Information Center
University of Missouri - Kansas City
2411 Holmes St., MG 200
Kansas City MO 64110-2792
(816) 235-5490
(816) 235-5491 (Fax)
E-mail: pjbryant@cctr.umkc.edu

Patrick J. Bryant, Pharm.D., is Director of the Drug Information Center at the University of Missouri-Kansas City. He is also associated with the School of Pharmacy as a Clinical Associate Professor and conducts research in the drug information and competitive intelligence areas. His 15 years' experience in the pharmaceutical industry includes research and development, licensing and business development, strategic planning, and 10 years' involvement with competitive intelligence activities. He led the conceptualization and implementation of a competitive technical intelligence unit for Marion Merrell Dow. Dr. Bryant is a member of the Society of Competitive Intelligence Professionals and sits on the editorial board for *Competitive Intelligence Review*.

Michel Callon
Centre de Sociologie
Ecole des Mines de Paris
62 Bd. Saint-Michel
75 006 Paris
FRANCE
(33-1) 40 51 91 90
(33-1) 43 54 56 28 (Fax)

Michel Callon is a professor of Sociology at the Ecole des Mines de Paris. He is a member of the Centre de Sociologie de l'Innovation, which he headed for 12 years. As an invited member of the School of Social Science, Institute for Advanced Study, Princeton, he and other colleagues developed the so-called actor-network theory. He has published widely in the sociology of science and technology and the economics of research and development. M. Callon is President of the Society for Social Studies of Science and, on several occasions, has been directly involved in defining, implementing, and evaluating policy on research in France.

James C. Coleman
Medical Research Manager/Scientist
Hoechst Marion Roussel, Inc.
10236 Marion Park Dr.
Kansas City MO 64137-1405
(816) 966-3251
(816) 966-3661 (Fax)

James C. Coleman has 5 years' experience in competitive intelligence activities in the pharmaceutical industry. Before joining the competitive intelligence unit at Marion Merrell Dow (now Hoechst Marion Roussel, Inc.), he was a principal investigator in the Research division at Marion Laboratories. Dr. Coleman is an adjunct professor in the School of Pharmacy at the University of Missouri-Kansas City. Dr. Coleman now holds a position in the U.S. Medical Research division of Hoechst Marion Roussel, Inc. He has a Bachelor's degree in chemistry; a Master's in forensic sciences; a Ph.D. in pharmacology; and a Master's of Business Administration.

Jean-Pierre Courtial
Université de Nantes
22 Rue Saint-Louis
44 300 Nantes
FRANCE
(33-2) 40 14 10 81
(33-2) 40 14 12 55 (Fax)

Jean-Pierre Courtial trained as an engineer at the Ecole Centrale des Arts et Manufactures. He has a degree in Mathematical Statistics and a doctorate in Social Psychology. He has worked as a management adviser, as well as in the field of quali-quantitative research on research evaluation, research management, competitive intelligence, and forecasting at the Centre de Sociologie at the Ecole des Mines de Paris. Over the past

10 years, he has developed a statistical tool, based on co-word analysis, that produces a series of programs called LEXIMAPPE. He has recently joined a research team on cognitive psychology at the University of Nantes.

Charles de Brabant
Project Manager
CM International
13 avenue Morane Saulnier
F-78140 Velizy-Villacoublay
FRANCE
(33-1) 30 67 23 29
(33-1) 30 67 23 39 (Fax)

Charles de Brabant is a project manager at CM International. He has been a consultant in strategy and technology for the last 4 years, working mainly in the fields of agro-foods, telecommunications, multimedia, and automobiles. In each of these areas, he has worked on competitive issues and, in many instances, has implemented competitive intelligence systems in his clients' organizations. He received an MBA from Stanford University and a Master's Degree in History from Oxford University. Prior to his graduate studies, he worked in development in Africa and Asia.

Thomas Durand
Professor
Ecole Centrale Paris
Paris
FRANCE
(33-1) 41 13 10 00
(33-1) 46 60 36 10 (Fax)

Thomas Durand has been a professor at the Ecole Centrale Paris since 1980. He also teaches at several other universities, including the Stockholm School of Economics and HEC. He heads the Strategy & Technology research center and the Technology & Management Masters. He has published numerous articles on business strategy and technology management. He has a wide range of consulting experience with French, European, and North American companies. A graduate of Ecole Centrale, he holds a DEA in Macroeconomics from the Sorbonne Pantheon, a specialists ECP diploma in Management-Economics, and an MS and Ph.D. from the University of Wisconsin-Madison.

François Farhi
Senior Partner
CM International
13 avenue Morane Saulnier
F-78140 Velizy-Villacoublay
FRANCE
(33-1) 30 67 23 15
(33-1) 30 67 23 39 (Fax)
E-mail: 101317.3460@compuserve.com

As a consultant with CM International for the last 7 years, François Farhi has led the implementation of competitive intelligence systems in various organizations and sectors. CM International is a consulting company that specializes in innovation and technology management; they have offices in Paris, Berlin, Detroit, and London. Mr. Farhi is an expert on innovation policies for the European Commission. He is also a member of the Institute for Research and Innovation Management and teaches Technology Management at Paris-Dauphine University. A graduate of Sorbonne University, Mr. Farhi spent his early career as a research engineer in INSERM, the French national health research organization.

Jan P. Herring
President
Herring & Associates
1338 Asylum Avenue
Hartford CT 06105
(860) 232-9080
(860) 232-4420 (Fax)

A pioneer and recognized expert in the field of business intelligence, Mr. Herring has written and lectured extensively on the topic, addressing both academic and business concerns. He is currently President of Herring & Associates and a Senior Fellow at The Futures Group. Mr Herring was the first Director of Intelligence at Motorola, where he designed and managed its modern business intelligence system. Before Motorola, he spent 20 years with the Central Intelligence Agency as a professional intelligence officer, where he was awarded the Agency's highest honor, the Medal of Distinction. He also holds the Society of Competitive Intelligence Professional's Meritorious Award, the society's highest award for private sector intelligence professionals

Bonnie Hohhof
Intelligent Information
517 Linden Street
Glen Ellyn IL 60137-4021
(630) 469-0732
(630) 469-0752 (Fax)

Bonnie Hohhof is a recognized expert in the design, development, and implementation of information systems that support business intelligence operations. She has more than 20 years' experience in information transfer at leading technology-intensive corporations, including the Corporate Strategy Offices of both Ameritech and Motorola. A charter member of the Society of Competitive Intelligence Professionals, she served on their Board of Directors and received the SCIP Fellow Award for contributions to the profession. She was the founder and executive editor of SCIP's *Competitive Intelligence Review* and author of *Competitive Information System Development*, the benchmark study in its field. Through her consulting firm, Intelligent Information, Ms. Hohhof has provided competitive information system support to numerous Fortune 500 companies.

Anne K. Johnson
Research Scientist
Pacific Northwest National Laboratory
901 D Street, S.W., Suite 900
Washington DC 20024-2115
(202) 646-5208
(202) 646-7825 (Fax)
E-mail: ak_johnson@pnl.gov

Since joining Pacific Northwest National Laboratory 6 years ago, Ms. Johnson has worked on a host of projects for the U.S. Department of Energy's Policy Office and the Office of Renewable Energy and Energy Efficiency. Ms. Johnson is co-author of a paper on monitoring science and technology for competitive advantage. Moreover, because of the nature of her work, she is a frequent user of electronic databases and other specialized research tools.

Bruce R. Kinzey
Senior Research Engineer
Pacific Northwest National Laboratory
901 D St., S.W., Suite 900
Washington DC 20024-2115
(202) 646-5231
(202) 646-7825 (Fax)
E-mail: br_kinzey@pnl.gov

As a senior researcher, Mr. Kinzey has had ample opportunity to hone his information search and retrieval skills. Mr. Kinzey was a primary investigator for the International Research Monitoring (IRM) program for the Office of Energy Efficiency and Renewable Energy (EERE), U.S. Department of Energy, whose purpose was to monitor international technology developments in the fields of energy conservation and renewable energy. For 4 years, he was also the editor-in-chief of the *IRMonitor*, the IRM program's primary communication to EERE. Mr. Kinzey has been with Pacific Northwest National Laboratory for 10 years.

Richard A. Klavans
Center for Research Planning
2405 White House Road
Berwyn PA 19312
(610) 251-2135
(610) 251-2136 (Fax)

Dr. Klavans has more than 20 years' experience formulating science and technology strategies for large firms. He began his career as a senior consultant for Pugh Roberts Associates, where he was responsible for technology forecasts for major industrial firms in the electronic, chemical, and paper industries. Now, as President of the Center for Research Planning, Dr. Klavans specializes in early warning techniques and blindspot analysis. He received an undergraduate degree in Mechanical Engineering from Tufts University, a Master's in Management from MIT, and a Ph.D. in Management from Wheaton. He has served on the editorial board of *Interfaces* and the *Competitive Intelligence Review* and has published numerous articles.

Thomas F. Krol
International Marketing
Hoechst Marion Roussel, Inc.
Route 202-206, Building M
P. O. Box 6800
Bridgewater NJ 08807-0800
(908) 231-3685
(908) 231-3304 (Fax)

Thomas Krol has more than 8 years' experience in competitive intelligence and related activities in the pharmaceutical industry. He played an integral role in the conceptualization and implementation of a competitive technical intelligence unit at Marion Merrell Dow Inc. He earned his Doctor of Pharmacy degree from the University of Utah, where he also completed a clinical pharmacy residency. Dr. Krol also completed a fellowship in clinical research and drug development at the University of North Carolina and Burroughs Wellcome Company. He is an adjunct professor at the College of Pharmacy at the University of Missouri-Kansas City and a member of the Editorial Board for *Competitive Intelligence Review*.

Christine Leboulanger
Université de Caen
Esplanade de la Paix
14032 Caen Cedex
FRANCE
(33-231) 31 45 55 55
(33-231) 31 93 37 42 (Fax)

Christine Leboulanger is Associate Professor of Management at the Université de Caen. She received her Master's degree in Economics, her M. Phil. in Management, and her Ph.D. in Management at the Université de Caen. Her principal areas of interest are bibliometric studies, technology management, and theories of organization.

D. William McDonald
423 Pythian Rd.
Santa Rosa CA 95409
(707) 538-5877
(707) 538-4358 (Fax)

Dr. D. William (Bill) McDonald is a consultant specializing in strategic planning, technology management, and technology intelligence. He is currently affiliated with the Richardson Consulting Group in Menlo Park, California. He was formerly an Associate of PA Consulting Group (Hightstown, New Jersey) and Deputy Director of the Technology Management Group of Pugh-Roberts Associates, Cambridge, Massachusetts. Before that, he was Director of Technology, Plastics Division, Monsanto Company, St. Louis, Missouri, and, subsequently, Director of Technology Planning, Corporate R&D Staff. He also served as Affiliate Professor of Technology Management at Washington University in St. Louis.

Mary Ellen Mogee
Mogee Research & Analysis Associates
11701 Bowman Green Drive
Reston VA 20190
(703) 478-2827
(703) 478-3253 (Fax)
E-mail: mogee@mogee.com

Mary Ellen Mogee is president of Mogee Research & Analysis Associates, a consulting firm specializing in technology policy and management. She previously served as a policy analyst at the U.S. National Science Foundation, the Congressional Research Service, the National Bureau of Standards, and the Patent and Trademark Office. She has published extensively in the field of technology indicators. She has a B.A. in Chemistry; an M.A. in Science, Technology, and Public Policy; and a Ph.D. in Political Science.

Hervé Penan
Centre de Sociology de l'Innovation
Ecole Nationale Supérieure des Mines de Paris
62 boulevard Saint Michel
75272 Paris Cedex 06
FRANCE
(33-1) 40 51 91 91
(33-1) 13 51 56 28 (Fax)
E-mail: penan@csi.ensmp.fr

Hervé Penan is a senior researcher at the Centre de Sociology de l'Innovation (Ecole des Mines de Paris) and has published numerous articles in the field of scientific and technological information analysis for R&D strategy. He has a wide range of consulting experience in competitive technologic intelligence activities with French and European companies. He is an expert on scientific and technological programme evaluation and has used this expertise in work for the European Commission (DGXII). He received his Doctorate of Management Science from the University of Toulouse (France). In addition, he completed a fellowship at the University of Pennsylvania (Management Science Program).

Françoise Perdrieu-Maudière
Université de Caen
Esplanade de la Paix
14032 Caen Cedex
FRANCE
(33-231) 31 45 55 55
(33-231) 31 93 37 42 (Fax)

Françoise Perdrieu-Maudière is Associate Professor of Management at the Université de Caen. She received her Master's degree in Law, her M. Phil. in Management, and her Ph.D in Management at the Université de Caen. Her principal areas of interest are bibliometric studies, technology management, and legal studies.

John L. Richardson
Richardson Consulting Group
2356 Branner Drive
Menlo Park CA 94025
(415) 854-1598
(415) 854-2136 (Fax)

Dr. Richardson, Principal of the Richardson Consulting Group, has a technology management consulting practice. In the last several years, he has developed and installed technology/competitive intelligence systems for major corporate clients. He has been a Senior Consultant Associate with PA Consulting Group (Hightstown, New Jersey) and Pugh-Roberts Associates (Cambridge, Massachusetts). Before his consulting work, Dr. Richardson spent 27 years in corporate functional and general management spanning five different industries.

Anne Sigogneau
Observatoire des Sciences et des Techniques
93 Rue de Vaugirard
75 006 Paris
FRANCE
(33-1) 42 22 30 30
(33-1) 45 48 63 94 (Fax)

Ms. Sigogneau studied Biology and Information Science at the University of Paris. She has worked at the Centre de Sociologie at the Ecole des Mines de Paris on several bibliometrics studies. She achieved her Ph.D. in collaboration with the Commissariat à l'Energie Atomique and the Observatoire des Sciences et des Techniques. She is now affiliated with the Observatoire. Her research subject concerns the demarcation of research fields by journal scientometrics studies.

Gary S. Stacey
Technology and Innovation
P.O. Box 39
1256 Troinex
Geneva
SWITZERLAND
(41) 22 7844354 (telephone and fax)

Dr. Stacey directed R&D and technology management programs for 25 years while a staff member at Battelle. He has experience in and teaches R&D management and strategy, vision and company learning, and scenario analysis. He consults with clients in the United States, Europe, and Japan in almost all industrial sectors and has worked with a number of government agencies and organizations in the United States and Europe. He is a member of the International Association for Impact Assessment and the Strategic Planning Society.

Jean Tibbetts
President
SEARCH Corporation
655 Mine Ridge Road
Great Falls VA 22066
(703) 759-3560
(703) 759-9778 (Fax)
E-mail: search1@ix.netcom.com

Ms. Tibbetts has been a research specialist in technological information and technology transfer since 1981 and president of SEARCH Corporation since 1983. SEARCH Corporation researches licensing and joint-venture prospects; tracks patent activity; identifies current markets, competition, and needs; conducts market research; locates distributors; finds experts; and reports on emerging technologies. Ms. Tibbetts developed investigative skills as a psychometrist with a specialty in psychological tests and measurements. She holds B.A. and M.A. degrees in psychology from the University of Virginia and George Mason University, respectively.

Index